Early Childhood Education and Care

Early Childhood Education and Care

MÁIRE MHIC MHATHÚNA AND MARK TAYLOR

Best wishes for your studies, Mónica,

Máire.

GILL & MACMILLAN

Gill & Macmillan
Hume Avenue
Park West
Dublin 12
with associated companies throughout the world
www.gillmacmillan.ie

9780717153244

Index compiled by Cover to Cover
Print origination by Carole Lynch
Printed in GraphyCems, Spain

The paper used in this book is made from the wood pulp of
managed forests. For every tree felled, at least one is planted,
thereby renewing natural resources.

A CIP catalogue record is available for this book
from the British Library.

Contents

Part 3 Pedagogy and Learning

Preface

Despite our country's economic difficulties, the last few years have been an exciting and a creative time for the early childhood education and care (ECEC) sector in Ireland. The state, for example, has introduced a free and universal pre-school year; Aistear, the curriculum framework for children from birth to six years, is now being used; and Síolta, the National Quality Framework for Early Childhood Education, is also in place.

Given these developments and the evidence highlighting the benefits of quality ECEC provision to children and society, it is therefore not surprising that recent years have also seen a big increase in the number of undergraduate students interested in working in the area of ECEC in Ireland. And it is primarily with these students in mind that this book has been produced.

This book aims to provide appropriate content for many of the modules on BA degree programmes in institutes of technology, colleges of education and universities; its purpose is to prepare ECEC undergraduate students to work with young children.

The idea for this book grew from discussions at the meetings of PLÉ, the organisation for lecturers on ECEC degree programmes founded in 2009. The acronym PLÉ stands for Pedagogy, Learning and Education and calls to mind both 'plé', the Irish word for discussion, and 'play', one of children's ways of exploring the world. All royalties received from the publication of this book will go to PLÉ, to support its work.

In this book, educators, practitioners and policy experts from across Ireland write on a broad range of academic and ECEC practice-related issues, identifying and setting out the knowledge, values and skills which are required to become a competent ECEC practitioner. Chapter authors are mindful that they are writing for those interested in working with young children, and so every chapter follows a similar structural format to engage students with the text and to aid their understanding and learning. The book is organised into four parts to consolidate students' learning:

- Part 1: Theoretical Underpinnings of Early Childhood Education and Care
- Part 2: Approaches to Early Childhood Education and Care
- Part 3: Pedagogy and Learning
- Part 4: Structures and Issues

Part 1 introduces students to the key concepts and theories in the various social science disciplines, enabling them to make sense of a child's place in the social world.

Part 2 demonstrates the richness and range of pre-school learning models; it draws a picture of the numerous theoretical and practical perspectives in care and education, which ECEC students can embrace to engage with young children in different ways and for various purposes.

Part 3 explores the different types of environments and situations which contribute to young children's learning and reminds the ECEC student of the need to constantly and consistently engage with parents and community – two key stakeholders in the working lives of ECEC practitioners.

Part 4 outlines the unique character of the ECEC sector in Ireland, while also highlighting the importance of ethics and the significance of diversity for ECEC practice.

We need to emphasise that while this book introduces a range of subjects to the reader, we expect and we want students to go elsewhere, to other texts and resources, to explore these subjects in more detail. This book should be seen as a resource to whet students' interest in ECEC, inviting them to embark in various directions to deepen their knowledge.

We would like to thank a number of people who supported the production of this book:

- Dr Perry Share, Head of the Department of Humanities, IT Sligo, inspired its creation and suggested the book's structure.
- PLÉ, who kindly and generously supported the book's inception, progression and publication.
- The contributors to the book, who have spent time researching, writing and revising their chapters, receiving no monetary reward for their dedication and effort.
- Marion O'Brien, from Gill & Macmillan, who has gently, capably and warmly held us by the hand from when we first approached her with the idea of this book.
- Catherine Gough, from Gill & Macmillan, for professionally and patiently seeing us through to the finish line.
- Jane Rogers, our brilliant and efficient copyeditor.
- All our colleagues at DIT and IT Sligo, who have supported and put up with us through the ups and downs of the book's production.
- Our ECEC students, who remain a constant inspiration, reminding us to stay focused on developing them to become capable and effective ECEC practitioners.
- Our families and friends, who have been there for us, providing emotional support and encouragement.

Finally, we hope that this book will contribute to the professional development of early years practitioners and through them to the optimal development of children, the main focus of all our work.

Máire Mhic Mhathúna and Mark Taylor
March 2012

Introduction: Children at the Centre of Practice

Nóirín Hayes

INTRODUCTION

There have been significant changes in the field of early childhood education and care (ECEC) in Ireland over recent decades. Responding to the increasing demands for provision, there has been unprecedented investment in the expansion of places and the infrastructure to manage such developments. The growth of local childcare support networks and improved co-ordination across the national voluntary organisations has given an increased visibility to the sector that was missing in the 1990s. The establishment in 2011 of the Department for Children – incorporating the Office of the Minister for Children and Youth Affairs (OMCYA) – should further enhance cohesion and integration across the variety of policy issues, including early years provision, that impact directly on young children's lives.

To a somewhat lesser extent there has been investment in supports for services to enhance the quality and sustainability of provision. This can be seen in the various financial supports available to childcare settings, including the introduction of the free pre-school year. Furthermore, the publication of *Síolta: The National Quality Framework for Early Childhood Education* (CECDE 2006) and *Aistear: The Early Childhood Curriculum Framework* (NCCA 2009) creates a rich basis for considering practice in services for young children. Finally, attention to the quality of staff working in the sector is captured by the commitments on training reported in the Workforce Development Plan (DES 2009) and offers an opportunity to follow other countries towards supporting and developing a graduate-led, diverse professional base to enhance the quality of service provision and the experiences of young children.

A number of international and national developments can be seen as directly influencing the daily work of practitioners in early childhood settings. Hayes and Kernan (2008) identified these developments as including:

1 The professionalising of the early years sector with expanded provision of higher-level training and the associated development of standards of good practice and ethics.
2 The growing heterogeneity of societies.

3 The almost universal ratification of the United Nations Convention on the Rights of the Child.
4 The notion of ECEC settings as sites of democratic practice where children and adults can participate collectively in interpreting experiences and shaping decisions affecting themselves (Moss 2007).
5 The centrality of the principles of social inclusion and respect for diversity in good-quality early childhood education.

These developments have been accompanied by a growing recognition of the importance of quality early childhood education experiences for all children in providing lasting educational, developmental and social benefits; and a view that access to quality ECEC is a right for all children.

EARLY YEARS PRACTICE

This chapter considers how theory and processes inform early years practice at a time when more young children are now spending more time in a range of settings outside the home. Evidence shows that the most effective early childhood practice is that which has a sound theoretical base. We know that the adult, and their style of engagement, has a profound impact on the learning experiences of children and sets the scene for their sense of engagement with the world. We also know a great deal about how children develop and learn and we recognise that early childhood experiences are important to children in their day-to-day life and into their future. Children are the social group most affected by the quality of early childhood services. While this seems like a truism, there is relative complacency about what actually happens to children in their everyday experiences and an assumption that by just attending early years settings they will develop and progress positively. In fact the quality of everyday experiences in the early years – wherever children are – has a profound influence on them. They are not merely recipients or consumers of a service but are deeply influenced, individually and collectively, by their early years experiences. The National Children's Strategy (DoH 2000) recognises that children are active agents in their development and that they affect and are affected by the environments within which they grow. They are active participants in our society and have a right to expect that early childhood settings will challenge and excite them, provide safety and security and enhance their overall development and learning. It is useful to review current understandings of how early childhood practices impact on children. Such a review can act as a stimulus for practitioners to reflect on their practice and the quality of provision for young children so that the experience of early childhood settings will be a positive and affirming one for all those involved.

Children develop in the midst of many different and interacting systems. Whilst the family is recognised as the central space for early development, an increasing number of families share the early care and education of their children with various types of service. These services grow and are supported as part of the wider society and have, to a greater or lesser degree, contacts with other educational, social and cultural settings in the wider community. They thus provide an important bridge for children and parents alike, particularly useful where services are provided for minority or marginalised parents and their children. While focusing on the role of the practitioner in respect of children attending settings it is also important to recognise the important potential of early childhood settings in creating these links across various systems.

INTERACTIONS BETWEEN CHILDREN, ADULTS AND ENVIRONMENTS

The interactions between individual children, the adults in their life and the various early years environments are critical spaces for learning. In Ireland 'early childhood education' refers to the development and learning of young children from birth through to the age of 6 years. This period of life has been defined internationally as the first stage in education. The contemporary view of children as active agents in their learning is an important one. It requires practitioners to recognise and respond to the reality that even the very youngest children contribute to the context and content of their own development. This is not to underestimate the dependence of the child or the very powerful protective role of the adult. It does, however, challenge adults to reconsider practice and to take account of the rich and diverse nature of each child when planning early education and care, designing learning environments and providing learning opportunities.

Viewing children as participants in the early childhood process allows adults to work with children as well as provide for them. It provides a context within which children can be seen as contemporaries and can be valued in the here and now. While it is important to consider the future – and practitioners are contributing to the foundations of future learning – it is the immediate, day-to-day experiences that are of most relevance: these are the experiences that matter. Children learn from the world around them; the ordinary has the potential to be extra-ordinary. The adult can contribute in making the experience of the ordinary a rich learning experience through expanding children's language, thinking and understanding.

Children trust adults and look to them for protection and guidance. Children are motivated to learn, to seek meaning in their world, and they expect that the adults they meet will assist them in this endeavour. They bring to the learning situation their own capabilities and will develop, through their experiences, the dispositions for learning that will contribute to their overall success among their peers and in new social environments. It is at this stage in their development that children come to understand their world. Their curiosity and desire for knowledge is evident in their play, their exploration, their questions and their behaviour. The adult has a valuable contribution to make in this regard. To make the most of the early years, children need adults who trust them, adults who are excited, inspired and challenged by them. The child becomes the centre of practice and the curriculum reflects this. Good practice requires that adults actively include children in the experiences of the early years setting, engage with children and learn from them as well as enhance the learning opportunities for them. This pedagogical approach is informed by a belief in the active nature of child development and includes the child as a partner in development.

The extent to which practice is responsive to learning opportunities in even the most mundane activity, such as nappy changing, transition from one space to the next or tidy-up time, will influence the quality of the experience for the child. Settings which recognise that learning is an ongoing process will engage children in day-to-day activities, will include them in planning and will expect them to contribute. The challenges of this approach to practice are recognised. It is not sufficient to make a plan for the day and follow it; the dynamic and interactive nature of development requires that practitioners are responsive and reflective throughout their engagement with children. The design, organisation and resourcing of the early years setting is central to the early learning process. Settings, both indoor and outdoor, should be safe whilst also providing rich and varied opportunities for exploration, play and risk-taking. Children thrive where they feel part of the learning environment and feel that they belong, and adults need to consider how best to make settings welcoming and familiar for all children, irrespective of their background. The planning necessary for such quality provision requires the creation of learning opportunities in a risk-rich, content-rich and language-rich environment. Such practice is most effective when it is relational and responsive to the child. This refocusing of practice requires a significant shift in approach away from the traditional styles.

THEORY TO PRACTICE

In research, the role of the early years setting in modern societies is under review. It is no longer seen as simply a safe place to have children minded while parents work. Rather, it is recognised as an influential institution for children, one where their rights and needs can be met in a way that recognises and respects them. Within such settings children have the opportunity to develop a sense of belonging beyond the immediate family group, a sense of contributing to a new social system. The quality of these opportunities can influence their sense of identity; the view they form of themselves. This reality places an obligation on adults to be alert to the immediate environment whilst at the same time remaining sensitive to the background experiences of children and the valuable contribution of such experiences, even for very young children.

Research continues to illustrate that successful early education facilitates the child in active learning in environments that are well planned, where staff are well trained, confident and supported in their work. Quality models of early education are characterised by underpinning principles which present a view of the child as an active partner in the integrated and ongoing process of learning, reflecting a strong commitment to developing the social and affective dimensions of learning as well as the more traditional emphasis on cognitive development. This reflects the views expressed by many (Bruner 1996; Hayes 2008; Hayes and Kernan 2008; Hayes and Bradley 2009; Sylva *et al.* 2004) that the most important learning in early education has to do with the affective and difficult-to-measure aspects of development such as aspirations, social skills, motivation, organisation, learner identity and confidence.

Rather than attending to the implementation of a given curriculum, research suggests that it is more effective to have a well-trained workforce, familiar with child development and subject material, who recognise and respond to the dynamic and individual nature of development in the early years and who can work with an emerging curriculum which is driven by the interests and experiences of the children and the opportunities afforded by the environment (OECD 2006). Cultivating positive learning dispositions and feelings in young children leads to positive outcomes in social, linguistic and cognitive development and the skills necessary for later school success. It is a holistic, adaptive and, ultimately, more effective approach to early education.

One of the difficulties in translating research findings into practice, however, is that practice happens in the real world and learning is a far more dynamic and messy process than any text can capture. Contemporary research and literature confirm the importance of attending to this dynamic and messy process and informing such attention by reference to our increased knowledge about and understanding of the components of the process and their interdependence. Early education models of practice have been guided by principles derived from the study of development and pedagogy, by societal values and by the aims that policymakers have for education.

The role of the adult in early childhood education is crucial and multi-faceted and has been characterised as a combination of listener, questioner, adviser, demonstrator, actor, sympathiser, negotiator, assessor and guide (Athey 1990). I would go further and contend that the adult in early childhood settings must also recognise their role as a 'learner', a reflective observer of children who learns from observation and uses this as the basis for pedagogical practice (Hayes 2008). To have a positive impact in the lives of young children, particularly those from disadvantaged backgrounds, requires understanding and respect for the fact that children are active agents and participants in their development. Recognising the child's active contribution to the process of learning reflects the rise in attention to children's participation in education that has emerged from psychological, sociological and rights research (Dahlberg and Moss 2005) and calls for a new pedagogical approach. Such a pedagogy presumes that all minds are capable of holding ideas and beliefs: and, through discussion and interaction, it can be moved towards some shared frame of reference and is child-sensitive, less patronising and more respectful of children's own role in their development. In the early years, understanding the dynamic development of individual children is critical as it presents insight into the varied levels of cognitive, affective and social development that are more typical than in later years; normative development affords a valuable benchmark against which to check the dynamic development of individual children, should such checks be necessary.

A NURTURING PEDAGOGY

If adults are to nurture children's learning as part of a caring educative process, they must develop skills of observation and reflection to allow for the non-intrusive planning and provision of a learning environment that supports and extends children's own learning and provides quality interactive opportunities. To nurture requires an engaged, bi-directional level of interaction and confers on the early years practitioner an enhanced educational role. Despite many recommendations highlighting the value of balancing the care and education elements of early education, there is a tendency to underestimate the educative role of caring. A significant shift in understanding the role of care in practice requires an explicit acknowledgement of the critical contribution of the interpersonal aspect of early education, the realisation in practice of the proximal process, the engines of development (Bronfenbrenner and Morris 1998). To emphasise this, it has been argued that there is a value in reconceptualising care as nurture in order that its status as an educative dimension be enhanced (Hayes 2006, 2008). Considering care as nurture gives it an active connotation, placing a responsibility on the adult to provide nurturance and foster learning rather than to simply mind or protect the child. Such a shift in emphasis would raise the expectations many have of early childhood care and education.

Reconceptualising care as nurture would strengthen the attention given to the educative value of care and allow for a more appropriate 'nurturing pedagogy' to emerge in early education learning environments (Hayes 2006, 2008; Hayes and Kernan 2008). Linking the term 'nurture' with pedagogy is intended to focus attention on the implications for practice. Although well known in educational theory through the work of authors such as Freire (1998/1970) and Bruner (1996), the term 'pedagogy' is a relatively new one in Irish early education discourse.

Pedagogy is a word that captures the multi-layered and dynamic practices necessary to support children's holistic development. The term 'pedagogy' is used to capture the integrated processes of caring, educating and learning alongside the principles, theory, values and approaches which underpin daily work with young children in the range of early childhood settings. Pedagogy encompasses the processes of children learning and adults creating learning opportunities and environments that engage, challenge and interest young children. It also focuses attention on the everyday learning in which adults themselves engage as they observe, reflect on and critically analyse the content and approach to their work with young children, alone and with other adults.

Central to a nurturing pedagogy are relationships and interactions: between children; between adults and young children; between adults and their colleagues and the parents of the children they work with; and between learners and the environments where learning takes place. A nurturing pedagogy is a style of practice that is explicit in engaging children, respecting them and integrating the learning opportunities provided across the care and education dimensions. It builds on the individual capabilities and dispositions of the child within the social context and derives from the belief that it is the close interactions, the proximal processes, between children and between children and adults that drive development and learning. Examples include feeding and comforting babies, playing with young children, facilitating child-to-child interactions, comforting those in distress, making plans, acquiring new knowledge and know-how. Responding to our understanding of early childhood development requires that we prioritise relationships and interactions over direct instruction and teaching as the cornerstone of early educational practice.

Combining the word 'pedagogy' with the term 'nurture' is intended to strengthen the early years professional space. The word 'nurture' has quite a different tone to it from the word 'care'. In comparing the meaning of the two words, 'nurture' is more engaging and active than 'care'. The verb 'to care' is almost custodial in tone and caring requires a minimum of interaction; the adult merely provides for and looks after the child. To nurture, on the other hand, conveys a far more engaged level of interaction and requires the adult to actively nourish, rear, foster, train and educate the child through his/her practice.

Skills of observation and reflection are central to a nurturing pedagogy. They enhance practice and planning and are manifest in well-managed and yet reasonably flexible practice, and in the provision of a learning environment that includes children and supports and extends children's learning. This allows for increased attention to positive interactions between both child and adult and child and child. It also allows for planning by the adult for future opportunities that might extend the child's own learning, giving a key role to the adult which takes the child, rather than the content, as central. It encourages the movement away from the more traditional, organisational/management role of the practitioner and strengthens the focus on the adult's pedagogical role, which is sometimes absent in more play-based settings. A nurturing pedagogy fosters the processes of interaction, dialogue and planning, leading to the shared construction of knowledge, between children and adults, within the context of an emerging curriculum responsive to the child in the immediate now. This pedagogy highlights the importance of initial and continuing professional development for the adult.

In settings where the adult is observing and listening to young children and reflecting on these observations, the curriculum plan is based on an assessment of children's interests and developmental level as well as their needs and the aims of education. A nurturing pedagogy encourages reflective practice in which the practitioner creates rich, interactive learning environments. In addition, it facilitates early identification of difficulties in individual development and early action to address them, either in the context of the setting or through outside interventions and supports. Implicit in the concept of a nurturing pedagogy is the idea that pedagogy is a guide to an emergent and responsive curriculum and is in itself a form of assessment. Finally, a nurturing pedagogy extends the underlying idea of respect for the child as a participating partner in the learning process while at the same time recognising and articulating a mechanism for respecting the dual nature of early education as care and education in practice.

References

Athey, C. (1990) *Extending Thought in Young Children: A Parent–Teacher Partnership*. London: Paul Chapman.

Bronfenbrenner, U. and Morris, P. (1998) 'The Ecology of Developmental Processes' in W. Damon and R.M. Lerner (eds), *Handbook of Child Psychology*, Vol. 1: *Theoretical Models of Human Development* (5th edn). New York: John Wiley and Sons, pp. 993–1028.

Bruner, J. (1996) *The Culture of Education*. Cambridge MA: Harvard University Press.

CECDE (Centre for Early Childhood Development and Education) (2006) *Síolta: The National Quality Framework for Early Childhood Education*. Dublin: CECDE.

Dahlberg, G. and Moss, P. (2005) *Ethics and Politics in Early Childhood Education*. London and New York: Routledge Farmer.

DES (Department of Education and Science) (2009) *Developing the Workforce in the Early Childhood Care and Education Sector: Background Discussion Paper*. Dublin: Stationery Office.

DoH (Department of Health) (2000) *Our Children – Their Lives: The National Children's Strategy*. Dublin: Stationery Office.

Freire, P. (1998/1970) *Pedagogy of the Oppressed*. New York: Continuum.

Hayes, N. (2006) *Perspectives on the Relationship between Education and Care in Early Childhood*. Background paper prepared for the National Council for Curriculum and Assessment. Dublin: NCCA.

— (2008) 'Teaching matters in early educational practice: the case for a nurturing pedagogy', *Early Education and Development* 19:3, 430–40.

Hayes, N. and Bradley, S. (2009) *Right by Children: Children's Rights and Rights-Based Approaches to Policy Making in Early Childhood Education and Care*. Dublin: CSER/DIT.

Hayes, N. and Kernan, M. (2008) *Engaging Young Children: A Nurturing Pedagogy*. Dublin: Gill & Macmillan.

Moss, P. (2007) *Bringing Politics into the Nursery: Early Childhood Education and Care as Democratic Practice*, Working Papers in Early Childhood Development. The Hague: Bernard van Leer Foundation.

NCCA (National Council for Curriculum and Assessment) (2009) *Aistear: The Early Childhood Curriculum Framework*. Dublin: NCCA.

OECD (Organisation for Economic Co-operation and Development) (2006) *Starting Strong II: Early Childhood Education and Care*. Paris: OECD.

Sylva, K., Melhuish, E., Sammons, P., Siraj-Blatchford, I. and Taggart, B. (2004) *The Effective Provision of Pre-School Education (EPPE) Project: Final Report*. London: Institute of Education/Surestart.

PART 1

THEORETICAL UNDERPINNINGS OF EARLY CHILDHOOD EDUCATION AND CARE

1

The Development of Early Childhood Education in Ireland in the Nineteenth and Twentieth Centuries

Maura O'Connor

Learning Objectives
After studying this chapter the reader should be able to:
* Map the development of early childhood education and care (ECEC) in Ireland from the nineteenth century to the second decade of the twenty-first century.
* Identify a number of factors influencing the advancement of ECEC services.
* Appreciate the changes and continuities over time in ECEC.
* Reflect on the historical and social constructions of the child and child-centred education.

INTRODUCTION

> All the great educational systems of the past embodied some unchanging truths and therefore something from each of them must be found to-day in any system worthy of general adoption. (Fynne 1924:1)

This chapter provides a historical analysis of the growth and development of early childhood education in Ireland from the beginning of the nineteenth century to the beginning of the second decade of the twenty-first century.

The main aim of the national system of education which was established in 1831 was to provide a basic education for all the children of Ireland. No reference was made in the early years of the system as to the age at which children could begin their formal education in primary (national) schools. As a result, until 1884, children as young as two years of age could begin their schooling in primary schools. In that year it was stated that no child under 3 years could be enrolled in a primary school, and no pupil aged over 7 years could be enrolled in an infant class. In 1934, the age of enrolment increased to 4 years.

CHILD-CENTRED EDUCATION

The evolution of the concept of the 'child' and 'child-centred education' that revolutionised the way the young child was perceived can be traced to Jean-Jacques Rousseau (1712–1778), Johann H. Pestalozzi (1746–1827) and Friedrich Froebel (1782–1852). These theorists, who are regarded as the pioneers of progressive education in Europe, contributed to new ways of thinking about teaching and learning (pedagogy), knowledge and curriculum, as well as the philosophy of education. They promoted the notion of a cultural or universal child, and regarded childhood as an important period in its own right and not as a preparation for any succeeding stage. The child was looked upon as being naturally good and naturally curious; consequently, his/her emotions, feelings and instincts were to be allowed full expression.

Pioneering educationalists in Ireland sought to modify and adapt the philosophies of these great educators to suit the particular needs of the Irish child. Richard Lovell Edgeworth (1744–1817) and his daughter Maria (1767–1849) were greatly influenced by the writings of Rousseau, and kept detailed records of their educational experiments and endeavours with the Edgeworth children in the late eighteenth century. These they published in a book entitled *Practical Education* (Edgeworth and Edgeworth 1798). The twenty-five chapters of the text represented a serious attempt by the Edgeworth family to put the psychology and the practice of education on a scientific basis.

Lady Powerscourt (1800–1836) established the first infant school in her estate in Enniskerry, County Wicklow in 1826 (Wilderspin 1832). Here she provided the young children with books, food, and a garden in which they could play. John H. Synge (1788–1845) was foremost among those in Ireland who were strongly influenced by the educational ideas of Pestalozzi. He was most impressed with what he witnessed when he visited Pestalozzi's school in Yverdun, and attempted in 1815 to introduce the Pestalozzian approach into this country when he set up a Pestalozzian elementary school in his estate in Roundwood, County Wicklow. He established a private press on which to print Pestalozzian textbooks and school charts and he prepared a detailed account, in English, of all he had learned from Pestalozzi and his educational endeavours (Synge 1815).

Eleonore Heerwart (1835–1911), who was trained as a kindergarten teacher by Froebel's second wife, opened a kindergarten and school in Dublin in 1862 to accommodate the needs of the children of the middle classes. Froebel coined the term kindergarten (*Kinder* – children; *Garten* – garden) to designate a garden where the child was presented as a human plant and the teacher as a careful gardener (Liebschner 1991). As well as endeavouring to educate her students according to Froebel's philosophies, in order to reach a wider audience Heerwart produced booklets offering guidance to those who wished to put Froebelian theories into practice (Heerwart 1883).

The private schools founded by the followers of the child-centred progressive educators of Europe could accommodate but a minority of children in the later decades of the nineteenth century. It was not until the creation in 1831 of a system of national education in Ireland, and the provision of mass schooling, that the majority of Irish children were afforded the opportunity of receiving any form of formal education.

THE NATIONAL SYSTEM OF EDUCATION (1831)

From the beginning of the national system it is evident that the value of infant education was recognised by members of the National Board of Education. In 1837, an Englishman named Samuel Wilderspin (1792–1866), who regarded himself as the 'Inventor of Infant Education', was appointed to introduce his system of infant education to Ireland, and to advise on the construction and appointment of the proposed model school and playground (McCann and Young 1982). In 1838, an advertisement inviting pupils for enrolment in the Model Infant School in Marlborough Street, Dublin, and outlining the rules of the school, appeared in the *Dublin Evening Mail* (O'Connor 2010:58).

Wilderspin, for a man of his time, had remarkable insights into the thinking and behaviour of young children. He had an appreciation of the part played by the teacher in supporting the intellectual development of the child. He recommended that instruction should be 'interesting, lively and inspiring'. To achieve this he advised the use of the gallery 'to teach the children simultaneously', giving lessons which appealed to the senses, so that each child, 'while literally at play', was 'acquiring a considerable amount of valuable knowledge' (Wilderspin 1852:79). Wilderspin remained in this country for a year and was succeeded by his son-in-law Thomas Urry Young.

In 1852, Young was commissioned to prepare a manual on the theory and practice of teaching infant classes (Young 1852). He was cognisant of the fact that children as young as 2 years old had to be accommodated in infant classes with children who were much older, so he wisely suggested that 'the Infant School legislates for its pupils in accordance with their age and state' (Young 1852:6). From a perusal of the text it is evident, however, that he saw teaching as a skill that, if acquired, would achieve positive results for those working with young children. Equipping the educators with teaching tips and ready-made solutions was inadequate preparation for day-to-day school organisation and management. Despite Young's best efforts, three decades after Wilderspin's return to England, the neglect of young children in infant classes was regarded as one of the weakest points in the Irish education system.

THE POWIS COMMISSION (1868–70) AND ITS AFTERMATH

The Powis Commission, which was set up 1868 to evaluate the system of education in Ireland, was most critical of the inadequacy of the system of infant education in this country. The Commissioners anticipated an improvement when the system of payment by results was introduced in 1872. According to the system a fixed sum of money would be paid for each pupil who passed an annual examination. The prescriptive programme for results–fees dictated the curriculum for the early years classes, and while the salaries of the teachers depended on the results their pupils obtained, the emphasis was to be on teaching rather than learning. Notwithstanding the best intentions of the Commissioners, the reports of the inspectorate in the 1870s continued to complain that young children were being introduced at an early age to a formal curriculum which prioritised reading, writing and arithmetic. Nevertheless, for many young children who had previously been ignored in school, this scheme meant an early introduction to literacy and numeracy.

Efforts were made in 1881 to introduce kindergarten into the infant programme when the Model Infant School in Marlborough Street, Dublin was organised along Froebelian lines (CNEI 1882). Prior to the introduction of the new approach, the headmistress of the Model Infant School, Miss Stephens, travelled to England to familiarise herself with this specialised method of infant education and organisation (CNEI 1884). In 1884, kindergarten became a component part of the programme for students in training to become teachers. In 1898, it achieved official recognition when it became a compulsory element of the curriculum for primary teachers. While its status was limited, it served to set the scene for future, more favourable, developments in ECEC.

THE COMMISSION ON MANUAL AND PRACTICAL INSTRUCTION (1897) AND THE REVISED PROGRAMME (1900)

In 1897, a Commission on Manual and Practical Instruction (the Belmore Commission) was set up to carry out wide-ranging enquiries into contemporary educational trends in Britain, Europe and America. Its general report reflected much of the child-centred movement, and particular emphasis was placed on the importance of educating children from their earliest years. A significant feature of the *Final Report of the Commission* (1898) was the recommendation that early childhood education should be accorded a much greater prominence than heretofore. It was advocated by the Commission that the Froebelian system of education be adopted in a modified form in the proposed new programme for primary schools. This would involve an intermixture of kindergarten with the work of reading, writing and arithmetic, while infant instruction should approximate as nearly as possible to the kindergarten ideal.

The introduction of the Revised Programme in 1900 heralded a whole new concept in Irish educational practice in relation to early childhood education, and presented a radical shift from the old didactic system of the nineteenth century. A new curriculum was now being introduced wherein reading, writing and arithmetic would remain as the core of a programme and attention would be given to the practical elements of the practical subjects, while at the same time new subjects would be guaranteed.

The prescribed occupations for junior and senior infant classes outlined by the Revised Programme (1900) were consistent with the Froebelian notion of quality kindergarten practice. Froebel's first, second, third and fourth 'Gifts' were to be introduced, while drawing, singing, school discipline and physical drill, cookery, laundry work and needlework were also placed on the syllabus. The programme in English included reading sections from the First Book, copying letters of the alphabet, and spelling words of two letters. In arithmetic, the numbers one to ten were to be explored using concrete materials on slates or paper (CNEI 1900).

As the Revised Programme (1900) was based on progressive theories, all those involved in early childhood education had to battle with such polarities as the education of the hand as distinct from the head, and the education of the child's body as opposed to his or her mind. In the early years of the twentieth century this proved to be a formidable task that demanded a major shift in mindset for teachers, inspectors, school managers and parents as they endeavoured to come to terms with the new concept of the young child and his or her needs and interests.

THE DALE REPORT (1904) AND ITS CONSEQUENCES

As early as 1903, Mr F. H. Dale, an inspector from England, was invited by the National Board to evaluate and report on the Irish system of primary education. His report offered some very descriptive information on the situation four years after the introduction of the Revised Programme (1900). Commenting on infant education, he complained that the teaching of the younger children was one of the weakest parts of Irish primary education. He saw an urgent need for an improvement in the education of young children in Ireland, advising that the intelligence of all children was largely determined by the education which they received in the infant classes (Dale 1904). The advice offered by Dale on improving infant education prompted the Board to action and steps were taken to implement his recommendations, with a greater emphasis being placed on early childhood education in schools.

In 1906, all schools with an average attendance of between thirty-five and fifty students were granted permission to appoint a junior assistant mistress, a new category of untrained female teacher who concentrated mainly on the instruction and care of the youngest children in school. It was anticipated that she would prove to be particularly valuable 'in regard to the care and education of children of very tender years' (CNEI 1905–06:20).

Miss Edith O'Farrell, who had received her education in a Froebelian college in England, was appointed as a kindergarten organiser in 1903. By 1912, the number of such organisers had increased to six (CNEI 1911–12). The organisers were largely responsible for the development and dissemination of kindergarten principles in the early decades of the twentieth century. While their efforts to improve infant education were almost heroic, their work was to a great extent hampered by the lack of resources available to infant schools as well as the inadequate accommodation and school furniture provided for young children. Nevertheless, they laboured tirelessly to propagate Froebelian theories by offering practical hints and suggestions to teachers of young children. The trajectory of the growth and development of kindergarten methods in this country would have been very different without their work in the early years of the twentieth century.

EARLY CHILDHOOD EDUCATION IN THE IRISH FREE STATE

The process of implementing the Revised Programme (1900) was interrupted in the early 1920s with the onset of independence for Ireland. The primary focus of the education policy of the Irish Free State in 1922 was centred on the restoration of the Irish language and in consequence the introduction of a child-centred curriculum was pushed to the background. A new programme, which evolved from the First National Programme Conference of 1921–2, recommended that in the two grades of infant classes all the work should be done through the medium of Irish. This was a rule that affected nearly 250,000 children whose home language in over 90 per cent of cases was English (Ó Cuív 1969).

Many teachers disagreed on educational grounds with this principle of teaching young children solely through Irish when that was not the language of the home. A small concession was made as a result of the Second National Programme Conference of 1926, which allowed instruction in English before 10.30 a.m. and after 2.00 p.m. With the publication of a *Revised Programme of Instruction* in 1934 (Department of Education 1934), the English language was once again diminished in infant classrooms at a time when it was the vernacular of the majority of the young pupils. In 1948, teachers of early years children were permitted to teach their pupils through the medium of Irish for half an hour daily. In 1960 each teacher of junior classes was given the right to choose between using Irish as a medium of instruction in such classes, and teaching Irish as a subject only.

In the late 1930s and early 1940s, teachers of young children in Irish schools were not, as yet, fully aware or convinced of the value of early childhood education. They were moved, however, by their own common sense and empathy with young children, and they were beginning to realise that the education of the young child, if it were to be constructive, could not be authoritative and dictatorial, but must certainly be focused on the young child's needs, interests and natural urge to play. During the 1940s, the nucleus of a conceptual framework for the reintroduction of the more child-centred curriculum was developing alongside the all-Irish policy in schools.

1948–1971: THE INFANT CLASSES GIVE THE LEAD

The publication of two policy documents – the *Revised Programme for Infants* (1948) (Department of Education 1948) and *An Naí-Scoil: The Infant School – Notes for Teachers* (1951) (Department of Education 1951) – marked a turning point in the history of infant education in Ireland. The *Revised Programme* (1948) placed less emphasis on nationalistic ideas and concentrated more on an activity-based, child-centred curriculum, as had been advocated in the *Revised Programme* of 1900. The designers of the programme wished to ensure that each child developed an oral competence in both Irish and English. It acknowledged that young children were most receptive to language acquisition, and that they could acquire two languages without apparent effort, provided they were in a suitable learning environment. Stress was placed on the use of play, handwork, art, number, songs, dance and music.

During the 1950s and 1960s an infant programme which was crucially important in its own right was implemented in the primary schools. This new curriculum offered a whole new concept of what constituted early childhood education. Its introduction was less revolutionary than the previous programmes of 1900, 1922 and 1926. Further, as had been the case in the early decades of the twentieth century, teachers of young children were supported in their endeavours to implement the programme by a group of female organising inspectors who travelled around the country offering professional development courses on classroom organisation, teaching approaches and methodologies, while focusing also on the holistic development of the child.

The advice and practical guidance provided by the organising inspectors seems to have been accepted and implemented by the teachers, because their pioneering work, and that of their more progressive colleagues, was acknowledged in the Primary School Curriculum of 1971 (Department of Education 1971), which stated that one of the most significant developments in the years after the publication of *An Naí-Scoil* in 1951 had been the application of these principles beyond the infant classes (Department of Education 1971:15). According to the curriculum of 1971, the junior and senior infant programme was to be extended upwards and outwards to incorporate all the classes of the primary school. It was suggested that the process should be gradual, systematic and organic, with no sharp wrench for the child between one stage of his or her development and the next. Teachers of junior and senior infants were advised that early childhood education, if it were to be successful, must be based on the child's instinctive urge to play, talk, imitate, manipulate materials, and make and do things.

The child-centred curriculum of 1971 was superseded by the 1999 Primary School Curriculum (Government of Ireland 1999). Like its predecessor, it placed greater emphasis on child-centred and quality education. In a socio-cultural environment, young children are encouraged to speak, to be active in their learning and to construct meaning with knowledgeable others.

THE DEVELOPMENT OF ECEC SERVICES FROM THE 1970S TO THE PRESENT

While innovations were taking place in the primary school system from the 1950s, in terms of provision and practice little state provision was made for the education and well-being of the pre-school child. This was perhaps because until the late 1960s the majority of children were cared for at home, primarily by the mother, until they attended primary school. Until 1940, there were only three day nurseries in Ireland (Cowman 2007). These included the Liberty Crèche, which was founded in 1892, Henrietta Street Nursery (1923), and St Brigid's Nursery (1939) (Cowman 2007). In the absence of state assistance and support, movements began from the late 1960s to provide services on a private or community basis (Douglas 1994). Such services included childminding, nurseries, community playgroups, grúpaí naíonraí and pre-schools. From small beginnings the movements grew and prospered.

In 1969, the Department of Education and the Van Leer Foundation initiated a pre-school intervention project in Rutland Street, Dublin (Holland 1979). During 1994 and 1995, the Department of Education and Science (DES) established a total of forty Early Start pre-schools attached to primary schools for children in areas of disadvantage. These were based mainly on the Rutland Street interventionist model. The Rutland Street pre-school continues to operate, as do the Early Start pre-schools. Primary school teachers and early years educators work closely with parents in these schools, which are funded by the Department of Education and Skills.

During the 1990s a consciousness in relation to children's rights was emerging. In 1992, the ratification by Ireland of the 1989 United Nations Convention on the Rights of the Child marked an important milestone in this regard. In 2000, the *National Children's Strategy* (DoHC 2000), which was rooted in the positive vision for childhood outlined by the Convention, set out a ten-year plan of action to improve the quality of children's lives. With the increased participation of women in the workforce in the late 1990s, private crèches became increasingly popular with parents, often providing a readily available form of childcare. A crèche usually offers education and care to young children up to the age of 5 years, with some providing care for older children. Crèches generally operate from 7.30 a.m. to 6.00 p.m., reflecting the working day of many parents. They provide a range of services which include full- or part-time day care, playgroups and after-school clubs, while some collect and return children to their homes.

In the late 1990s, a wide range of policy documents and initiatives focusing on the needs of the young child were introduced, many of them as a result of the workings of the National Forum on Early Childhood Education (Coolahan 1998), which was held in 1998. This forum provided the first opportunity in Ireland for diverse groups and organisations with an interest in early childhood education to unite. It explored a broad range of issues related to the provision of early childhood education for children from birth to the age of 6 years old (Coolahan 1998; DJELR 1999). It was attended by organisations, including service providers, parents, teachers, teacher educators, care workers, statutory and voluntary agencies and social partners. The report of the forum provided the basis for the publication of the White Paper on Early Childhood Education, *Ready to Learn* (DES 1999). The establishment of a Centre for Early Childhood Development and Education (CECDE) in 2002, whose objective was to develop and co-ordinate early childhood care and education, accommodated many of the recommendations of the White Paper. In 2006, Ireland's first quality framework, entitled *Síolta: The National Quality Framework for Early Childhood Education* (CECDE 2006) was produced by CECDE.

In 2004, the Organisation for Economic Co-operation and Development's *Thematic Review*, reporting on practice in the early childhood education system of primary schools, declared that the approaches 'appeared to be directive and formal' (OECD 2004:58). One of its main recommendations was the formulation of a common quality framework that early years educators should follow. This led to the creation of *Aistear: The Early Childhood Curriculum Framework* (NCCA 2009), which sets out a curriculum framework for all children from birth to 6 years old across the range of early childhood settings. It provides ideas, suggestions and guidance to support all those engaging with young children.

In 2011, the National Voluntary Childcare Collaborative (NVCC: www.nvcc.ie) comprises eight national non-governmental organisations, each of which fosters and promotes childcare and early learning for young children by providing support, resources and education to those working with young children. The NVCC was created in 1999, with a view to establishing excellence and quality in Irish childcare services. The organisations comprising NVCC are the Irish Preschool Play Association (www.ippa.ie), Forbairt Naíonraí Teo (www.naoinrai.ie), National Children's Nurseries Association (www.ncna.ie), Childminding Ireland (www. childminding.ie), St Nicholas Montessori Society of Ireland (www.montessoriireland.ie), Irish Steiner Kindergarten Association (www.steinerireland.org), Children in Hospital Ireland (www.childreninhospital.ie) and Barnardos (www.barnardos.ie). Other supportive organisations which promote early childhood care and education and help shape educational thought in relation to young children are Start Strong (www.startstrong.ie), the World Organisation for Early Childhood Education (OMEP) (www.omepireland.ie) and the Children's Rights Alliance (CRA) (www.childrensrights.ie).

In 2009, the government announced a new programme to provide for a free pre-school year with effect from January 2010. In June 2011 the Department of Children and Youth Affairs was formally established. One of the key areas of interest of the Department is the provision of high-quality early childhood education and care. In spite of economic difficulties, it is stated that the free pre-school year is firmly established as an essential building block of early care and education (www.dcya.gov.ie).

The vital importance of educating young children from birth to 6 years of age is recognised to a much greater degree in the twenty-first century than it has been until now. However, it stills needs to be consolidated and in the future it will be crucial that what has been achieved is retained. History shows us that the sensitive, studied development of our young children is of vital importance. Those who are convinced of the great value of early childhood education should be active in highlighting the great benefits that derive from it.

Key learning points
- To develop an awareness of the chronology of events, debates and challenges in reforming ECEC in Ireland.

- To appreciate the influences on thinking and practices in ECEC.
- To recognise how the factors that influence policy and practice in ECEC interact and sometimes conflict.

References

Belmore Commission (Commission on Manual and Practical Instruction in Primary Schools under the Board of National Education in Ireland) (1898) *Final Report of the Commissioners* [C.8924]. Dublin: Alexander Thom and Co. Ltd.

CECDE (Centre for Early Childhood Development and Education) (2006) *Síolta: The National Quality Framework for Early Childhood Education*. Dublin: CECDE.

CNEI (Commissioners of National Education in Ireland) (1882) *Forty-ninth Report*.

— (1884) *Fifty-first Report*.

— (1894) *Sixty-first Report*.

— (1900) *Sixty-seventh Report*.

— (1905–6) *Seventy-second Report*.

— (1911–12) *Seventy-eighth Report*.

Coolahan, J. (ed.) (1998) *Report of the National Forum for Early Childhood Education*. Dublin: Stationery Office.

Cowman, M. (2007) *Growth and Development: Nurturing by Love, Language and Play*. Dublin: Daughters of Charity of St Vincent de Paul.

Dale, F.H. (1904) *Report of Mr. F.H. Dale, His Majesty's Inspector of Schools, Board of Education, on Primary Education in Ireland* [Cd.1981]. Dublin: Alexander Thom and Co. Ltd.

Department of Education (1922) *National Programme of Primary Instruction*, issued by the National Programme Conference. Dublin: Educational Company.

— (1926) *Report and Programme Presented by the National Programme Conference*. Dublin: Stationery Office

— (1934) *Revised Programme of Primary Instruction*. Dublin: Stationery Office.

— (1948) *Revised Programme for Infants*. Dublin: Stationery Office.

— (1951) *An Naí-Scoil: The Infant School – Notes for Teachers*. Dublin: Stationery Office.

— (1971) *Primary School Curriculum: Teacher's Handbooks*. Dublin: Stationery Office.

DES (Department of Education and Science) (1999) *Ready to Learn – A White Paper on Early Childhood Education*. Dublin: Stationery Office.

DoHC (Department of Health and Children) (2000) *The National Children's Strategy. Our Children – Their Lives*. Dublin: Stationery Office.

DJELR (Department of Justice, Equality and Law Reform) (1999) *National Childcare Strategy: Report of the Partnership 2000 Expert Working Group on Childcare*. Dublin: Stationery Office.

Douglas, F. (1994) *The History of the Irish Pre-Schools Playgroups Association 1969–1994*. Dublin: IPPA.

Edgeworth, R.L. and Edgeworth, M. (1798) *Practical Education*. London: J. Johnson.

Fynne, R.J. (1924). *Montessori and Her Inspirers*. London: Longman, Green and Co.

Government of Ireland (1999) *Primary School Curriculum*. Dublin: Government of Ireland.

Hayes, N. and Kernan, M. (2008) *Engaging Young Children: A Nurturing Pedagogy*. Dublin: Gill & MacMillan.

Heerwart, E. (1883). *Lecture to the Elementary School Teachers in Burton-on-Trent*. London: John Walker.

Holland, S. (1979) *Rutland Street: The Story of an Educational Experiment for Disadvantaged Children in Dublin*. Oxford: Pergamon Press; The Hague: Bernard Van Leer Foundation.

Liebschner, J. (1991) *Foundations of Progressive Education: The History of the National Froebel Society*. London: Lutterworth Press.

McCann, P. and Young, F. (1982) *Samuel Wilderspin and the Infant School Movement*. London: Groom Helm.

NCCA (National Council for Curriculum and Assessment) (2009) *Aistear: The Early Childhood Curriculum Framework*. Dublin: NCCA.

O'Connor, M. (2010) *The Development of Infant Education in Ireland, 1838–1948: Epoch and Eras*. London and Bern: Peter Lang.

Ó Cuív, B. (ed.) (1969) *A View of the Irish Language*. Dublin: Stationery Office.

OECD (Organisation for Economic Co-operation and Development) (2004) *OECD Thematic Review of Early Childhood Education and Care Policy in Ireland*. OECD.

Synge, J. (1815) *A Biographical Sketch of the Struggles of Pestalozzi to Establish His System*. Dublin: William Folds.

Wilderspin, S. (1852) *The Infant System for Developing the Intellectual and Moral Powers of all Children from One to Seven Years of Age*. London: James S. Hodson.

Young, T.U. (1852) *The Teacher's Manual for Infant Schools and Preparatory Classes*. Dublin: McGlashan & Gill.

Further Reading

Akenson, D.H. (1970) *The Irish Education Experiment: The National System of Education in the Nineteenth Century*. London: Routledge and Kegan Paul.

Coolahan, J. (1981) *Irish Education: Its History and Structure*. Dublin: Institute of Public Administration.

Parkes, S. (2010) *A Guide to Sources for the History of Irish Education, 1780–1922*. Dublin: Four Courts Press.

2

Theoretical Perspectives on Children's Development During the Early Years

Dorit Wieczorek-Deering and Ann Marie Halpenny

Learning Objectives
- To introduce early years students to the nature of child development and highlight some of the core questions addressed by developmental psychologists.
- To raise early years students' awareness that adopting a theoretical stance is essential for understanding, explaining and predicting young children's development.
- To introduce five key theoretical perspectives: biological, learning, cognitive, socio-emotional and ecological theories of child development.
- To illustrate some of the practical implications of gaining an understanding of theoretical perspectives on children's development for early years professionals.

INTRODUCTION

This chapter aims to provide an introduction to the main theoretical perspectives on children's development during the early years and to illustrate their relevance for early years professionals.

THE NATURE OF CHILD DEVELOPMENT

Key questions addressed in this section are:

- What is development?
- Is a child's development determined by patterns built in at birth or is it shaped by experiences after birth?

When we speak about child development, we are referring to the process through which children change biologically and psychologically – a process which is gradual, orderly in its sequence and, in most cases, facilitates over time greater competence in terms of children's abilities. Normative development refers to the general, expected patterns of growth which are experienced by most children. However, it is also essential to consider that each child is different and these differences make it impossible to make generalisations about all children. Some theories conceptualise development as a continuous process, while others emphasise discontinuity through a focus on qualitative differences in children's abilities at specific ages and stages of their development. Views about the extent to which development is influenced by nature (biology) or nurture (environment) also differ from one theoretical perspective to another. Increasingly, development is understood to be the result of a complex interaction of biological and environmental influences. Recent theories have also placed much greater emphasis on the child's active contribution to their own development, in terms of both their individual biological make-up and their subjective interpretation or representation of their experiences.

THEORIES OF CHILD DEVELOPMENT

This section introduces students to the importance of explaining and predicting children's age-related changes within a theoretical framework. Five specific theoretical perspectives on child development (biological, learning, cognitive, socio-emotional and ecological) are explored and their specific contributions to our overall understanding of young children's development are illustrated. These theoretical approaches are reviewed with reference to their main proponents and key principles, placing particular emphasis on their practical implications for early years professionals.

BIOLOGICAL THEORIES

Development is best understood as an interaction between biological structures and environmental experiences (Bukato and Daehler 2004). However, certain patterns of behaviour seem to be universal, in so far as they are evident across different cultures, and such patterns are often most apparent during the early years of a child's development. Signalling behaviours, such as crying and smiling in infancy, can be found across a wide range of different cultures, and tend to appear at approximately the same stage of development in all cultures. These behaviours are highly significant in facilitating communication between infants and adult caregivers and are believed to have a biological basis (Durkin 1995). Theories which place an emphasis on biological influences on development may, therefore, help us to address the following questions.

- Why do certain aspects of children's development follow identical patterns despite the different social and cultural contexts in which they occur?
- How can we explain the fact that children's development follows an orderly sequence?

- Are there particular periods in young children's development which are critical or sensitive in terms of the development of certain abilities?
- Do individual differences in babies' and young children's behaviour have a biological basis?
- How can knowledge about brain development help us enhance children's learning in the early years?

Arnold Gesell (1880–1961) was a psychologist, paediatrician and educator who in the 1940s developed a theory of *maturation*, which had its roots in the biological, physiological and evolutionary sciences. Maturation refers to instinctive behaviour patterns which appear at a particular point in development (Smith, Cowie and Blades 2003). These patterns of behaviour are determined to a large extent by genetic instructions, so that when a certain growth point is reached, some fixed behaviour patterns emerge. According to this theory, each child's individual and unique genetic and biological make-up, rather than the environment in which they are developing, determines the pace and pattern of development. Maturational theorists highlighted the orderly sequence in which key aspects of development occur. For example, children crawl before walking; children babble before producing one-word utterances and ultimately progressing to speak complex sentences. Maturationists also believed that this sequence is largely determined by the biological and evolutionary history of the species.

In order to effectively support and promote children's development in the early years, an understanding of periods which may be optimal or ideal in terms of specific learning outcomes for children is invaluable. The principle of *critical* or *sensitive* periods for aspects of children's development is highlighted in ethological theories. Ethology is the study of human and animal behaviour, with a view to understanding behaviour and development from an evolutionary perspective. Konrad Lorenz (1903–1989), in a series of well-known experiments, discovered that newborn geese are genetically programmed to become attached to the first moving object they see after hatching. Through these experiments Lorenz identified the concept of *imprinting* – rapid, innate learning within a limited critical period of time that involves attachment to the first moving object seen.

Biological theories have generated consideration of the importance of biological determinants in influencing behaviour patterns. *Neuroscience* is a growing discipline which involves the study of the nervous system, including the brain, in order to further our understanding of human behaviour, thought and emotion. Blakemore and Frith (2005) point out that knowledge of how the brain learns can have a positive impact in transforming educational strategies and optimising learning opportunities for children. With particular reference to language-learning abilities in infancy, Patricia Kuhl, co-director of the Institute for Learning and Brain Sciences at the University of Washington, has drawn attention to the profound importance of the interaction of biological influences and environmental experiences in infants' ability to discriminate sounds across the first year of their lives.

Of particular interest for early years professionals is the work of temperament theorists, who have identified the presence of biologically rooted individual differences in behaviour tendencies which are present very early in life and are relatively stable across various situations and over the course of time (Bates 1989). For instance, Buss and Plomin (1984) have argued that individual differences in emotionality (the arousal of the sympathetic nervous system), sociability (the tendency to prefer the company of others) and activity (the tempo and vigour of movement) have a strong constitutional basis and show some degree of continuity across the life span. A child's genotype (i.e. genetic make-up) and environment are seen to interact in three complex ways (Scarr 1992): first, passive genotype–environment interactions (parents who are genetically related to the child and who also provide the child's rearing environment); second, evocative genotype–environment interactions (a child's genotype eliciting certain types of physical and social environmental reaction); and finally, as children get older, active genotype–environment interactions (in which they themselves seek out environments they find compatible with their own temperamental disposition).

LEARNING THEORIES

Learning theories, also known as behaviourist theories, have had a powerful influence on many early childhood educators' views of learning (Waller 2009). While biological theories focus on innate characteristics of the child, learning theories emphasise the external world and how the environment shapes children's development.

Learning theories may help us address the following questions.

- In what way are children conditioned to behave in certain ways through interactions with their environment?
- Why are the perceived consequences of actions so powerful in influencing children's future behaviour?
- When are children more likely to imitate other children's behaviour?
- Are children influenced by violence or aggression that they see on television?

Behavioural theories influenced child-rearing strategies in the early part of the twentieth century by highlighting the notion that a child is more likely to repeat a behaviour if adults or the environment reinforce or reward it in some way. In this way, learning theories have helped us to gain insight into how children acquire social skills, emotional self-control, reasoning strategies, and the physical skills of walking and running. However, these early learning theories tended to conceptualise the child as passive with little influence or control over their development.

Classical Conditioning

Classical conditioning is a basic behavioural process in which certain stimuli or events in the environment generate a response in the person experiencing them. Key theorists such as Ivan Pavlov (1849–1936) and John Watson (1878–1958) carried out experiments which illustrated how a neutral stimulus can be manipulated to create a particular response in humans. For example, the smell of baking bread may produce a feeling of hunger in someone passing by. In this case the feeling of hunger could be called an *unconditioned response*, as it is a naturally occurring response. However, in some cases, particular responses to stimuli may be altered or manipulated if they are continually paired with another stimulus. This may be illustrated by a famous experiment carried out by John Watson in the 1920s. Little Albert was an eleven-month-old infant who was conditioned to become afraid of a rat. When little Albert was first presented with the rat, he showed no fear. However, after being repeatedly shown the rat, accompanied by a very loud noise, he began to cry in fear. Finally, Albert cried in fear at just the sight of the rat. The repeated pairing of the loud noise with the sight of the rat had induced in little Albert a fear of rats.

Classical conditioning helps us to understand how certain behaviours are learned by children. In particular, responses of fear may be based on previous experience in a child's life: for example, a child who has in the past been to the doctor for an injection and who cries at the sight of a needle in future contexts.

Operant Conditioning

Operant conditioning differs from classical conditioning in its emphasis on actively shaping behaviour by using reward and punishment to increase desirable behaviour and, conversely, decrease undesirable behaviour. B. F. Skinner (1904–1990) and Edward Thorndike (1874–1949) carried out experiments using animals as their subjects and established clearly the phenomenon of increasing certain behaviours through rewarding those behaviours. Parents and teachers who praise a child for tidying away his or her toys are likely to increase such prosocial behaviour in a child in future contexts. Similarly, learning theories have drawn attention to the phenomenon of decreasing behaviours by withholding rewards. Children also learn, through their experiences with others and with the environment, that certain behaviours generate negative consequences and so they are more likely to avoid such behaviours in future contexts. A child, for example, who burns his or her hand on a hot hob while attempting to reach for an object nearby may learn to avoid similar dangerous actions in the future. Many of the strategies adopted by early years professionals to support the development of prosocial behaviour in children have been refined beyond the fundamental principles of learning theories to include greater emphasis on communication and children's agency or active role in their own development.

Social Learning Theory

Social learning theory provides a more recent model of behavioural theories, and puts forward the view that children choose, to some extent, the behaviours they wish to adopt. From this perspective, children take on an increasingly active role in controlling their development. Albert Bandura (b. 1925) is the main theorist associated with social learning theory, which highlights the importance of observing and modelling the behaviours of others. The role and power of imitation in shaping children's behaviour is apparent in most early childhood settings. A toddler banging an object on a table, curious at the sound and impact this action produces, may well set off a chain of similar actions in other young children looking on. However, Bandura emphasised that children play an active role in choosing who to imitate and when to imitate an action. A young child may observe another child gain access to an object through coercion or force. Whether this child chooses to imitate such coercive action will most likely depend upon the degree of similarity between the children – are they of similar age and gender? And is the action perceived to be beneficial to the child? Bandura was very interested in the effects of media on children and, most specifically, in the effects of media violence on children's behaviour.

COGNITIVE THEORIES

The rapid technological advances of the twentieth century have contributed to our understanding of cognitive development – how the mind processes, stores and retrieves information. Cognitive theories may help us address the following questions.

- What processes are involved in children's thinking in the early years?
- How do children's thinking and problem-solving abilities change as they get older?
- In what ways are children agents of their own thinking and learning?
- What role do adults play in supporting children's cognitive development?

Jean Piaget (1896–1980) was one of the main theorists to draw attention to children's cognitive development, with particular reference to four age-related stages and the particular abilities associated with each of these stages of development. Piaget's approach to children's development was constructivist, in that it emphasised the child's own construction of his/her mental representation of the world (Oates, Wood and Grayson 2005). For Piaget, children developed their cognitive abilities through their actions on the environment. This theory emphasises two particular processes: the *organisation* of our experiences and the *adaptation* of our thinking to incorporate new ideas. Piaget put forward the notion that we organise our thinking through *schemas*, or mental structures, that contain information relating to certain aspects of the world. For example, a young toddler may have a simple schema for dogs which includes any animal with four legs. As a result, the young child may exclaim 'Big doggie!' when seeing a horse for the first time. Children, through their experiences with the concrete world around them, adapt their schemas through *assimilation* (understanding something new by comparing it with what is already known) and *accommodation* (understanding something new by changing what is already known).

Children's thinking moves through four stages, according to Piaget, each of which is characterised by key features.

These four stages are:

1 Sensorimotor stage (0–2 years).
2 Pre-operational stage (2–7 years).
3 Concrete operational stage (7–11 years).
4 Formal operational stage (11 years onwards).

The *sensorimotor stage* (0–2 years) is characterised by a focus on physical sensation and learning to co-ordinate our bodies (Jarvis and Chandler 2001). One of the most widely documented abilities which Piaget highlighted during this stage of development is *object permanence*, the understanding that objects exist permanently even when they are no longer visible.

The *preoperational stage* (2–7 years) is characterised by a shift to symbolic thought, supported through the emergence of language. Observing children's play can provide insight into the differences between sensorimotor thinking and preoperational thinking. For example, in the sensorimotor stage, children will explore playdough for its sensory and tactile properties. However, the young preoperational child might roll the playdough to a specific shape and then hold it up to show their teacher, exclaiming 'bun', demonstrating the emergence of symbolic thought. Preoperational children are still egocentric, experiencing the world predominantly with reference to themselves.

The *concrete operational stage* (7–11 years) is characterised by a shift to understanding conservation, the process through which children understand that even though the appearance of something may change, its underlying properties remain the same. Cognitive developmental psychologists explain this profound change in reasoning in terms of children acquiring new ways of understanding their world (Bukato and Daehler 2004).

Finally, the *formal operational stage* (11 years onwards) is characterised by the ability to engage in abstract reasoning.

While Piaget's theory has made a very significant contribution to our knowledge of child development, it has been criticised for underestimating, to some extent, children's cognitive competences (Donaldson 1984).

Around the same time as Piaget was developing his cognitive developmental theory, Lev Vygotsky (1896–1934) put forward a socio-cultural cognitive theory. Like Piaget, Vygotsky saw children as active in their own development, but he placed more emphasis on the role of social and cultural influences on development and learning. A key aspect of Vygotsky's theory was the notion that children's social interaction with more skilled adults or peers is central to facilitating and supporting cognitive development. In this way, Vygotsky can be seen as a social constructivist as he places emphasis on social interaction in supporting children's learning and development. One key aspect of his emphasis on social interaction and the importance of learning with more expert others was what he termed the *zone of proximal development* (ZPD). This refers to the difference between what a child can achieve alone and what it can achieve when supported by an adult or more expert peer or sibling. Using a term coined by Jerome Bruner, Vygotsky promoted the term 'scaffolding' for children's learning through providing appropriate support for their learning and adjusting that support as children's abilities increase. Language was a central tool of thinking for Vygotsky, as it facilitated communication and, ultimately, the internalisation of knowledge.

More recent cognitive theories have placed emphasis on the concept of mental states in cognitive development. Specifically, *theory of mind* researchers have explored children's understanding and awareness of their own and others' beliefs, intentions and desires (Astington, Harris and Olson 1988; Wellman 1990).

SOCIO-EMOTIONAL THEORIES

Whilst it is important for early years professionals to gain an understanding of young children's cognitive development and learning, it is vital to the role of the early years professional to support and promote children's emotional, social and personality development; this is seen as one of the most central developmental tasks in childhood (Schaffer 2006). Key assumptions about the processes of socio-emotional and personality development will be briefly reviewed here in the context of psychoanalytic and psychodynamic perspectives, as well as attachment theory.

Psychoanalytic and Psychodynamic Theories

Some of the key questions addressed by psychoanalytic and psychodynamic theorists are:

- How can we explain contradictory and irrational behaviour?
- Why does the development of some children regress (e.g. after the arrival of a new baby a toilet-trained 3-year-old starts wetting his pants again)?
- Why is it a constant struggle to keep babies from putting everything in their mouth?
- What role does weaning and potty training play in children's development?
- What are the milestones in young children's psychosocial development?
- Do individual differences in young children's psychosocial development have an impact on later socio-emotional and personality functioning?

Key proponents of the 'family' of psychoanalytic and psychodynamic theories are Sigmund Freud (1856–1939), his daughter Anna Freud (1895–1982), Melanie Klein (1882–1960) and Donald Winnicott (1896–1971). A hallmark of all psychoanalytic and psychodynamic theories is the emphasis on the formative role of early experience in subsequent socio-emotional development and the claim that behaviour and experiences are often strongly influenced by the dynamic interplay of forces within our mind that are *outside* our conscious awareness and intentional control. Psychodynamic perspectives help early years professionals to recognise and understand the presence of conflicting motives and contradictory behaviour. For instance, an abusive mother may also be very devoted to her child. Furthermore, in the view of psychodynamic thinkers, defence mechanisms also play a critical role in young children's psychosocial adjustment. Defence mechanisms are unconscious strategies that are not based on reality and that operate outside of consciousness to help young children cope when faced with overwhelming anxiety. For instance, a child may be unable to recall or remember physical or sexual abuse suffered in early childhood because of repression, which removes deeply traumatic events from consciousness. Other important defence mechanisms are regression (a child behaving in a way that is not in accordance with his or her developmental stage), projection (seeing one's own behaviour or beliefs in others), and displacement (directing emotion to an object or person other than the person who provoked it).

A more controversial notion of Sigmund Freud's psychoanalytic theory is that children's sexual feelings play a critical role in their personality development. He proposed that, arising from maturational processes, children's development progresses in an orderly, fixed sequence through three psychosexual stages: the oral (first year of life), anal (1–3 years) and phallic (3–6 years) stages. At each stage, young children's primary motivation is to gratify their own internal drive for physical pleasure, which is referred to as libido. During the oral stage the mouth, lips and tongue are the focus of the drive for physical pleasure and the major developmental task is weaning. As maturation progresses the libido is said to shift to the anus and later to the genitals. The major developmental task during the anal stage is toilet training, whilst identification with the same-sex parent is seen to be the developmental task during the genital stage. According to Freud, either *too little* or *too much* responsiveness to a young child's pleasure drive at a particular stage can lead to a developmental arrest in which the child may become unable to move on to the next developmental task, with long-term implications for personality development. For instance, children whose development has become fixated at the oral stage are thought to develop an oral–passive personality, i.e. they tend to be very dependent on others and often retain an interest in 'oral gratifications' such as eating, drinking and smoking. In contrast, individuals with an anal personality are described as especially clean, perfectionist and stubborn.

One of the most influential neo-Freudians, Erik Erikson (1902–1994) built on the strengths of Freud's theory while attempting to avoid some of its limitations. Like Freud, he assigned an important role to early experiences and proposed that each stage builds on the outcome of the previous stages. However, in Erikson's view children do *not* become fixated, and developmental issues are much broader. Specifically, he proposed that children move through three successive psychosocial stages in the first six years of life as a function of maturation *and* experience:

1   trust versus mistrust (from birth to first year of life)
2   autonomy versus shame and doubt (1–3 years of age)
3   initiative versus guilt (3–6 years of age).

Each stage is characterised by a specific developmental challenge which may be resolved in terms of two opposing dimensional outcomes, associated with *more* or *less* optimal psychosocial functioning. Early years professionals can play a critical role in helping young children to achieve positive developmental outcomes, such as: the development, during the first year of life, of basic trust in the outside world and of hope; followed in the second year of life by the promotion of self-confidence, assertiveness and self-control; and finally, during the pre-school years, the enhancement of a growing sense of agency and purpose. According to Erikson (1995), the extent to which a developmental crisis is successfully negotiated (or not) will have important implications for the successful resolution of all subsequent stages during childhood and across the life span.

Attachment Theory

Some of the key questions addressed by attachment theorists are:

- Why do *all* babies usually develop attachment to one or more of their caregivers?
- Why do babies get upset when separated from their mother figure when 6 months or older but *not* before?
- Are there individual differences in the *quality* of attachment which young children develop, and if so, why?
- Do individual differences in the quality of infant attachment have an impact on children's later socio-emotional development and personality functioning?

Freud's psychoanalytic views on the importance of early relationships exerted a strong influence on John Bowlby (1907–1990). Bowlby also integrated ideas from ethology, evolutionary theory, cognitive psychology and control systems theory into his evolutionary–ethological theory of attachment. Attachment theorists define attachment as 'a deep-seated emotional tie that one individual forms with another, binding them together in space and enduring over time' (Ainsworth *et al.* 1978:302) and refer to all behaviours (e.g. crying, crawling) that promote physical closeness to the attachment figure(s) as attachment behaviours. In contrast to learning and psychoanalytic perspectives, attachment theorists maintain that the formation of close emotional ties between babies and their attachment figure(s) – 'a preferred individual, who is usually conceived as stronger and far wiser' (Bowlby 1977:203) – has a strong evolutionary basis. According to this view the biological predisposition of infants to seek physical proximity to their attachment figure(s) – when hungry, tired or frightened – enhanced their chances of survival in the human race's distant past. Whilst the attachment figure provides a secure haven in times of danger, in the absence of perceived physical or psychological threat the attachment figure is also used as a secure base from which the baby begins to explore the world and to which it can return at any time when in need of security and comfort.

According to Ainsworth *et al.* (1978) the baby's attachment emerges gradually in four distinct stages and is based on the ability to differentiate between familiar, regular caregiver(s) and strangers:

1 The initial pre-attachment phase (from birth to 8–12 weeks of age).
2 The phase of attachment-in-the-making (from 8–12 weeks to 6 months).

3 The phase of clear-cut attachment (during the second half of the first year)
4 The phase of goal-corrected partnership (3–4 years).

Once babies have developed a clear-cut attachment to one or more caregivers, they start protesting or crying when being separated from their attachment figure and show increased levels of cortisol – a biological marker of distress (Ahnert and Lamb 2003). Separation anxiety tends to rise in frequency from 6 to 8 months onwards until about 12 to 18 months of age.

Attachment theorists maintain that whilst the tendency to form attachments and the stages in their development are universal, there are four different patterns in the *quality* of attachment: secure; insecure-avoidant; insecure-resistant; and insecure-disorganised attachment. Ainsworth proposed that babies who experience warm and responsive care develop secure attachment and develop a belief that they can obtain care when needed. In contrast, infants whose caregivers do not respond to their distress signals in a sensitive, responsive manner develop an insecure attachment and may doubt their own abilities. Whilst Bowlby's model of developmental pathways acknowledges that change always remains possible, these early adaptational patterns are held to play an important role as new situations are thought to be interpreted in light of previously formed expectations about the self and others.

As a result of Bowlby's and Ainsworth's very influential writings, attachment has become one of the central concepts in developmental psychology and has many important implications for early years professionals. For instance, attachment theory explains the timing of the emergence of separation anxiety and highlights that babies aged 6 months or older may need longer to adjust to day care than younger babies. Furthermore, it clearly indicates the critical importance of early years professionals' responsiveness to young children's need for physical closeness when tired, hungry or upset.

ECOLOGICAL THEORY

The different theoretical perspectives reviewed above all aim to examine and explain the developmental processes underlying individual differences in young children's current functioning. In contrast, Bronfenbrenner's (1979) ecological systems theory is concerned not with development per se, but with the *context* in which individual differences in child development emerge (Bronfenbrenner 1979). According to this perspective some of the key questions are:

• What environmental influences exist beyond the young child's immediate family?
• How does the social ecology contribute to individual differences in child development?
• What role do historical events play in young children's lives?

According to Bronfenbrenner (1979) it is necessary to broaden the rudimentary conception of the environment in which the developing child lives and grows beyond the mother–child relationship to a complex hierarchy of five nested levels of influence: microsystem, mesosystem, exosystem, macrosystem and chronosystem. Bronfenbrenner emphasises that the developing child *both* influences *and* is influenced by these different environmental systems in contexts ranging from direct relationships within the family, the early years setting, the neighbourhood setting in which young children spend their everyday lives, to the broad-based inputs of culture and the historical time and place in which young children are growing up.

Table 2.1 Bronfenbrenner's (1979) ecological systems perspective

Ecological systems	Definitions	Examples
Microsystems	Part of the environment with which young children are directly in contact	Child's relationships with mother, father, siblings, grandparents, peers and early years professionals
Mesosystems	Links between microsystems	Parents' relationship with early years professionals
Exosystems	Settings in which young children do not directly participate, but which nevertheless exert an indirect influence on their development	Mother's or father's work conditions
Macrosystems	Overarching structures of the particular culture which influence young children's development	Parental belief systems, customs and lifestyles
Chronosystem	Historical context which has an impact on a child's life course	Periods of economic prosperity versus economic recession

CONCLUSION

As we have seen above, developmental and ecological theories help to explain young children's age-related changes within their social contexts and provide the basis for predicting their further development. Specifically, theories help to decide *which* research questions are important to ask and *how* to ask them when describing the course of development during the early years. The theoretical perspectives reviewed above differ in their emphasis on specific developmental domains (e.g. biological, cognitive and socio-emotional), the core dimensions of development (e.g. normative versus individual differences) and the extent to which the child is seen as an active agent in his or her own development.

Whilst there is no single, universally accepted theory of child development, *each* of the specific theoretical perspectives reviewed above provides a valuable contribution to early years professionals' overall understanding and knowledge of how to facilitate young children's development.

Key Learning Points

- The extent to which development is seen to be shaped by biological or environmental sources of influences varies from one theoretical perspective to another.
- Biological theories help us understand how children who grow up in very different social and cultural contexts share similarities in aspects of their development. These theories also help us to become aware of sensitive/critical periods in young children's development and to acknowledge the role of biologically rooted individual differences in behaviour tendencies.
- Learning theories provide us with insight into how children's behaviour is shaped by their environment. Specifically, these theories demonstrate how young children learn by association, reinforcement and observation of behaviours.
- Cognitive theories focus on how young children's thinking changes and becomes more complex over time. These theories help us understand that particular cognitive abilities are associated with specific ages and stages of a child's development.
- Socio-emotional theories highlight the importance of children's emotional, social and personality development during the early years and its implications for subsequent functioning across the life span.
- The ecological perspective emphasises environmental influences which exist beyond the young child's immediate family, as well as the historical context in which child development occurs during the early years.

References

Ahnert, L. and Lamb, M. (2003) 'Shared care: establishing a balance between home and child care settings', *Child Development* 74:4, 1044–9.

Ainsworth, M.D.S., Blehar, M.C., Waters, E. and Wall, S. (1978) *Patterns of Attachment*. Hillsdale, NJ: Erlbaum.

Astington, J.W., Harris, P.L. and Olson, D.R. (1988) *Developing Theories of Mind*. New York, NY: Cambridge University Press.

Bates, J.E. (1989) 'Concepts and Measures of Temperament' in G.A. Kohnstamm, J.E. Bates and M.K. Rothbart (eds), *Temperament in Childhood*. John Wiley & Sons.

Blakemore, S.J. and Frith, U. (2005) *The Learning Brain: Lessons for Education*. Oxford: Blackwell.

Bowlby, J. (1977) 'The making and breaking of affectional bonds', *British Journal of Psychiatry* 130, 201–10.

Bronfenbrenner, U. (1979) *The Ecology of Human Development: Experiments by Nature and Design*. Cambridge, MA: Harvard University Press.

Bukato, D. and Daehler, M. (2004) *Child Development: A Thematic Approach*. Wadsworth Cengage Learning.

Buss, A.H. and Plomin, R. (1984) *Temperament: Early Developing Personality Traits*. Hillsdale, NJ: Erlbaum.

Donaldson, M. (1984) *Children's Minds*. London: Fontana.

Durkin, K. (1995) *Developmental Social Psychology: From Infancy to Old Age*. Oxford: Blackwell.

Erikson, E. (1995) *Childhood and Society*. Berkshire: Cox & Wyman.

Jarvis, M. and Chandler, E. (2001) *Angles on Child Psychology*. Nelson Thornes.

Oates, J., Wood, C. and Grayson, A. (2005) *Psychological Development and Early Childhood*. Oxford: Blackwell.

Scarr, S. (1992) 'Developmental theories for the 1990s: development and individual differences', *Child Development* 63:1, 1–19.

Schaffer, R.H. (2006) *Key Concepts in Developmental Psychology*. London; Thousand Oaks, CA: Sage.

Smith, P.K., Cowie, H. and Blades, M. (2003) *Understanding Children's Development*. Oxford: Blackwell.

Waller, T. (2009) *An Introduction to Early Childhood: A Multi-Disciplinary Approach*. London: Sage.

Wellman, H.M. (1990) *The Child's Theory of Mind*. Cambridge, MA: MIT Press.

Further Reading

Baillargeon, R. and De Vos, J. (1991) 'Object permanence in young infants: further evidence', *Child Development* 62, 1227–46.

Bee, H. and Boyd, D. (2011). *The Developing Child*. Allyn and Bacon.

Bowlby, J. (1969) *Attachment and Loss*, Vol. 1: *Attachment*. London: Hogarth; and New York: Basic Books.

Bronfenbrenner, U. and Ceci, S. (1994) 'Nature–Nurture reconceptualized in developmental perspective: a bio-ecological model', *Psychological Review* 101:4, 568–86.

DeHart, G.B., Sroufe, L.A. and Cooper, R.G. (2004) *Child Development: Its Nature and Course* (5th edn). New York: McGraw-Hill.

Freud, A. (1968) *Ego and the Mechanisms of Defense*. Hogarth Press.

Freud, S. (2005) *The Unconscious*. London: Penguin.

Hayes, N. (2011) *Early Childhood Education: An Introductory Text*. Dublin: Gill & Macmillan.

Keller, H., Poortinga, Y. and Schoelmerich, A. (2002) *Between Culture and Biology: Perspectives on Ontogenetic Development*. Cambridge University Press.

Klein, M. and Mitchell, J. (1986) *The Selected Melanie Klein*. New York, NY: Free Press.

McCartney, K. and Phillips, D. (2005) *The Blackwell Handbook of Early Childhood Development*. New York: Wiley Blackwell.

Shonkoff, J. and Phillips, D. (2000) *From Neurons to Neighbourhoods: The Science of Early Childhood*. Washington: National Academy Press.

Santrock, J. (2011) *Child Development: An Introduction* (11th edn). New York: McGraw Hill.

Winnicott, D. (1982) *Playing and Reality*. London: Routledge.

Useful Websites

http://childdevelopmentinfo.com/index.shtml

International Society for the Study of Behavioural Development – www.issbd.org/

Society for Research in Child Development – www.srcd.org/

3

Understanding Child Health and Well-being

Jennifer (Sturley) Pope

Learning Objectives

After studying this chapter the reader should be able to:

- Recognise the importance of child health and well-being to the overall development of young children and to adults in later life.
- Understand the broad determinants of health in young children and families and the impact that poverty and social inequality can have on children's health and well-being.
- Examine the relationship between parental, familial and community 'wellness' and the 'wellness' of children.
- Consider strategies to promote children's health in an ecological framework.
- Identify major child public health problems such as the rise of obesity and asthma in young children.

INTRODUCTION

Rather than concentrating predominantly on illness and disease, this chapter will focus on ideas about optimising the health and well-being of children. Based on a significant body of research (CDC 2010; Marmot 2010; Barker 1994, 2000) it is now well acknowledged that the foundations of lifelong health begin *in utero* and that experiences in early childhood have a significant impact on both the physical and emotional health and well-being of adults in later life. Many factors, including poverty and social inequality, influence children's lives and it is essential that those working directly with young children and their families have a fundamental understanding of the broader factors or social determinants that influence the health and well-being of young children.

DEFINING HEALTH

If you were to define health, would you take a negative perspective (the absence of disease) or would you take a broader view? The World Health Organisation (WHO) definition of health reflects a broad perspective: 'a state of complete physical, mental and social well-being, and not merely the absence of disease or infirmity'. A more contemporary view expands on the WHO definition:

> . . . an evolving human resource that helps children and adults adapt to the challenges of everyday life, resist infections, cope with adversity, feel a sense of personal well-being and interact with their surroundings in ways that promote successful development. (CDC 2010:2)

Many different factors in children's lives influence their health and well-being and a broader definition such as this one helps us to consider how factors such as family health and relationships, poverty, the early childhood setting, the local community and social capital, cultural perspectives and national and international policy work together. This is often referred to as an *ecological* approach. The wellness of children is strongly influenced by the wellness of parents and caregivers, families, communities and societies at large (Blair *et al*. 2010). Ireland has a high rate of child poverty and poverty is strongly associated with poorer health outcomes; for example, adults from lower socio-economic groups are significantly more likely to die younger (Marmot 2010). The relationship between income and child health is highlighted throughout this chapter.

THE IMPORTANCE OF PRE-CONCEPTION AND PRENATAL EXPERIENCES

Genetic factors obviously play a role in our health status; however, lifestyle factors before conception, *in utero* and in early childhood have a significant long-term impact (CDC 2010). It would appear that there are 'sensitive or critical periods' *in utero* and in early childhood when factors such as teratogens or nutritional deficiencies can cause significant damage. Taking folic acid prior to conception and for the first twelve weeks after conception facilitates the formation and closure of the neural tube, reducing the risk of neural tube defects such as spina bifida. Certain factors (known as teratogens) can have adverse effects on healthy development during pregnancy, for example drugs (both illegal and some prescription drugs), smoking, viruses (such as rubella), radiation and alcohol. Alcohol consumption during pregnancy increases the risk of alcohol-related birth defects, cognitive and behavioural problems in childhood and foetal alcohol spectrum disorders (Mullally *et al*. 2011). Conditions that develop in adulthood, such as cardiovascular disease, type 2 diabetes and certain respiratory conditions, have also been linked to early life experiences (Barker 1994, 2000). Undernutrition in foetal and early life may permanently alter the physiology of the body, impact on metabolism and increase the risk of such chronic conditions in adulthood.

Case Study: Low Birth Weight

In Ireland, women from lower socio-economic groups (SEGs) are twice as likely as women from other social groups to give birth to babies of low birth weight (less than 2.5kg/5.8lb) (McAvoy, Sturley and Burke 2006). These babies are more vulnerable to a range of illnesses and cognitive impairment in childhood and later life (McAvoy, Sturley and Burke 2006). Poor maternal nutritional status and smoking during pregnancy are known risk factors in low birth weight. Despite health warnings on cigarette packets and increased public awareness of the dangers of smoking during pregnancy, of the mothers surveyed by the *Growing Up in Ireland* study (Williams *et al.* 2010), 18 per cent smoked at some stage during pregnancy and 13 per cent smoked during all three trimesters. Mothers with lower levels of education were more likely to report smoking during pregnancy and continuing to smoke when the child was an infant (Williams *et al.* 2010). A simple solution such as educating mothers on healthy behaviour is not sufficient. Graham (2009:153) highlights the complexity of the issue, stating that smoking 'provides a resource which can be accessed instantly when caring responsibilities are many and material resources are few'.

When a person is stressed, they produce higher levels of the chemical cortisol, which may have an impact on the healthy growth and development of the foetus. Women from lower SEGs may be more at risk of the effects of stress due to: physically demanding work; lifestyle stresses, including the impact of poverty; and poor nutrition during pregnancy.

Reducing inequalities in birth weight is complex and requires a multidisciplinary approach. Socio-economic factors, good nutrition, smoking during pregnancy and levels of stress are all intertwined. There would appear to be a 'low birth weight cycle' or an intergenerational predisposition, similar to a poverty cycle, whereby women who were low birth weight themselves are more likely to have low birth weight babies.

Study Question

Why is it important to promote the health of young women before and during pregnancy?

THE FOUNDATIONS OF CHILDREN'S HEALTH

The foundations of health for children include appropriate nutrition, safe environments and stable and responsive relationships. (CDC 2010)

APPROPRIATE NUTRITION

Healthy growth and development throughout life is influenced by nutrition. Appropriate nutrition is particularly important in periods of rapid growth and brain development, most notably during pregnancy, in infancy and during early childhood.

A substantial body of evidence has highlighted the optimal role that breast milk plays in the development of young children. Breast milk is an incredibly complex substance containing antibodies that confer protection against infection. The composition changes from feed to feed and also during a feed. The initial milk released in a feed serves to quench thirst, and is followed by a more nutrient-dense main course. Night-time feeds are less calorific than breakfast feeds; they adjust to meet the energy requirements of the baby (Goddard Blythe 2008). Breastfeeding would appear to promote cognitive and neurological development and play a protective role against gastroenteritis, respiratory infections, ear infections, digestive disorders, diabetes, obesity and heart disease. The benefits of breastfeeding may be long-lasting and give protection from conditions not just in infancy but also in later childhood and adulthood (Goddard Blythe 2008). Research indicates that breastfeeding may also reduce mothers' risk of certain cancers.

In line with WHO recommendations, the Department of Health recommends exclusive breastfeeding for the first six months. In recent years, the number of mothers breastfeeding on discharge from maternity hospitals has increased; however, this figure drops significantly within the first few months. Breastfeeding rates in Ireland still fall considerably behind those in many other countries and a significant socio-economic difference is apparent: women with higher education levels are more likely to breastfeed (Williams *et al.* 2010).

Student Exercise
- Consult the document *Breastfeeding in Ireland: A Five-Year Strategic Plan* (2005) (available on the Department of Health website, www.dohc.ie).
- The mission statement of this plan is 'to improve the nation's health by ensuring that breastfeeding is the norm for infants and young children in Ireland' (p.7). Do you think that breastfeeding is the norm in Irish society? Give reasons for your answer.

Many parents and practitioners sometimes find planning appropriate menus for young children and dealing with 'fussy eaters' problematic. The book *Feed Your Child Well* (Dunne, Farrell and Kelly 2008) offers very practical advice. Two common problems in young Irish children are iron-deficiency anaemia and constipation. Iron deficiency can sometimes result in behavioural issues, poor concentration and irritability. Making connections between health, social, emotional and cognitive behaviours and linking the child's behaviour with other factors such as diet, volume of milk consumed, etc. can help practitioners recognise the root of problems rather than focusing on addressing the behaviour in isolation. In relation to constipation, parents or practitioners often focus on dietary factors such as increasing fibre intake; however, toileting routines are usually the underlying issue (Nicholson and O'Malley 2009). For example, the child may feel under pressure to perform, the situation may be too rushed, or they may feel uncomfortable with the particular adult present.

From an early childhood education and care (ECEC) perspective, practitioners should also be making the most of mealtimes as golden opportunities for learning and for fun. Involving children in activities such as preparing healthy food and table setting not only encourages them to eat the food but is also a valuable way of introducing mathematical concepts in an informal way (for example dividing the fruit into equal parts, working out how many spoons will be needed, etc.).

From a global perspective, there are major inequalities in the distribution of food to children and malnutrition still plays a major role in the cause of deaths of young children.

Case Study: Obesity in Childhood – A Major Public Health Problem
Figure 3.1 Factors associated with childhood obesity

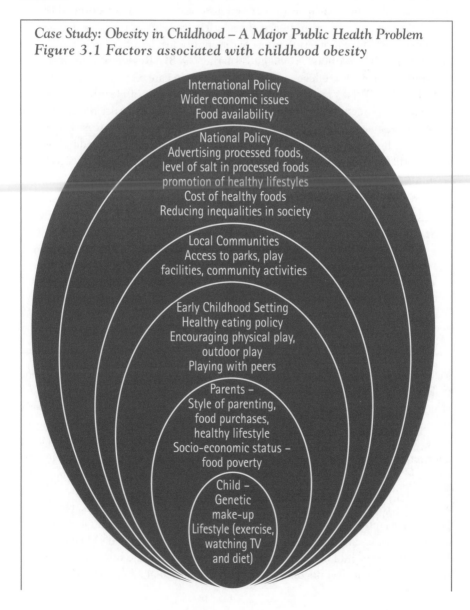

Establishing healthy behaviours in early childhood can have long-term consequences. Obesity has now become a major public health problem in adults and children. In Ireland, almost one in four boys and over one in four girls are either overweight or obese (Whelton, Harrington *et al.* 2007). Obesity in childhood is associated with psychological ill health, cardiovascular problems, asthma, chronic inflammation, diabetes, orthopaedic problems, liver problems and premature death (Reilly 2006). Addressing the issue of obesity is multifaceted and requires an ecological strategic approach. Figure 3.1 summarises some of the many factors associated with obesity in childhood.

Study Question
What recommendations would you suggest to reduce the levels of obesity in your local area?

Case Study: Asthma and Allergies
Asthma is a complex disease usually characterised by episodes of wheezing, breathlessness, chest tightness and coughing. Asthma and allergies such as rhinitis and eczema are all part of the same atopic family and these conditions often co-exist in a child. A global study highlighted Ireland as having the fourth highest prevalence of childhood asthma in the world; the UK, Australia and New Zealand were all in the top five (ISAAC 1998). Approximately one in five children in Ireland have asthma and, although there is a strong genetic predisposition, an increase in recent decades of asthma and allergies in children has led to greater attention being paid to the role of environmental factors in the development of asthma and allergies (Sturley 2006). Asthma is an immune condition and research is being undertaken on factors that may influence our immune system and cause asthma. One theory is the 'hygiene hypothesis', which maintains that due to better hygiene practices, less exposure to rural, outdoor environments, smaller families and fewer infections, our immune systems are not being stimulated enough in early life. Other avenues of research include examining dietary factors and a possible link with obesity (due to an increase within a similar timeframe).

It is important that people working with young children have accurate information about possible triggers and know what to do if a child has an asthma attack. It is also important to understand the impact that chronic (long-lasting) conditions can have on children. Having accurate and reliable information will promote the quality of life for the child and family, and working in partnership with parents is important to ensure that the child does not feel alienated or very different from other children.

SAFE ENVIRONMENTS

Unintentional injuries (accidents) are a major cause of morbidity and mortality in children.

> If a disease were killing our children at the rate that unintentional injuries are, the public would be unbelievably outraged and demand that this killer be stopped. (Koop 2001, cited in WHO 2008)

The UN Convention on the Rights of the Child states that 'every child has the right to a safe environment and to protection from injury and violence'. Based on unintentional injury statistics, boys are significantly more at risk, as are children from families with a lower socio-economic status. Children may be influenced by the media, and unrealistic depictions of accidents in cartoons may affect their risk-taking behaviour.

It is essential that parents and adults working with young children make every effort to anticipate and eliminate potential dangers while also providing a challenging and stimulating learning environment. This can be a difficult balancing act and we may sometimes ask if we are playing it too safe.

Student Exercise
- Consult the WHO (2008) World Report on Child Injury Prevention (www.who.int/violence_injury_prevention/child/injury/world_report/en/).
- In Ireland, do you think that we are adopting the measures to prevent child injury that are suggested in this document?

Protecting Children through Immunisation

In Ireland at present, the vaccination schedule for young children includes immunisation against the following conditions: tuberculosis (BCG), diphtheria, tetanus, pertussis (whooping cough), polio, Haemophilus influenzae type b (Hib), hepatitis B (the six in one); pneumococcal disease (PCV); meningitis; measles, mumps, rubella (MMR). Because some of these conditions are no longer common in Ireland, there is a widespread misconception that it is no longer necessary to vaccinate against them; but the reason that they are uncommon is because we do vaccinate against them.

In recent years, there have been concerns over the safety and potential side effects of certain vaccines, most notably the MMR vaccine. One particular study in 1998 suggested a possible link between the MMR vaccine and autism. It transpired that the researcher had falsified the findings for personal gain: no such relationship between the vaccine and autism had actually been observed. The article was later deemed fraudulent and was retracted (Godlee *et al.* 2011). Several large studies undertaken since the publication of the original article have not found a link between the vaccine and autism.

Student Exercise
- Consult the document *Immunisation Guidelines for Ireland 2008* (with amendments 2011) at www.immunisation.ie.
- Consider what effects the conditions discussed in the guidelines would have if children were not vaccinated against them.

Sudden Infant Death Syndrome (SIDS)

SIDS, formerly known as cot death, is the sudden, unexpected and unexplained death of an apparently healthy infant. The Back to Sleep campaign recommends that babies should sleep on their back in order to reduce the risk of SIDS. This recommendation is based on a significant body of evidence from many different countries: a decreased incidence of SIDS was observed in each country that adopted a 'Back to Sleep' public campaign. In Ireland, the rate of SIDS has fallen by 76 per cent since the 1980s; however, it is still a significant cause of death in infants (NPMRI 2011). According to the *Growing Up in Ireland* study (Williams *et al.* 2010), 76 per cent of mothers usually put their baby to sleep on their back. This figure ranged from 66 per cent of mothers in the lowest income group to 84 per cent of mothers in the highest group. Children from lower socio-economic groups are at greater risk from SIDS, as are low birth weight and premature babies; and smoking in the home is also a significant risk factor (McDonnell 2002).

RESPONSIVE AND STABLE RELATIONSHIPS

Not only is it important that children grow up in a physically safe environment, but children also need a safe and secure emotional environment. Research evidence suggests that negative early life experiences such as highly stressful situations may impact on the body's regulatory responses such as the immune system and inflammatory responses in childhood and in later life (CDC 2010). It is not possible to differentiate between physical health and emotional health as they are inextricably linked. In terms of a child's biological development, relationships in early childhood can have lifelong implications for emotional health, stress responses, competency of the immune system and appropriate health-related behaviours (CDC 2010). Therefore, it is argued that supports for families and appropriate training and education for those working with young children is essential, not just for quality learning environments but also for improved health outcomes throughout life (CDC 2010).

Based on research findings examining the social dimension of health, it would appear that social relationships have potentially health-enhancing qualities. Individuals who report positive social relationships and good social networks are also more likely to report good health-related quality of life. The level of social cohesion, trust and co-operation in communities is often referred to as 'social capital' and this is now recognised as a relevant public health concept (Underdown 2007). The more social inequalities there are in a society, the more health inequalities are evident (Wilkinson and Pickett 2007).

Student Exercise
- Consult the document 'The foundations of lifelong health are built in early childhood' (CDC 2010) (www.developingchild.harvard.edu).
- Consider the strategies presented in the document to strengthen the capacities of caregivers and communities.

CHILDREN'S PERCEPTIONS OF THEIR OWN HEALTH AND WELL-BEING

Investigating children's perceptions of their own health and well-being is an integral part of understanding and acknowledging how children feel about their lives. Gaining the opinions and personal insights of children and adults is also an important part of the democratic process, and acknowledging and valuing the experiences of our young citizens is very much in keeping with a participatory approach. Gaining insights into how they feel about their lives, their relationships and experiences also indicates that we recognise that young children have valuable opinions and contributions to make.

CHILDREN HAVE THE RIGHT TO A HEALTHY CHILDHOOD

Children represent the future, and ensuring their healthy growth and development ought to be a prime concern of all societies. (WHO 2008)

Although this chapter has highlighted that the health and well-being of young children has direct implications for health in adulthood, it is important that a future-focused perspective is not the sole point of view (Collins and Foley 2008). From a social justice and moral perspective, children have the right to a healthy childhood, as specified in Article 24 of the UN Convention on the Rights of the Child (UN 1989). From a cultural perspective, there have been some cases in recent years of clashes over parents' rights and children's rights, for example in cases of female genital mutilation and blood transfusions and surgical intervention.

Student Exercise
- Consult the UN Convention on the Rights of the Child (UN 1989), Article 24.
- Do you think that all the rights in this article are addressed in Irish society?

PROMOTING CHILD HEALTH AND WELL-BEING IN SOCIETY

Strategies to promote the health and well-being of children must be ecological in design if they are to be effective. In order to reduce inequalities in health and improve the health and well-being of all in our society, Marmot (2010) specifies these six policy objectives:

1 Give every child the best start in life.
2 Enable all young people and adults to maximise their capabilities and have control over their lives.
3 Create fair employment and good work for all.
4 Ensure a healthy standard of living for all.
5 Create and develop healthy and sustainable living places and communities.
6 Strengthen the role and the impact of ill health prevention.

> *Student Exercise*
> - Consult the document *Fair Society, Healthy Lives* (Marmot 2010) (www.marmotreview.org).
> - Examine the six policy objectives listed above from an Irish perspective. To what extent do you feel that these objectives are being addressed in Irish society at present?

According to UNICEF (2007):

> The true measure of a nation's standing is how well it attends to its children – their health and safety, their material security, their education and socialisation, and their sense of being loved, valued and included in the families and societies into which they are born.

It is important that those working with young children and families appreciate the many different factors that influence the health and well-being of young children so that we can build healthy foundations for our society and also because children have a right to a healthy childhood.

Key Learning Points
- The environments that children grow up in (including before birth) can significantly impact on their health and well-being in childhood and in later life.
- Many different factors determine a child's health and well-being. In order to promote health and well-being we need to adopt an ecological approach.
- The foundations of health for children include appropriate nutrition, safe environments and stable and responsive relationships.

- It is important that we respond to research findings in order to develop a strong evidence-based approach to practice in terms of promoting children's health and well-being.
- A social gradient exists in Ireland and in other countries in terms of child health: children from lower socio-economic groups are more at risk of poorer health in childhood, and this may persist into adulthood.
- Children have the right to a healthy childhood.

References

Barker, D.T.P. (1994) *Mothers, Babies and Health in Later Life*. Edinburgh: Churchill Livingstone.

Barker, D.T.P. (ed.) (2000) *Fetal Programming: Influences on Development and Disease in Later Life*. New York: Marcel Dekker.

Blair, M., Stewart-Brown, S., Waterston, T. and Crowther, R. (2010) *Child Public Health*. Oxford University Press.

CDC (Center on the Developing Child), Harvard University (2010) 'The foundations of lifelong health are built in early childhood'. CDC Harvard.

Collins, J. and Foley, P. (eds) (2008) *Promoting Children's Well-being: Policy and Practice*. Bristol: Policy Press.

Dunne, T., Farrell, P. and Kelly, V. (2008) *Feed Your Child Well*. Dublin: A&A Farmar.

Goddard Blythe, S. (2008) *What Babies and Children Really Need*. Gloucestershire: Hawthorn.

Godlee, F., Smith, J. and Marcovitch, H. (2011) 'Wakefield's article linking MMR vaccine and autism was fraudulent', *British Medical Journal* 342:c7452.

Graham, H. (ed.) (2009) *Understanding Health Inequalities*. Berkshire: Open University Press.

ISAAC (International Study of Asthma and Allergies in Childhood) Steering Committee (1998) 'Worldwide variation in prevalence of symptoms of asthma, allergic rhinoconjunctivitis and atopic eczema', *Lancet* 351, 1225–32.

Marmot, M. (2010) *Fair Society, Healthy Lives*. London: Marmot Review Strategic Committee.

McAuley, C. and Rose, W. (eds) (2010) *Child Well-being*. London: Jessica Kingsley.

McAvoy, H., Sturley, J. and Burke, S. (2006) *Unequal at Birth*. Dublin: Institute of Public Health in Ireland.

McDonnell, M. and Matthews, T. (2002) 'Smoking: the major risk factor for SIDS', *Irish Medical Journal* 95, 111–13.

Mullally, A., Cleary, B., Barry, J. and Murphy, D. (2011) 'Prevalence, predictors and perinatal outcomes of peri-conceptual alcohol exposure – retrospective cohort study in an urban obstetric population in Ireland', *BMC Pregnancy and Childbirth* 11:27.

National Committee on Breastfeeding (2005) *Breastfeeding in Ireland: A Five-Year Strategic Plan*. Dublin: Department of Health and Children.

Nicholson, A. and O'Malley, G. (2009) *When Your Child is Sick*. Dublin: Gill & Macmillan.

NPMRI (National Paediatric Mortality Register in Ireland) (2011) *National SIDS Register Annual Report*. Dublin: Children's University Hospital.

Reilly, J. (2006) 'ABC of obesity', *British Medical Journal* 333:7580, 1207–10.

Sturley, J. (2006) 'An investigation into the relationship between early life experiences (both ante and postnatal) and the development of asthma and allergic disorders in children in Cork'. PhD thesis, University College Cork.

UN (United Nations) (1989) *Convention on the Rights of the Child*. Geneva: UN.

Underdown, A. (2007) *Understanding Children's Health and Well-being*. Berkshire: Open University Press.

UNICEF (2007) *Child Well-being in Rich Countries*. Geneva: UNICEF.

Whelton, H., Harrington, J. *et al.* (2007) 'Prevalence of overweight and obesity on the island of Ireland', *BMC Public Health* 7:187.

WHO (World Health Organisation) (2008) *World Report on Child Injury Prevention*. Geneva: WHO.

Williams, J., Greene, S., McNally, S. *et al.* (2010) *Growing Up in Ireland: Infant Cohort*. Dublin: Office of the Minister of Children and Youth Affairs.

Wilkinson, R.G. and Pickett, K.E. (2007) 'Child well-being and income inequality in rich societies: ecological cross-sectional study', *British Medical Journal* 335:1080.

Useful Websites
Department of Health – www.dohc.ie

For a more global perspective:
UNICEF – www.unicef.org
WHO – www.who.int
Pubmed, a very useful, freely available online database –www.ncbi.nlm.nih.gov/pubmed/

4

Sociological Perspectives on Childhood

Karen Smith

Learning Objectives

After studying this chapter the reader should be able to:

- Identify the key concerns of the academic discipline of sociology.
- Understand the main approaches to the sociology of childhood and what they can tell us about early childhood.
- Describe different forms of childhood inequality.
- Appreciate the benefits to the early years practitioner of adopting a sociological perspective on early childhood.

INTRODUCTION

The aim of this chapter is to explore the relevance of *sociology* to the study of early childhood. We will briefly look at the key characteristics of sociology as an academic discipline before examining the most important sociological perspectives on childhood and their relevance to early years theory, policy and practice.

WHAT IS SOCIOLOGY?

Sociology can be broadly defined as the *study of society*. There are many different perspectives within the discipline of sociology; for example some perspectives view society in terms of stability and consensus, while others see conflict and inequality. While not all sociological perspectives are compatible with each other, they share a concern with humans as *social* beings; that is, as people interacting within a complex network of diverse relationships. It is this network of social relationships connected by a common culture or way of life that we think of as 'society' (Giddens 2009:1133–4). Sociologists view human behaviour as influenced by societal factors rather than as simply the result of individual choice or 'natural' characteristics (Macionis and Plummer 2008:4–10). From a sociological standpoint, aspects of human behaviour which might be seen as universal or innate are viewed in the context of the various cultural and social arrangements which shape – and are shaped by – human interaction within societies.

Traditionally, developmental psychology has been the main form of knowledge employed by early years practitioners. For a student of early childhood education it can seem a challenging task to look at childhood from a sociological rather than a psychological perspective. Psychologists are typically interested in children's development across a range of dimensions, for example cognitive, emotional or moral. Although concerned with both the social context of development and children's social interaction, the primary concern of developmental psychology is the interior world of the individual child as s/he progresses towards maturity. Sociologists, by contrast, have a direct concern with the relationship between children and society. For the early years practitioner, sociology provides the conceptual tools to begin viewing children as 'social beings' and to explore the broader societal context influencing early years policy and provision.

SOCIALISATION

Until relatively recently, thinking about childhood in sociology was largely centred on socialisation. Socialisation of children refers to the process by which the young learn the cultural rules or 'norms' which allow them to 'fit into' society as adults. The concept of socialisation is particularly associated with *functionalism*. This sociological perspective takes as its starting point the idea of society as a system of discrete but interconnected elements such as political institutions, educational institutions and families. Each element is regarded as having distinct *functions* which contribute to the overall functioning of society (Macionis and Plummer 2008:29). From a functionalist perspective, socialisation of the young is the means by which society reproduces itself. This function is carried out in the first instance by families (and increasingly early childhood institutions) and in later years by schools, religious institutions, peer groups and the media (Giddens 2009:284–91).

Functionalism came to particular prominence (in the form of structural-functionalism) in the United States in the mid-twentieth century and it reflects the assumptions of this specific time and place, in particular assumptions about the respective roles of men and women. From the vantage point of structural-functionalism, 'role specialisation' by gender along breadwinner/carer lines represents the most efficient means of meeting the 'needs' of society for adequately socialised individuals (Giddens 2009:370). From a *feminist* perspective this ignores the inequalities associated with traditional gender roles – indeed lack of attention to inequality and social conflict is a criticism that has been made of the functionalist view of society generally.

In contrast to functionalism, *conflict* perspectives see society in terms of competing interests and are particularly concerned with inequality. These include inequalities based on social class, but also those based on other social divisions such as gender or race/ethnicity. From a conflict perspective, socialisation serves as the means by which individuals come to accept inequalities as 'natural' or unavoidable. Here socialisation is seen as a process through which knowledge/ideas that support the position of elites in society achieve taken-for-granted status (Clarke 2004:79).

Whether looked at from a functionalist or conflict perspective, the starting point of socialisation is society (James, Jenks and Prout 1998:23). This means that there is limited recognition of people – especially children – as *agents*, i.e. as beings possessing the capacity to act and create change (Wyness 2006:133). From the vantage point of socialisation, children appear primarily as future adults – the emphasis is on what children will *become*, rather than on who they are in the present (Prout and James 1997). This is a criticism which has also been levelled against developmental psychology, an important influence on theories of socialisation (Prout and James 1997; James, Jenks and Prout 1998). Prout and James (1997:10–14) note that from a developmental perspective childhood has traditionally been represented as a more or less universal series of stages on the route to adulthood; they argue that this not only tends to reduce childhood to a preliminary phase in the life course, but also underplays the diversity found in the experience and understanding of childhood across different societies.

THE SOCIOLOGY OF CHILDHOOD

In recent decades a number of different perspectives on childhood have emerged within sociology that aim to transcend the perceived limitations of socialisation theories and developmental psychology and to develop a distinct 'sociology of childhood'. According to Prout and James (1997:8), while there are significant differences between the various approaches, they share some basic assumptions; among the most important of these are the idea of childhood as 'socially constructed' and the notion that children are 'social actors'. James, Jenks and Prout (1998) identify four distinct approaches within the sociology of childhood: *social constructionist* and *social structural* approaches are primarily interested in the idea of childhood as socially constructed; the notion of children as social actors is of more direct concern to *ethnographic* and *child standpoint* approaches.

CHILDHOOD AS 'SOCIALLY CONSTRUCTED'

To state that childhood is 'socially constructed' is to acknowledge that the experience of childhood is not universal, but varies in accordance with diverse social, economic and cultural conditions. This can be understood on at least two different levels. The first level relates to the *meaning* accorded to childhood; this is of interest from a *social constructionist* perspective. The second relates to the impact on childhood of the structural conditions (e.g. political, economic, legal, social or cultural) of society, which is the concern of *social structural* perspectives on childhood.

Social Constructionist Perspectives on Childhood

To examine childhood from a social constructionist perspective is to explore the meaning which individuals attribute to childhood within a particular cultural context. Human beings convey meaning through images and language; the key assumption of this approach is that the images and words we use are not neutral, but reflect the values and interests of particular cultures or ways of life. Recognition that the meaning of childhood changes over time and across cultures is particularly associated with the work of French historian Philippe Ariès. In *Centuries of Childhood*, Ariès (1962:128) argued that in the medieval world childhood did not exist. What Ariès meant by this is that the notion of childhood as a separate, protected stage in the life course is a modern 'invention', closely associated with the rise of schooling. While a number of scholars have disagreed with Ariès, his work has inspired others to explore further historical and cultural variation in 'constructions of childhood'.

Among the most important cultural influences which have shaped ideas of childhood in modern Western societies are Christianity and science. For instance, the doctrine of original sin has had a profound impact on how children have been perceived in the West, but so too have alternative religious views of children as innately innocent. The image of the 'innocent child' became particularly influential from the eighteenth century following the publication of Rousseau's *Émile* and the rise of the Victorian Romantic movement (Jenks 2005). The Romantic emphasis on the connection between children and nature was an important influence on pioneers in the field of early childhood education.

With the rise of scientific thinking came more formal approaches to the study of childhood and by the twentieth century developmental psychology had emerged as the dominant form of knowledge about children. Looked at from a social constructionist perspective, the notion of the 'developing child', associated with psychology and the work of Piaget in particular, represents childhood in terms of deficiency (James, Jenks and Prout 1998:17–19). In recent years this conception of childhood has been challenged by the image of the child as 'competent social actor' associated with sociological and children's rights perspectives, but also increasingly influential in psychology.

It should be clear that multiple different ways of conceptualising childhood co-exist at any one time, although some may be more influential than others (Jenks 2005:61). The field of early childhood education and care (ECEC) is influenced by prevailing assumptions about childhood, with knowledge drawn from psychology particularly important. From a social constructionist perspective the knowledge we access – whether drawn from religion, psychology or sociology – must be regarded as partial and tied to particular social and cultural contexts. The implications for ECEC theory and practice are that we must always be willing to question 'taken-for-granted' assumptions about children and childhood.

Student Exercise
Which 'constructions of childhood' do you think inform ECEC policy in Ireland today (e.g. Síolta/Aistear)? Which 'constructions of childhood' inform your own practice?

Social Structural Perspectives on Childhood

The starting point for social structural perspectives on childhood is that *all* children in society have in common membership of the social category of childhood. This perspective is most closely associated with Jens Qvortrup, who argues that children *as a group* are affected by societal conditions and not necessarily in the same way as adults (Qvortrup 2008). This means that researchers need to focus specifically on children when gathering statistical data. To this end Qvortrup has argued that 'generation' should be used as a variable in statistical research in the same way as 'gender' or 'class'. In this way, when gathering data – on poverty, for example – researchers can compare the position of children and adults in the same way as using gender as a variable allows us to compare between men and women.

From a social structural perspective the structure or 'shape' of childhood varies over time and in different countries (Qvortrup 2008). At the macro (large-scale) level, childhood is shaped by the political, economic and cultural conditions of society, while the structure of childhood in turn strongly influences children's lives at the individual level (Qvortrup 2008). Macro-level issues of significance might include labour market trends such as unemployment levels or female participation rates. Other relevant issues might be taxation and social welfare policy, poverty trends or technological advances. Research from a social structural perspective uses statistical methods to provide us with information on the general impact on children of these macro-societal issues. This kind of data is vital in developing early years policy and planning services in a way which places children at the heart of provision.

Student Exercise
What kinds of 'macro-societal' trends do you think are most important in shaping Irish childhood today? What are the implications for ECEC policy and provision?

CHILDREN AS SOCIAL ACTORS

The idea that children, even very young children, are competent social actors capable of exercising *agency* represents a profound shift from traditional assumptions about childhood. In recent years a wide literature has emerged in sociology which tries to capture some of the diverse ways in which children exercise agency. We can identify two main approaches within this literature. *Ethnographic* approaches typically look at children's interaction within peer group contexts, while the *child standpoint* perspective is concerned with the manner in which children's agency is both facilitated and constrained by prevailing patterns of child–adult relations.

Ethnographic Perspectives on Childhood

Ethnography is an approach to social research which aims to gain a view of social life from the perspective of those being studied. It is often utilised in studying communities or groups whose values or lifestyles are perceived as somewhat different from those of 'mainstream' society. The main research method used is *participant observation*, which involves researchers taking part in the everyday activities of research participants. Obviously this poses challenges for adults studying children – researchers may try to observe children's interaction unobtrusively, but may also use methods which actively involve children in the research process (see Emond 2005).

Ethnographic approaches to the study of childhood take a certain amount of inspiration from *symbolic interactionism* (Prout and James 1997). This sociological perspective is concerned with the ways in which individuals actively create the social world in their interaction with each other. Human beings interact through language: this 'symbolic interaction' allows us to generate shared meanings which form the basis for the social values, norms and structures that make up society (Giddens 2009:25). Researchers studying childhood from an ethnographic perspective are interested in observing how children construct shared 'cultural worlds' with rules and structures which are distinct from those of adult society (Wyness 2006). So while this approach shares the assumption that childhood is socially constructed, the focus is the role of children themselves in actively shaping childhood (Wyness 2006).

One of the leading exponents of ethnographic research with children is William Corsaro. Corsaro's work is particularly relevant for ECEC as he has carried out research in early years settings. Corsaro's work has led him to take a radically different view on socialisation from the perspectives discussed earlier. He uses the term 'interpretative reproduction' to capture the active engagement of children with the wider culture, arguing that children do not passively absorb knowledge and values, but instead actively *interpret* the adult world, which provides the basis for their own 'peer worlds and cultures' (Corsaro 2005:24). For early years practitioners, ethnographic research assists us in recognising children as competent, creative beings. It also helps us to appreciate that forms of child behaviour which adults might see as irrational or even 'bold' might be perfectly logical within the framework of rules and structures which children themselves have developed (Wyness 2006:169–70).

Student Exercise
Think about the way children interact with each other in your own placement setting. Have children developed particular 'rules' around their interaction with each other?

The Child Standpoint Perspective

The child standpoint perspective is directly concerned with child–adult relations, with an explicit focus on inequalities of power. This approach derives mainly from the work of Leena Alanen and Berry Mayall, who draw from feminist theory in developing their approach. Just as feminists distinguish between *sex* and *gender*, Alanen and Mayall suggest that the concept of *generation* can be used to differentiate socially derived disparities between children and adults from those linked to biological difference. The assumption here is that inequalities of power between children and adults are linked to prevailing social arrangements rather than biological difference alone.

The child standpoint approach is explicitly politicised and emancipatory in intent. It is guided by the aim of revealing and *challenging* inequitable child–adult relations, with a strong emphasis on children's rights. Similar to ethnographic approaches, the basic starting point is that children are competent social actors and therefore deserving of rights, including participation rights. At the same time, this perspective emphasises the ways in which children's capacities to act and participate are affected by the different social roles accorded to children and adults. Alanen and Mayall advocate an approach to research which combines a focus on the macro structures that shape and constrain children's actions with children's own perspectives on issues that concern them (see Alanen 1998). This emphasis on giving a *voice* to children is a defining characteristic of the child standpoint approach.

Children as a group have traditionally had little power – adult politicians and policymakers pass laws and make decisions concerning children typically with little consultation. The institutions in which children are cared for and educated – schools and early years settings – have been designed by adults, often with adult needs and interests as the primary concern. Looking at society from a child standpoint perspective challenges anyone who works with the young – including early years practitioners – to reflect on the unequal distribution of power in their relationships with children, to consider the effects of unequal generational relations and to think about how to bring about change.

Student Exercise

Think about your own placement setting. Are inequalities of power between children and adults evident? Are attempts made to reduce inequalities between children and adults in the setting (perhaps through a children's rights approach)?

CHILDHOOD INEQUALITY

Childhood inequality can be observed on a number of levels. In addition to thinking about inequality between children and adults, as in the child standpoint approach, we can think about the various forms of inequality – such as those based on social class, gender, ethnicity or (dis)ability – which cut across childhood and which have a profound impact on the resources and opportunities available to different groups of children. A near universal feature of human societies is that they are *stratified* (Macionis and Plummer 2008:232). By this we mean that societies are arranged hierarchically, with some groups having greater status, resources and/or power than others. In democratic capitalist societies stratification is informal and is usually conceptualised in terms of *social class*. Social class is defined mainly in terms of economic resources or, following Marx, in terms of people's relationship to the means of production. While the idea of social class is primarily linked to income and occupation, class is also viewed as connected to social status, educational levels, lifestyle, beliefs and values (Tovey, Share and Corcoran 2007:180–2). We typically conceptualise classes in a hierarchy moving downwards from the professional/managerial classes to non-manual workers, skilled manual workers and finally unskilled manual workers and the unemployed.

In Ireland inequalities linked to social class are evident across a number of dimensions. For example, a baby born to an unemployed woman has a greater than average risk of low birth weight, which has long-term implications for health (www.publichealth.ie). Educational qualifications increasingly determine individual life chances and sociological research reveals that success in the education system is strongly linked to social class, for example the number of points attained in the Leaving Certificate is closely linked to parental occupational status. Irish society could also be said to be stratified on the basis of social divisions such as gender, race/ethnicity and disability; these forms of inequality intersect and reinforce disadvantage (e.g. a young girl from a low-income Traveller background is disadvantaged on the basis of gender, class *and* ethnicity).

On a global scale, the vast disparities that exist in income and wealth have profound implications for children, particularly those in the global South. The starkest indicator of inequality is that every single day 22,000 children under the age of five die, mostly from preventable causes (www.unicef.org). Adopting a sociological perspective can help us to gain a greater understanding of childhood inequality at local, national and global levels, allowing us to move beyond approaches that focus on the characteristics or behaviour of the disadvantaged to look at the economic and social structures that create inequality. This means that we cannot tackle disadvantage simply by providing assistance to those affected – we need to effect change at the societal level. The implications of this for ECEC is that while high-quality early years provision certainly has a part to play in tackling disadvantage it cannot – as is sometimes implied by policymakers – serve as a panacea for social ills (Dahlberg and Moss 2005).

Student Exercise
Which group of children do you think are most disadvantaged in the Irish context and why? Could ECEC play a role in tackling the disadvantaged position of this particular group?

CONCLUSION

Sociology offers a number of perspectives from which childhood can be viewed. While no one perspective can tell us everything we need to know about children and childhood, each helps to shed light on particular aspects of the relationship between children and society. These include the variable cultural meanings attached to childhood and the impact of political, social and economic conditions on children's lives, as well as the creative ways in which children engage in social interaction and the effects of prevailing patterns of child–adult relations. Sociology also helps us to appreciate that disadvantage is socially produced and not simply determined by the characteristics or behaviour of those affected. For the early years practitioner, sociological perspectives are vital in understanding the impact of social and cultural factors on children's lives.

Key Learning Points

- Sociology is an academic discipline concerned with the study of society. Adopting a sociological perspective helps us to see children as 'social beings' whose lives are profoundly influenced by societal factors. Sociology also helps us examine how children themselves shape the childhood they experience.
- Socialisation refers to the acquisition of social values and norms as children are 'inducted' into society.
- The idea that childhood is socially constructed refers to the considerable variation in the meaning and experience of childhood over time and across cultures. Looking at childhood in this way helps us to question assumptions about childhood and to think about the societal factors which shape early childhood and early childhood provision in Ireland.
- The idea that children are 'social actors' means that children are social beings capable of carrying out actions and creating change. This is linked to the contention that children are rights-holders. These ideas have strong implications for ECEC policy and practice.
- Childhood inequality can be understood in a number of ways – between children and adults, between different groups of children and on a global level between children in affluent and poor countries. Each of these forms of inequality can be regarded as 'socially produced' rather than simply the consequence of innate differences.

References

Alanen, L. (1998) 'Children and the Family Order: Constraints and Competencies' in I. Hutchby and J. Moran-Ellis (eds), *Children and Social Competence*. London: Falmer Press, pp. 30–47.

Ariès, P. (1962) *Centuries of Childhood*. London: Random House.

Clarke, J. (2004) 'The Sociology of Childhood' in D. Wyse (ed.), *Childhood Studies: An Introduction*. Oxford: Blackwell, pp. 77–82.

Corsaro, W. (2005) *The Sociology of Childhood* (2nd edn). Thousand Oaks: Pine Forge Press.

Dahlberg, G. and Moss, P. (2005) *Ethics and Politics in Early Childhood Education*. Abingdon: RoutledgeFalmer.

Emond (2005) 'Ethnographic Research Methods with Children and Young People' in S. Greene and D. Hogan (eds), *Researching Children's Experiences: Methods and Approaches*. London: Sage, pp. 123–40.

Giddens, A. (2009) *Sociology* (6th edn). Cambridge: Polity Press.

James, A. Jenks, A. and Prout, A. (1998) *Theorising Childhood*. Cambridge: Polity Press.

Jenks, C. (2005) *Childhood* (2nd edn). London: Routledge.

Macionis, J. and Plummer, K. (2008) *Sociology: A Global Introduction* (4th edn). Harlow: Pearson Education.

Prout, A. and James A. (1997) 'A New Paradigm for the Sociology of Childhood? Provenance, Promise and Problems' in A. James and A. Prout (eds), *Constructing and Reconstructing Childhood* (2nd edn). Basingstoke: Falmer Press, pp. 7–33.

Qvortrup, J. (2008) 'Macroanalysis of Childhood' in P. Christensen and A. James (eds), *Research with Children: Perspectives and Practices* (2nd edn). London: Routledge, pp. 66–86.

Tovey, H., Share, P. and Corcoran, M. (2007) *A Sociology of Ireland* (3rd edn). Dublin: Gill & Macmillan.

Wyness, M. (2006) *Childhood and Society: An Introduction to the Sociology of Childhood*. Basingstoke: Palgrave Macmillan.

Further Reading

Abbott, P., Wallace, C. and Tyler, M. (2005) *An Introduction to Sociology: Feminist Perspectives* (3rd edn). Abingdon: Routledge.

Alanen, L. and Mayall, B. (eds) (2001) *Conceptualising Child–Adult Relations*. London: RoutledgeFalmer.

Kehily, M.J. (ed.) (2009) *An Introduction to Childhood Studies* (2nd edn). Maidenhead: McGraw Hill.

Wells, K. (2009) *Childhood in a Global Perspective*. Cambridge: Polity Press.

Useful Websites

www.sociology.ie
www.socioweb.com
www.omc.gov.ie
www.childrensrights.ie
www.unicef.org

5

The Legal Framework for Early Childhood Education and Care

Moira Jenkins

Learning Objectives
After studying this chapter the reader should be able to:
- Describe the legal regulation of early childhood education and care (ECEC) provision in Ireland.
- Identify how various laws relevant to early childhood are made, interact and are implemented – the Constitution, legislation, case law and international law.
- Appraise the key provisions of the Child Care Act 1991 (as amended) together with the implementing Regulations against the internationally prescribed rights of the child.
- Generate a list of operational policies and procedures for a pre-school service to ensure legal compliance.
- Evaluate the contribution of legal regulation in early years education with reference to current reform debates.

INTRODUCTION

Child law in Ireland, including early childhood law, has undergone rapid and radical change in the last twenty years. Globally, early childhood services are considered to have received insufficient priority from governments in the past, with responsibility fragmented between government departments, delivery largely provided by the private and voluntary sector with inadequate co-ordination, regulation or resourcing (OHCHR 2005:10).

As a result of the growing recognition of the young child as a rights-holder and of the value of early childhood education, the law has undergone fundamental change. This process continues.

It is now crucial that the childcare provider has a current and comprehensive knowledge of the relevant legislation regulating the sector. There is a formidable body of minimum statutory requirements that the early childhood professional must comply with in providing childcare services. The student on placement should note how most policies have a foundation in legal obligation.

In addition to sector-specific laws such as Part VII of the Child Care Act 1991 and the Pre-School Regulations, laws of general application in the areas of employment, equality, health and safety at work, fire safety, food regulations, data protection and freedom of information apply to a pre-school service. This legislative regulation applies on top of so-called 'common law' – legal obligations under the law of negligence and other torts, contract law and criminal law. The rate of change from no specific regulation of the sector to monitoring/enforcement of detailed regulations has been welcomed by childcare workers as necessary to safeguard the vulnerable younger child, but criticisms of the regulatory system remain, especially with regard to the lack of minimum qualifications for workers and how inspection/enforcement occurs. This chapter aims to equip the student with an awareness of the key legislative requirements that are the foundations of a regulatory structure for ECEC in Ireland. The focus is mainly functional and applied – what laws dictate the policies and procedures you will encounter on placement or when first working – but the chapter also considers the child as a person with rights and the childcare provider as a champion of those rights. This chapter is not legal advice on the interpretation or likely application of the law in any particular case. The law and practice are stated as at 1 October 2011.

OVERVIEW OF LEGAL REGULATION OF ECEC IN IRELAND

The Child Care Act 1991 Part VII marked the first regulation of child care services in Ireland. Under the Act the Health Service Executive (HSE) is made responsible for the welfare and development of children attending pre-schools, playgroups, day nurseries, crèches, day care facilities, childminders and drop-in services. Section 50 of the Act gives power to the Minister to enact regulations to specify the minimum requirements for childcare provision. The Act provides for criminal penalties for non-compliance with Part VII and/or the Regulations.

The pace and extent of regulation of the sector was further accelerated in the last five years with the introduction by the Minister of new Pre-School Services Regulations in 2006, which became operational in September 2007 (DoHC 2006). The 2006 Regulations replaced the earlier 1996/1997 Regulations and introduced a greater emphasis on the learning, development and well-being of the child (Regulation 5) with 'regard to the age and stage of development of the child and the child's cultural context'. The current Regulations also introduced mandatory Garda vetting for all staff together with requirements for references for staff, students and volunteers. Significantly, the Regulations do not require minimum specialised training of staff. Regulation 8(1) requires only that 'a sufficient number of suitable and competent adults are working directly with the pre-school children in the pre-school service at all times'.

It is important to make the distinction between what is a statutory requirement and must be done (the Act and Regulations are law) and guidelines/codes of practice/standards which will assist in complying with the law and may help a court decide whether you have broken a law but do not have the force of law in themselves.

THE IRISH LEGAL SYSTEM

WHAT IS LAW?

Law has been described as 'the cement of society and also an essential medium of change' (Smith 2010). Law is dynamic in that it changes to reflect what the people in a society value. The view of the child as the possession of his/her parents evolved into early child welfare provisions in the 1908 Children Act and then, very slowly, into a more enlightened view of the child as a person with child-specific rights with the passing of the Child Care Act 1991 and the ratification of the United Nations Convention on the Rights of the Child (UNCRC) (UN 1989) by Ireland in 1992. This evolving view of the child as an individual with rights distinct from those of the family unit now demands recognition in the paramount law of the state – the Constitution.

Student Exercise

Access and read the *Case for Constitutional Change* on the Barnardos website, www.barnardos.ie, for an insight into the long-standing argument for constitutional change to enshrine the rights of the child in our Constitution.

Law is mandatory – if a court finds it to have been breached or broken, after a fair hearing, the state can enforce a punishment on a criminal wrongdoer or enforce a remedy to compensate an innocent party.

Sometimes the law is very slow to react to change and sometimes structural deficiencies, such as the cost of accessing justice or lack of awareness of legal rights, rather than inherent flaws in the law itself, prevents justice according to the law. Article 34.1 of the Irish Constitution states that justice is to be administered in public save in exceptional circumstances as prescribed by law – this means that we are all entitled to attend court to see justice being administered in our name (*in camera*, or closed, court hearings, usually those involving family law and/or children, will be clearly marked as such).

Student Exercise

Log on to the Courts Services website (www.courts.ie), select 'Courts' from the drop-down menu and look up 'District Court' to see the jurisdiction or authority of that court. Under 'terms and sittings' see if you can identify when your nearest District Court sits and consider a visit to see justice being administered.

A STRUCTURAL OVERVIEW

Ireland is a parliamentary democracy with a written Constitution guaranteeing certain fundamental rights and establishing the institutions of the state. The Constitution, the fundamental and paramount law of the state, is rigid and can only be changed by popular referendum. All power in the state derives from the people – we have popular sovereignty rather than parliamentary sovereignty – and the institutions of the state are bound by the laws and the Constitution.

> *Student Exercise*
> Visit the Citizens' Information website (www.citizensinformation.ie) and locate Bunreacht na hÉireann under the 'Government in Ireland' section. Find the provisions on education in the text.

SOURCES OF LAW IN IRELAND

The Constitution

The Constitution was enacted by the people in a referendum held in 1937. Article 6 of the Constitution provides for the separation of powers of government between the legislative function (the law-making power, i.e. the Dáil, Seanad and President); the executive function (which executes/implements the law, i.e. the government: the Taoiseach and his/her cabinet); and the judicial function (interpretation and application of the law, i.e. the judiciary and the courts). This division of power between the different organs/institutions of the state is designed to provide a system of checks and balances, with each institution overseeing and supervising the actions of the others. The courts are empowered to interpret and uphold the Constitution and can strike down a law (or a proposed law: a Bill) as unconstitutional and therefore invalid.

Legislation

Legislation consists of both primary or statute law – Acts/Statutes of the Oireachtas – and secondary/delegated legislation – regulations, by-laws/statutory instruments/orders. Under an Act a Minister or other body can be given power to create regulations to implement the policies and principles of the parent Act. Such delegated law-making is permissible so long as it is implementing the parent Act, putting the 'flesh on the bones' of the primary Act, otherwise the statutory instrument is *ultra vires*, or beyond the power of the delegate, and can be struck down by the courts. The Child Care Acts (1991–2007) are examples of primary Acts and the Child Care (Pre-School Services) (No. 2) Regulations (2006) an example of delegated legislation.

> **Student Exercise**
> Log on to www.irishstatutebook.ie.
> 1 Find the Child Care Act 1991 – No.17/1991 – and research the duty of a person carrying on a pre-school service as set down in Section 52.
> 2 Source the Child Care (Pre-School Services) (No.2) Regulations 2006 and check what the Regulations require on behaviour management under Regulation 9.

Precedent/Case Law

Imposition of English common law eventually supplanted the indigenous Brehon laws in Ireland. In time the enactment of the 1937 Constitution shed the remnants of colonial rule, but the Irish legal system retained the bulk of legal rules/principles, known as the common law, developed in thousands of judgments down through the centuries. Case law precedent or judicial precedent is the following of decisions in similar past cases – *stare decisis* or 'let the decision stand'.

The doctrine of precedent requires that cases must be decided the same way when the same material facts arise in a subsequent case. This doctrine provides for predictability, consistency and equality in the application of the law. It is worth noting that even where legislation has been passed to regulate an area, the meaning of such a law will not be 'settled' until the courts have interpreted and applied the provision in question, thereby setting a precedent for the future.

European Community/Union Law

In 1973 Ireland amended the Constitution to allow that, if a topic is covered by the Treaties establishing the European Communities (EC), European law takes precedence over national law. The primary law of the EC is contained in the Treaties themselves. The secondary law of the EC takes the form of regulations, directives and decisions. The European Court of Justice, sitting in Luxembourg, interprets and applies EC law.

International Law

Ireland is 'dualistic' in terms of international law. This means that the state can sign up to an international treaty but an individual cannot go into an Irish court and rely on that treaty unless and until domestic legislation has been passed to implement the terms of the treaty or international agreement. Ireland has implemented aspects of the United Nations Convention on the Rights of the Child (UNCRC) 1989, for example in relation to juvenile justice and in creating the role of the Ombudsman for Children. The European Convention on Human Rights Act (2003) incorporated that Convention into domestic law, albeit at a sub-constitutional level.

Divisions of Law

Criminal vs. Civil Law

Criminal law is a public law matter. Prosecution for a criminal offence involves the state and is usually commenced by an agent of the state, e.g. a guard. The standard of proof is beyond reasonable doubt. The sanction imposed on conviction is punitive – meant to punish. Sentencing in Ireland is governed by maximum or mandatory penalties set down in statute and by precedent. So, for example, if an HSE inspection reveals non-compliance with the Pre-School Regulations the Inspector can recommend prosecution under the Child Care Act 1991. Section 57 of the Act provides that a person who refuses admission to an authorised HSE inspector, or who obstructs an inspector, or who breaches the requirements of Part VII of the Act or the Regulations shall be guilty of an offence and on conviction in the District Court can be fined a maximum of £1,000. Under the Act the Court can also prohibit that person from operating a pre-school service for a stated period of time in addition to any other penalty.

Civil law is a private law process between two private parties – a plaintiff and a defendant/respondent. The standard of proof is on the balance of probabilities, a lower standard than that required in criminal law. The sanction sought is restitutionary, usually financial compensation, although other remedies such as an injunction or declaration may be ordered.

One incident can lead to criminal prosecution and later to civil claim. For example, a failure to take all reasonable measures to safeguard a child in a pre-school service, resulting in injury, could lead to HSE inspection, prosecution and sentence and to the family of the child taking civil proceedings seeking compensation for personal injuries to the child caused by alleged negligence.

Substantive and Procedural Topics of Law

The study of law is divided into substantive topics or subject areas such as family law, property law, criminal law and employment law. Procedural law, in contrast, involves study of the machinery by which laws are enforced in the courts.

THE RIGHTS OF THE CHILD

In little more than one hundred years, legal recognition of the rights of the child has developed from virtual non-existence to comprehensive, international treaty recognition in the UNCRC. This growth in awareness of rights of the child, distinct from the rights of the child within the family, led to political commitment to give express recognition of the rights of the child in the Irish Constitution. An information pack on children's rights, updated in summer 2008, is available on the Barnardos website and details important developments in the recognition of children's rights internationally and at home (Kilkelly and Barnardos 2008).

The following survey highlights some mechanisms by which the rights of the child have been recognised and advanced in law.

THE UNCRC

The UNCRC, ratified by Ireland in 1992, stipulates the civic, political, economic, social and cultural rights of the child and the state's duty to protect the child from abuse and exploitation (UN 1989). The Convention sets out minimum standards for the well-being of every child and is governed by four guiding principles: non-discrimination (Article 2); adherence to the best interests of the child (Article 3); rights to life, survival and development (various articles including Article 6); participation rights (Articles 12 and 13). All children have the same rights and all rights are interconnected and of equal importance. Children have a responsibility to respect the rights of others.

Student Exercise

1 In groups of three or four, discuss what you believe the specific rights of the child should be. Compare your summary with the child-friendly version of the Convention on www.unicef.org/rightsite/files/uncrcchildfriendly language.pdf.

2 A group of independent experts, called the Committee on the Rights of the Child, report on the degree of countries' compliance with the Convention. Summarise some of the key subjects of concern and recommendations of this committee on Ireland's performance in realising the rights of the child as noted in Concluding Observations by UNCRC on Ireland's Second Report (2006), available at www.dcya.gov.ie.

3 In 2006 the Committee on the Rights of the Child published an influential document, (2005) Implementing Child Rights in Early Childhood: General Comment No. 7 (OHCHR 2005) to encourage recognition of early childhood as a critical period for the realisation of these rights. Access the General Comment and consider the relevance to Ireland of the comments on policies and programmes for early childhood at paragraph 22 (www2. ohchr.org/English/bodies/crc/comments.htm).

CHILD PROTECTION

The core piece of legislation to promote the welfare and protection of children is the Child Care Act 1991 (as amended). As mentioned above, Part VII of that Act regulates pre-school services. The 1991 Act provides that the welfare and protection of children is of paramount importance; that parents are responsible for their children's welfare, and that within the family is the best place for a child to grow up and be cared for wherever possible; that the HSE must support families in protecting and caring for children; that where a child is at risk of harm the HSE and Gardaí and others have a duty to protect children, and these bodies are given powers to intervene subject to rigorous criteria applied by a court. In 1999 the Department of Health and Children produced guidelines aimed at helping people in identifying and reporting child abuse – *Children First: National Guidelines for the Protection and Welfare of Children* (DoHC 1999). In July 2011 the Office of the Minister for Children and Youth Affairs published a revised version of *Children First* online. There have been numerous calls for the *Children First* guidelines to given legal status – to be legislated for. The Guidelines and the accompanying publication, *Our Duty to Care*, are intended to assist the development of best practice in child protection. All organisations providing services to children have responsibilities to report reasonable concerns, develop and implement child protection policies and procedures, appoint a designated person and provide child protection training to staff and volunteers. Whilst *Children First*, at the time of writing, lacks a legislative base, other legislation does exist to reinforce and complement the provisions of the Child Care Act and to safeguard the welfare of the child.

Student Exercise

Log on to the website of the Department of Children and Youth Affairs, www.dcya.gov.ie, select 'Child Welfare and Protection' and then 'Child Protection Guidelines' from the drop-down menu and open the document 'Children First: National Guidelines for the Protection and Welfare of Children'. Access 'Appendix 7: Relevant legislation' and identify the legislative protection given to someone reporting a child protection concern in good faith.

CONSTITUTIONAL RIGHTS

At the time of writing (October 2011) a referendum on the rights of the child is promised by the new coalition government and Minister for Children. A constitutional amendment to state/express the rights of the child has been recommended and campaigned for over many years by most child rights organisations, including Barnardos and the Ombudsman for Children. Whilst the proposal has received widespread and cross-party political support, the wording of any amendment is still unknown. In that light the following overview serves merely to highlight some aspects of the debate behind the drive for constitutional amendment to express the rights of the child in Bunreacht na hÉireann.

Children enjoy all the rights expressed in the Irish Constitution – human rights do not commence at the age of 18 years. In addition, it has been held that certain unenumerated rights (i.e. rights that are not written in the text of the Constitution but discovered/declared as inherent in the Constitution by the courts), including unenumerated rights of the child, are protected by the Constitution. However, the rights of the child in Irish law to date have been described as 'patchwork in appearance and beset with difficulties' (Shannon 2005:2).

EQUALITY AND DIVERSITY

It was noted above that a foundational principle of the UNCRC is non-discrimination – that the rights of all children be respected and promoted irrespective of the child's (or the child's parent's or guardian's) race, colour, sex, language, religion, political beliefs, property, disability, birth or other status. Similar assertions in law of rights to equality before the law and non-discrimination exist in the Irish Constitution (Articles 40.1 and 44 for example) and in legislation: the Employment Equality Acts 1998–2008; the Equal Status Act 2000; the Equality Act 2004; and the Disability Act 2005. These legal principles of non-discrimination and equality have further resonance in the Pre-School Services Regulations (Regulation 5 on the health, welfare and development of the child), in the Síolta standards – see standards 1, 7, 14 and 15 – and in the National Children's Strategy in the 'Whole Child' perspective.

Student Exercise

Under the Equal Status Act 2000, as amended, discrimination in the supply of goods and provision of services is prohibited on any of nine grounds. Access the Diversity and Equality Guidelines for Childcare Providers at www.dcya. gov.ie/documents/childcare/diversity_and_equality.pdf and list the nine grounds. Read the overview of the legislative framework in Ireland on equality as provided on page 53.

REGULATION OF PRE-SCHOOL CHILDCARE SERVICES IN IRELAND

THE CHILD CARE ACT 1991, PART VII

Under Part VII of the Child Care Act 1991, as amended by the Child Care (Amendment) Act 2007, the HSE is legally required to ensure the health, safety and welfare of pre-school children attending services. The 'pre-school child' is defined as a child under the age of 6 years who is not attending a school or equivalent. Pre-school services include sessional services, full- and part-time day care services and childminders caring for more than three pre-school children from families other than their own. The Act requires that pre-school providers must notify their local HSE 'in the prescribed manner' that they are operating or intend to operate a pre-school service and that the HSE must supervise and inspect pre-school services and provide information on pre-school services. Section 52 states:

> It shall be the duty of every person carrying on a pre-school service to take all reasonable measures to safeguard the health, safety and welfare of pre-school children attending the service and to comply with regulations made by the Minister under this Part.

THE CHILD CARE (PRE-SCHOOL SERVICES) REGULATIONS 2006

The Regulations (DoHC 2006) are set out in statutory instruments numbers 604/06 and 643/06. There are thirty-three Regulations in total, arranged in six parts, addressing the areas of the health, welfare and development of the child; notification to the HSE and numbers of children who may be catered for; record keeping and information for families; standards of premises and facilities; inspection and administration including insurance. Students should read the Regulations and the accompanying explanatory guide to the requirements in their entirety. The following is an overview of some key legal responsibilities.

1 Health, Welfare and Development of the Child

Regulation 5 requires that 'each child's learning, development and well-being is facilitated within the daily life of the service' through the provision of age- and culturally appropriate opportunities, experiences, activities, interactions and materials and equipment. The Explanatory Guide makes reference to play as 'a powerful learning vehicle for young children' and to the Síolta framework. Further, the 'whole child' perspective under the National Children's Strategy is specified in the Explanatory Guide. The Interim Code of Practice in Determining Compliance (HSE 2007) emphasises the need for regular, positive and meaningful interactions with children by staff in over two pages of criteria for assessing compliance with Regulation 5. It has been observed that environmental and safety aspects of service provision (sometimes referred to as 'static variables' of quality: Mahony and Hayes 2006) are easier to define, quantify and monitor than matters of communication, pedagogical approach and the day-to-day experience of the child (the 'process variables' of quality (Mahony and Hayes 2006), but Regulation 5 is an attempt to incorporate into the regulations significant developments in perspectives on quality in early childhood.

Regulations 6 and 7 require a suitable first aid box to be on the premises and arrangements to be in place for administration of medicine and summoning medical assistance. The Explanatory Guide details the recommended content of a first aid box; that a person trained in first aid be on the premises at all times and available on outings; written parental consent to be secured for medical assistance and the administration of medicine.

Regulation 9 on behaviour management strictly prohibits corporal punishment of the pre-school child or any practice that is 'disrespectful, degrading, exploitive, intimidating, emotionally or physically harmful or neglectful'. Written policies and procedures must be in place to deal with challenging behaviour in an age- and developmentally appropriate way. The Explanatory Guide makes reference to Article 2.2 of the UNCRC and notes that *Children First* requires clear written guidelines on identifying and reporting child abuse.

2 Management and Staffing

Regulation 8 requires that there must be a designated person in charge and a designated deputy, one of whom should be on the premises at all times; that all staff, students and volunteers with access to the child have Garda vetting and two recent validated references from 'reputable sources' and that 'a sufficient number of suitable and competent adults are working with the pre-school children' at all times. A 'competent' adult is stated to be someone over 18 with adequate, appropriate experience in caring for children under 6 years and/or who has appropriate qualifications. The Explanatory Guide suggests that centre-based services 'should aim' to have at least 50 per cent of their staff appropriately qualified. Whilst the Regulations do require written policies on management, recruitment, training and staff absences, there are no minimum standards in law on the educational qualifications of staff. The European Commission Network on Childcare set a target that a minimum of 60 per cent of staff working directly with children in collective services have at least three years' training. The number of suitable staff required is dictated by the minimum staff:child ratios set down in Regulation 12 in light of age, group size and space requirements per child.

Table 5.1 Adult:child ratios in pre-school settings

Full-time and part-time services	
0–1 year	1:3
1–2 years	1:5
2–3 years	1:6
3–6 years	1:8
Sessional and drop-in services	
0–1 year	1:3
1–2.5 years	1:5
2.5–6 years	1:10

3 Record Keeping and Information for Families

A copy of the Child Care Act and the Regulations must be kept at the service and parents/guardians have also the right to information about staff qualifications and experience (including students and volunteers) and staff:child ratios, policies and procedures, the type of programme and facilities provided, fees and details as to their child's activities during the day, including any accident that occurred. The parent/guardian is entitled to inspect the register, but only as it relates to their own child. Confidentiality in relation to children and their families must be respected at all times except where child protection procedures require otherwise.

Regulation 13 details the matters to be included in the Register of Pre-School children. As well as the name, address and contact number of a parent/guardian authorisation for collection, details of any illness/disability/allergy or special need, contact details for the child's general practitioner, immunisations (if any) and written parental consent for appropriate medical treatment must be included in the Register, which must be updated as necessary. The Regulations also require records to be kept in relation to all staff (including vetting and references details); details of daily attendances and staff rosters; details of staff:child ratios; opening hours and fees; accidents/incidents; facilities available and type of care/programme provided (see also Regulation 25); administration of medicines; and fire safety measures, including fire drills and maintenance of fire equipment and smoke alarms. Staff must be trained in the use of equipment, and staff and children should know evacuation procedures.

4 Childcare Premises

The Regulations require that anyone operating a pre-school service ensures that premises are sound and stable and suitable for the 'purpose of providing a pre-school service' – including compliance with building regulations. Importantly, access and egress should be planned to ensure safe drop-off and collection of children. Regulation 18(b) requires 'adequate space per child', which is detailed in the Explanatory Guide and relates to clear floor space per child. Fixtures, premises and fittings, furniture and work/play surfaces must all be kept in a proper state of repair, be non-toxic and be clean and hygienic. Adequate and suitable facilities must be available for the child to rest and to play indoors and outdoors during the day. Requirements are also imposed as to suitable and adequate heating, ventilation and lighting, and sanitary facilities.

5 Safety, Facilities for Rest and Play, Food Safety and Insurance

Regulation 27 and Appendix G specify measures to ensure safety of the child, including that heat-emitting surfaces are guarded or thermostatically controlled; hot water for use by the child is thermostatically controlled; all external play areas and ponds or pits are made safe and/or fenced; steps are to be taken to prevent the spread of infection and procedures are in place for the safe conduct of any outings, including appropriate supervision.

It is important to note that other legislation will complement the requirements of the Pre-School Regulations; for example, the Safety, Health and Welfare at Work Act (2005) and its implementing regulations cover a wide range of matters to ensure the safety of 'persons at work' including safe systems of work such as manual handling.

Regulation 28 deals with sleeping arrangements (where relevant) and requires that children should have daily access to the outdoors, weather permitting.

Regulation 26 obliges the pre-school to ensure that 'suitable, nutritious and varied' food is available and that all legislation and sector specific guides as to food hygiene and safety are adhered to. Statutory minima as to provision of food apply according to the length of time the child is in attendance.

Finally, Regulation 30 mandates that adequate insurance cover be secured, including public liability (including cover for outings) and fire and theft.

Student Exercise
1 Locate and detail the recommended contents of a first aid box for children in Appendix C to the Explanatory Guide.
2 Individually, and then in a small group, generate a list of the written policies a full day care service requires to ensure day-to-day compliance with the Regulations. Compare your completed list with the suggested list in Appendix C of the recent National Standards for Pre-School Services published by the Standards Working Group. Note that the Standards exceed the strict legal requirements of the 2006 Pre-School Regulations.

CONCLUSION

The wide scope of relevant regulation has been noted, but organisations such as Start Strong argue that much remains to be done. The lack of regulations for inspection of childcare for school-going children, the absence of a legislative basis to *Children First*, regulation of all paid childminders and publication of inspection reports are seen as immediate issues. The future direction of law reform in this area is well put in the 2005 General Comment of the Committee on the Rights of the Child:

> State parties must ensure that the institutions, services and facilities responsible for early childhood conform to quality standards, particularly in the area of health and safety and that staff possess the appropriate psychosocial qualities and are suitable, sufficiently numerous and well trained. . . . Work with young children should be socially valued and properly paid, in order to attract a highly qualified workforce, men as well as women. (OHCHR 2005:11)

Legal regulation of pre-school services to date has contributed greatly to setting minima in the care and education of the young child. The next challenge is incorporating legal requirements for a specialist, professional and supported body of early childhood educators.

Key Learning Points
• The pre-school child has rights and protections under Irish law.
• The early childhood professional must comply with a set of minimum statutory requirements in providing childcare services.

- In addition to laws of general application, the Child Care Act (as amended) and the Pre-School Services Regulations impose sector specific requirements inspected by the HSE and ultimately enforced by criminal prosecution in the courts.
- The UNCRC applies equally to all children. The Committee on the Rights of the Child has highlighted the importance of the realisation of the rights of the child in early childhood.
- The law governing early childhood care and education is developing rapidly, and the student and practitioner should participate in the law reform debate on how best to promote the well-being of the young child.

References

DoHC (Department of Health and Children) (1999) *Children First: National Guidelines for the Protection and Welfare of Children*. Dublin: DoHC.

— (2002) *Our Duty to Care: The Principles of Good Practice for the Protection of Children and Young People*. Dublin: DoHC.

— (2006) *Child Care (Pre-School Services) (No. 2) Regulations 2006 and Explanatory Guide to Requirements and Procedures for Notification and Inspection*. Dublin: Stationery Office. Available at: www.dohc.ie.

HSE (Health Service Executive) (2007) *Interim Code of Practice in Determining Compliance with Child Care (Pre-School Services)(No. 2) Regulations 2006 for the Pre-School Inspectorate*. Dublin: HSE. Available at: www.hse.ie.

Kilkelly, U. and Barnardos (2008) *Information Pack. Children's Rights*. Barnardos. Available at: www.barnardos.ie.

Mahony, K. and Hayes, N. (2006) *In Search of Quality: Multiple Perspectives*, CECDE Research Series. Dublin: CECDE.

OHCHR (Office of the UN High Commissioner for Human Rights) (2005) Committee on the Rights of the Child: *Implementing Child Rights in Early Childhood: General Comment No. 7* CRC/C/GC/7. UN. Available at: www2.ohchr.org/English/bodies/crc/comment.htm

Shannon, G. (2005) *Child Law*. Dublin: Thomson Round Hall.

Smith, A.T.H. (2010) *Glanville Williams: Learning the Law* (14th edn). London: Sweet & Maxwell.

UN (United Nations) (1989) *Convention on the Rights of the Child*. UN, Treaty Series 1577, p. 3. Available at: www2.ohchr.org/English/bodies/crc/comment.htm.

Further Reading

Davenport, R. (2008) *Make that Grade: Fundamentals of Irish Law*. Dublin: Gill & Macmillan.

DoHC (Department of Health and Children) (2000) *Our Children – Their Lives: The National Children's Strategy*. Dublin. Stationery Office. Available at: www.dohc.ie.

— (2010) *National Standards for Pre-School Services*. Dublin: DoHC. Available at: www.hse.ie.

Donohoe, J. and Gaynor, F. (2007) *Education and Care in the Early Years. An Irish Perspective* (3rd edn). Dublin: Gill & Macmillan.

Doolan, B. (2007) *Principles of Irish Law* (7th edn). Dublin: Gill & Macmillan.

Fox, G. and Kingston, C. (2010) *Our Children First. A Parent's Guide to the National Child Protection Guidelines*. Dublin: Barnardos.

HSE (Health Service Executive) (2007) *Pre-School Inspection Tool and Inspection Outcome Report: Guidance Note Child Care (Pre-School Services) (No. 2) Regulations 2006*. Dublin: HSE. Available at: www.hse.ie.

Office of the Minister for Children (2006) *National Childcare Strategy 2006–2010. Diversity and Equality Guidelines for Childcare Providers*. Dublin. Available at: www.dcya.ie.

O'Kane, M. (2005) 'The effect of regulation on the quality of early childhood services in Ireland', *Child Care in Practice* 11:2, 231–51 <www.childrensdatabase.ie> accessed 17 December 2010.

Willoughby, M. (2007) *A Parent's Guide to the Child Care (Pre-School Services) Regulations 2006*. Dublin: Barnardos.

Useful Websites

Aistear – www.ncca.ie/earlylearning

Barnardos – www.barnardos.ie

Children's Database – www.childrensdatabase.ie

Citizens' Information – www.citizensinformation.ie

Department of Children and Youth Affairs – www.dcya.gov.ie (the Early Years Education Policy Unit reports to the Department of Education and Science)

Food Safety Authority of Ireland – www.fsai.ie

Government of Ireland – www.irlgov.ie

Health Service Executive – www.hse.ie

Irish Statute Book – www.irishstatutebook.ie

Office of the Ombudsman for Children: established to investigate complaints regarding actions by public bodies and to provide research and policy advice on child-related matters – www.oco.ie

Síolta – www.siolta.ie

6

Social Policy and Early Childhood Education and Care

Mark Taylor

Learning Objectives

After studying this chapter the reader should be able to:

- Briefly explain what social policy is.
- Demonstrate the relevance of studying social policy for early childhood education and care (ECEC) students and practitioners.
- Consider the issue of social justice.
- Discuss how a theory of social justice, namely the 'capabilities approach', can be applied by an ECEC student at his/her practice placement.
- Outline the policy instruments the state has at its disposal to improve the lives of children in the area of ECEC.

INTRODUCTION

An ECEC degree programme consists of both theoretical and practical elements; it provides you with a number of disciplinary perspectives and placement opportunities, preparing you to become an ECEC practitioner by increasing your understanding of the lives of younger children. My intention in this chapter is to demonstrate how understanding social policy enhances your ECEC practitioner training.

WHAT IS SOCIAL POLICY?

If you type 'Define Social Policy' into Google, Bing or another internet search engine, you will find links to many web pages. Clicking on these links, however, might confuse you in your attempt to work out what social policy is all about. And this would be a shame: social policy is a subject which has a great deal to offer you.

The subject of social policy centres on the concept of social justice, a concept examined in more detail later in this chapter. Social policy, consequently, asks us to identify better ways in which society can function.

By drawing on concepts, theories and models from a range of disciplines (e.g. economics, sociology, political philosophy, management and psychology), social policy as a subject frequently looks at the impact of the state's social policies in areas such as health, education, work, family life, social welfare, housing and the community. For example, a social policy analyst might want to examine whether increases in third-level registration fees deter people in certain socio-economic groups from attending college or influence their choice of course. Alternatively, a social policy analyst might want to assess the validity of the state's claim that the free pre-school year promotes social inclusion, prepares children for later schooling and frames the long-term foundations for a skilful workforce and a stronger economy.

This chapter focuses on the relevance of social policy to ECEC and to your future career as an ECEC practitioner. While other subjects on your course help you to think about, for example, young children's development (e.g. psychology) or their interaction with their environment (e.g. sociology), social policy challenges us to think about the issue of social justice in relation to children's lives.

At the same time we need to be mindful that we do not *only* reflect on social justice – social policy is also about action. Not only does social policy provide the ECEC practitioner with an understanding of some of the key concepts associated with social justice (e.g. equality, citizenship, well-being), it also encourages the practitioner to consider some of the steps which can be undertaken to improve younger children's lives, both in society and in the ECEC workplace. Therefore, social policy as a subject offers you a framework, encompassing theoretical and practical dimensions, with which to address the issue of social justice in relation to younger children. Later on in the chapter you will read about one such framework, namely the 'capabilities approach' – arguably one of the most important theoretical developments in social policy over the past twenty-five years – and I will consider how this approach could be used by you in your ECEC practice placement.

In the meantime, here is a puzzle for you.

Student Exercise

Anne, Bob and Carla are nine years old. They are arguing over who should get a flute. Anne claims the flute on the grounds that she is the only one of the three who knows how to play it (the others do not deny this). Bob demands it on the basis that he is so poor – unlike the others, he has no other toys to play with, and it would mean a lot to Bob if the flute was given to him. Carla says that it belongs to her because she has made it.

Who do you think should get the flute?

SOCIAL POLICY AND ECEC

The Nobel Prize-winning economist Amartya Sen introduced his book, *The Idea of Justice* (2009:12–14), by asking readers to consider this puzzle (see student exercise above); and when a class of ECEC students examines this brainteaser, we often find a range of answers emerging. Some students suggest that Anne should be awarded the flute because she or society would get the greatest pleasure or benefit from her ownership – literally, music to our ears. Other students think that Bob should be entitled to receive it because he appears to be the poorest and has no other toys; giving him the flute may also reduce his inequality in relation to Anne and Carla. Sometimes students feel that Carla should have the right of possession since she made the flute (with some suggesting that Anne (or her parents) could buy it from her or that the state could purchase it for Bob). And one or two students take a slightly different approach, proposing a shared ownership of the flute – resolving subsequent arguments between the children may require further exploration by ECEC students!

The difference of opinion over who gets the flute is not surprising; our views and values are informed by our upbringing and life experiences, and sometimes we are unaware of how powerful these influences can be. It may (or may not) be reassuring to know that social policy analysts have spent years trying to analyse and solve similar, but larger-scale, puzzles, often without reaching agreement.

These variances occur because the question of 'What is the fairest distribution of a resource?' is not an easy one to answer. Yet the absence of a straightforward answer should not be surprising because in social policy, as in the rest of the social sciences, there is no single, objective way of viewing and making sense of the social world. Different theoretical perspectives of social life are present, and these go hand in hand with different 'constructions' of social problems. For example, social policy analysts offer a range of explanations for the existence of poverty and for its resolution.

Nevertheless, a key aspect of social policy involves considering how resources should be distributed in society and for what purpose (Lister 2010:243). Central to all this is the role of the state, and a social policy analyst, thinking about ECEC issues from a societal or macro level, is likely to grapple with the following dilemmas (which, if you look closely, are not a million miles away from the flute puzzle):

- Given that children come from a range of backgrounds (e.g. rich or poor) or have different needs (e.g. special needs), should the state ensure that every child is provided with an equal opportunity to thrive?
- Given that children come from a range of backgrounds or have different needs, should the state ensure that a minimum level of care and education is provided to all? Arguably, it is up to parents, members of the wider family or the local community to provide further support.
- Although children come from a range of backgrounds or have different needs, should the state take any responsibility for them? Arguably, since they have brought them into the world, parents have sole or primary responsibility for children's well-being.

SOCIAL JUSTICE

Although there are a number of important concepts in social policy, such as need, equality and citizenship (Lister 2010:167), this chapter focuses on the concept of social justice, arguably the key concept in social policy. Unfortunately, social justice is not easy to define: people use the term in different ways for different purposes, frequently drawing on ideas from other disciplines, such as political philosophy, to support their own conceptualisations (Piachaud 2008:34). Furthermore, some commentators (e.g. Lister 2010:242; Le Grand, Propper and Smith 2008:168) argue that social justice is an 'overarching concept', in the sense that it subsumes other concepts (e.g. need, citizenship, equality). On the other hand, other commentators suggest that links can be made between social justice and concepts such as human rights or globalisation (e.g. Alcock, Daly and Griggs 2008:467). However, irrespective of how social justice is conceptualised, it is nearly always inextricably linked to the way in which resources are distributed in a society, raising the question, 'What are resources for?'

Reflecting on our understanding of human freedom or autonomy is one way of trying to make sense of social justice and why people need to have access to sufficient resources. While the relationship between social justice and freedom is complex, thinking about social justice in relation to freedom ultimately opens up a debate about the extent of the state's role in the lives of younger children. As a way of introducing an exploration of the relationship between social justice and freedom, please have a look at the next exercise.

Student Exercise

Imagine a world where you are free to do what you want as long as your actions do not have a negative impact on the lives of others. Imagine a world where you pay minimal taxes and where the state spends resources primarily on protecting you or your property, on safeguarding your freedom and on defending your country. In such a world, you are responsible for your actions and for how your life turns out, responsible for your successes and failures, responsible, ultimately, for your well-being. In such a world it is primarily up to you – and not the state – to support yourself and your family; you do this by working in the private market. If the state intervenes to 'help', it does so by providing a minimal safety net for the destitute and people living with severe disabilities.

Some people suggest this type of world is fair or socially just. What do you think?

SOCIAL JUSTICE, NEGATIVE FREEDOM AND CLASSICAL LIBERALISM

'Classical liberalism' (see Alcock, Daly and Griggs 2008:194) is the term usually given to classify the set of ideas in the student exercise (see above), even if there is some disagreement over the extent of the state's involvement in people's lives. These ideas have been around, going in and out of fashion, since the sixteenth century. Recently, they have been rebranded as 'neo-liberalism', forming an important strand of 'new right' thinking (see Lister 2010:42).

Social justice aligned to a classical liberal perspective advances a particular type of freedom and rests on a number of assumptions:

- People are rational and moral.
- People treat one another with respect.
- People find work and act in their own self-interest.
- People require little or no support from the state because the free market (i.e. an economic system where prices and wages are settled, without state interference, by the laws of supply and demand; in other words, wage levels are determined by the demand from employers for workers and by the supply of available workers) will provide welfare.
- Parents make provision for children.

The classical liberal perspective draws on a particular set of principles from economics and political philosophy, which, at their centre, value certain forms of freedom and individualism. Economically, free markets are considered to provide a superior source of welfare than the state because 'the market is regarded as the most efficient producer and allocator of resources' (Lister 2010:32). Politically, there is criticism of the state's role as a primary source of welfare because 'general and individual welfare is best promoted by allowing individuals to associate and contract and exchange freely with one another through markets or other forms of voluntary action' (Alcock, Daly and Griggs 2008:187).

However, a major criticism of the classical liberal perspective is that a restrictive form of liberty or freedom is valued. In a helpful contribution, Berlin (1969) draws a distinction between two kinds of liberty or freedom: negative and positive (discussed below). Negative freedom is about protecting people from the interfering and constraining actions of others or the state; in many ways this echoes the classical liberal position. From a negative freedom standpoint, a state's support of ECEC services may be seen as unfair because such an intervention undermines freedom! As the state needs to find money to fund ECEC services, taxpayers' incomes are reduced, and, consequently, they have less freedom because they have less money either to save or to spend.

SOCIAL JUSTICE, POSITIVE FREEDOM AND THE CAPABILITIES APPROACH

At the same time, some argue that the safeguarding of negative freedoms requires the state to be *more* actively involved in our lives. For example, in an explanation of Plant's (1990) argument in favour of social rights, Lister (2010) suggests the objective of negative freedom is to protect individuals' autonomy, which 'is to enable individual citizens to pursue their own ends' (Lister 2010:108). For this to happen, 'negative freedom cannot be separated from the *ability* [my italics] to pursue those ends' (Lister 2010:208). In other words, it is all very good for people to be 'free', but what can people achieve in their lives if they have insufficient resources or opportunities? For example, parents may have the freedom to send their children to a pre-school service, but without sufficient resources – and if the state does not fund the service – they will be unable to do so. What sort of freedom is that? Is this fair?

In this regard, Berlin's (1969) notion of positive liberty or freedom becomes evident in the sense that individuals need access to sufficient resources, opportunities and support to attain greater autonomy and control over their lives. Freedom without access to sufficient resources to achieve well-being is a partial freedom. For example, it is all very well for parents to be free to decide to send their children to a pre-school service; they also need to have access to resources to carry out their decision to ensure that their children profit in both the short and long term.

Moreover, there is an acceptance that private markets – without state intervention – are not always the most efficient in generating benefits in areas such as health and education (Le Grand, Propper and Smith 2008:179–84). A number of economic explanations account for this: for instance, individuals may have imperfect information on particular services. Many parents, for example, are unaware of the significance of 'quality' in ECEC settings for the longer-term prospects of their children. Where its significance is appreciated, many parents would still be unable to compare the quality of different ECEC services without state assistance in the form of pre-school inspection reports. The individual and the private market, therefore, may both require some form of state intervention for positive freedoms to be realised (see also Chapter 30 for a discussion on the economic benefits of the state's involvement in ECEC).

There are a number of ways in which the relationship between social justice and positive freedom have been considered, for example mapping out the link between citizenship and social rights (Marshall 1963); thinking about the 'needs' of individuals (Doyal and Gough 1991); establishing principles of social justice (Rawls 1972). And for children in recent years, there has been a growing emphasis on the rights of the child (for a very interesting account of children's rights, see Chapter 5). But for the purposes of this chapter, I want to discuss in detail the 'capabilities approach', an important and user-friendly social policy theory, which can be applied by ECEC students in their practice placements.

THE CAPABILITIES APPROACH

Martha Nussbaum's (2011:18) version of the *capabilities approach* can be viewed as a theory of social justice which aims to improve the quality of life or well-being of people. Social justice, from a capabilities perspective, focuses on freedom in terms of choices, 'holding that the crucial good societies should be promoting for their people is a set of opportunities, or substantial freedoms, which people then may or may not exercise in action: the choice is theirs' (Nussbaum 2011:18). Influenced by the political and ethical thought of the philosopher Aristotle, Nussbaum believes that the goal of public policy is less about the attainment of human survival and more about people having access to a life in which they are able to fully function or in which 'a kind of basic human flourishing will be available' (Nussbaum 2011:34).

Specifically, Nussbaum suggests that public policies should centre on the question, 'What are the people of the group or country in question actually able to do and to be?' (Nussbaum 2011:34). In other words, how can the state help people to flourish or fully function as human beings? In answering this question, Nussbaum suggests that we can specify the activities or functions which are undertaken by human beings that constitute a life which is truly human. For Nussbaum, a life without these activities or functions cannot be regarded as fully lived.

Nussbaum's theory is more than an abstract political or philosophical ideal, and therefore of use to ECEC undergraduate students, for she attempts to mark out the activities or functions of a life that is truly human. Unlike Sen (2009), who is also an advocate of the capabilities approach but takes a different focus (e.g. quality of life comparisons), Nussbaum has developed a list of ten central capabilities (see student exercise below) in an effort to specify, at a practical level, the dimensions of a 'dignified and minimally flourishing life' (Nussbaum 2011:18). All citizens should be able to secure these capabilities, whatever else they have or pursue. It is important to realise that she acknowledges that this is a list of capabilities rather than of actual functionings, because she suggests that capability, not functioning, should be the goal of public policy. For instance, public policy should ensure that people have the capability to be nourished rather than to be fed: for example, forcing a person to eat who has for religious reasons chosen to fast would reduce their well-being and would therefore be unjust.

Nussbaum notes that all the central capabilities are of significant importance and all are distinct in quality. Although some may be linked to each other, trade-offs between them are limited. The capabilities approach, as she conceives it, claims that a life that lacks any one of the ten central capabilities, no matter what else it has, will fall short of being a good human life (Nussbaum 2011:42). In other words, a shortfall in any capability limits the possibility of a person being able to flourish as a human being.

A fair criticism which can be levelled against any state adopting the capabilities approach is that someone has to pay for its realisation. Not all of the resources required, however, are monetary, for as Nussbaum (2011:18) suggests, the 'most important elements of people's quality of life are plural and qualitatively distinct'. Nevertheless, if a state were willing to fully embrace the capabilities approach, it is likely that there would be significant resistance from those reluctant to pay the level of taxes required to ensure its successful implementation.

While Nussbaum proposes that the capabilities approach should be taken up by governments, I would suggest that this theory of social justice could also be adopted by ECEC practitioners, to reflect on whether they, their colleagues or their local pre-school settings could be doing more to create opportunities for children. For that reason, we now turn to how Nussbaum's capability approach could be used by you in your ECEC practice placement.

Student Exercise

The capabilities approach – linking a social policy theory to your ECEC practice placement experience

During your ECEC practice placement you might want to reflect on these two questions:

1 What *are* you or others currently doing to help young children or their families to flourish or to improve their well-being?
2 What *could* you or others do now and in the future to help young children or their families to flourish or to improve their well-being?

But what do improvements in well-being look like? What does flourishing look like? Nussbaum's list of ten central capabilities (see below) is an attempt to articulate a rich, practical vision of well-being and flourishing for adults; it can also be considered for children. The list of ten central capabilities is consequently important: it gives us a language to think about what people require to achieve a life of dignity; it also enables us, in a practical sense, to reflect on whether ECEC settings are creating life-enhancing opportunities for children.

The purpose of this student exercise is to help you to reflect on what you or others (e.g. your supervisor, other workers, the pre-school owner or trustees, parents, other children, volunteers, the agency itself, other agencies, your college, funders (e.g. the state), etc.) are doing to help children to flourish during your ECEC practice placement experience. Look at Nussbaum's list of central capabilities and think about what you and others are doing during your practice placement to help children develop these various capabilities. For example, look at Capability No. 9 (Play: Being able to laugh, to play, to enjoy recreational activities). Think about and write down what you or others are doing during your ECEC practice placement to help children to play in the way Nussbaum describes.

Try to complete Table 6.1 during your ECEC practice placement. Don't worry if you are unable to fill all the boxes, as some of the capabilities may not be age appropriate for younger children. Alternatively, the pre-school setting may not be the most suitable environment to promote particular capabilities. However, central Capabilities Nos 4,5,7,8 and 9 (see below) seem particularly relevant to the ECEC environment. Once you have completed the exercise, think about what else you or others could do in your placement agency to further support children or their parents to flourish.

Table 6.1 Supporting social justice in ECEC for children and families: linking Nussbaum's capabilities approach to your reflections on your ECEC placement experience

Ten central capabilities (Nussbaum 2011:33–4) Numbers 4,5,7,8 and 9 seem particularly relevant to the ECEC environment	For each capability, try to write down what you or others *are* currently doing during your ECEC practice placement to help young children or their families to flourish or to improve their well-being. (Don't worry if some of the boxes remain empty.)
1 Life Being able to live to the end of a human life of normal length; not dying prematurely, or before one's life is so reduced as to be not worth living.	
2 Bodily Health Being able to have good health, including reproductive health; to be adequately nourished; to have adequate shelter.	
3 Bodily Integrity Being able to move freely from place to place; to be secure against violent assault, including sexual assault and domestic violence; having opportunities for sexual satisfaction and for choice in matters of reproduction.	

4 Senses, Imagination and Thought
Being able to use the senses, to imagine, think, and to reason; and to do these things in a 'truly human' way, a way informed and cultivated by an adequate education, including, but by no means limited to, literacy and basic mathematical and scientific training. Being able to use imagination and thought in connection with experiencing and producing works and events of one's own choice – religious, literary, musical and so forth. Being able to use one's mind in ways protected by guarantees of freedom of expression with respect to both political and artistic speech, and freedom of religious exercise. Being able to have pleasurable experiences and to avoid non-beneficial pain.

5 Emotions
Being able to have attachments to things and people outside ourselves; to love those who love and care for us, to grieve at their absence; in general, to love, to grieve, to experience longing, gratitude and justified anger. Not having one's emotional development blighted by fear and anxiety. (Supporting this capability means supporting forms of human association that can be shown to be crucial in development.)

6 Practical Reason
Being able to form a conception of the good and to engage in critical reflection about the planning of one's life. (This entails protection for the liberty of conscience and religious observance.)

7 Affiliation **A** Being able to live with and towards others, to recognise and show concern for other human beings, to engage in various forms of social interaction; to be able to imagine the situation of another. (Protecting this capability means protecting institutions that constitute and nourish such forms of affiliation, and also protecting the freedom of assembly and political speech.)	
B Having the social bases of self-respect and non-humiliation; being able to be treated as a dignified being whose worth is equal to that of others. This entails provisions of non-discrimination on the basis of race, sex, sexual orientation, ethnicity, caste, religion, national origin.	
8 Other Species Being able to live with concern for and in relation to animals, plants and the world of nature.	
9 Play Being able to laugh, to play, to enjoy recreational activities.	

10 Control Over One's Environment **A Political** Being able to participate effectively in political choices that govern one's life; having the right of political participation and protections of free speech and association.	
B Material Being able to hold property (both land and movable goods), and having property rights on an equal basis with others; having the right to seek employment on an equal basis with others; having the freedom from unwarranted search and seizure. In work, being able to work as a human being, exercising practical reason and entering into meaningful relationships of mutual recognition with other workers.	

ECEC SERVICES AND THE ROLE OF THE STATE IN PROMOTING SOCIAL JUSTICE

So far we have considered Nussbaum's capabilities approach, thinking about its utilisation at an agency or a practitioner level. However, theories of social justice, such as Nussbaum's, primarily place demands on the state to intervene constructively in our lives. And while state interventions are not always perfect (see Le Grand, Propper and Smith 2008:185–91), governments do have a number of tools at their disposal (see Ledbury et al. 2006) to improve the lives of younger children, including the use of:

* information
* financial instruments
* legislation, regulations and policies.

These tools can be seen as ways in which the state intervenes to enhance the opportunities available to younger children and their families, thereby promoting their capabilities and thus social justice.

INFORMATION

The state can inform parents and the general public of the benefits for you
children of ECEC. For example, in July 2009, the Office of the Minister for Childre
and Youth Affairs published a brief guide for parents to the free pre-school year, in
advance of the scheme's commencement. The guide provided information on
eligibility, enrolment and cost, and highlighted the potential benefit of the service
to children.

Pre-schools, play groups and crèches are regularly inspected by Health Service
Executive (HSE) pre-school inspectors. Parents should be able to access and read
these inspection reports on different pre-school services before deciding where to
send their children. Without comprehensible, updated and independently researched
information, how can parents make sufficiently informed ECEC choices?

At a more local level, the state funds the thirty-three City and County Childcare
Committees (CCCs), established in 2001. The CCCs serve a number of functions,
which include providing information to parents on the pre-school services in their
area and offering information, advice and training resources to pre-school providers.

FINANCIAL INSTRUMENTS

The state has at its disposal a number of financial tools which can be used to improve
the well-being of younger children in ECEC.

Indirect Funding of Services

The government introduced the Early Childcare Supplement (ECS) in the 2006
Budget. The purpose of the supplement was to financially support families with the
cost of raising younger children. Parents were given €1,000 per annum (reduced to
€500 per annum towards the end of the scheme) for each child up to the age of 5
years. The ECS can be seen as a form of subsidy to parents of younger children.
Parents could decide on how they wanted to spend the supplement – it did not have
to be spent on ECEC. The free pre-school education scheme replaced the Early
Childcare Supplement (ECS) in 2010.

Direct Funding of Services

In January 2010 the Irish state introduced a pre-school education scheme for children
aged between 3 and 4 years. This scheme – the free pre-school year in ECEC – is free
to all parents; the state pays pre-school centres to provide the service. The level of
payment received by a provider is dependent upon the number of children using a
service and the qualification levels of staff. An attractive feature of the free pre-
school year is its universality: the service is free to all children irrespective of a
family's ability to pay. The free pre-school year is a step in the right direction when

l justice in the context of developing the capabilities and
ildren. Unsurprisingly, since the scheme's inception, the
ds using pre-school services has risen considerably.
universal ECCE services, governments can also decide to
ar population groups for different reasons. For example, the
ubvention (CCS) programme, which was introduced in
taged and low-income parents in accessing affordable
funding to community childcare services. The level of
subvention resuits iii a decrease of up to €100 per week in the cost of each full day
care place; as a result, 'these children are availing of a second pre-school year'
(OMCYA 2011:27). The Childcare Education and Training Support (CETS)
scheme was introduced in 2010 and supports the childcare needs of participants
attending training and educational courses provided by FÁS (Ireland's national
training and employment authority) and the Vocational Educational Committees
(VECs).

The state introduced the National Childcare Investment Programme 2006–2010
(NCIP) in 2006 to improve and expand the childcare infrastructure in the country.
Grants were given to private and community providers to increase the number of
childcare places. Large-scale capital funding to new applicants was stopped in 2009
due to the economic downturn. The total capital expenditure made through the
NCIP programme was approximately €185m, and about 25,000 childcare places were
created (OMCYA 2011:27).

LEGISLATION, REGULATIONS AND POLICIES

Legislation, regulations and policies in Ireland also play a significant role in
influencing the quality and standards of the pre-school sector and, in turn, making
a positive contribution to the lives of children. The Child Care Act 1991 is an
essential piece of Irish legislation which promotes the welfare and protection of all
children. Of particular relevance to the ECEC sector are the Child Care (Pre-School
Services) Regulations 2006, which govern the HSE's role in the inspection of pre-
school services. In practice, the HSE prepares a standardised pre-school inspection
outcome report which indicates whether or not a particular service is compliant with
a range of regulations, in areas such as the health, welfare and development of
children.

In December 2010, the Office of the Minister for Children and Youth Affairs
introduced the National Quality Standards for Pre-School Services, based on
statutory requirements. This policy framework supports ECEC providers to work
toward high standards in pre-school settings (OMCYA 2011:27). Legislation and
regulations can also change. For example, the state could increase the qualification
levels required by practitioners to work in the free pre-school scheme. Other recent
initiatives supported by the state, and discussed elsewhere in this book, include Síolta
and Aistear.

CONCLUSION: SOCIAL POLICY AND THE ECEC PRACTITIONER

On one level, this chapter may seem irrelevant to your future career as an ECEC practitioner. You may feel that the issue of social justice is for others to consider – perhaps, for example, politicians, policymakers or campaigners. And while I would agree that those working in the Dáil, civil service or advocacy organisations have an important role to play in developing policies – at a societal or macro level – to improve children's lives, I also believe that the ECEC practitioner has an equally important role to play in helping children to thrive. In fact, it could be argued that ECEC practitioners, by fulfilling their role in an authentic, creative and life-affirming way, are acting as agents of social justice. Heckman (2008:4) warns us that children are more likely to fail in adulthood if they are not 'motivated to learn and engage early on in life'. Indeed, Nussbaum (2011:26) suggests that when it comes to children, more emphasis should be placed on them achieving 'functionings', as these lay the foundations of a fulfilled adulthood.

On another level, irrespective of whether you find social policy an attractive subject, the issues that are addressed in your social policy lectures and classes are likely to have important consequences for your future career. For example, we know that, all things being equal, children in pre-school settings do better when staff are more highly qualified. But we also know that pay and conditions in the sector are not at a satisfactory level for degree-educated practitioners. Therefore, it could be argued that if the state wants to maximise the capabilities of younger children at a pre-school level, it is currently failing to do so: many highly qualified ECEC graduates are not entering or remaining in the sector. Certain conceptualisations of social justice can, for that reason, be used to advocate for a well-trained and appropriately remunerated ECEC workforce.

Finally, the subject of social policy considers many more issues than have been examined in this chapter. For example, little or no attention has been paid to considering the specific benefits of ECEC to children from socially deprived backgrounds (see Chapter 18 for a fuller discussion). At the same time, by focusing on a particular conceptualisation of social justice – namely the capabilities approach – I hope you can see how social policy as a subject has something practical to offer you, both during your practice placements and in your future ECEC career.

Key Learning Points
- The subject of social policy is primarily concerned with the issue of social justice.
- Social justice is not easily definable.
- Advocates of different theories of social justice draw on ideas from political philosophy, psychology, sociology and other disciplines to support their perspectives.

- Theories of social justice are closely associated with different conceptualisations of freedom.
- The capabilities approach – a social justice theory – can be used by ECEC practitioners to justify the creation of opportunities in ECEC settings to support children to thrive or to flourish.

Thanks to Anamika Majumdar, London South Bank University, and Toby Wolfe, Start Strong, for their wise suggestions on improving this chapter: all errors continue to be mine.

References

Alcock, C., Daly, G. and Griggs, E. (2008) *Introducing Social Policy* (2nd edn). Harlow: Pearson Education.

Berlin, I. (1969) *Four Essays on Liberty*. Oxford: Oxford University Press.

Blakemore, K. (2003) *Social Policy: An Introduction* (2nd edn). Maidenhead: Open University Press.

Doyal, L. and Gough, I. (1991) *A Theory of Human Need*. Basingstoke: Macmillan.

Heckman, J.J. (2008) 'Schools, Skills, and Synapses' <www.voxeu.org/index.php?q=node/5642> accessed 12 June 2011.

Ledbury, M., Miller, N., Lee, A., Fairman, T. and Clifton, C. (2006) 'Understanding Policy Options' <www.hm-treasury.gov.uk/d/2(6).pdf> accessed 12 June 2011.

Le Grand, J., Propper, C. and Smith, S. (2008) *The Economics of Social Problems* (4th edn). Basingstoke: Palgrave Macmillan.

Lister, R. (2010) *Understanding Theories and Concepts in Social Policy*. Bristol: Policy Press.

Marshall, T.H. (1963) 'Citizenship and Social Class' in *Sociology at the Crossroads and Other Essays*. London: Heinemann.

Nussbaum, M.C. (1998) *Sex and Social Justice*. New York: Oxford University Press.

— (2011) *Creating Capabilities: The Human Development Approach*. Cambridge, MA: Belknap Press, Harvard University.

OMCYA (Office of the Minister for Children and Youth Affairs) (2011) 'Briefing Material for Minister for Children: Roles and Functions of the Office of the Minister for Children and Youth Affairs' <www.rte.ie/news/2011/0404/healthbriefingdoc.pdf> accessed 12 June 2011.

Piachaud, D. (2008) 'Social Justice and Public Policy: A Social Policy Perspective' in G. Craig, T. Burchardt and D. Gordon (eds), *Social Justice and Public Policy*. Bristol: Policy Press, pp. 33–52.

Plant, R. (1990) 'Citizenship and Rights' in R. Plant and N. Barry (eds), *Citizenship and Rights in Thatcher's Britain: Two Views*. London: Institute for Economic Affairs Health and Welfare Unit, pp. 1–32.

Rawls, J. (1972) *A Theory of Justice*. Oxford: Clarendon Press.

Sen, A. (2009) *The Idea of Justice*. London: Allen Lane.

Taylor, M. (2009) 'Pre-school Needs to be Classy', *Irish Times* <www.irishtimes.com/newspaper/health/2009/0623/1224249330632.html> accessed 12 June 2011.

Wolff, J. (2008) 'Social Justice and Public Policy: A View From Political Philosophy' in G. Craig, T. Burchardt and D. Gordon (eds), *Social Justice and Public Policy*. Bristol: Policy Press, pp. 17–32.

Further Reading

Judt, T. (2010) *Ill Fares The Land*. London: Penguin Books.

Moore, S. (2002) *Social Welfare Alive!* (3rd edn). Cheltenham: Nelson Thornes.

Useful Websites

www.eurochild.org/
www.freechild.org/index.htm
www.socialjustice.ie/
www.onlinesocialjustice.com/
www.socialjusticeinearlychildhood.org/
www.startstrong.ie/

PART 2

APPROACHES TO EARLY CHILDHOOD EDUCATION AND CARE

7

Síolta: The National Quality Framework for Early Childhood Education

Maresa Duignan

> *Learning Objectives*
> After studying this chapter the reader should be able to:
> - Demonstrate an understanding of the rationale for and context of the development of Síolta.
> - Describe the structure and content of Síolta.
> - Discuss the Síolta Quality Assurance Programme.
> - Discuss the relationship between Síolta and other relevant national policy.
> - Understand how Síolta supports the professional role of the adult in an early childhood education and care (ECEC) setting (e.g. reflective practice).

INTRODUCTION

Síolta is an Irish word meaning 'seeds'. It was chosen as the title for the national framework for quality in early childhood education because it captures the concept of potential for growth and development that can be enhanced in ECEC settings through quality improvement processes. It also represents the potential of each child and adult, which is enabled and nurtured in a high-quality ECEC environment.

Síolta was developed over a three-year period from 2002 on behalf of the Department of Education and Skills. The main policy driver for this initiative is *Ready to Learn: The White Paper on Early Childhood Education* (Department of Education and Science 1999). In this policy document, which itself was the final output of a national consultation process on early childhood education begun in 1998, the development of a national quality assurance programme was recommended to fulfil a number of functions:

> Firstly it will improve the quality of early childhood education provision generally. Secondly . . . it will signal that a provider has achieved certain standards and is subject to inspection and evaluation [and] parents can be

confident that their child will receive a quality early education. (Department of Education and Science 1999:54)

Síolta was developed to promote and support the improvement of quality provision and practice in early childhood education across all settings where children aged from birth to 6 years are present.

The context of the ECEC sector in Ireland at the time Síolta was being developed was that a wide diversity of types of ECEC provision existed, ranging from full day care for working parents, which catered for children from infancy to school age, to sessional playgroups and pre-schools, which mainly provided for children aged 3–5 years. Practice within these settings was informed by a very wide range of theory, philosophy and pedagogical practice including Montessori, Steiner, HighScope, Reggio Emilia and Naoínraí (Irish language-medium pre-schools). The majority of ECEC settings in Ireland were operated by the community and voluntary and private sectors, funded in the main by parental fees but in some cases, particularly the community and voluntary sector, subsidised by state aid for a range of targeted interventions designed to support children deemed to be at risk of social exclusion or educational disadvantage.

The diversity of the ECEC sector was also reinforced by a range of membership and support organisations, usually referred to as voluntary childcare organisations (VCOs), which emerged over time to support groups of practitioners who had similar goals and objectives for their practice; for example the Irish Pre-school Play Association (IPPA), which supports and promotes the development of play in ECEC settings; and Childminding Ireland, which represents the views of childminders working in their own homes and in children's homes. Several of the VCOs developed quality improvement or quality assurance programmes in the period that preceded and coincided with the development of Síolta and, whilst all had a high degree of common content (CECDE 2005), a variety of implementation methods and processes were employed. It was in this dynamic and rapidly developing and changing context that Síolta was developed.

THE CONTENT OF SÍOLTA

The Síolta Framework is built around three distinct but interconnected elements:

- defining quality
- assessing quality
- supporting quality.

Each element provides a set of tools that support staff in ECEC settings to engage in a continuous process of quality improvement. This process is illustrated in the Síolta quality improvement spiral in Figure 7.1.

Figure 7.1 The Síolta quality improvement spiral

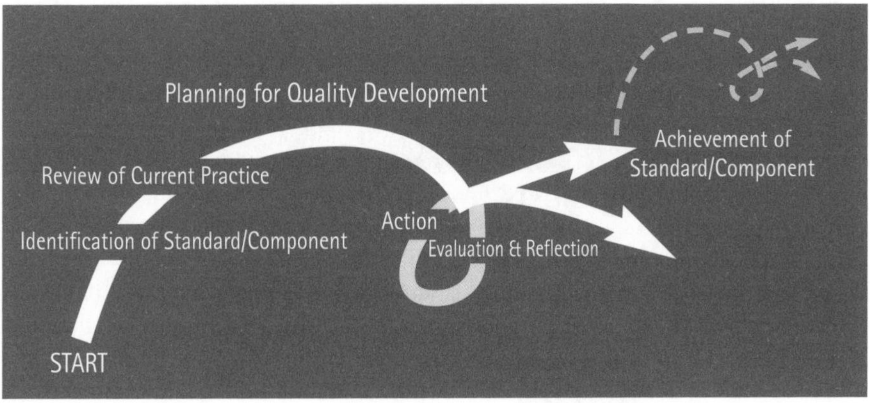

Source: CECDE 2006:29.

Defining Quality

Síolta presents an agreed national set of indicators of quality in practice in ECEC settings. These indicators comprise:

- twelve Principles – present an overarching vision for quality in practice
- sixteen Standards – translate the vision into the reality of everyday activities in an ECEC setting
- seventy-five Components – break down the Standards into more detailed elements of quality within each Standard.

Each of the Standards and Components is accompanied by a set of 'Signposts for Reflection', which are open-ended questions designed to prompt staff in ECEC settings to think in a critical and challenging way about their practice in relation to each Component and Standard. There are also a set of 'Think-about' suggestions for activities or actions that might be relevant to good practice. Figure 7.2 illustrates the layout of these materials. It is taken from Standard 1 of Síolta, which deals with the rights of the child, and states:

> Ensuring that each child's rights are met requires that s/he is enabled to exercise choice and to use initiative as an active participant in her/his own development. (Department of Education and Skills 2010:13)

This Standard has three Components: the third of these is detailed below.

Figure 7.2 'Signposts for Reflection' and 'Think-abouts'

Component 1.3

Each child is enabled to participate actively in the daily routine, in activities, in conversations and in all other appropriate situations, and is considered as a partner by the adult

Signposts for Reflection

→   **General**

1.3.1   How do you enable each child (including the child with special needs) to participate with her/his peers?

See 5.1

1.3.2   How do you show responsiveness and sensitivity to the child when you are engaged with her/him?

See 5.4

→   **Birth–18 months**

1.3.3   How do you ensure the child is responded to sensitively, with loving care?

1.3.4   Can you give a description of responding to the child's actions (such as babbling, moving, etc.) with affection and playfulness through nonsense sounds, songs, baby games, hugs, etc.?

→   **12–36 months**

1.3.5   How do you ensure that each child joins in the shared activities in a way that suits her/his own disposition?

See 5.2

!   **Think about: (e.g.)**

• Supporting each child's participation in a group activity
• Managing difficulties which arise among children during group activity.

Source: DES 2010.

Whilst the Síolta Standards and Components are relevant to all ECEC settings where children aged birth to 6 years are present, they are presented in four different manuals targeting the following setting categories:

- full- and part-time day care
- sessional services
- childminding
- infant classes in primary schools.

The rationale behind the separate manuals is that the content of each manual will be more meaningful for staff in the relevant setting if the language used reflects their particular practice environment. For example, in full day care settings, it is possible that staff will be working with children across the entire birth to 6 years age range and will therefore have to think about the quality of their practice in the context of the quite different needs and interests of children at different ages. While childminding will have similar challenges, the language of Síolta will be more meaningful if it relates to the context in which childminding usually takes place – the environment of a family home. In the infant classroom or sessional setting it is likely that all the children will be within the 3–6 age range; however, in the infant class, the familiar language will usually be that of the wider primary school context. The three age ranges that are used in Síolta mirror those used in Aistear, the Early Childhood Curriculum Framework (NCCA 2009).

SUPPORTING AND ASSESSING QUALITY

The definitions of quality provide a set of benchmarks against which any practitioner in an ECEC setting should be able to reflect on and assess their own practice; however, if these activities are to be meaningful and contribute to quality improvement in practice, they need to be supported by structured processes which scaffold the practitioner and ECEC setting to work towards achieving positive change. A number of materials have been developed to support both informal and formal processes of using Síolta in an ECEC setting.

Informal Processes

Any ECEC practitioner or setting can purchase the Síolta manual most relevant to their setting and read its contents with a view to changing and improving their own practice. However, because the content of the Síolta Principles, Standards and Components may contain language or ideas and concepts that are new or unfamiliar, a set of research digests was developed to help practitioners to understand the theory behind each Síolta standard and to translate this theory into practical activities and ideas in their everyday work (CECDE 2007). These research digests can also be used to support team meetings and planning in the workplace, and discussion groups about improving quality in network meetings of groups of ECEC practitioners. This type of activity is described as informal because it usually involves internal processes on the part of either the individual practitioner or the ECEC setting. If an external perspective on this internal quality improvement work is sought, the activity takes on a more formal structure.

Formal Processes

The Síolta Quality Assurance Programme (QAP) is the formal, structured method of engagement with Síolta. It involves an ECEC setting working through a series of steps culminating in an external validation process. Figure 7.3 illustrates these steps.

Figure 7.3 The Síolta Quality Assurance Programme

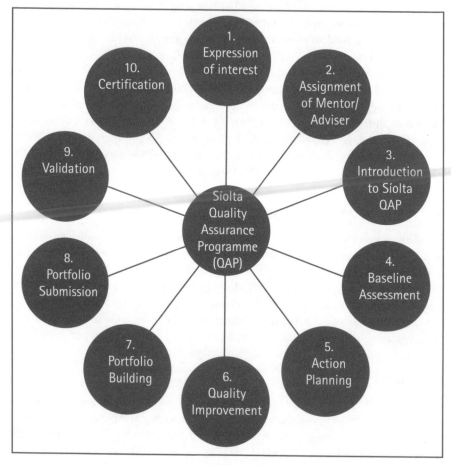

Formal engagement with Síolta through the QAP is supported by a mentor/adviser. This role is central to the QAP and must be undertaken by an individual who has achieved graduate-level qualifications or equivalent in ECEC, has at least five years' experience of delivering ECEC services and has undertaken specialised training for this specific role. The overarching task of the mentor is to support the ECEC setting and staff to take ownership of the quality of their practice and to acquire the skills necessary to ensure that they can effectively carry out all steps of the Síolta QAP. In many ways the challenge for the mentor is to mirror the type of good pedagogical practice that we advocate for early childhood education: a partnership approach that is respectful of the contribution of all parties, which builds on the skills, strengths and interests of the staff in the ECEC setting and which is well planned and documented. Once the ECEC setting has become familiar with the Síolta Principles, Standards and Components, they will carry out the following activities, with support from their mentor.

- *Self-assessment* – a specially designed self-assessment tool asks staff in ECEC settings to: critically reflect on their practice against each of the 75 Components of Quality; write a short description of what they do and then rate themselves against a four-point rating scale. Exemplars drawn from practice are provided as a guide.
- *Action planning* – based on the outcome of their self-assessment, staff in the ECEC setting will develop a concrete plan of quality improvement work around each Component and Standard.
- *Portfolio building* – involves documenting the quality of practice in the ECEC setting. It includes: gathering together evidence of practice related to each Síolta Component; reflecting on this evidence; and selecting materials that best describe the level of quality practice in the setting.
- *Portfolio submission* – once the setting is happy that they have reached a point in their quality improvement journey whereby they are ready to seek external validation of their self-assessed ratings, they will submit their Quality Portfolio. This involves connecting the evidence to the written description in the self-assessment tool, organising the evidence in a logical sequence and putting it together into a portfolio/presentation.
- *Validation* – the final stage in the Síolta QAP is validation, where the internal self-assessed ratings and accompanying portfolio of evidence from an ECEC setting are reviewed by an external expert validator. This review, combined with a validation visit to the ECEC setting, forms part of the validation process, which is completed when an ECEC setting is issued with a validation certificate detailing the ratings they have achieved for each Síolta Standard.

The Síolta QAP is being tested in practice in 2011 and an evaluation of this national field test is expected to be made by the end of the year. The objectives of the evaluation are to test the reliability and validity of the Síolta materials and processes across the diverse range of ECEC settings where children aged from birth to 6 years are present. It will also report on the relevance and effectiveness of the Síolta QAP and will focus in particular on the role of the mentor/adviser. On completion of the field test and evaluation, the implementation of Síolta in the national policy context of the ECEC sector in Ireland will be decided.

SÍOLTA AND STATUTORY REGULATION

Síolta has been designed to promote and support compliance with all statutory regulations applicable to ECEC settings. These settings include infant classes in primary schools that are inspected as part of the Whole School Evaluation (WSE) process carried out by the Department of Education and Skills Inspectorate and the wide variety of non-school-based settings that are regulated under the Child Care (Preschool Services) (No. 2) Regulations 2006. If we think about quality improvement as a continuum, compliance with statutory regulations is the necessary first step along this continuum. Síolta can support services at any stage, to achieve compliance with regulations and to move forward to achieve higher standards of quality across all dimensions of practice.

SÍOLTA AND AISTEAR

Síolta and Aistear are complementary sets of practice guidelines. Whilst each was developed with a different focus – Síolta takes a broad view of all factors that can influence the quality of practice in an ECEC setting while Aistear specifically addresses issues related to curriculum and assessment – they have both been developed through extensive processes of research and consultation with the ECEC sector and are built upon very similar values and goals. When used together, they are a rich resource for guiding, supporting and encouraging the delivery of high-quality early childhood education experiences for children. For further information on Aistear, see Chapter 8.

SÍOLTA AND THE FREE PRE-SCHOOL YEAR SCHEME

In 2010 the Irish government instituted the first ever universal free pre-school provision for all children aged between 3 years 3 months and 4 years 7 months in the year before enrolment in primary school. This policy initiative provides a clear rationale for the implementation of Síolta and Aistear. Universal pre-school provision is focused on the interests of the child and seeks to afford all children the benefit that can accrue from attendance at a high-quality pre-school. This initiative is concerned not just with the number of ECEC places created, but with the quality of the programme that is delivered. To this end, qualification requirements for the pre-school leader in the ECEC setting and adherence to the principles of Síolta were made contractual obligations for those ECEC settings delivering the free pre-school year scheme.

SÍOLTA AND THE NATIONAL LITERACY AND NUMERACY STRATEGY

In 2011 the Department of Education and Skills published a national strategy document on the issue of literacy and numeracy (Department of Education and Skills 2011). The significance of this strategy for Síolta is that for the first time, early childhood and ECEC settings were identified as an important context within which children's literacy and numeracy should be developed and supported. The strategy also recognised that developing high-quality ECEC environments would make an important contribution to achieving the strategy's aims and objectives.

SÍOLTA AND PROFESSIONAL PRACTICE

Síolta makes very clear statements in Standard 11 about the essential indicators of quality in terms of professional practice. These statements have been developed through a review of national and international research and therefore are not simply reflective of our national perspective, but are also in tune with international developments, particularly those in Europe. Standard 11 reads as follows:

> Practicing [sic] in a professional manner requires that individuals have skills, knowledge, values and attitudes appropriate to their role and responsibility within the setting. In addition, it requires regular reflection upon practice and engagement in supported, ongoing professional development. (CECDE 2006)

This standard identifies that being a professional in ECEC is a demanding role that must be informed by specialised knowledge and skills. It also makes clear that the professional knowledge and skills need to be regularly updated and refreshed to take account of new insight and practical guidelines offered by research. The professional ECEC practitioner values partnership and democracy as central aspects of good practice and uses reflection in and on practice as the main tool of self-regulation and quality improvement in the workplace.

The reflective questions attached to each Síolta Component prompt self-awareness and critical thinking on the part of the ECEC practitioner. The repeated focus throughout Síolta on planning and documentation of practice are designed to channel this self-reflection into practical actions which not only improve the quality of practice in the ECEC setting but also support continuous professional development. The reflective questions can also be used to support the development of team working by encouraging all staff to become comfortable with challenging their practice in a non-judgemental, supportive environment.

Síolta promotes leadership in ECEC settings that is characterised by democratic principles. Good leaders are those who seek to empower and enable staff to reach their full potential and who promote a climate of openness and transparency in decision making. The ECEC setting is transformed through such leadership into a learning community where debate and sharing of ideas and information is welcomed.

CONCLUSION

In modern society there are many definitions of quality; for example, value for money, 'doing what it says on the tin', or something accessible only by the privileged or wealthy. Síolta is based on a definition of quality that is described as 'the pursuit of excellence that has the capacity to transform'. This means that engaging with the principles, standards and components of quality that constitute the heart of Síolta will begin to change the quality of practice in the ECEC setting immediately and will also encourage positive attitudes to continuous improvement in practice for the long term.

REVISION QUESTIONS

1 What was the policy rationale for the development of Síolta?
2 What are the four setting manuals that Síolta has been mediated for?
3 How many Principles, Standards and Components comprise Síolta?
4 What is the Síolta Quality Assurance Programme?
5 Describe briefly how Síolta supports the implementation of other national policies.
6 What are the characteristics of professional practice promoted by Síolta?

References

CECDE (Centre for Early Childhood Development and Education) (2005) *Insights on Quality. A National Review of Policy, Practice and Research Relating to Quality in Early Childhood Care and Education in Ireland 1990–2004*. Dublin: CECDE.

— (2006) *Síolta: The National Quality Framework for Early Childhood Education in Ireland*. Dublin: CECDE.

— (2007) *Síolta Research Digests*. Dublin: CECDE.

Department of Education and Science (1999) *Ready to Learn: The White Paper on Early Childhood Education*. Dublin: Stationery Office.

Department of Education and Skills (2010) *A Workforce Development Plan for the Early Childhood Care and Education Sector*. Dublin: Department of Education and Skills.

— (2011) *Literacy and Numeracy for Learning and Life: The National Strategy to Improve Literacy and Numeracy among Children and Young People 2011–2020*. Dublin: Stationery Office.

Department of Justice, Equality and Law Reform (2002) *Quality Childcare and Lifelong Learning: A Model Framework for Education, Training and Professional Development in the Early Childhood Care and Education Sector in Ireland*. Dublin: Stationery Office.

Duignan, M. and Walsh T. (2005) *Insights on Quality: a National Review of Policy, Practice and Research Relating to Quality in Early Childhood Education in Ireland*. Dublin: CECDE.

NCCA (National Council for Curriculum and Assessment) (2009) *Aistear: The Early Childhood Curriculum Framework*. Dublin: NCCA.

8

Aistear: The Early Childhood Curriculum Framework

Mary Daly and Arlene Forster

> *Learning Objectives*
> After studying this chapter the reader should understand:
> - What Aistear is and who it is for.
> - Why and how Aistear was developed.
> - The contents of Aistear and how these can help practitioners in supporting and nurturing children's early learning and development.
> - The key messages in Aistear about assessment and planning.
> - The purpose of the Aistear Toolkit.

INTRODUCTION

Aistear is Ireland's curriculum framework for all children from birth to 6 years. The White Paper on Early Childhood Education *Ready to Learn* (DES 1999a) recommended the development of national curriculum guidelines for the early childhood sector to ensure that early childhood provision would be structured, developmental and of high quality. The guidelines were to provide information on enhancing all aspects of children's development and were to include appropriate teaching methodologies together with a focus on play.

In response, the National Council for Curriculum and Assessment (NCCA) (whose remit is to advise the Minister for Education and Skills on curriculum for early childhood education and primary and post-primary schools) developed a curriculum framework in partnership with the early childhood sector in Ireland. Since early childhood marks the beginning of children's lifelong learning journeys, this curriculum framework is called Aistear, the Irish word for journey. Published in October 2009, the curriculum framework describes the types of learning that are important for children, and shows how these experiences can be provided in different types of setting, including:

- childminding settings
- full- and part-time day care settings

- sessional services
- infant classes in primary schools.

Aistear can also support parents as they help their children to learn and develop through everyday routines and activities.

DEVELOPMENT OF AISTEAR

The partnership process between the NCCA and the early childhood sector in Ireland and abroad (see Daly and Forster (2009) for more information) enabled the NCCA to develop a curriculum framework based on research in early childhood education and care (ECEC), and on evidence from practice. This resulted in a curriculum framework which connects with the day-to-day experiences of those working in the sector in Ireland, and which illustrates how the quality of these experiences can be improved for the benefit of children.

The partnership process included a number of different elements. A technical working group made up of nine experts from the field of ECEC in Ireland was established to guide the preparatory work for the curriculum framework. In 2004 a wide-reaching consultation was held with the early childhood sector (NCCA 2005). Following the consultation an Early Childhood Committee representing the sector in Ireland was established to support the NCCA's work in developing Aistear.

In addition, children as young as 9 months contributed through a research study called *Listening for Children's Stories: Children as Partners in the Framework for Early Learning* (NCCA 2007). Three articles (Brennan *et al.* 2007; Daly *et al.* 2007; and Daly *et al.* 2008) describe the study and highlight its key messages, including the importance of:

- holistic learning and development through play and active exploration
- relationships, in particular the crucial role of parents
- communication
- a sense of identity and belonging
- observing and listening to children in order to support their learning and development, and the importance of building this into the development of Aistear.

This research study helped the NCCA to gain a greater understanding of what life was like for the children involved. In this way, the voices and experiences of very young children in Ireland informed the development of the curriculum framework. Four research papers were also commissioned by the NCCA to set out the theory behind Aistear:

- *Perspectives on the Relationship between Education and Care in Early Childhood* (Hayes 2007).
- *Children's Early Learning and Development* (French 2007).

- *Play as a Context for Early Learning and Development* (Kernan 2007).
- *Supporting Early Learning and Development through Formative Assessment* (Dunphy 2008).

The papers and their executive summaries are available on the NCCA website, www.ncca.ie/earlylearning. All of the different elements of the partnership process culminated in a curriculum framework called Aistear.

AISTEAR'S CONTENTS

Aistear comprises four elements:

1 *Principles and Themes* describes what children learn.
2 *Guidelines for Good Practice* focuses on partnerships with parents, interactions, play and assessment.
3 *User Guide* gives practical information on using the curriculum framework.
4 *Key Messages from the Research Papers* summarises important points from research used in developing Aistear.

The *Principles and Themes* and the *Guidelines for Good Practice* are the most important of these elements.

PRINCIPLES

Aistear is based on twelve early childhood principles as outlined in Table 8.1.

Table 8.1 Aistear's twelve principles

Children's lives in early childhood	Connections with others	Learning and developing
• The child's uniqueness • Equality and diversity • Children as citizens	• Relationships • Parents, family and community • The adult's role	• Holistic learning and development • Active learning • Play; hands-on experiences • Relevant and meaningful experiences • Communication and language • The learning environment

These principles are similar to the principles underpinning *Síolta: The National Quality Framework for Early Childhood Education* (CECDE 2006) and the Primary

School Curriculum (DES 1999b). Audits of Aistear and the Primary School Curriculum (NCCA 2009b) and of Aistear and Síolta (NCCA 2009c) are available on the NCCA website at www.ncca.ie/earlylearning. The audits focus on the main similarities and differences between the documents. In doing this, they provide initial insights into how practitioners might use the frameworks and curriculum together to support children's early learning and development.

THEMES

Aistear describes what children learn through four interconnected themes:

1 *Well-being* is about children being confident, happy and healthy.
2 *Identity and Belonging* is about children developing a positive sense of who they are, and feeling that they are valued and respected as part of a family and community.
3 *Communicating* is about children sharing their experiences, thoughts, ideas and feelings with others with growing confidence and competence in a variety of ways and for a variety of purposes.
4 *Exploring and Thinking* is about children making sense of the things, places and people in their world by interacting with others, playing, investigating, questioning, and forming, testing and refining ideas.

Each theme is presented using four aims (sixteen in total) and six learning goals (ninety-six in total).

Figure 8.1

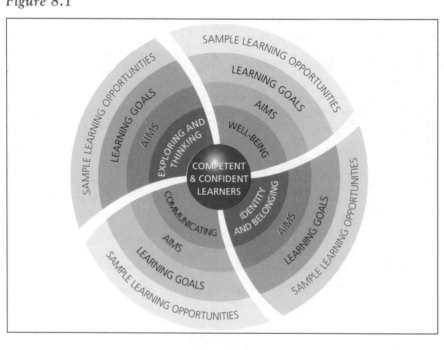

Together, these aims and goals describe the dispositions, skills, attitudes and values, knowledge and understanding that are important for children in early childhood. Aistear emphasises in particular the development of dispositions or habits of mind (Katz and Raths 1985; Katz 1993; Carr 1999). Positive dispositions such as curiosity, creativity, self-motivation and resilience are key to children's learning and development. Because of this the development of positive dispositions receives particular attention in Aistear, and the framework shows how the adult can support and nurture these important 'habits of mind' in children from birth.

Each Aistear theme offers ideas and suggestions for the types of learning activity that practitioners might provide for children in working towards its aims and goals. These ideas are called *sample learning opportunities* and are presented for three overlapping age groups:

- babies (birth to 18 months)
- toddlers (12 months to 3 years)
- young children (2½ to 6 years).

The sample learning opportunities can be adapted for different types of setting and can be used either indoors or outdoors.

GUIDELINES FOR GOOD PRACTICE

Four sets of guidelines offer support to practitioners and parents in using Aistear's principles and themes. The themes provide the 'what' of learning, while the guidelines provide the 'how' of learning by focusing on:

- building partnerships between parents and practitioners
- learning and developing through interactions
- learning and developing through play
- supporting learning and development through assessment.

The guidelines begin by focusing on partnerships: parents are children's primary carers and educators, and good co-operation and collaboration between parents and out-of-home settings are essential to support children's early learning and development. The guidelines describe good practice and use a number of stories called *learning experiences* to show Aistear in action. These can be viewed on the NCCA website at www.ncca.ie/earlylearning, where they are organised according to:

- setting type
- age group of children
- Aistear theme.

While each learning experience is based in a particular type of setting and focuses on a particular age group of children, as well as on one of the four themes, many of them can be adapted to suit other age groups and other types of setting.

Reflecting on practice is important in order to identify what works well, what doesn't work and how practice can be continually improved. To support this, *thinking about my practice* questions are presented throughout Aistear's guidelines to help the practitioner reflect on what s/he is doing to support children's learning and development.

SUPPORTING LEARNING AND DEVELOPMENT THROUGH ASSESSING AND PLANNING

Assessment is part of the practitioner's day-to-day interactions with the children. Aistear defines assessment as 'the on-going process of collecting, documenting, reflecting on, and using information to develop rich portraits of children as learners in order to support and enhance their future learning' (NCCA 2009a:72). These assessment actions overlap and often happen at the same time. Aistear points out that while much assessment is done intuitively, some is planned for a particular purpose.

Through assessment the practitioner makes judgements about the children's learning and development and over time builds a picture of each child's progress and achievements. This picture is shaped by information the practitioner collects about how the child learns (the learning dispositions) as well as what s/he learns (skills, knowledge, understanding and values/attitudes). The practitioner documents information, reflects on it and uses it to make important decisions about how to help each child take the next steps in his/her learning and development.

Aistear describes two principal approaches to assessment, shown in Table 8.2.

Table 8.2 Approaches to assessment

Assessment *for* Learning (AfL)	Assessment *of* Learning (AoL)
• Using evidence on an **ongoing** basis to inform teaching and learning • A range of feedback and '**feed-forward**' to show, motivate and help the child make progress • Part of the **daily flow** of teaching and learning • **Learner** actively involved	• Measuring and reporting on **achievement** • **Awarding** grades or scores • At the **end** of the learning period • **Practitioner**-led

Both approaches involve the practitioner in making judgements. What the practitioner does with these judgements is what distinguishes one approach from the other. Assessment *for* learning (AfL) is about planning for, nurturing and supporting learning and development by reflecting on the assessment information to shape the actions the practitioner and child can take to improve learning. Assessment *of* learning (AoL), on the other hand, is the process of simply measuring. The measurements may be interesting to compare and analyse, but, in themselves, they do not affect learning and development. As the old saying goes, 'weighing the pig does not make him fatter'. For this reason Aistear's guidelines focus on the practitioner using AfL on a daily basis to help children progress in their learning and development across Aistear's four themes.

Aistear's guidelines outline several features of good assessment practice (NCCA 2009a:73), as shown in Table 8.3.

Table 8.3 Features of good assessment practice

Assessment	The adult:
Benefits children	• gives feedback to children on their learning and development as part of his/her daily interactions with them • makes decisions that build on past experiences and support new learning and development
Involves children	• talks with children to understand their learning and development • gives children opportunities to think about what they did, said, made and learned, and helps them plan what they will do next
Makes sense for children	• assesses as part of everyday activities, events, routines and interactions, and uses objects, places and people which are familiar and interesting to children
Involves children's families	• provides parents with insights into their children's learning and gives suggestions for how they might support learning at home • gives parents opportunities to share information about their children's learning and development

Assessment	The adult:
Uses many methods	• uses methods such as self-assessment, conversations, observations, tasks and tests • uses methods in a way that is appropriate, given children's ages, backgrounds and stages of learning and development
Happens over time	• collects and uses information on a daily basis • over time, builds a rich portrait of each child as a learner
Celebrates the breadth and depth of children's learning and development	• provides evidence of children's learning and development across the dispositions, skills, attitudes and values, knowledge, and understanding set out in Aistear's themes.

Aistear emphasises that assessment benefits children and that it should be manageable and useful for the practitioner in helping children to progress in their learning and development. A key aspect of ensuring that assessment meets these criteria is that it guides the practitioner's planning work.

DOCUMENTING

The practitioner has to document relevant assessment information in order to build a picture of the child's learning and development (what children understand, can do, say, make, and how they approach tasks and experiences), which will support planning for the next stage in learning. Sometimes the practitioner records in detail children's involvement in particular events or activities. Aistear refers to this approach as the *storytelling approach*, which can be especially useful in early childhood as it creates a fuller picture of the richness and complexity of early learning and development.

Aistear outlines a number of different ways of documenting assessment. These include:

- *Samples of children's work* – things children make, write, draw.
- *Notes* – brief notes, often just key words, about an event, activity or task.
- ICT: *photographs and video or audio records* – photographs sometimes in sequence to show progress in a particular activity, snippets of video or audio.
- *Stories* – detailed information about a child's involvement in a particular event, activity or task.

- *Daily diaries or records of care* – information about children's care routines, responses, activities. The diary or record is shared with parents on a daily basis and parents can add to it.

Examples of these different types of documentation can be found in the learning experiences in Aistear's assessment guidelines. Documentation can be organised and stored in a portfolio. The portfolio can take the form of a folder, box or something similar. The information stored in it can be shared with children and with parents and is used to plan for future learning.

ASSESSMENT METHODS

Aistear presents a continuum of five methods of gathering assessment information (see Figure 8.2).

Figure 8.2 Aistear's assessment methods

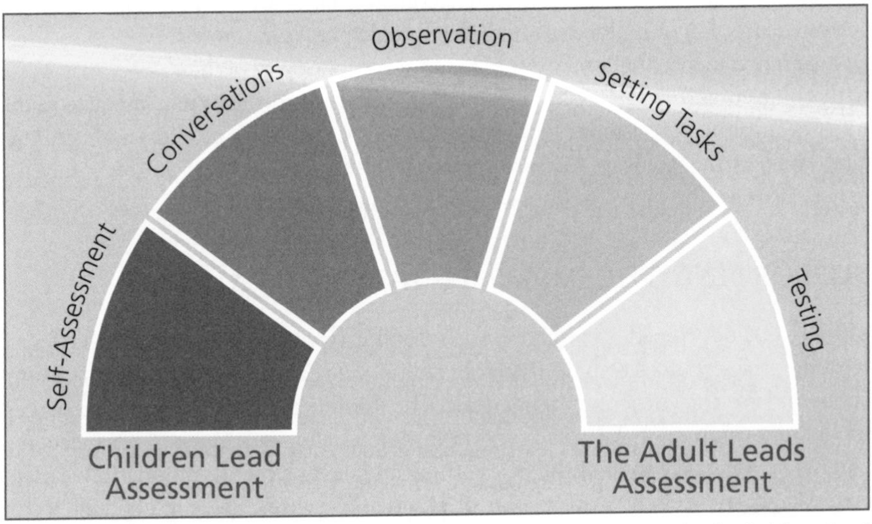

These methods range from self-assessment and conversations, in which children lead the assessment process (on the left of the graphic), to observation, setting tasks and testing, in which the practitioner leads the process (on the right of the graphic). Information on each method is provided by answering three questions:

1 What is the method?
2 How do I use it?
3 What age group can it be used with?

Each method ends with learning experiences. A table outlining the challenges and strengths of each of the methods ends the guidelines. No one assessment method on its own will provide sufficiently useful information. A practitioner needs to use a combination of methods over time to gain a full picture of the child's progress.

THEORY UNDERPINNING AISTEAR'S ASSESSMENT GUIDELINES

While all the papers that underpin Aistear impacted in different ways on the development of the framework's elements, the fourth and final paper in particular informed Aistear's assessment guidelines (Dunphy 2008). A paper called 'Assessment in Aistear: the Early Childhood Curriculum Framework' (Daly and Forster 2011) synopsises the key messages from the paper and outlines some of the challenges and possible responses to using assessment for learning in early childhood settings.

PLANNING

Information on planning in Aistear is outlined in the *User Guide* (available at www.ncca.ie/earlylearning), which provides a description of long-, medium- and short-term plans, as well as Individual Educational Plans (IEPs), and daily and activity plans. It also includes a number of sample plans for different types of setting. Aistear recommends that practitioners make assessment part of their day-to-day work with children and that they use information collected through assessment to plan. In assessing, the practitioner looks for evidence of children's progress and uses the aims and learning goals in Aistear's themes to interpret and build on the children's experiences as s/he plans for future learning and development.

SUPPORTING THE IMPLEMENTATION OF AISTEAR

The NCCA developed an online Aistear Toolkit (www.ncca.ie/aisteartoolkit) as a repository of resources to help the early childhood sector, including parents, learn about and use the curriculum framework. The Toolkit includes a range of resources including examples of Aistear in action in different types of setting, tip sheets for parents on aspects of their children's learning and development, information leaflets on Aistear, and podcasts on aspects of practice. New resources are added to the Toolkit on an ongoing basis.

A small number of primary school teachers have become Aistear tutors and provide workshops on Aistear through the Network of Education Centres. Many teachers are using Aistear to implement play as a key teaching and learning methodology in infant classrooms by incorporating an hour of play a day into their infant timetable.

The NCCA continues to collaborate with other organisations in supporting the sector to use Aistear. One of these important collaborations involves working with Early Childhood Ireland (formerly IPPA, the Irish Pre-school Play Association, and the National Children's Nurseries Association) to gather examples of Aistear in action in different types of setting.

The NCCA also works closely with the Early Years Education Policy Unit, co-located in the Department of Education and Skills and the Department of Children and Youth Affairs.

AISTEAR'S CONNECTIONS WITH NATIONAL DEVELOPMENTS

Aistear complements and supports many other developments in the early childhood sector in Ireland. In particular, it supports:

- The Early Childhood Care and Education Scheme (free pre-school year).
- *Revised Child Care (Pre-School) Regulations* (Department of Health and Children, 2006)(in particular Article 5's focus on well-being, learning and development).
- *Síolta: The National Quality Framework for Early Childhood Education* (CECDE 2006).
- The Infant Level in the *Primary School Curriculum* (DES 1999b).

CONCLUSION

The publication of Aistear in 2009 marked a significant milestone in ECEC in Ireland. The purpose of this curriculum framework is to help practitioners and parents in supporting and nurturing children's early learning and development. This chapter on Aistear highlighted:

- the collaborative way in which Aistear was developed
- the importance of nurturing positive dispositions in children alongside skills, attitudes and values, knowledge and understanding
- the critical role the practitioner plays in enriching and extending learning and development so that children reach their full potential
- the role of assessment in planning for and supporting progression in children's learning and development, and the importance of good documentation as part of the assessment process.

Aistear complements and supports many other developments in the early childhood sector in Ireland and is a key resource in ensuring children in early childhood settings are given rich and varied experiences to support and progress their learning and development. Let your Aistear journey begin.

References
Brennan, P., Daly, M., Forster, A., Maxwell, M., Murphy, R., O'Connor, E. and Sweeney A. (2007) 'Listening for Children's Stories: The NCCA's Portraiture Study' in *Vision into Practice: Making Quality a Reality in the Lives of Young Children*. Dublin: CECDE.

Carr, M. (1999) 'Being a learner: five dispositions for early childhood', *Early Childhood Practice* 1:1, 82–99.

CECDE (Centre for Early Childhood Development and Education) (2006) *Síolta: The National Quality Framework for Early Childhood Education*. Dublin: CECDE.

Daly, M. and Forster, A. (2009) 'The story of the Framework for Early Learning: partnership in action', *An Leanbh Óg (OMEP Ireland Journal of Early Childhood Studies)* 3:1, April, 55–73.

— (2011) 'Assessment in Aistear: the Early Childhood Curriculum Framework', *An Leanbh Óg (OMEP Ireland Journal of Early Childhood Studies)* 4:1, April, 51–62.

Daly, M., Forster, A., Murphy, R. and Sweeney, A. (2008) 'The NCCA's portraiture study – key messages', *An Leanbh Óg (OMEP Ireland Journal of Early Childhood Studies)* 2:1, April, 73–86.

Daly, M., Forster, A., Murphy, R., Sweeney, A., Brennan, P. and O'Connor, E. (2007) 'Children's voices in the Framework for Early Learning – a portraiture study', *An Leanbh Óg (OMEP Ireland Journal of Early Childhood Studies)* 1:1, April, 57–71.

DES (Department of Education and Science) (1999a) *Ready to Learn*: White Paper on Early Childhood Education. Dublin: Government Publications.

— (1999b) *Primary School Curriculum*. Dublin: Government Publications.

Department of Health and Children (2006) *Revised Child Care (Pre-School) Regulations*. Dublin: Government Publications.

Dunphy, E. (2008) *Supporting Early Learning and Development through Formative Assessment*. Research paper, Framework for Early Learning, commissioned by the NCCA. Available at www.ncca.ie/earlylearning.

French, G. (2007) *Children's Early Learning and Development*. Research paper, Framework for Early Learning, commissioned by NCCA. Available at www.ncca.ie/earlylearning.

Hayes, N. (2007) *Perspectives on the Relationship between Education and Care in Early Childhood*. Research paper, Framework for Early Learning, commissioned by the NCCA. Available at www.ncca.ie/earlylearning.

Katz, L.G. (1993) *Dispositions as Educational Goals*. ERIC EDO-PS-93-10 <http://ceep.crc.uiuc.edu/eecearchive/digests/1993/katzdi93.html>

Katz, L.G. and Raths, J. (1985) 'Dispositions as goals for education', *Teaching and Teacher Education* 1:4, 301–307.

Kernan, M. (2007) *Play as a Context for Learning and Development*. Background paper, Framework for Early Learning, commissioned by the NCCA. Available at www.ncca.ie/earlylearning.

NCCA (National Council for Curriculum and Assessment) (2005) *Towards a Framework for Early Learning: A Consultative Document*. Dublin: NCCA.

— (2007) *Listening for Children's Stories: Children as Partners in the Framework for Early Learning*. Dublin: NCCA. Available at www.ncca.ie/earlylearning.

— (2009a) *Aistear: The Early Childhood Curriculum Framework*. Dublin: NCCA. Available at www.ncca.ie/earlylearning.

— (2009b) *An Audit of Aistear and Síolta*. Dublin: NCCA. Available at www.ncca.ie/earlylearning.

— (2009c) *An Audit of Aistear and the Primary School Curriculum*. Dublin: NCCA. Available at www.ncca.ie/earlylearning.

Further Reading

Black, P. and William, D. (1998) *Inside the Black Box: Raising Standards Through Classroom Assessment*. London: NFER Nelson.

Bruce, T. (2001) *Learning through Play: Babies, Toddlers and the Foundation Years*. UK: Hodder & Stoughton.

Carr, M. (1998) *Assessing Children's Experiences in Early Childhood: Final Report to the Ministry of Education*. Wellington, New Zealand: Ministry of Education.

— (2001) *Assessment in Early Childhood Settings*. London: Paul Chapman Publishing.

Carr, M., Duncan, J., Smith, A.B., Jones, C., Lee, W. and Marshall, K. (2009) *Learning in the Making: Dispositions and Design in Early Education*. Boston: Sense Publishers.

Carr, M., Haye, H. and Podmore, V. (2000) *Learning and Teaching Stories: Action Research on Evaluation in Early Childhood: Final Report to the Ministry of Education*. New Zealand: Council for Educational Research.

Carr, M., May, H. and Podmore, V. N. with Cubey, P., Hatherly, A. and Macartney, B. (2000). *Learning and Teaching Stories: Action Research on Evaluation in Early Childhood* ERIC 447930. Wellington: New Zealand Council for Educational Research and Ministry of Education.

Clarke, A. and Moss, P. (2001) *Listening to Young Children: The Mosaic Approach*. London: National Children's Bureau.

David, T. (ed.) (2003) *Early Years Research: Pedagogy, Curriculum and Adult Roles, Training and Professionalism*. UK: British Educational Association Early Years Special Interest Group.

Dockett, S. and Fletcher, M. (2002) *Play and Pedagogy in Early Childhood: Bending the Rules*. Australia: Nelson.

Fleer, M. (1995) *Staff–child interactions: A Vygotskyan Approach*. Reading: Addison-Wesley.

Goldschmeid, E. and Jackson, S. (2004) *People Under Three: Young Children in Daycare* (2nd edn). New York: Routledge.

Hall, K. and Burke, W. (2003) *Making Formative Assessment Work: Effective Practice in Primary Classrooms*. UK: Open University Press.

IPPA (Irish Pre-School Play Association) (2004) *The Power of Play*. Dublin: IPPA.

Manning-Morton, J. and Thorp, M. (2003) *Key Times for Play: The First Three Years*. Bershire: Open University Press.

McNaughton, G. (2003) *Shaping Early Childhood: Learners, Curriculum and Context*. Berkshire: Open University Press.

— (2011) *Parents and Professionals in Early Childhood Settings*. New York: McGraw-Hill.

McNaughton, G. and Williams, G. (2004) *Teaching Young Children: Choices in Theory and Practice*. Berkshire: Open University Press.

Moyles, J. (1989) *Just Playing? The Role and Status of Play in Early Childhood Education.* Milton Keynes: Open Universtiy Press.

— (ed.) (2005) *The Excellence of Play* (2nd edn). Maidenhead: Open University Press.

National Children's Nurseries Association (2007) *Guiding Childcare Practitioners through Observation, Planning and Reflection.* Dublin: NCNA.

Pluckett, M.B. and Black, J.K. (2000) *Authentic Assessment of the Young Child* (2nd edn). USA: Prentice Hall.

Sayeed, Z. and Guerin, E. (2000) *Early Years Play: A Happy Medium for Assessment and Intervention.* London: David Fulton.

Wood, E. and Attfield, J. (2005) *Play, Learning and the Early Childood Curriculum* (2nd edn). London: Paul Chapman.

Useful Websites

www.ncca.ie
www.ncca.ie/earlylearning
www.ncca.ie/aisteartoolkit

9
Engaging with Early Childhood Education Models

John McGarrigle

> **Learning Objectives**
> After studying this chapter the reader should be able to:
> - Discuss the concept of a model of early childhood education and care (ECEC).
> - Describe the connection between quality, play, education and care.
> - Explain the role of active learning, play and the role of the adult in early learning curricula.
> - Discuss implications for best practice in relation to the Irish early learning curriculum.

INTRODUCTION

The practice of early childhood education has in many countries, including Ireland, evolved over the past century to become child-centred and focused on the developing child's needs. A great deal of argument and research during periods of major social change have led to this recognition of childhood as a valued time. Froebel, Steiner and Montessori have influenced our vision of how children should be treated in order to develop and grow to their full potential; and major theorists in the area of human development, such as Piaget, Vygotsky, Bruner, Donaldson, Gardner and Bronfenbrenner, have created debate about how children learn, which has influenced early years practice in different countries.

Many arguments are made for the benefits that will accrue to society in the future if children are provided with the wherewithal to develop into socially responsible citizens. There are a number of models of ECEC around the world, from HighScope in the USA to Te Whariki in New Zealand and Reggio Emilia in Europe: and other examples of how ECEC is practised in different countries can be found in Bennett (2004) and in research papers at the Centre for Early Childhood Development and Education (CECDE). Yet each country, including Ireland – with Aistear (NCCA 2009) and Síolta (CECDE 2006) – has its own model of early childhood provision that fits into the particular political, legal and social framework of the time.

WHAT IS IN A MODEL OF ECEC?

Before we consider the various models of ECEC it is useful to consider the concept of a 'model': what do we mean when we use this term?

Davidson and Elliott (2001), in the context of nursing, describe a model of care as a conceptual tool that is 'a standard or example for imitation or comparison, combining concepts, belief and intent that are related in some way' (p. 121). For our purposes, we can note that care and education are related when considering children's development. In the document *Quality Childcare and Lifelong Learning* (DJELR 2002:6) reference is made to a growing international consensus that '"care" and "education" are inseparable concepts and that quality services for children necessarily provide both'. (OECD 2001, cited in DJELR 2002) From this we can make an assumption that care, education and quality are conceptually linked.

Epstein, Schweinhart and McAdoo (1996) note that choosing the principles to guide quality practice requires combining creative and scientific approaches – it is both an art and a science. They suggest that 'A curriculum model has a theory and knowledge base that reflects a philosophical orientation and is supported, in varying degrees, by child development research and educational evaluation' (Epstein, Schweinhart and McAdoo 1996:10).

Some practitioners adhere to one particular model, while others combine elements and activities in an eclectic approach. Some focus on programme ingredients such as length of free play periods or the ways in which children are grouped, while others emphasise elements related to programme context, such as location, physical setting, social context or type of agency. Epstein, Schweinhart and McAdoo also refer to Frede (1985), who suggests that practitioners may go through a four-stage process of development in using a curriculum model where initial attempts to learn, master and implement a model eventually lead to the confidence and competence to adapt and modify it to suit a particular purpose or setting.

PEDAGOGY AND CURRICULUM

We can describe the content of a programme for early learning as *curriculum* and the way it is delivered as *pedagogy*. Put simply, these together are 'what we do with children and how we do it'. Sometimes it is hard to separate the two. How we prepare the environment for young children is influenced by what we think they should be doing – our philosophy. Early learning curricula are often described as taking a *holistic* approach, which means that a child learns in a variety of areas at the same time. For example, the Te Whariki curriculum in New Zealand uses the symbol of a woven mat to show how principles such as family and community, empowerment, holistic development and relationships run through a curriculum; and the strands of well-being, belonging, contribution, communication and exploration are evident in the themes of our own Aistear curriculum. Applying the holistic view to our practice, we might for example consider what is involved for a child in listening to a story in circle time. How is this helping them cognitively, emotionally, socially? How can it benefit their well-being or sense of belonging?

UNDERLYING CHILD DEVELOPMENT THEORY

Different theorists emphasise different aspects of child development. For example, Jean Piaget was interested in how children learn to think and he focused on cognitive aspects of development. During the 1970s a number of researchers, such as Margaret Donaldson in Scotland and Jerome Bruner in the USA, pointed out how difficult it is to separate social aspects from cognitive aspects of child development, as children tend to make sense of the world by taking cues from the social context. As the work of Russian psychologist Vygotsky became better known, the social aspect of understanding the world received more attention. Gardner (2006) focused debate on how in formal education a narrow focus on academic subjects largely ignores the natural musical, dance and creative abilities of many learners, and he introduced the idea of *multiple intelligence*. Bronfenbrenner drew attention to the interactions between the individual child and the social systems in which they find themselves, such as the family and the school, and the impact of these social systems on development.

Looking to the future, influential thinkers on early childhood development give us ideas concerning nature and growth which see development as a gradual unfolding of what is within as the child responds to the world around him/her. The idea of the absorbent mind resonates with the concept of assimilation that Piaget proposed in relation to cognitive development. So as adults our role in preparing the environment for the child to experience becomes vital and leads to a consideration of the essential ingredients for stimulating children's natural desire to learn and play.

ACTIVE LEARNING AND SCAFFOLDING

One major concept of ECEC is that a child's understanding arises out of active experiences, which leads us to the question, 'What environment will lead to children having enjoyable experiences from which they can learn and develop?' This pinpoints the difficulty of thinking about ideas, concepts and underlying intentions in the abstract when referring to something that is experienced, which comes to the fore when we start talking about something like play. It can lead to ambiguity and misunderstanding and requires us to be clear and rigorous in our descriptions and definitions. What exactly did Montessori or Piaget or Vygotsky say about play?

Many models refer to how children and adults construct their knowledge of the world and a vital concept in this knowledge construction is Vygotsky's 'zone of proximal development', which is defined as the stage in a task just before it becomes achievable alone. Rather than merely providing experiences for children to construct their ideas of the world on their own as they might in a state of solitary concentration, this suggests that children are also likely to check what is going on with adults and other children. In a class of young children we can observe children at a range of different developmental abilities – some seem to do things with little instruction while others are unsure and watch what others do. As adults we may demonstrate or lead by example, as Steiner proposes; and children may imitate, as the observational or social learning theory of Bandura suggests. Thus children may be at different places in terms of the zone of proximal development and can assist each other in learning. Here we can also see why play is at the heart of the early learning curriculum because, according to Vygotsky, a child in play can operate at a higher level of functioning. For example, a group of children playing at shop may act out or imitate what they have seen or heard and each child can suspend reality to try out their competencies in language. This view elevates the status of play to a higher role than in Piaget's thinking, who views it as inadequate egocentric thinking in the preoperational stage.

CONCLUSION

What are the important points we should take from models of education? It seems that we can adopt a practical disposition that places the child's physical, emotional and developmental needs at the centre of our practice. We hope to develop our sensitivities to the ways children learn so that we can arrange an environment where children feel valued and can choose to participate in enjoyable learning experiences to develop to their full potential. We can acknowledge that children learn best through playful experiences, making play the basis of the early learning curriculum. As adults working in the area we can also use this pedagogy in our learning. The reader is encouraged to engage with the following activities and co-construct with their colleagues.

ACTIVITIES

Student Exercise 1
A daytime radio programme is doing a phone-in with the title 'Play – are we wasting our children's time?' Each student should take a role: radio announcer; male parent; female parent; pre-school manager; researcher; politician, etc. and prepare what they will say. After the role play, discuss the issues in justifying play-based practice in the early years.

Student Exercise 2
Refer to Elizabeth Wood's podcast on 'Understanding Play' (available on the National Council for Curriculum and Assessment website, www.ncca.ie). Write a reflective essay with the title 'Why play is at the heart of my practice'.

Student Exercise 3
Write an essay on 'Is pre-school preparing for school or preparing for life?'

Key Learning Points

- An ECEC model includes underlying philosophy, concepts, ideas, beliefs and intentions about childhood and indicates a desired approach to inform our practice.
- Early education models promote child development through preparing environments that stimulate active exploration using the senses and emphasise informal learning through play.
- Nature, care, play, choice, knowledge construction and the role of the adult are vital concepts in a model of ECEC.
- The theories of Piaget, Bruner, Vygotsky, Donaldson, Gardner and Bronfenbrenner influence models of ECEC.

References

Bennett, J. (2004) *Starting Strong – Curricula and Pedagogies in Early Childhood Education and Care*. Paris: OECD.

Bronfenbrenner, U. (1979) *The Ecology of Human Development: Experiments by Nature and Design*. Cambridge, MA: Harvard.

CECDE (Centre for Early Childhood Development and Education) (2006) *Síolta: The National Quality Framework for Early Childhood Education in Ireland*. Dublin: CECDE. Available at: www.siolta.ie.

Davidson, P. and Elliott, D. (2001) 'Managing Approaches to Nursing Care' in E. Chang and J. Daly (eds), *Preparing for Professional Nursing Practice*. Sydney: Churchill Livingstone Elsevier.

DJELR (Department of Justice, Equality and Law Reform) (2002) *Quality Childcare and Lifelong Learning: Model Framework for Education, Training and Professional Development in the Early Childhood Care and Education Sector*. Dublin: DJELR.

Epstein, A., Schweinhart, L.J. and McAdoo, L. (1996) *Models of Early Childhood Education*. Michigan: HighScope Press.

Gardner, H. (2006) *Multiple Intelligences – New Horizons*. New York: Basic Books.

Ministry of Education, New Zealand (1996) *Te Whariki*. Wellington, NZ: Learning Media.

NCCA (National Council for Curriculum and Assessment) (2009) *Aistear: The Early Childhood Curriculum Framework*. Dublin: NCCA. Available at: www.ncca.ie.

OECD (Organisation for Economic Co-operation and Development) (2001) *Starting Strong: Early Childhood Education and Care*. OECD.

Weikart, D. (1998) 'Changing early childhood development through educational intervention', *Preventive Medicine* 27:2, 233–7.

Useful Websites

Aistear – www.ncca.biz/Aistear/
Síolta – www.siolta.ie/
Irish Pre-school Playgroup Association – www.ippa.ie/

Developmentally appropriate practice – www.youtube.com/watch?v=a-h4IHIqkcc&
   feature=related

FernAvery, 'All they do is play' – www.youtube.com/watch?v=75Kan48OftU&
   feature=channel

Reggio Emilia – www.reggioemiliaapproach.net/about.php#reading

Wood, E. (2010) 'Understanding play' – www.nccastore.info/Aistear/understanding
   play/player.html

HighScope – www.highscope.org/

Reggio Emilia –www.ltscotland.org.uk/resources/r/genericresource_tcm4242154.asp

Te Whariki – www.educate.ece.govt.nz/learning/curriculumAndLearning/TeWhariki.
   aspx

10

The Montessori Approach to Early Childhood Education

Máire Mhic Mhathúna and Mark Taylor

Learning Objectives

After studying this chapter the reader should have an understanding of:

- Maria Montessori's life and contribution to early childhood education.
- Montessori's educational philosophy.
- Montessori education and training in Ireland.
- The areas of learning in the Montessori curriculum.
- The links between the Montessori curriculum and Síolta and Aistear.

INTRODUCTION

This chapter will give an overview of the Montessori approach to early childhood education. The term 'Montessori' is sometimes treated as synonymous with early childhood education in Ireland, but it should be used by early childhood educators to describe the specific approach that Maria Montessori (1870–1952) developed in the early twentieth century. Although significant advances have been made in psychology and education since that time, many of Montessori's basic principles still stand. Maria Montessori wrote extensively on her approach and students are encouraged to read some of her original work, such as *The Absorbent Mind* or the *Discovery of the Child* in order to understand her philosophy. Her work has been reinterpreted by modern commentators including Lillard (1988), Gettman (2003) and Isaacs (2010) and this commentary forms the basis of the current chapter.

HISTORY OF MONTESSORI EDUCATION

Maria Montessori is one of the best known and influential figures in early childhood education worldwide. Her influence is so extensive that many of her ideas have been adopted in general early childhood education practice and are no longer recognised as being Montessori in origin. These include child-sized furniture, graded approaches to problem solving and a focus on active learning.

Maria Montessori was a pioneer in many areas of life, including medicine, women's role in society and education. Born in 1870 in the province of Ancona in Italy, she was the first woman to graduate as a medical doctor from the University of Rome (1896) and joined the university's psychiatric clinic. There she worked with children with learning difficulties and saw the need for a stimulating environment. She studied the work of Jean Gaspard Itard and Eduard Seguin and developed her ideas on graded learning exercises that were tailored to suit the needs of individual children. She set up and worked in a special school for children with learning difficulties. Her son Mario was born in 1898 and, in keeping with the custom of that time and society, he was fostered as she was not married.

In 1907 Maria was appointed director of a day care centre for children aged 3–7 years in San Lorenzo, a disadvantaged area of Rome. She called the centre 'Casa dei Bambini', the Children's House. She observed how children absorbed knowledge from their environment and how they preferred to work independently on her graded exercises (Lillard 1988). From her observations, she concluded that children can teach themselves and learn when in an atmosphere of love and freedom, so laying down the foundations of the Montessori approach to early childhood education (Lillard 1988).

Montessori's ideas on early childhood education spread around the world and she visited centres in Ireland, the United States, Spain, England, the Netherlands and India, meeting staff and children and giving lectures (Hayes 2010). Two Irishwomen attended one of her courses in London in 1919, Mrs Eleanor Gibbons and Sr Gertrude Allman of the Mercy Order. Sr Gertrude founded the first Montessori school in Ireland, in Waterford, in 1920. Maria Montessori visited the school in 1927 and other famous visitors included W. B. Yeats, who referred to Sr Gertrude and the children in his poem 'Among Schoolchildren'.

> I walk through the long schoolroom questioning;
> A kind old nun in a white hood replies;
> The children learn to cipher and to sing,
> To study reading-books and histories,
> To cut and sew, be neat in everything
> In the best modern way.

Many more Montessori schools were founded around the country and the first training course was provided in Dominican College, Sion Hill, Dublin in 1934. The St Nicholas Montessori Training Centre was founded in Dún Laoghaire, County Dublin in 1970.

Maria Montessori was confined under house arrest in India during the Second World War but resumed her work after the war. She later lived in the Netherlands with her son Mario and his family and died there in 1952. Her educational ideas live on in a more modern guise today and her basic concepts can be rephrased and summarised as active learning, the importance of motivation and of a high-quality early education environment (Isaacs 2010).

CURRENT MONTESSORI TRAINING OPPORTUNITIES IN IRELAND

Many Montessori-trained practitioners work in private crèches and pre-schools: a small number work in publicly funded services. Some Montessori qualifications are recognised by the Department of Education and Skills, allowing practitioners to work in special schools or units. Montessori training colleges are listed below: for further details about all Montessori courses and their validation, please contact the colleges direct.

AMI Montessori College Dublin

Mount St Mary's
Dundrum Road
Milltown
Dublin 14
www.montessoriami.ie
Association Montessori Internationale (AMI) was founded by Maria Montessori in 1929 to promote and safeguard her educational approach. AMI Montessori College Dublin is the only formally recognised AMI centre operating in Ireland. AMI Montessori College Dublin trains teachers of 3- to 12-year-old children through a three-year course. It also offers a one-year graduate course.

Liberties College

Bull Alley Street
Dublin 8
www.libertiescollege.ie
Liberties College offers a one-year Montessori Diploma course or a two-year course (combined with childcare) in Montessori, accredited by the Montessori Accreditation Council for Teacher Education.

St Nicholas Montessori College Ireland

16 Adelaide Street
Dún Laoghaire
Co Dublin
www.snmci.ie
St Nicholas Montessori Training College offers a range of courses including a BA Degree in Montessori Education and a one-year Higher Diploma in Arts in Early Childhood Montessori Education for graduates.

MONTESSORI PHILOSOPHY

The Montessori method of education advocates 'freedom of choice and independence for children' (Pound 2011:42–3). This self-determination is aided by an educator's readiness to observe and plan activities for children, and it is reinforced when children interact with the learning materials and witness what practice can achieve. Maria Montessori's empirical approach to developing an educational method for children was influenced by her medical training and by her early work with young children from deprived backgrounds. Following a period of observation, Montessori suggested that young children exhibited a number of developmental characteristics. Specifically, she saw children (see Isaacs 2010:9) as:

- being capable of extended periods of concentration
- enjoying repetition and order
- revelling in freedom of movement and choice
- enjoying purposeful activities (preferred work to play)
- self-motivated, displaying behaviours that did not require either punishments or rewards
- taking delight in silence and harmony in the environment
- possessing personal dignity and spontaneous self-discipline
- being capable of learning to read and write.

Nurturing these characteristics, Montessori believed, supports children's learning, development and independence. Consequently, practitioners must tailor their approach to recognise and respond to these characteristics, noting that the Montessori approach to education promotes a number of key themes (Bradley *et al.* 2011:74):

- the child's independence
- learning through active play
- the ability to think creatively and the ability of children to educate themselves
- developing children's concentration
- the adult's respect for the child as a unique individual
- the adult's use of observation
- the environment prepared according to individual children's needs.

These themes find expression in the three key areas associated with Montessori's approach to education:

- the child
- the teacher
- the environment.

THE CHILD

Montessori suggested that children progress through four main developmental stages. Each stage has its own unique features, requiring receptive learning environments and flexible responses from adults to optimise children's development. The four stages are outlined by Bradley *et al.* (2011:75):

1 The '*absorbent mind*' (conception to age 6): imaginatively and sentiently exploring, the child's mind readily absorbs impressions and information from their environment, creating and expanding their own perspective of the world.
2 *Childhood* (age 6 to 12): a time of composed expansion of previous development. Learning through the use of their intellect, the child is keen to discover the world.
3 *Adolescent* (age 12 to 18): another creative period.
4 *Early adulthood* (age 18 to 24): a further stage, marked by a time of calm development of what has been previously learned and understood.

During the stage of the 'absorbent mind' (i.e. 0–6 years), the child's disposition directs them to develop particular human 'skills and abilities' (Isaacs 2010:16) during six key 'sensitive periods':

1 order
2 movement
3 small detail
4 language
5 refinement of the senses
6 the social aspects of life.

Sensitive periods are episodes of heightened interest when children focus on particular activities and objects, thereby providing opportunities for learning and development. Montessori saw these key moments in children's lives as being closely connected: some sensitive periods occurring simultaneously, some peaking at different times. Isaacs (2010:16) outlines how the 'sensitive period' for language might unfold:

> For example the sensitive period for language starts in the womb, when the baby recognises their mother's voice. Babies are pre-disposed to respond to human language. They listen attentively before their first word is uttered. Then between eighteen and thirty-six months the child's language unfolds and explodes, from passive to active vocabulary, ability to use grammar and syntax, using language appropriately within the social context.

The developmental stages and sensitive periods form the basis of educational planning in the Montessori method. By looking out, for example, for indications of sensitive periods, Montessori practitioners can create sufficient learning opportunities in the pre-school environment to respond to the needs of younger children. Without these opportunities, children may not be able to reach their full potential.

THE TEACHER

During a training course for teachers in the USA in 1913, Dr Montessori told participants that 'the teacher in our method is more an observer than a teacher' (Feez 2010:24). A key part of Montessori teacher training is therefore learning how to observe, and Feez (2010:24) suggests that observations need to be recorded to capture:

- everything that interests each child, no matter how apparently insignificant
- how long a child sustains interest in each activity they choose, whether for seconds, minutes or hours
- how a child moves, especially movement of the hand
- how many times a child repeats the same activity
- how a child interacts with others.

Following observations of a child's needs, interests and behaviours, and taking into account their developmental stage and sensitive periods, the Montessori practitioner devises her lesson plan or 'Montessori Presentation'. Presentations, according to Bradley *et al.* (2011:80), 'identify how the learning environment is to be organised, building on each child's prior achievements in small steps, specifying materials and indicating the level of adult support'.

Presentations normally constitute the first stage of a Montessori exercise, and Feez (2010:61) submits that nearly all Montessori exercises for younger children follow a three-stage pattern.

1 The teacher's presentation of the exercise, usually to an individual child.
2 The child's independent work.
3 The child's use of the knowledge in another context.

The developmental characteristics identified by Montessori inform the creation of exercises and activities. For example, central to developing the three-stage pattern is the view that children learn through concentrating on and repeating actions and by using their imagination. Children can work for extended periods which are often not demarcated by a break.

Day-to-day activities for children to practise include cooking, gardening, dressing and cleaning. Sensory experiences are also important, and according to Pound (2011:44), 'a wide range of structured materials are used to heighten olfactory, oral, visual and kinaesthetic awareness and discrimination'. Activities have also been developed to support four areas of language development: talking, listening, reading and writing. Pound (2011:44) also notes that a familiar feature of the Montessori method is the use of sandpaper letters, as an aid to support sensory and phonic learning.

The challenge for the teacher is to identify the appropriate level of her involvement: on the one hand, she is expected to develop the learning environment based on her awareness of children; on the other hand, she must resist the temptation to intervene too much, as 'every useless help is an obstacle to development' (Montessori 1946:59–60), in the sense that unnecessary praise or criticism can act as a barrier to ego development. Therefore, the capacity to reflect is an important aspect of Montessori practice, a key skill supporting a constant cycle of observation, planning and activity.

THE ENVIRONMENT

Feez (2010:25) suggests that the most lasting Montessori contribution to early childhood education and care (ECEC) is 'a series of learning environments full of interest for young children at different ages and stages of development'. The Montessori approach proposes that the capacity of children to learn is influenced by their environment, and so attention must be given by the teacher to creating an environment which responds to the unique needs of each child, enabling active learning to take place. According to Bradley et al. (2011:78), a good Montessori environment:

- is accessible and available to the child
- provides freedom of movement and choice
- enables the child to take personal responsibility for looking after the environment
- provides real materials and a natural environment
- possesses beauty and harmony.

Feez (2010:39) also suggests that the Montessori setting is created to:

- make it possible for children to learn through their own activity
- provide motives for purposeful activity that requires concentration.

The prepared environment is sympathetic to the developmental characteristics identified by Montessori. The setting must be attractive and welcoming. The atmosphere, while not silent, promotes self-directed activities, requiring focus and attention. Montessori believed that three-dimensional objects promote learning and that these should be made, as far as possible, from natural objects. In practice, Montessori was a revolutionary in terms of changing our ideas about the space that children occupy: furniture and equipment at a child's scale; room sightlines from a child's perspective; the floor as a learning tool. In a Montessori setting, Pound (2011:44) suggests:

The environment, indoors and out, is carefully arranged so that children can choose from an appropriate range of structured learning materials. Order and an absence of clutter are thought to minimise distractions. Children select structured apparatus from a range provided and are given the opportunity to repeat the same experience time after time.

AREAS OF LEARNING IN THE MONTESSORI CURRICULUM

Each activity in the Montessori classroom has specific aims, geared to the development of the individual child (Gettman 1987). Most Montessori classrooms have designated areas for:

- practical life
- refinement of the senses
- communication, language and literacy
- numeracy
- cultural aspects of life
- creativity.

PRACTICAL LIFE

The practical life activities mirror activities that take place in the home and allow children to contribute to the daily life of the classroom. They include care of the environment, care of self and grace and courtesy. Through participating in activities involving pouring, sweeping and getting dressed, children perfect these skills and attain independence. These tasks are practised by the children in set and graded exercises and then can be used to keep the classroom neat and tidy, serve food for themselves and other children or assist in other ways. This experience helps children to become independent and contribute to the social life of the group (Isaacs 2010). The Montessori directress shows the children how the exercises can be carried out and then leaves the children free to try things out for themselves.

REFINEMENT OF THE SENSES

The aim of the sensory exercises is to help children organise and classify their experiences of the environment. Children work with the Pink Tower of graded bricks, sets of knobbed cylinders and colour tables and so learn in concrete ways about size, shape and order. Each piece of equipment is designed to teach particular skills and can only be assembled in the correct sequence. This control of error allows the child to find out for him/herself how things work, and the exercises form the basis of later mathematical learning (Isaacs 2010).

COMMUNICATION, LANGUAGE AND LITERACY

Being involved in conversations is one of the important ways of helping children develop their language and of laying the foundation for reading and writing at a later stage. Montessori (1949) advocated teaching reading and writing simultaneously (now termed the 'whole language' method) and based her method on the phonics (sounds) approach. Isaacs (2010) suggests that children should be encouraged to learn how to read and write through the phonics method only if they show an interest in this area. Montessori developed a series of sandpaper letters and sound boxes that isolate certain sound patterns in language. Isaacs (2010) stresses that a great deal of preparatory work has to be carried out on phonic awareness before beginning work on the sandpaper letters. However, most early years educators prefer to follow the child's lead in learning literacy and suggest responding to children's interest in the initial letters of their own names and those of their friends, for example, rather than a more formal approach to phonics.

NUMERACY

Many of the sensory materials promote mathematical understanding of shapes, size and sequence. Materials include number rods, sandpaper numbers and spindles, as well as geometric solids and inset boards. Montessori emphasised the importance of working with solid three-dimensional shapes before moving on to two-dimensional geometric inset boards. All mathematical activities are presented to the child through the use of objects, while building up an understanding of number. Children are then encouraged to use their mathematical knowledge in everyday situations in the classroom such as counting cups, cooking and gardening.

CULTURAL ASPECTS OF LIFE

This area covers topics that interest the children, including nature, history and geography. Young children will be interested in many aspects of their local environment and in other topics such as dinosaurs, insects or vehicles. The Montessori curriculum encourages staff to explore these topics in age-appropriate ways.

CREATIVITY

Modern Montessori approaches value children's creativity and self-expression (Isaacs 2010). Painting, drawing and collage are all encouraged and the Montessori directress encourages the child to develop the necessary skills, such as cutting and gluing, to carry out these activities. Music and storytelling are often carried out at children's request. Most Montessori classrooms do not have adult-chosen role play areas such as shops or garages as Montessori believed that role play functions best when it emerges spontaneously from children's ideas or interests. Montessori did not believe in fantasy and her writings do not encourage reading fairy tales or nursery rhymes to young children (Hayes 2010). She believed that children learn best by first becoming knowledgeable about the real world. This approach to reality is further reflected in the use of real tools, utensils and crockery in a Montessori classroom.

THE MONTESSORI APPROACH AND SÍOLTA AND AISTEAR

The two framework documents for early childhood education, *Síolta: The National Quality Framework for Early Childhood Education in Ireland* (CECDE 2006) and *Aistear: The Early Childhood Curriculum Framework* (NCCA 2009) both allow for a variety of approaches to early childhood education.

The Montessori Alliance (www.montessorialliance.ie) has prepared templates that allow Montessori practitioners to see how the links with Síolta work in practice. Two examples are given below.

SÍOLTA STANDARD 1: RIGHTS OF THE CHILD

Ensuring that each child's rights are met requires that she/he is enabled to exercise choice and to use initiative as an active participant and partner in her/his own development and learning. (CECDE 2006)

The Montessori Alliance (2011) suggests that the component in each child's right to develop in his/her own ways according to his/her abilities be put into practice through the provision of a variety of materials/exercises matched to the child's unique stage of development. An individual educational plan should be created and revised as the practitioner observes the child's interaction with the exercises. In regard to respecting the environment, the practitioner should model respectful behaviour and should create opportunities and exercises to foster respect and appreciation of every environment that the child inhabits (home, school, community, etc.).

SÍOLTA STANDARD 2: ENVIRONMENTS

Enriching environments, both indoor and outdoor (including materials and equipment) are well-maintained, safe, available, accessible, adaptable, developmentally appropriate and offer a variety of challenging and stimulating experiences. (CECDE 2006)

There are many connections to the Montessori curriculum in regard to the environment and the Montessori Alliance (2011) recommends that a broad range of musical instruments that reflect a wide variety of cultures be presented to the children and that practitioners provide Montessori sound boxes and CD players for children's use so that they can explore music making and listening. Outdoor areas should be safe and pleasing to the eye. Opportunities should be provided for children to decorate, organise, maintain and create their outdoor space. Themed areas such as the Home Corner, woodwork or arts and crafts areas may need to be rotated if space is at a premium. Links should be made between the themed areas and practical life exercises, with added materials as the child's skills and dexterity develop (Montessori Alliance 2011).

At the time of writing (August 2011), there are no publicly available documents making specific links between the Montessori curriculum and Aistear. However, Montessori principles are in keeping with Aistear principles and with other curriculum frameworks such as the Early Years Foundation Stage in England (DCSF 2008). Remarks by Isaacs (2010) on the links between the Montessori approach and the Foundation Stage have been adapted to refer to two similar principles in Aistear.

AISTEAR PRINCIPLE: CHILDREN AS CITIZENS

> Children are citizens with rights and responsibilities. They have opinions that are worth listening to, and have the right to be involved in making decisions about matters which affect them. In this way, they have a right to experience democracy. From this experience they learn that, as well as having rights, they also have a responsibility to respect and help others, and to care for their environment. (NCCA 2009)

Self-confidence and self-esteem are nurtured in the Montessori curriculum through fostering independence in self-care, practical life exercises and care of the environment. Some of these actions can be done independently and others require some adult assistance. This participation fosters a reciprocal relationship with the Montessori directress and promotes peer learning and respect for the environment.

AISTEAR PRINCIPLE: COMMUNICATION AND LANGUAGE

> The ability to communicate is at the very heart of early learning and development. Communication helps children learn to think about and make sense of their world. They communicate from birth using many different ways of giving and receiving information. Each of these ways is important in its own right. Learning to communicate in early childhood is shaped by two main factors: children's own ability and their environment. (NCCA 2009)

Maria Montessori recognised the importance of language as a cognitive tool and as a means of communication (Montessori 1989). The Montessori approach promotes conversation, discussion and dialogue (Isaacs 2010). Children's vocabulary is enriched through the wide range of sensory experiences provided and they are encouraged to talk about their work and to ask questions.

CRITICISMS AND BENEFITS OF MONTESSORI EDUCATION

A number of criticisms have been made of the Montessori method. First, Montessori approaches 'are sometimes criticised for being overly prescriptive and rigid. This means that practice, rather than being dynamic and open to change, can become ossified, or over-rigid' (Pound 2011:44). However, supporters of the Montessori method claim that its underpinning principles have to be situated in a historical context, in that structure and coherence were provided to young children who were frequently living in chaotic circumstances.

Second, the Montessori approach has also been criticised for being too work-focused. According to Bradley *et al.* (2011:82), for example, there is some concern that the attention given to day-to-day practical activities reduces the opportunities for imaginative play for children. In contrast, Isaacs (2010:34) suggests that Montessori made a clear distinction between children's work and adults' work, with the child more interested in the process of doing things than with the product of its endeavours. The child becomes more skilful through repeating an activity. For Isaacs (2010:35), Montessori classroom activities form part of the developmental work of growing up.

Third, Pound (2011:45) notes that Montessori's work has been criticised on the grounds that it introduces phonics to children too early. The background to this early introduction, Pound (2011:45) suggests, is that the Italian language 'in which Montessori developed her ideas, is entirely phonetic while written English is not at all regular'. Interestingly, an early introduction to phonetic awareness is common in many current ECEC policies.

A number of studies have considered the benefits of the Montessori method. For example, in a US study Lillard and Else-Quest (2006) evaluated the outcomes for children aged 5 and 12 years attending either a Montessori school or a mainstream school. They found that children from the Montessori school developed better social and academic skills and a better sense of social justice. Lillard and Else-Quest (2006:1894) concluded that 'when strictly implemented, Montessori education fosters social and academic skills that are equal or superior to those fostered by a pool of other types of schools'. Pound (2011:46) also notes that many parents suggest the Montessori approach 'gives children the ability to behave quietly and purposefully as they go about their self-chosen activities'.

Dohrmann *et al.* (2007), in another US study, revealed that young people who attended a Montessori school from pre-school to fifth grade (i.e. aged 10–11 years) performed better at maths and science in high school compared to those students who attended a non-Montessori school. However, there were no significant performance differences between the groups in English or social studies.

Barber (2005), in a UK study, examined the transition of children from a Montessori pre-school setting to a non-Montessori primary school environment. Her research found that Montessori-educated children coped satisfactorily with the transition, but that primary schools needed additional information about the Montessori approach to prepare for the transfer more effectively.

CONCLUSION

Montessori has made a significant contribution to early years education in Ireland and around the world, particularly in relation to child-sized furniture, sensory development and in highlighting the importance of early childhood (Hayes 2010). The Montessori philosophy has stood the test of time. It is popular with parents and it is recognised as one of the principal strands of thinking offering an imaginative, practical and structured approach to working with young children.

The knowledge, skills and dispositions developed through the Montessori curriculum remain relevant to children today and are compatible with the principles of Síolta and Aistear.

Key Learning Points

- Maria Montessori was a pioneer in many areas of life.
- Her philosophy and methods were informed by her observations of young children.
- Her contribution to early childhood education includes a recognition of the importance of a stimulating environment for young children, of sensory development and of using child observation as the basis of planning educational work.
- Montessori principles are compatible with the principles of Síolta and Aistear.

References

Barber, H. (2005) 'Joining the "Mainstream": Transferring from a Montessori Nursery School to a State Reception Class' in K. Hirst and C. Nutbrown (eds), *Perspectives on Early Childhood Education: Contemporary Research*. Stoke-on-Trent: Trentham.

Bradley, M., Isaacs, B., Livingston, L., Nasser, D., True, A.M. and Dillane, M. (2011) 'Maria Montessori in the United Kingdom: 100 Years On' in L. Miller and L. Pound (eds), *Theories and Approaches to Learning in the Early Years*. London: Sage.

CECDE (Centre for Early Childhood Development and Education) (2006) *Síolta: The National Quality Framework for Early Childhood Education in Ireland*. Dublin: CECDE.

DCSF (Department for Children, Schools and Families, UK) (2008) *The Early Years Foundation Stage*. Annesley: DCSF Publications.

Dohrmann, K.R., Nishida, T., Gartner, A., Lipsky, D. and Grimm, K. (2007) 'High school outcomes for students in a public Montessori program', *Journal of Research in Childhood Education* 22, 205–17.

Feez, S. (2010) *Montessori and Early Childhood*. London: Sage.

Gettman, D. (1987/2003) *Basic Montessori: Learning Activities for the Under-Fives*. Oxford: ABC-Clio.

Hayes, N. (2010) *Early Childhood: An Introductory Text* (4th edn). Dublin: Gill & Macmillan.

Isaacs, B. (2010) *Bringing the Montessori Approach to your Early Years Practice* (2nd edn). London: David Fulton.

Lillard, A. and Else-Quest, N. (2006) 'Evaluating Montessori education', *Science* 313:5795, 1893–4.

Lillard, P.P. (1988) *Montessori: A Modern Approach*. New York: Schocken Books.

Mooney, C. (2000) *Theories of Childhood*. St Paul, MN: Redleaf Press.

Montessori, M. (1912/1994) *The Discovery of the Child*. Oxford: ABC-Clio.

— (1946) *Education for a New World*. Madras, India: Kalakshetra Publications.

— (1949/1989) *The Absorbent Mind*. London: BN Publishing.

Montessori Alliance (2011) 'Síolta Standards' <www.montessorialliance.ie/practitioners/siolta> accessed 11 August 2011.

NCCA (National Council for Curriculum and Assessment) (2009) *Aistear: The Early Childhood Curriculum Framework*. Dublin: NCCA.

Pound, L. (2011) *Thinking about Early Childhood Education*. Maidenhead: Open University Press.

11

The HighScope Approach to Early Learning

Geraldine French

Learning Objectives

After studying this chapter the reader should be able to:

- Describe the historical origins, the longitudinal research, and the theoretical underpinnings of the HighScope approach.
- Identify the teaching strategies adopted by HighScope educators.
- Appreciate the curriculum content.
- Understand the HighScope approach to the assessment of children's learning.
- Consider some criticisms of the HighScope research and approach to early learning.

This chapter aims to provide an overview of the HighScope curriculum. It is presented in order of the learning objectives listed above.

SETTING THE CONTEXT: HISTORY, RESEARCH AND THEORY

The name 'HighScope' refers to the high purposes and far-reaching mission of a model of education originating in the USA. Its goal is to improve the life chances of children and young people by promoting high-quality educational programmes. The HighScope approach was designed by David Weikart and colleagues, beginning in 1962, '. . . in response to the persistent failures of high school students from Ypsilanti's poorest neighbourhoods' (Hohmann and Weikart 1995:3).

Weikart was a director of special services in Ypsilanti Public Schools, Michigan. He believed that the low scores of some students on academic and intelligence tests were due to a lack of educational opportunities and inadequate school preparation rather than a lack of innate intelligence. Furthermore, he believed that poor performance at secondary schools correlated with attendance at elementary schools in poor neighbourhoods. An intervention to prevent school failure for 3- to 4-year-old children was established with a classroom secured in the Perry Elementary School from 1962 to 1968. It became known as the HighScope Perry Preschool Project. A longitudinal study was designed to compare the progress of children attending the Project with those who did not receive the pre-school experience. A hundred and twenty-three children were randomly assigned to programme (58 children) or no-programme (65 children) control groups. This strategy of random assignment means that children's experiences at the experimental Perry Preschool Project remain the best evidence for the subsequent differences that were observed in social and intellectual performance between the control and the programme group. In addition to the high-quality programme delivered by trained teachers, children's families received regular home visits. Figure 11.1 details the main study findings for the programme participants at age 40.

Figure 11.1 Major findings of the Perry Preschool Study

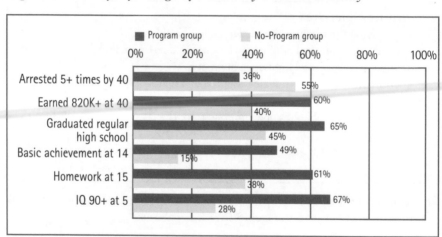

Source: Schweinhart *et al.* (2007)

In a monograph on the research, which measures the outcomes for the children from age 3 to age 41, Schweinhart and his colleagues concluded that:

> High-quality preschool programs for young children living in poverty contribute to their intellectual and social development in childhood and their school success, economic performance, and reduced commission of crime in adulthood. This study confirms that these findings extend not only to young adults, but also to adults in midlife. It confirms that the long-term effects are lifetime effects. (Schweinhart *et al.* 2005:5)

The HighScope Educational Research Foundation was founded in 1970 by Weikart to continue the research and programme activities he had originally initiated. The foundation engages in research, curriculum development, publishing, training and communication. Centres for the dissemination of HighScope materials and ideas are located in twenty countries outside the USA, including Ireland.

The HighScope approach to learning is grounded in research, theory and practice and is continually updated (Epstein 2007). In designing the curriculum, Weikart and his colleagues initially drew extensively from Piaget's research on child development and John Dewey's philosophy of progressive education. Piaget's theory on cognitive development supported the originating team's philosophy that theory and practice must support each child's capacity to develop through active learning (Hohmann and Weikart 1995). Dewey's influence is seen in the prominence in the HighScope approach of playful active engagement in real-life experiences using real materials. Currently HighScope is underpinned by more recent research on cognitive development and on brain activity. The former emphasises learning pathways related to specific content, such as early number and vocabulary, and the latter on the importance of children's interactions with people, things, experiences and, later, ideas (Epstein 2007). Since learning happens in the socio-cultural milieu in which it occurs, the work of Vygotsky and his followers now influence the teaching practices of HighScope educators (Epstein 2007).

TEACHING STRATEGIES

The HighScope approach for babies and toddlers (children from approximately 6 weeks to approximately 3 years of age) and for pre-schoolers (children from approximately 2½ years to the beginning of formal schooling at approximately 6 years of age) share core components.

The cornerstone of the HighScope approach to early childhood education is the belief that *active participatory learning* through play is fundamental to the full development of human potential. It occurs most successfully in environments that are appropriate to the context of children's development. Children in active learning environments experience enjoyment, control, interest, probability of success, feelings of competence and self-confidence. To evaluate whether activities are truly appropriate to the context of development and provide active learning experiences, the following ingredients of active learning were developed by HighScope researchers and educators (Epstein 2007). Abundant, age-appropriate *materials* that appeal to children's senses and can be used in a variety of ways are provided: HighScope argues that learning grows out of the child's direct actions on and thinking about the materials. Children have opportunities to explore, *manipulate*, combine and transform the materials chosen. Since learning results from the child's attempts to pursue personal interests and goals, the opportunity for children to *choose* activities and materials is considered to be essential. Through their *language and thought*, children are encouraged to think about and communicate, in words and actions, what they are doing. Children integrate new experiences into an existing knowledge base, and seek the co-operation of others in their activities. Through *adult* scaffolding, educators recognise and encourage the child's reasoning, problem solving and creativity. In

HighScope, educators 'first validate what children already know, and then challenge them to extend their thinking to the next level' (Epstein 2007:18).

The *learning environment* in a HighScope setting, indoors and outdoors, is carefully planned to provide children with the optimum opportunities to work independently, to make choices and decisions and to solve problems. Children are actively encouraged to use the materials in creative ways. For example, it is just as valid to stack pieces of a jigsaw as it is to make the jigsaw. The indoor and outdoor space is organised into specific *areas* of interest to support children's involvement with activities such as building, pretending and role play, 'reading' and 'writing', playing with sand and water, drawing and painting, counting, sorting, climbing, singing and dancing. The areas are stocked with a wide variety of easily accessible, open-ended natural, found, real-life and commercial materials, which reflect children's home cultures and interests and can be used in creative and purposeful ways, providing ample opportunities for problems to be solved. These materials are *labelled* and *stored* so that children can find, use and return materials they need. Children are encouraged to combine materials from different areas.

HighScope advocates that the *daily routine* provides a common framework of support for children of diverse abilities as they pursue their interests and engage in various learning experiences. The daily routine consists of specific time segments allotted to certain activities and is designed to support children's initiatives and to be flexible. The routine enables children to anticipate what happens next and gives them control over what they do in each part of the day. For babies and toddlers the daily schedule is centred on care-giving routines and is flexible but predictable. The routine includes sensitive arrivals and departures, feeding and mealtimes, bodily care routines, nap times, choice times, outside time, and group times. For preschoolers it includes the *plan–do–review* process unique to HighScope, which enables children to express their intentions, carry them out and reflect on what they've done. *Small-group time* provides educator-initiated learning experiences based on observations of children's interests, key developmental indicators and local events. In *large-group time*, educators and children initiate music and movement activities, storytelling and so on. Other aspects of the routine include greeting time, tidy-up time, outside time, break and transition times.

Research evidence suggests that the engagement of parents and families in their child's education improves children's academic performance and their motivation. *Parental participation* leads to higher adult expectations and increased parental confidence and aspirations (Schweinhart *et al.* 2005). HighScope programmes offer a variety of meaningful opportunities for fathers, mothers and educators to work together, sharing information on *how* to extend children's learning and development. These opportunities can include: daily conversations; family group meetings; conducting home visits; parents' or educators' observations, using a diary or film as a focus for discussion (given due ethical considerations for the confidential nature of the material), or attending key concept sessions (perhaps on an aspect of child development). Epstein (2007) suggests that occasions which develop relationships with children's families can build bridges between the setting and home, enhance parents' and educators' understanding of children and encourage learning opportunities in the home (for example, shopping as a literacy experience identifying listed items, or unpacking the shopping into presses as a mathematical exercise in spatial awareness). Finally, parental participation enriches the programme. Importantly, parents' sharing of information supports educators' planning for children's learning which builds on children's interests in the home.

To support and extend babies' and toddlers' play, recommended HighScope *adult–child interaction* strategies include offering children comfort and contact, participating in play, and conversing with children. Educators share control with pre-school children, focus on their strengths, form authentic relationships with them and support their play. Throughout the day educators use a problem-solving approach, for example asking, 'How will you stick that page up?', 'How can you get this juice carton open?' In addition, educators use encouragement and a problem-solving approach to social conflict, as opposed to praise, punishment or reward, for the management of children's behaviour.

CURRICULUM CONTENT

Key developmental indicators (KDIs), previously known as key experiences, are developed by HighScope to organise the content of children's learning. They are a series of statements describing the overall development of children. In other words, they describe what children do as they play and learn in early childhood settings. They guide educators as they observe, support and plan experiences for children and as they evaluate their early childhood practices. KDI statements are available for babies and toddlers, pre-schoolers and elementary (school-age) children.

HighScope identifies forty-two baby and toddler KDIs organised within six content areas, and fifty-eight pre-school KDIs within eight content areas. For example, babies and toddlers develop their *approaches to learning*, learning 'what is me and what is not me' through to the concept of 'I can do it myself'. They achieve healthy *social and emotional development* through forming close attachments, building relationships and interacting with adults and peers. Babies and toddlers experience *physical development and health* through developing muscle control and listening to steady beat. They learn *communication, language and literacy* skills from gestures, 'cooing' to 'talking', listening and responding and exploring print. Babies and toddlers enhance their *cognitive development* by exploring objects, through mouths, hands and feet. They learn about early number concepts; a toddler experiences 'more' by putting more than one object into a box. They begin to learn about time; for babies time is 'now'; toddlers begin to anticipate – 'putting on coats means going for a walk'.

Through the *creative arts*, children imitate and pretend. By experiencing many times what a banana tastes, feels and looks like, babies and toddlers get a mental picture of a banana and can identify it in photos; later they can draw its image. Each statement highlights an active learning experience that is essential for the fundamental abilities that emerge during childhood. The content areas into which the pre-school KDIs are organised are:

- approaches to learning
- language, literacy and communication
- social and emotional development
- physical development and health
- mathematics
- creative arts
- science and technology
- social studies.

Both sets of KDIs are arranged to correspond to the National Goals for Education in the USA. They equally relate to Aistear, the early childhood curriculum framework in Ireland.

ASSESSMENT

In the HighScope approach careful daily observation of children's experiences is seen as essential to planning, teaching and learning. The KDIs are used as the basis for the HighScope record-keeping process. Educators record brief, precise anecdotes or capsule summaries of children in action as they play, build, pretend, explore and talk. These narratives are then arranged within the main KDIs and cross-referenced if appropriate (acknowledging the complexity and integrated nature of children's learning and development). Selected anecdotal notes can then be transcribed into the *child observation record* (COR). The COR is a comprehensive and validated assessment tool. It affords a systematic assessment of young children's abilities and knowledge, incorporating all areas of development. In addition to the anecdotal notes, portfolios and other evidence of children's work can be included. The COR is administered as a baseline assessment when children have settled into the setting and is ideally followed by two further assessments throughout the year. The KDIs and hence the COR can be recorded electronically.

CRITICISM OF THE HIGHSCOPE RESEARCH AND APPROACH

In relation to the HighScope Perry Preschool Study, questions have been raised about, for example, the study's internal and external validity, the small sample size and thus its significance, and the study's generalisability and replicability. These questions have been robustly defended (Schweinhart 2007). Other criticisms centre on the tension between maintaining *any* educational approach and modifying it, if it is written down. In other words, if changes are made to the programme, at what point does it stop being HighScope (Pound 2005)? Perry participants may have outperformed their control group counterparts, but they could be considered to have performed poorly in comparison with mainstream children (Olsen 2003). Furthermore, the approach has been criticised as being underpinned by a compensatory approach to education. Such an approach aims to compensate for educational inequality or poverty as opposed to being aimed at *all* children (Pramling Samuelsson and Asplund Carlsson 2008). Nonetheless, the HighScope approach contains components of high-quality early childhood education which is emulated in other robust studies (for example Siraj-Blatchford *et al.* 2002).

Key Learning Points

- HighScope is continually being updated to reflect the latest child development research, the experience of practising educators, the development of new theories and the curriculum content standards of state and professional associations.
- Central to HighScope are: the provision of opportunities for active participatory learning; attention to the learning environment; the establishment and adoption of a consistent but flexible daily routine; working with families sharing educational experiences; and modelling respectful ways of interacting with others.
- Ongoing observation and assessment of children's learning as they engage in their everyday experiences is essential to the approach. Staff teams share their observations and assessments to plan for further learning experiences and interactions.
- Training in the HighScope approach and continuing professional development through communities of practice is necessary in implementing the HighScope (or any) approach.

References

Epstein, A. (2007) *Essentials of Active Learning in Preschool*. Ypsilanti, MI: High/Scope Press.

Hohmann, M. and Weikart, D. (1995) *Educating Young Children*. Ypsilanti, MI: High/Scope Press.

Olsen, P. (2003) 'Understanding the Promise of Universal Preschool' in A. Reynolds, M. Wang and H. Walberg (eds), *Early Childhood Programs for a New Century*. Washington: Child Welfare League of America Inc., pp. 329–52.

Pound, L. (2005) *How Children Learn*. Leamington Spa: Step Forward.

Pramling Samuelsson, I. and Asplund Carlsson, M. (2008) 'The playing learning child: towards a pedagogy of early childhood', *Scandinavian Journal of Educational Research* 52:6, 623–41.

Schweinhart, L.J., Montie, J., Xiang, Z., Barnett, W.S., Belfield, C.R. and Nores, M. (2005) *Lifetime Effects: The High/Scope Perry Preschool Study through Age 40*, Monograph 14, High/Scope Educational Research Foundation. Ypsilanti, MI: High/Scope Press.

Siraj-Blatchford, I., Sylva, K., Muttock, S., Gilden, R. and Bell, D. (2002) *Researching Effective Pedagogy in the Early Years*, Research Report No. 356. London: Department for Education and Skills.

Further Reading

French, G. and Murphy, P. (2005) *Once in a Lifetime: Early Childhood Education and Care for Children from Birth to Three*. Dublin: Barnardos.

Schweinhart, L.J. (2007) *The High/Scope Perry Preschool Study Through Age 40: Summary, Conclusions, and Frequently Asked Questions* <www.highscope.org>.

Useful Website

HighScope – www.highscope.org

12

Reggio Emilia

Doireann O'Connor

Learning Objectives

After studying this chapter the reader should:

- Have a clear overview of the Reggio Emilia approach to early childhood education.
- Understand how the centres operate and how the individuals in them act to produce a communal and positive learning experience for all.
- Appreciate the importance of the learning environment and understand its role in a Reggio Emilia context.
- Understand the importance of documentation as a pivotal task for the Reggio Emilia practitioner and understand the connection between this documentation and professional reflective practice.

WHAT IS REGGIO EMILIA?

Reggio Emilia is a city in northern Italy that has a unique and internationally admired approach to early childhood learning. Early childhood education services in the city are supported by the municipality – an organisation similar to an Irish county or city council.

STAFF STRUCTURE

There are six professional roles in Reggio Emilia centres:

1 infant practitioner
2 toddler practitioner
3 pre-school practitioner
4 artist in residence (atelierista)
5 educational philosopher (pedagogista)
6 cook.

All practitioners must be qualified early childhood practitioners before taking an apprenticeship position in a Reggio early learning centre, where they will be trained on site in the Reggio approach.

Atelieristas (artists in residence) must have a degree in art and experience of individual and group art. They are there to support the children in art projects each day.

The pedagogista, a pedagogical or teaching philosophy specialist, works with the practitioners in a group of settings (between three and five centres).

The cook manages the food budget and the weekly menus and prepares and serves all food. All meals are communal, with all age groups eating together in a large central piazza.

Each centre also has a number of volunteers and helpers who support each area of work in the centre. These are usually parents, grandparents or community members.

THE REGGIO EMILIA LEARNING ENVIRONMENT

The Reggio Emilia approach is centred on the belief that learning is enabled by human interaction, the physical environment and the cultural environment (Project Zero 2001).

THE PHYSICAL LEARNING SPACE

A Reggio Emilia centre of early childhood learning is primarily a place of beauty and light. The aesthetics of the physical space are of paramount importance, and creating and developing its beauty is seen as the collective responsibility of all staff and children.

Every Reggio centre has lots of space – both indoor and outdoor – and plenty of natural light. Mirrors are used to maximise the sense of space and light that is central to the principle of beauty everywhere. This principle is further evident in hundreds of small details throughout each centre. Scented candles, hanging crystals spraying rainbows, handmade shell and mirror mobiles tinkling in windows, muslin sheeting draped from the ceiling, beautiful china and pottery delph, essential oil burners, atmospheric and classical music, handmade curtains, cushions and tablecloths in beautiful materials, freshly cut flowers in vases, plants, cared-for spaces and equipment and countless other small details that combine to create a beautiful physical environment are all evident in any Reggio Emilia setting.

The large physical space allows for free and confident movement by the children throughout the building, where they are free to wander, engage with the adults in any room, join other groups, help younger children and learn from older children.

The centres are of a free-flowing design. This is achieved by the creation of a large central space called the piazza. All other rooms lead off this space. The piazza is used for the morning assembly, inter-group socialising, eating together, events and large group projects.

Every centre also has an art space called an atelier or mini atelier. This is a space where art is the central theme. All children have access to this space and can create art projects on their own or in consultation with the atelierista. The mini ateliers are smaller spaces adjacent to each classroom.

A dress-up area is also a feature in each centre. This is a space where role-playing and story-telling projects are supported by the provision of costumes and props.

Each centre has a reading area where soft seats, couches and bean bags are available beside a large, varied, well-cared-for collection of books on easily accessible shelving. The children can seek out books and spend time here alone or with friends. The practitioner also uses this space to read aloud to the children.

Other designated areas include a shop area and a home play area. There is also a separate room for sleeping and resting. The majority of spaces in the school are spacious, free play areas whose function can be determined by the children's imaginations on an ever-evolving and changing basis.

LEARNING MATERIALS AND EQUIPMENT AS AN ELEMENT OF THE PHYSICAL ENVIRONMENT

The equipment used is largely made up of natural and recycled materials. The purpose of materials is seen as supporting a landscape of possibility and suggestion. Therefore raw materials (boxes of shells, buttons, spools, stones, sticks, pieces of material, mesh, bottles, sand, water, leaves, clay, elastic, wood, blocks, bricks, coloured glass, string) make up the majority of equipment in a Reggio Emilia setting. Used materials such as old and cleaned engines, pipes large and small, barrels, nuts and bolts, spare parts and metal are all used in construction, engineering and invention projects. Many of the materials are sourced free of charge through the Remida Centre – Reggio's creative recycling centre. Children also have access to paper, pens, pencils, paints, glue, scissors, paper and all manner of art support materials in the atelier.

Every centre has at least one *projection box*, an electric light-filled box with an opaque top, with which all materials can be examined in minute detail and with great clarity. All materials are provided with the aim of enabling the children to pose questions and develop hypotheses and of fostering their innate desire to experiment, create and learn (Project Zero 2001).

CULTURE, ATMOSPHERE AND ENERGY AS AN ELEMENTS OF THE LEARNING ENVIRONMENT

A school is a very complex and fluid organism. It is made up of individuals, spaces, rhythms, desires, expectations and emotions (Project Zero 2001).

The culture, atmosphere and energy of a centre come from the people within it, both adults and children. Being aware of this helps the often unperceived to be seen and understood. The feelings and values that exist at any one time are what creates an ever-evolving culture within each centre.

In this way, happiness, curiosity, possibility, fun, desire, individuality, belonging, identity, love, affection, friendship, intimacy, peace, autonomy, confidence and freedom together with rights, responsibilities, stimulation, understanding, respect, diversity, equality, openness, trust, nurturing, mindfulness, care, integrity, attention, democracy, beauty and comfort all combine to create an *amiable school*. An amiable school is one where the children, staff and parents are happy; and an amiable school is the Reggio Emilia goal (Malaguzzi 1993).

This happiness, enabled by the culture of the centre, is a central component of the learning environment as it frees all in the centre to enjoy and learn. It also underlines the principle of respect for the children and their families as citizens of the democratic children's centre, where it is understood that they have rights as well as needs.

DOCUMENTATION AND REFLECTIVE PRACTICE

Documentation plays a key role in the Reggio Emilia philosophy of both teaching and learning. It is most valued as a recall tool (Project Zero 2001). Documentation that allows for recall enables both practitioners and children to revisit and progress projects through examination, analysis and discussion. This process allows for all involved to reflect on their work and its meaning. In this way it is also a form of ongoing research and as such has contributed to a body of publications and exhibitions.

Documentation provides material which enables the practitioners to reflect on each project. This reflection enriches their input and guidance through thorough and informed awareness of each child's learning.

Documentation refers to any record of the children's projects, interactions, work and processes. Often these are written notes but audio and video recordings, as well as photographs and copies of the children's work, are also kept and used for reflective purposes by children and practitioners alike, in groups and individually. The function of this reflective practice is to seek the *meaning* in what the children are doing. Once the meaning is identified, it is the practitioner's role to understand it so that it can be employed as a tool·for maximising both the children's enjoyment and their learning. It also plays an important role in the practitioner's learning process and allows the Reggio principle of reciprocal learning to flourish for both the children and their educators.

Observing, listening and paying careful attention are therefore key skills of the Reggio Emilia practitioner. Writing up notes after each session, attaching other forms of supporting documentation to them and making the time to revisit them and reflect on their content as an exercise in ascertaining the meaning of the work for each child is a commitment made by Reggio Emilia practitioners and a skill built up over their training and apprenticeship.

THE DAILY ROUTINE IN A REGGIO EMILIA CENTRE OF EARLY CHILDHOOD LEARNING

Children and their parents arrive between 7.30 a.m. and 9.00 a.m. This period of time is viewed as the welcoming time. Children and their families are welcomed with warmth and delight. The atmosphere is one of *overall softness* (Ceppi and Zini 1998), which is described as an ecosystem where there is diversification, stimulation and a great welcome, where children open to their group but where there are also spaces for privacy and opportunities for pause from the general rhythms of the group.

Respect and listening to children is paramount in a Reggio setting, to the extent that a *pedagogy of listening* is employed by practitioners at all times. The principle of overall softness serves to ensure that the centre is a serene, amiable, liveable place.

The children wait for friends to arrive. Groups are organically formed in this space and projects spontaneously initiated or continued from previous work.

The practitioners warmly greet each arrival, and they are also available to support any of the children's organically developed activities. In addition, they spend this time talking with colleagues, discussing possibilities for the day, based on preceding days, sharing ideas, offering advice and making decisions about arising issues.

By 9.00 a.m. all the children have arrived and together with the practitioners they tidy up the morning's work, put away the materials and shelve works in progress for continuation another time. Children in the middle of a project or game are given time to wind it up naturally and join the group when they have done so.

Usually by 9.15 a.m. all are ready to sit down for morning assembly, a time for discussing the day ahead. During the assembly, fruit is served and the children eat and discuss their ideas for the day ahead. Projects from previous days are examined and how to progress them is discussed.

An outline structure is given to the day with set resting and eating times, but otherwise the children's interests and desires determine the activities and how they progress. Different groups of children can embrace different activities and follow divergent paths for the day.

The morning assembly is seen as an important element of democratic learning. It gives the children a sense of participation and inclusion that leads to a higher degree of self-regulation and lower levels of challenging behaviour as it promotes a sense of belonging which results in lower aggression levels (Project Zero 2001).

After assembly, the children and practitioners organise themselves in accordance with the plans they have made. Projects are developed that can last for minutes, hours, days, weeks or even months. A project I observed during a study visit to Reggio Emilia is a good example of how projects evolve. This project involved a group of children working on self portraiture. First they drew a series of pictures of themselves, then they painted self portraits. They traced the outline of their bodies onto large sheets of paper, they sculpted their image in clay, they photographed their face and body, their belongings and clothes, they videoed interviews with themselves. They stopped regularly to discuss their progress and their learning with their practitioner, each other and their atelierista. They helped each other with cameras, materials and equipment. The project was still going on when I left Reggio Emilia. The children did not know when it would end. It would reach its own natural conclusion, they felt. Children can work on more than one project simultaneously, deciding at the morning assembly how much time they wish to give to each project that day.

Lunch is served at noon and the children all take a siesta after lunch. Children who do not wish to sleep rest in their bed and enjoy a quiet time. This resting period lasts for two hours. Most of the children sleep, with even those electing to 'rest' slipping in and out of a snooze. The staff use this time to reflect on the morning, discuss projects, share information and ideas as well as archive documentation on the children's work.

Projects continue after siesta until going-home time, with a snack being served in the piazza at 3.30 p.m. The day's projects are discussed at the following day's morning assembly and so the learning continues.

Key Learning Points
- The environment in a Reggio Emilia school is a place of beauty, light and space.
- The equipment is predominantly natural, and recycled materials are used.
- An atmosphere of *overall softness* is a key component of the learning environment.
- Democratic learning through freedom is a key principle. This is actualised through the process of *morning assembly* and the *pedagogy of listening and attentiveness*.
- Documentation through notes, photographs, videos and art work is a key element of *reflective practice* and ongoing research.

References

Ceppi, G. and Zini, M. (1998) *Children, Spaces, Relations – Metaproject for an Environment for Young Children*. Reggio Emilia: Reggio Children.

Katz, L. and Cesarone, B. (1994) *Reflections on the Reggio Emilia Approach*. Urbana, IL: ERIC/EECE.

Malaguzzi, L. (1993) 'For an education based on relationships', *Young Children* 49:1, 9–12.

Project Zero (2001) *Making Learning Visible: Children as Individual and Group Learners*. Reggio Emilia: Reggio Children.

Useful Websites

www.reggiochildren.it

National Children's Nurseries Association, a member of Reggio Children International Network – www.ncna.ie/reggio-children/

The view of children as competent learners and communicators is underpinned most vividly in Loris Malaguzzi's 'One Hundred Languages of Children', also known as 'No Way the Hundred is There', available at www.thewonderoflearning.com/history/?lang=en_GB

Information on the Remida Centre can be found at www.ncna.ie/reggio-children/remida-centre/

13

Friedrich Froebel and Early Childhood Education

Claire Nolan

Learning Objectives
- To introduce Friedrich Froebel's model of early education.
- To examine his educational approach and the implications for early childhood practice today.
- To link Project EYE with Froebel's social/traditional model of early education.
- To emphasise the importance of adopting a Froebelian approach to educating young children.

INTRODUCTION

This chapter introduces Friedrich Froebel (1782–1852) and outlines his educational philosophy and his influence on early childhood education and care (ECEC) in Ireland, Project EYE, the primary school curriculum, Síolta and Aistear. It begins with an overview of his life and then discusses his educational philosophy. This chapter also introduces Project EYE as a means of understanding Froebel's influence on early years education today. The chapter concludes that Froebel taught us to discover and to respect the unity of the child and he 'demonstrated that play has an integral place in a child's curriculum' (Manning 2005:376).

FROEBEL'S LIFE

Friedrich Froebel was born on 21 April 1782 in Oberweissbach, a small village in the Thuringian forest, Germany (Manning 2005; Douglas 2008). 'He was one of the most influential educational reformers of the 19th century' (Douglas 2008:27). Froebel was driven by questioning the purpose of the education system.

> [He] spent his formative years in a tumultuous Europe, contending with policies of a divided Prussia and the reactions to the ideas of individualism embraced

in the American and French Revolutions. German Romanticism, which embraced the idea of the harmony of nature, man and God, was the dominant philosophy. (Manning 2005:371)

Froebel wrote that throughout his life he was always seeking the hidden connections and an underlying unity in all things, which he failed to find in studies of school.

FROEBEL'S PHILOSOPHY

Froebel's educational philosophy was influenced by 'the idea of the child as an innocent, in need of special care and protection in contrast to the medieval notion of the child as miniature adult' (Braun and Edwards 1972, cited in Manning 2005:372) Froebel searched for an educational theory based on the psychological understanding of the child. His efforts led to an increasing appreciation of the sanctity of childhood. At a more fundamental level, his educational theories resulted in child-centred curricula in which the emphasis was on self-activity, continuity, movement, creativity and happiness.

> [Froebel's] views on children, their natural position in the order of things, his recognition of the value and importance of childhood in itself, and his views on the roles of adults as guides, facilitators and learners influenced both early education and primary education. (Hayes 2010:8)

Froebel influenced both the primary school curriculum in Ireland and the education and care of children in various childcare settings, for the first time bringing to our attention in his writings the importance of being 'child-centred' in our work with children (DES 1999; CECDE 2006; NCCA 2009).

He disagreed with an educational system which anchored children to textbooks and fed them with mouthfuls of knowledge. He felt that this reduced children and his theory of education resulted from his idea that human nature is an expression of divine activity. Froebel compared:

> . . . the growth of the child to the growth of a plant, to be tended and cared for as the gardener cares for his seedlings, and he emphasised the importance of play for the young child, leading to purposeful activity in the classroom. Above all, education should lead to harmony with God and nature. (Lawrence 1969:22)

The healthy growth and development of children through self-activity, connectedness and continuity, creativeness and physical activity, in happy and harmonious surroundings, is vital. Froebel saw education as essentially a process of growth, dependent upon self-activity. 'The infant's playfulness, exploration and energy were finally seen as an indication of the self-evolving unity of nature and mind within a dynamic universe' (Douglas 1994:56).

He argued that the true theory of education should acknowledge and respect the child's real nature and the laws of his/her development. In his view, the first condition of education is the utmost freedom for the child. 'Given this freedom he would actively and continually seek growth by the successive deployment and exercise of his faculties. Such activity, Froebel termed "play"' (Douglas and Horgan 1995:55). According to Froebel, play is the medium and instrument through which the child, out of his/her own impulses and inward resources, effects his/her growth in every direction that is open to him/her. Froebel emphasises 'the value of observing children's play, for it is in this activity . . . that children reveal their present selves and the aspects of life with which they are coping, both successfully and unsuccessfully' (Bruce *et al.* 1995:119). Through play children come to understand their world and their position in it. Play helps develop of vocabulary and conversational skills, and social skills such as waiting, sharing and turn-taking. Play also helps children work out how to solve problems. However, play needs to be guided and structured (Hayes 2010; Manning 2005; Douglas 2008).

Froebel's contribution to ECEC can be seen in the social/traditional model of early education, which 'stresses the notion of child-centred education in a nurturing environment' (Hayes 1999:182). In this approach the social development of the child is encouraged through providing various play experiences to enhance their social skills while also enabling them to mature socially. The environment is planned and many pre-schools reflect this philosophy in practice (Hayes 1999). Project EYE (Douglas, Horgan and O'Brien 2000) provides 'a developmental curriculum for three- to four-year-old children in Ireland' (Douglas, Horgan and O'Brien 2000:5) and has links with Froebel's social/traditional approach to educating young children.

> The development of the child's social world can be greatly enhanced through socio-dramatic play which involves the following components: imitative role play; make-believe in regard to objects; make-believe in regard to actions and situations; interaction with play partners; verbal communication related to the play episode; and persistence in the play episode. These attributes can be encouraged by the Educator through the provision of a suitable play environment and possibly, intervention at appropriate times. (Douglas, Horgan and O'Brien 2000:13)

Froebel emphasised the productiveness of the child's self-activity and he devised the kindergarten, or 'garden of children', the first of which was opened in Blankenburg in 1837. This kindergarten was built around the child. Its central feature was that children played. According to Froebel:

> [The kindergarten] is a place where a child may grow and develop in body and mind, a place where there is alternation between systematic occupation and play, where the balance is held between restraint and freedom, where the rights of the individual are duly respected and also the rights of the community, where all are occupied according to their strength, and as a natural consequence it is

a place where children are simply and really happy. They find in the kindergarten kindly sympathy and direction, and a suitable field for the exercise of their growing powers. (Bishop 1914:147, cited in Bruce *et al.* 1995:126)

Froebel created certain games and occupations which formed the core of the kindergarten curriculum and which were graded to ensure increasing complexity for the maturing child. This approach stemmed from Froebel's theory that all education revolves around religion, nature, language and arts. The first group of activities consists of 'gifts' and 'occupations': these are intended to familiarise the child with inanimate things (Manning 2005; Douglas 2008; Towler 2009).

The gifts, while providing for the children's play, also trained them in dexterity and movement, and taught them something of the laws of nature. The gifts comprised balls, blocks for building, coloured tablets for design, coloured papers to cut and fold, pencils and paint, clay and sand. All of these items were arranged in a series to capitalise on skills acquired by previous activities. The occupations consisted of paper folding, drawing (using perforated paper designs and squared paper), weaving, folding and cutting. Peawork, sticklaying, cardboard and clay modelling were also included.

Froebel's second group of activities, intended to be conducted outdoors, included various gardening activities and the care of pets to encourage empathy with plants and animals.

In 1843, he published a book of *Mother and Nursery Songs*. This collection of action songs and singing games was based on folk music and the occupations and objects the children saw around them. It formed the third group of activities.

FROEBEL AND THE PRIMARY SCHOOL CURRICULUM IN IRELAND

Froebel's educational philosophy is a fundamental part of our *Primary School Curriculum* (DES 1999); *Síolta: The National Quality Framework for Early Childhood Education* (CECDE 2006); and *Aistear: The Early Childhood Curriculum Framework* (NCCA 2009). Towler (2009) identifies a number of principles highlighted in these documents that reflect Froebel's philosophy.

The first principle highlighted in these documents recognises 'the uniqueness and potential of each child' (Towler 2009:136). Second, childhood is to be acknowledged as a distinct period 'in its own right' (Towler 2009:136; DES 1999; CECDE 2006). Froebel's third principle – that the child should be viewed as part of a wider context – is also incorporated in our current policy in relation to the care and education of children. These policy documents clearly reflect Froebel's views on childhood in stating that 'enriching environments, both indoor and outdoor, the importance of play and self activity in learning, and the significant role which staff and teachers contribute to the child's education' (Towler 2009:137). Towler (2009) specifically draws our attention to the subject SESE (Social, Environmental and Scientific

Education) in the Irish primary school curriculum (DES 1999) and highlights that this subject 'shows striking similarities to the activities in Froebel's school and Kindergarten. The subject of the curriculum is subdivided into geography, history and science' (Towler 2009:138). During these activities the child explores, investigates and uses natural materials to create an understanding of or a unity with the world around them. These are all aspects of how Froebel believed the child should be educated.

CONCLUSION

In conclusion, Froebel made us aware that the 'child presents himself to us in many ways, a body, a mind, a spirit, is always one person, and that whatever affects him in any one part of his being affects him in all' (Bruce *et al.* 1995:114).

Key Learning Points
- Students should be aware of the influence of Froebel in ECEC today.
- Students can apply the Froebelian philosophy/approach to their work practice in order to facilitate children's learning.
- Students should develop an understanding of child-centred practice and the importance of preparing the environment for the child to learn.
- Students should gain an understanding of the role and importance of play in young children's development.

References
Bruce, T., Findlay, A., Read, J. and Scarborough, M. (1995) *Recurring Themes in Education*. London: Paul Chapman.

CECDE (Centre for Early Childhood Development and Education) (2006) *Síolta: The National Quality Framework for Early Childhood Education*. Dublin: CECDE.

DES (Department of Education and Science) (1999) *Primary School Curriculum*. Dublin: Government Publications.

Douglas, F. (1994) *The History of the Irish Pre-school Playgroups Association*. Dublin: IPPA.

— (2008) 'Some implications of the Froebelian and Montessorian methods of educating young children for effective schooling today', *An Leanbh Og (OMEP Journal of Early Childhood Studies)* 2:1, April.

Douglas, F. and Horgan, M.A. (1995) *Early Childhood Education: Issues and Concerns*. Dublin: INTO.

Douglas, F., Horgan, M. and O'Brien, C. (2000) *Project EYE; An Irish Curriculum for the Three- to Four-Year-Old Child*. Cork: Early Years Unit, Education Department, University College Cork.

Hayes, N. (1999) *Early Childhood: An Introductory Text* (2nd edn). Dublin: Gill & Macmillan.

— (2010) *Early Childhood: An Introductory Text* (4th edn). Dublin: Gill & Macmillan.

Lawrence, E. (1969) *Friedrich Froebel and English Education*. London: Routledge & Kegan Paul.

Manning, J.P. (2005) 'Rediscovering Froebel: a call to re-examine his life and gifts', *Early Childhood Education Journal* 32:6, June.

NCCA (National Council for Curriculum and Assessment) (2009) *Aistear: The Early Childhood Curriculum Framework*. Dublin: NCCA.

Towler, M. (2009) 'Friedrich Froebel: a relic from the past, a vision for the future', *An Leanbh Og (OMEP Ireland Journal of Early Childhood Studies)* 3:1, April.

14

Steiner Waldorf Early Years Education

Jonathan Angus

Learning Objectives

After studying this chapter the reader should:

- Develop a clear understanding of the basic pedagogical principles underlying the Steiner Waldorf approach to early childhood education.
- Recognise the importance of creative play, as presented in Steiner Waldorf early years educational settings, for cognitive and social development.
- Recognise the value of an early years educational setting that foregoes early academic instruction.

INTRODUCTION

Steiner Waldorf is a unique and vibrant, salutogenic (health-giving) approach to education. Beyond a thorough view of human development that addresses what to teach when, the approach calls for a fundamentally different relationship of the teacher to his/her work and to the children in his/her care.

The objectives for this chapter are to develop a useful and contextualised picture of the educational philosophy that stands behind Steiner Waldorf early years education and to identify best practices and adaptations used in Steiner Waldorf settings.

WHAT IS STEINER WALDORF EDUCATION?

The founder and chief early proponent of Steiner Waldorf education was Rudolf Steiner (born 1861 in Austria, died 1925 in Switzerland). Combining a thoroughly practical contemporary scientific background with unique philosophical insights, he became a popular author and lecturer, presenting his ideas on broad themes of human and cosmic spiritual evolution to diverse groups of people throughout Europe. His reforming ideas, fruits of active research encompassing an astonishing variety of subjects, still have exceptional relevance. Steiner developed a methodology to systematically research psychological and spiritual phenomena based on direct observation, which he considered to be a path of self development with practical applications in many areas of human activity, including education, medicine and agriculture.

Rudolf Steiner was asked in 1919 to create a school for the children of the workers at a factory in Stuttgart, Germany. One feature of the school's remit was to educate children together, without regard to religious, economic or gender-based differences. In the following years, that school catered to the needs of children aged 4–18 years, and its approach was emulated in other schools in Europe and elsewhere. Since then, a worldwide reputation has been built by Steiner Waldorf schools as educators of creative and clear-thinking individuals with a strong interest in contributing to their communities.

One of the greatest strengths of Steiner Waldorf schools is their adaptability, both to reflect the cultural values of the peoples in particular regions and to meet the changing climate of educational needs. Another attribute of the Steiner Waldorf approach is its reliance on the individual teacher to design a unique curriculum for his/her class.

Early childhood is the most vulnerable time in life, as the transformation and growth that takes place during the first seven years of life is far greater than in any subsequent period. The educator needs to be aware of this vulnerability, and to most effectively meet the needs of the child, s/he must have a deep understanding of what those needs are.

At the root of the Steiner Waldorf pedagogy is a spiritually influenced picture of child development. The concept of developmental phases in childhood was subsequently explored by both Jean Piaget and Arnold Gesell, though each man's perspective has fundamental differences from that of Rudolf Steiner. In Steiner's picture, the years before adulthood are schematically broken into three seven-year cycles.

Around our seventh year we begin to lose our first set of teeth. Steiner observed that this dramatic event is one sign of the complete conversion of a physical body given to us by heredity at birth to one that is remade by the soul and spirit of the individual (Steiner 1924). Steiner saw these shifts as more than just physical changes; he viewed them as thresholds into new ways of experiencing the world, calling for fundamental changes to the way in which education of the child should be approached.

Throughout this first seven-year phase of life, it is the educator's task to address the volition or *will* of the child. Steiner connects free will in our actions to moral imaginations (Steiner 1924). To this end, an attempt is made to structure the whole learning environment inspired by the quality of *goodness*.

A central concern in Steiner Waldorf centres is *aesthetics*. Arts not only bring beauty to learning, but also home in on a child's tendency to learn through mental pictures. An environment rich in music, poetry, painting, drama and dancing helps to develop this imaginative picture-making quality in the child, an essential skill in full-person formation. It's no good being able to read if you can't visualise the story.

The formal or didactic teaching of reading and writing is developed in an age-appropriate fashion in Steiner Waldorf education as the child progresses through the school, and does not usually begin before the seventh year. The social and political pressures educators experience to bring the age of immersion in schooling ever downward are believed, from the Steiner Waldorf point of view, to arise from an economic argument, rather than a pedagogical one.

The contemporary bias toward intellectual precociousness in early childhood goes against copious evidence that this is a cause of great stress to young people (Elkind 1992; Pearce 1992).

Steiner Waldorf theorists and practitioners believe that this social ill can be countered with an educational approach that meets the whole of the young child, nourishing his/her sense of wonder, even reverence, for all that is good in the world.

The three Rs as fundamental principles of Steiner Waldorf early childhood education are *rhythm*, *repetition* and *reverence*. As described below, these principles refer to aspects of experience that are natural to the young child, and working with these healthy inclinations in early childhood settings brings great satisfaction to all.

Rhythm

With *rhythm* comes predictability. The growing child is nourished by regularity. Because activities are taken as a matter of fact and become habits, strong rhythms result in a great reduction in discipline issues, as the children feel confident and content in the warm embrace of a 'breathing' structure. There is daily structure and routine such as a gentle song to announce time to put away toys, followed by washing hands, helping to serve the food, a blessing on the meal, then enjoying the food prepared on that day. But there is also a weekly rhythm, which might involve baking bread on Tuesdays and making vegetable soup on Wednesdays; or activities such as watercolour painting or a puppet show might have their own predictable place in the week. And then there are seasonal rhythms as well, expressed through traditional craft projects using nature's bounty, and the annual celebration of festivals.

Repetition

Through *repetition* of experience, children learn about the world. This managed microcosm – simple experiences, repeated (with very little imposed variety) – is a tool to replicate key experiences so that they can become familiar, and the knowledge gained through the meticulous efforts of the child goes very deeply. Children intuitively seek repetitive experiences, and often ask for stories or songs to be presented again and again, until the child masters the delivery him/herself, and will do so seemingly ad infinitum.

REVERENCE

The Steiner Waldorf approach does not equate *reverence* with religiosity, but it works out of the notion that everything, visible and invisible, which surrounds children has an impact on them. Steiner Waldorf practitioners create an environment that is calm, peaceful, dependable and unhurried. This not only boosts children's intellectual development but also teaches them life skills. The mindful work of carers creates an atmosphere that is both protective and nurturing, making it a sacred space for children to inhabit. The work of sweeping the floor or mending a torn cloth is done in the children's presence as part of the day's work, and is carried out in a mood of calm attentiveness. This can be seen as reverence for the tasks of life, and Steiner Waldorf practitioners believe that more is gained by the children experiencing this in their environment than would be gained through admonitions about how one 'should' behave.

THE ART OF STORYTELLING

Waldorf emphasises orality in the early years, as it is recognised as the fundamental basis for cognitive development. Discussion is a key element, and informal and frequent opportunities are provided in which children are encouraged to speak and listen to one another. More formal recitation, which models and exercises clear and dynamic speech, is also practised daily. Stories offered by the adults, with a rich vocabulary and told from memory rather than read from books, give rise to a broad range of emotional responses.

Rudolf Steiner placed great emphasis on the development of imagination in the early years of life, as a precursor to more advanced levels of knowing. Sloan (1983) argues that it is only through imagination, the image-making power of the mind, that we have any knowledge whatsoever, for it shapes our everyday perception of the world, and there is no perception separate from interpretation.

It is Schwartz's (1997) contention that the efficacy of a beautiful and meaningful story to convey ideas and ethical concepts with economy and elegance is a tenet that has been both understood in all religions throughout the ages and recently rediscovered by a number of educators. He goes on to warn that a culture whose stories are trivial and negative will inculcate just those attitudes, particularly in very young audiences.

CREATIVE PLAY

Play, language, activity and the manipulation of a variety of materials are central to early childhood learning and help to maintain a learning continuum between home and the school. Friedrich Froebel, who gave us the lovely word 'kindergarten' to describe a child-caring centre, emphasised the importance of children gaining proficiency in the language of things before the language of words.

Free, imaginative play is crucial to develop self-control and socialisation, and no single factor has been shown to have greater impact on the healthy development of a child's future educability. As is often said in Steiner Waldorf pedagogy (and in many developmental psychology courses), play is the young child's work. The opportunity to develop the capacity for make-believe is all too often sacrificed to bring worksheets and standardised assessment to the under-7s.

A distinction should be made between the types of play scenarios created and directed by adults for children versus wholly child-created play activities. In Steiner Waldorf settings, the children are routinely allowed and encouraged to play amongst themselves, while the adult carers engage in domestic work in the shared environment (baking or cleaning, gardening or woodworking), observing the children's activities and intervening as needed. A framework for play is certainly provided, but this is a subtle encouragement that comes through the availability of simple and 'unfinished' toys, basic costumes and natural environments. The children are also encouraged to join in with adult 'work', in order to teach them social and domestic skills and develop motor and practical abilities. Helping with household tasks and daily activity around the home is an excellent foundation for later life. Often children prefer to help gather kindling for a fire or dig a bed for cabbages to playing a role in a fairy tale or piloting a plane across the mountains. In this setting, there's plenty of time to engage in both types of activity.

Steiner Waldorf practitioners have long understood the fundamental importance of play for children's growing cognitive functioning. Janni Nicol, an expert in Steiner education, explains that play is integral to a child's mental, emotional, social, intellectual and physical development. She points to studies showing that children who score highest in socio-dramatic role playing demonstrate the highest intellectual competence, longest attention span and most innovative and creative thinking. They think with their entire physical being, and learn through doing.

STEINER WALDORF EARLY YEARS EDUCATION IN IRELAND

The first early years centre using Steiner Waldorf principles in Ireland was established more than forty years ago. According to the Irish Steiner Kindergarten Association, there are currently twenty early years centres in the Republic and Northern Ireland. These include four in County Clare; three each in Cork, Dublin and Down; two in Kilkenny; and one each in Sligo, Tyrone, Kildare, Wexford and Wicklow. Of these twenty centres, five are directly connected to Steiner Waldorf primary schools.

With the advent of two Steiner Waldorf national schools recognised and funded by the Department of Education and Skills in 2008, signs point towards an increase in the availability of this type of early childhood education in Ireland over the coming years.

CONCLUSION

Steiner Waldorf offers a unique and vibrant educational approach to working with young children. Today, there are more than 1,500 Steiner Waldorf early years centres worldwide, representing possibly the fastest growing non-government education system in the world. In a time of increasing pressures to hurry children through childhood, the Steiner Waldorf method provides a rich and nourishing environment that is truly centred on the developmental needs of the child, that meets the small child with respect and dignity, and that is equally rewarding and satisfying for childcare practitioners.

Key Learning Points

- Steiner Waldorf early childhood education arises from a view of human development that recognises the first seven years as the most important period of life.
- Storytelling and the modelling of conscientious engagement with domestic tasks are two means of conveying social responsibility and ethical attitudes that are of far greater power and significance than confrontation, criticism or moralising.
- Creative play builds imaginative capacity, social facility and cognitive flexibility. It is the very work of young childhood.
- Rather than introducing early academics into pre-school settings, the three Rs of Steiner Waldorf early childhood education are rhythm, repetition and reverence.

References

Clouder, C. (ed.) (2003) *Rudolf Steiner Education: An Introductory Reader*. Forest Row, Sussex: Rudolf Steiner Press.

Elkind, D. (1992) *The Hurried Child: Growing up Too Fast Too Soon*. Reading, MA: Addison-Wesley.

Pearce, J.C. (1992) *Evolution's End: Claiming the Potential of Our Intelligence*. San Francisco: HarperCollins.

Schwartz, E. (1997) *Why the Setting Sun Turns Red and Other Pedagogical Stories*. Fair Oaks, CA: AWSNA.

Sloan, D. (1983) *Insight–Imagination: The Emancipation of Thought and the Modern World*. Westport, CT: Greenwood.

Steiner, R. (1924) *The Kingdom of Childhood: Introductory Talks on Waldorf Education: Seven Lectures of August 12th to 20th 1924 in Torquay, England*, trans. H. Fox (1995). New York: Anthroposophic Press.

Further Reading

Froebel, F. (1895) *Pedagogics of the Kindergarten*. New York: D. Appleton & Co.

Jaffke, F. (1996) *Work and Play in Early Childhood*. Edinburgh: Floris.

Nicol, J. (2010) *Bringing the Steiner Waldorf Approach to Your Early Years Practice* (part of a series of comparative approaches to early childhood education). London: Routledge, David Fulton.

Oldfield, L. (2001) *Free to Learn: Introducing Steiner Waldorf Early Childhood Education*. Stroud, Gloucestershire: Hawthorn Press.

Useful Websites

Irish Steiner Kindergarten Association – www.steinerireland.org

Steiner Waldorf Schools Fellowship of the UK and Ireland – www.steinerwaldorf.org.uk

International Association for Steiner/Waldorf Early Childhood Education – www.iaswece.org

15

Na Naíonraí

Máire Uí Chonghaile

Learning Objectives

After studying this chapter the reader should be able to:

- Demonstrate an understanding of the historical development, objectives and provision of Naíonraí as an immersion education programme.
- Analyse and evaluate immersion education as practised in the Naíonra setting.
- Name and categorise the main advantages of an immersion education programme.
- Critically evaluate the methodologies and activities used to promote second language acquisition and the role of the stiúrthóir (leader) and parents in this process.

INTRODUCTION

This chapter describes the background to the development of the Naíonra movement (see www.naionra.ie) in Ireland since the 1970s. It explains the Naíonra experience, underpinned by research which highlights the advantages of early immersion education. This is followed by an examination of the range of activities that promote second language acquisition. Finally, the centrality of both stiúrthóir and parents in the child's language learning process is discussed.

A Naíonra is a group of children between 3 and 5 years of age who come together for a few hours each day, under the guidance of a stiúrthóir, to play and to learn through play. The objective of the Naíonra is to structure the environment to ensure that all facets of the child's holistic development are catered for, while giving the child the opportunity to acquire Irish naturally through the medium of play. The Naíonra's emphasis on language acquisition is placed in the context of the child's overall social, cognitive and physical development.

HISTORICAL OVERVIEW

In the 1960s concerns were expressed about the shift away from the use of the Irish language and from Irish-medium education. The success of the Welsh pre-school immersion programme prompted the setting up of the Naíonra movement in the 1970s. In an attempt to revitalise the language, an organisation known as Na Naíscoileanna Gaelacha was founded in 1974. Its aim to establish Irish-medium pre-schools throughout the country and to instruct its members about the principles of immersion education was soon realised. By 1978, twenty-six Naíonraí had been successfully established. A name change to Na Naíonraí Gaelacha drew attention to the pedagogical approach practised, placing greater emphasis on the principles of play in the holistic development of the child.

In 1978 this organisation, Naíonraí Gaelacha, jointly with Bord na Gaeilge (a state body responsible for the promotion of the Irish language), became known as An Comhchoiste Réamhscolaíochta. The remit of this committee was to act as a co-ordinating and training body, to provide services and resources to Naíonraí and to oversee the expansion of the movement.

As a successor to An Comhchoiste Réamhscolaíochta, Forbairt Naíonraí Teoranta was established in 2003. This all-Ireland voluntary organisation supports the establishment of a range of services through the medium of Irish, primarily Naíonraí but also after-school services, crèches, summer camps and parent/toddler groups.

September 2010 saw the establishment of an unprecedented number (eighteen) of new Naíonraí. A total of 168 Naíonraí are now in existence with over four thousand children attending. A further forty-five (approximately) Naíonraí are located in Gaeltacht areas with almost a thousand children enrolled. In recognition of their important role in Irish language acquisition and maintenance in these increasingly bilingual communities, the Gaeltacht Naíonraí receive a subsidy from Údarás na Gaeltachta for each child attending.

The majority of children in Gaeltacht Naíonraí are from English-speaking homes. Children with special needs or children who have come from abroad also enrol in Naíonraí. In general, Naíonraí are experiencing an increasing number of children attending who have a limited understanding of the language (Mhic Mhathúna and Mac Con Iomaire, 2009). This presents a challenge for Naíonra providers to facilitate the acquisition of the language across a wide range of competencies and abilities.

THE NAÍONRA AS AN IMMERSION PROGRAMME

Immersion education refers to the use of children's non-native language as a medium of instruction. Various types of immersion programme exist, from early immersion (pre-school stage) to late immersion (children aged about 7 years). Further classifications are total immersion, in which all instruction is given through the medium of the second language; and partial immersion, in which only some subjects are taught through the second language. It is acknowledged that total immersion produces better results than partial immersion and that early immersion produces better results than late immersion (Baker 2011).

The Naíonra philosophy emphasises the acquisition of Irish as distinct from teaching Irish in the traditional manner. Irish is spoken at all times by the stiúrthóir, who understands everything the child says in his/her first language but answers him/her in the second language. During this interaction every opportunity is taken to provide the child with the necessary vocabulary in the second language. The Irish s/he hears is associated with the immediate environment, for example the activities, play, songs, rhymes in which the child is involved and the equipment being used. This context gives meaning to the language and the child picks up phrases, formulae and words informally as a child would when acquiring her first language. Hence, a child's linguistic development within the Naíonra is attributed to the ability to make word associations through experience. The child will begin to use Irish when s/he is ready, each child at his/her own pace.

THE ADVANTAGES OF IMMERSION EDUCATION

Most studies favour immersion education, and they indicate the linguistic, cognitive, cultural and social benefits of learning another language in the early years (Johnson and Swain 1997; Johnstone 2002). It has been found that children develop greater fluency not just in the new language they are learning, but also in their mother tongue (Bialystok 1986). They develop an awareness of how language works, which contributes to improved flexibility and creativity in thinking.

Interestingly, the findings of two Irish studies (Horgan 1987; Horgan 1995) further strengthen the case for early immersion programmes. Horgan (1995:188) found that children in junior infant classes in Gaelscoileanna were in communication with each other for over 42 per cent of the total time they were at school, a figure that far surpasses the amount noted by Horgan (1987:194) in junior infant classrooms in standard primary schools. This statistic shows that the immersion education setting places more emphasis on children being actively involved in the language learning process.

Moreover, children in the immersion environment were engaged in cognitively stimulating activities for 28 per cent of their time compared with children in standard classrooms, where 17 per cent of the time was devoted to highly challenging activity (Horgan 1987:201). From these and several other recorded findings in these two studies, it can be tentatively argued that participation in an immersion education promotes intellectual development.

With respect to overall scholastic achievement, results of research indicate that an immersion experience does not necessarily have negative effects on curriculum attainment. In fact, it has been found that most children gain a second language without cost to their performance in other areas of the curriculum. Baker (2011:273) compares immersion education to cooking: 'the ingredients, when mixed and baked, react together in additive ways'. In this context it has been found that children learn a third and fourth language more easily when they have experienced early immersion education.

Children are exposed to a wider cultural experience when they learn a second language. Irish culture is rich in music, song, dance and folklore, all of which are used as media for developing children's understanding and enjoyment of the language. An appreciation of Irish cultural identity can engender a respect for people of different backgrounds, an important factor as Ireland becomes more multicultural. Furthermore, many non-Irish-national pupils have successfully studied the Irish language.

It is well documented that early immersion programmes have played a significant role in assisting the language revitalisation movement not only in Ireland but also in a number of other countries, for example Wales and New Zealand. Early immersion education has also boosted the demand for primary school immersion education (Gaelscoileanna Teo). Consequently, there has been unprecedented growth of all-Irish primary and post-primary schools both in Ireland and in Northern Ireland over the past twenty-five years. Approximately 40,000 children are currently receiving education through the medium of Irish in 173 primary schools and forty post-primary schools outside the Gaeltacht.

THE ROLE OF THE STIÚRTHÓIR IN PROVIDING ACTIVITIES THAT PROMOTE SECOND LANGUAGE ACQUISITION

Routines in the daily activities of the Naíonra assist in the acquisition and mastery of language. There are many advantages cited in the literature with regard to the establishment of routines, namely: children know what to expect; it assists them to work independently; it helps to develop memory skills; and it fosters self-esteem. Equally, the repetition of commonly used phrases during daily routines (arriving, lunchtime, tidy-up time, going home time and frequent activities such as washing hands) enhances the language acquisition process. Consistent use of the same phrases augments learning.

A further principle that underpins the acquisition of Irish in the Naíonra setting is the involvement of pupils in a specified range of activities. Hickey (1997), in a survey conducted among stiúrthóirí, found that activities involving the home corner, jigsaws, brick and building materials were the most frequently employed: over 80 per cent of children engaged in these activities daily.

In the same survey, the author sought the views of stiúrthóirí on the most effective activities for promoting language acquisition. Songs and rhymes, story telling, home corner, group games and card matching were identified. This points to a disparity between what is considered productive in promoting language competence and what is actually being implemented, since Naíonraí tend to focus more on object-centred activities (involving jigsaws, bricks, etc.) than on language-centred activities (story telling, drama, puppetry).

Therefore, children need to be exposed to a language-rich environment to ensure the development of their language competency. The stiúrthóir plays a significant role in this process. Supporting activities to meet the language needs of children, providing them with phrases, songs and poems, preparing the environment and supplying resources for activities are daily aspects of their work routine. Coupled with this, the stiúrthóir is expected to listen to children, be alert to their comments, affirm and guide them during activities, and promote enjoyment, interest and fun.

There is evidence to indicate that where the competence of the stiúrthóir in Irish is rated as satisfactory to weak, children tend to perform less well in language skill development. Hickey (1997) found that 18 per cent of stiúrthóirí and 44 per cent of assistants in the Naíonra had low levels of Irish. The positive link between the fluency of the stiúrthóir and the acquisition of Irish comprehension and production by children in the Naíonra is an indication that competency in Irish should be a priority in the training of stiúrthóirí. Each stiúrthóir undertakes an eighty-hour intensive training course to qualify for registration. This consists of one full week course and one weekend course. Forbairt Naíonraí Teoranta is a FETAC-recognised training centre and provides training at Level 5 and Level 6 through the medium of Irish.

Notwithstanding the above, Hickey (1997) found that children make significant advances in Irish during their time in the Naíonra. However, she also cautions against unrealistic expectations, noting that it should not be assumed that children will emerge as balanced bilinguals after twelve to twenty-four months in the Naíonra setting. Comprehension of basic Irish phrases and an ability to produce some phrases is an achievable outcome and a good basis for further learning. Children who attend Naíonraí begin primary school having made significant progress in Irish acquisition.

THE ROLE OF PARENTS

Advantages which accrue from increased parental involvement in the education of their children have been well documented. Hickey (1997) found that 20 per cent of parents chose to send their children to a Naíonra for general development/education reasons rather than for language reasons, while 60 per cent of parents selected the Naíonra for both language and general development reasons. She further noted that parents were very satisfied with their children's progress in Irish and also with their holistic advancement. These parents reported that there was a significant increase in the use of Irish in the home after their children started in the Naíonra.

Nevertheless, it is noteworthy that parental involvement in the life of the Naíonra is low (Hickey 1997). Consequently, it is important that the stiúrthóir develops strategies to engage parents more fully. Such activities might include information booklets, compilations of rhymes and songs, self-help Irish material, Irish classes, involvement in policy development and helping to organise events and tours. A wide range of high-quality resources are also available to support parents in promoting the language in the home (www.naionrai.ie).

CONCLUSION

Effective early immersion programmes are child-centred, holistic, play-based, interactive and language-rich. They provide a valuable service to children whose parents wish them to acquire or develop further their competence in Irish at an early age. Moreover, a partnership with parents is central to their success. The Naíonra can also be considered a vital link in the chain of language revitalisation. The balance of research evidence indicates that early immersion education is an excellent way of introducing a second language while also enhancing other cognitive and social skills. Indeed, children in Naíonraí experience a wide range of activities which promote their overall development.

Naíonraí have shown an exponential rate of growth over the last decade. This recent growth has come about as a result of the convictions and persistence of those who value the Irish language. Crucially, the Naíonra, a high-quality provider of early immersion programmes, gives each child the right to receive care and education through the medium of Irish.

Key Learning Points
- Historical background of the Naíonra movement.
- Advantages of immersion education.
- The Naíonra experience.
- Activities that promote second language acquisition.
- Role of the stiúrthóir in the Naíonra setting.
- Importance of parental involvement.

References

Baker, C. (2011) *Foundations of Bilingual Education and Bilingualism* (5th edn). Bristol: Multilingual Matters.

Bialystok, E. (1986) 'Factors in the growth of linguistic awareness', *Child Development* 57.

Uí Ghrádaigh, D. (ed.) (2004) *Cúnamh Tacábhar Cúram Leanaí 0–6*. Dublin: Forbairt Naíonraí Teo.

Gaelscoileanna Teo [nd] *Excellent Education Immersion Education*. Information leaflet.

Hickey, T. [nd] 'An Tumoideachas', cited in *Cúram agus Oideachas Luathóige Treoirleabhar*. Gaillimh: Údarás na Gaeltachta.

— (1997) *Early Immersion Education in Ireland: Na Naíonraí*. Institiúid Teangeolaíochta Éireann.

Horgan, M.A. (1987) 'A Study of the Importance of Play in Junior Infant Class Children in Cork City and County', MEd thesis, University College Cork.

Horgan, S.E. (1995) 'A Study of the Linguistic and Cognitive Development of Junior Infant Class Children in Gaelscoileanna in Cork City and County', MEd thesis, University College Cork.

Johnson, R.K. and Swain, M. (1997) *Immersion Education: International Perspectives.* Cambridge University Press.

Johnstone, R. (2002) *Immersion in Second or Additional Language at School: A Review of the International Research.* Stirling: Scottish CILT.

Mhic Mhathúna, M. and Mac Con Iomaire, M. (2009) *Developing a Language Planning Scheme in Gaeltacht Naíonraí,* cited in *An Leanbh Óg* (OMEP Ireland *Journal of Early Childhood Studies*) 3:1, April.

Further Reading

Uí Ghrádaigh, Déirdre (2005) *Lámhleabhar do Stiúrthóirí Naíonra Eagarthóir.* Forbairt Naíonraí Teo.

Mhic Mhathúna, M. (1997) 'Early Steps in Bilingualism: Learning Irish in Irish-Medium Pre-schools', *Early Years* 19:2, 38–50.

Useful Websites

Forbairt Naíonraí Teo – www.naionrai.ie

National Council for Curriculum and Assessment – www.ncca.ie

Gaelscoileanna Teo – www.gaelscoileanna.ie

Comhluadar – www.comhluadar.ie

16

Learning to Play and Playing to Learn

Carmel Brennan

Learning Objectives

After studying this chapter the reader should be able to:

- Identify key elements of the play-based approach to early childhood education and care (ECEC).
- Engage with a socio-cultural perspective to further inform practice.
- Discuss the significance of socio-dramatic play from that perspective.
- Plan and implement related roles and strategies for the play-based ECEC practitioner.

INTRODUCTION

Aistear, the early childhood curriculum framework (NCCA 2009) focuses on the play-based approach to early childhood education. It outlines the characteristics of play, identifies categories and types of play and offers multiple exemplars of learning through play. This chapter proposes to add to the understanding in Aistear by introducing a socio-cultural perspective and exploring the pedagogic directions that emerge.

WHAT IS MEANT BY A PLAY-BASED APPROACH TO ECEC?

The term 'play-based approach' or 'play-based curriculum' is used to describe an approach to ECEC that recognises that children learn through play and builds on their play experiences to promote further learning. It is an emergent curriculum (Jones and Nimmo 1994) and therefore responds to children's interests, abilities and negotiations. Other concepts congruent with the emergent curriculum include:

1 Children's own self-initiated play, particularly pretend play, is central.
2 Learning is holistic and integrated, with the principle aim of promoting well-being.
3 The focus is on process rather than product, on promoting a spirit of enquiry.

4 Children learn in varied and multiple ways. While play is central, it is supported
   by observation, imitation, direct instruction, experimentation and exploration.

The play-based curriculum has over the last sixty years drawn largely on Piaget's
(1937/1971) theory of cognitive development. Vygotsky's (1933/1976) socio-cultural
theory, which placed in the foreground the role of social interaction and culture in
children's learning, brings a new perspective. It focuses on how children use play to
make sense of the world, to connect, contribute and belong in community. In the
next section, we explore this perspective.

VYGOTSKY AND PLAY

Vygotsky (1933/1976) positions play as the leading source of development and the
zone of proximal development (ZPD) for many reasons. In play, for example, children
manage to do what they cannot do in real life – they operate beyond their real-life
capabilities and therefore in the ZPD. At the same time, they enjoy the emotional
satisfaction of being what they want to be. In cognitive terms, in making one thing
stand for another in play (for example a stick might be a horse), children learn to
create and give meaning to signs and symbols, thereby developing imagination,
language and abstract thought.

He also introduces the idea that children's play is rule-bound. 'What passes
unnoticed by the child in real life becomes the rules of behaviour in play' (Vygotsky
1933/1976:9). There are rules for being a mother or father, a doctor or astronaut,
being in a restaurant, a church or school. Children enjoy the experience of living the
role and they learn that when they live by the rules of the role other players know
what to expect and how to respond. Living within the rules provides a framework for
behaviour and interaction that helps them to connect, understand each others'
initiatives and collaborate. Being connected in a shared story is very satisfying for
children. Consequently, Vygotsky tells us, they voluntarily and happily live by the
social rules. In their play, children learn to regulate their behaviours and emotions
and to co-ordinate them with the behaviours and emotions of other people. In the
process, they internalise the rules as a natural way of thinking – they learn to think
in a shared way.

CO-CONSTRUCTING THE WORLD FROM THE BEGINNING

This theory of play flows from Vygotsky's (1978) more general socio-cultural theory
of learning. He believed that through their relationships and activities with other
important people in their lives, children learn to be part of a culture. They develop
in ways that help them to fit in and belong in family and community. This process
begins in first relationships, when parent and child share experiences and create
meaning together.

From the beginning, they engage in pretend play. They play the game 'Pretend we're
having a conversation and pretend I understand you and you understand me' (Brennan,

2010). The rules of the game are: (i) you follow my initiatives (my sounds, actions, emotions) and I'll follow yours; (ii) we'll take turns; and (iii) we'll talk about what we're doing and feeling, and the people, things and happenings around us. In this play-based approach, the baby learns the skills of connection, the skills of intersubjectivity and self–other regulation. In these interactions babies are developing a sense of selfhood and building an identity as communicators, contributors and emotionally connected people. 'A desire to know more and to gain skills in ways that other trusted people recognise and encourage . . . is the defining feature of young, human nature' (Trevarthen 2004:29). The experience of intersubjectivity satisfies a basic human need to feel part of community and drives development and identity in cultural ways. Children then bring these ways of participating and thinking, these experiences and skills, to their peer relationships in play.

CO-CONSTRUCTING THROUGH PLAY IN ECEC SETTINGS

Entering the pretend play world with peers in ECEC settings, however, is generally more challenging than play at home. The children are moving into unfamiliar places with other young children. Playing together and co-ordinating a play story requires that they listen to one another, understand and share one another's ideas and intentions, and collaborate. They must contribute ideas that others find interesting and understandable. They need to know how various characters act and talk. When children use these skills successfully, they feel competent and they have an identity as a welcome player and friend. These are the foundations of every child's well-being. This ability to share ideas with others, to empathise with and follow their reasoning and intentions develops in peer play and facilitates all learning.

In the pretend world, while playing mammies and daddies, doctors, shopkeepers, astronauts, superheroes, princes and princesses, children create real-life and fantasy contexts to which they bring their experiences, knowledge and skill (see Brennan 2004a, 2004b and IPPA 2006 for examples). They abstract them from one situation and situate them in another so that they can reflect on them, test them and open them to other perspectives. Together with their co-players, they change and adapt them and renegotiate their meaning, importance and usefulness. It is a process of co-construction that changes the way they see the world.

In enacting roles, children adopt the practices, tools and persona of the role. The doctor uses a stethoscope, injections and prescriptions and speaks to patients in a particular way. Lave and Wenger (1991) describe this as a community of practice (CoP). Children participate in multiple CoPs through their play (Brennan 2004b) and engage with their distinctive ways of knowing and practising. It is a very complex, holistic, authentic way of learning. The medium of learning is participation in pretend play and the outcome is more skilled participation in both the pretend and real world. So how do ECEC practitioners support this participation?

Pedagogy with Play

As we can see, this socio-cultural perspective centralises the importance of relationships, connection and collaboration, roles and contexts in play. Within this perspective, the role of the ECEC practitioner is principally as facilitator, co-constructor and mentor. S/he supports the development of:

- *Well-being, identity and belonging* (NCCA 2009). First and foremost the pedagogue has the responsibility to ensure that each child has the opportunity and the skills to participate. Exclusion has long-term negative impacts.
- *Self–other regulation, connection, communication and collaboration*. Play provides the best opportunity for practitioners to teach the skills of connection and of building relationships in everyday interaction moments.
- *Co-constructing and reconstructing ways of knowing the world*. The pedagogue is a co-constructor with the children, helping children to explore and interpret the adult world and reconstruct the peer world.
- *Play skills and knowledge*. S/he helps children to enter and extend play by sharing with them the ideas, knowledge and skills they need to enact their roles more fully.
- *Reflection, questioning and abstraction*. Children play out their experiences in pretend scenarios and roles to revisit them and make sense of them. The pedagogue observes children's play and uses their ideas to generate questions, dialogue, reflection and further learning.
- *Symbolic and abstract thinking*. The pedagogue offers materials and practices that children can adapt and use symbolically and creatively in their play. S/he helps children to draw on their knowledge and experience and transfer them to new play contexts.
- *Valued practices*. The pedagogue locates practices and resources in play contexts, e.g. shopping lists, weighing scales, etc., to support the valued practices of literacy, numeracy, science, etc.
- *Emotions*. The pedagogue recognises the emotional quality of participation in play and listens to, guides and supports children.
- *Assessment*. The pedagogue reviews their play with children, sharing feedback on their contributions and engaging children and their families in their learning.

REFLECTION AND DISCUSSION

The following is an example of a pre-school play episode and practitioner supports that facilitate and extend the children's learning. Consider a play episode that you have observed and discuss what children might be learning in the episode and possible ways you could enrich and extend that learning.

Case Study: 'Holidays' (Brennan 2008)

Prompted by a new travel bag in the home corner, Laura and Anne play 'holidays'. They pack the bag and baby's buggy to bursting point, select magazines and proceed to the airport. Toys are purchased at the duty free shop to keep baby amused. Waving goodbye, they board the plane for Portugal. On arrival, they exude excitement and head for their hotel. The girls are very collaborative, building on one another's ideas and communicating their pleasure in each other's company.

Pedagogic supports:

- The play is prompted by a new travel bag as a play prop. The children use available books to symbolise magazines and the book corner as the airport. The practitioners know that equipment can generate ideas and help children to connect and initiate a shared play theme.
- The enclosed play space protects their game from too many interruptions so they can stay focused.
- The practitioner notes some details from their play for later discussion in the 'small group' session. S/he sees an opportunity to extend their knowledge of holiday travel, to build their language and pre-reading skills, to introduce geographical concepts and affirm the girls' collaboration skills. S/he poses questions:
  - 'Tell me about "going on holidays".' S/he invites other children to talk about their holidays. S/he shares brochures and stories with them.
  - 'Who had the idea to play holidays – to bring magazines, etc.?' S/he affirms that they listened to one another and shared their ideas.
  - 'What happens at an airport?' They talk about money, tickets, security checks, X-rays and conveyor belts. S/he extends their knowledge, builds their store of ideas and enriches their language. Dramatising the security procedure and making the conveyor belt becomes a project.
  - 'Where is Portugal?' Children talk about places that are nearby and far away.
  - 'When you play again, what could you do?' They could make props, involve others or represent their ideas through painting, building an airport, etc.

CONCLUSION

Children through the ages and across cultures engage in play. It is their way of co-constructing the practices, skills and knowledge of their communities so that they make sense and are useful in their world. Play is both a context and medium for co-constructing this learning. The skilled practitioner works with children's play to enrich, mentor and extend the meaning that they make and to nurture their identity and their ability to connect and develop a sense of belonging. This perspective on play relocates it as central to learning in childhood.

Key Learning Points
- The essential components of the play-based approach.
- How children learn to play.
- How and what children co-construct in their play.
- How play supports well-being, identity, belonging, communicating, exploring and thinking (NCCA 2009).
- What the pedagogue can do to enrich and extend children's learning.

References
Brennan, C. (ed.) (2004a) *Power of Play: A Play Curriculum in Action*. Dublin: IPPA.
— (2004b) 'Playing the Way into Communities of Practice', *An Leanbh Óg* (OMEP *Ireland Journal of Early Childhood Studies* 192–207.
— (2008) 'Partners in Play: How Children Organise their Participation in Sociodramatic Play'. Unpublished PhD thesis, DIT, Dublin.
— (2010) 'The Power of Pretence', IPPA AGM and Conference, Dublin, April.
IPPA (Irish Preschool Play Association) (2006) *Nurture through Nature: Promoting Outdoor Play for Young Children*. Dublin: IPPA.
— (2008) *Inspiring Play*. Dublin, IPPA.
Jones, E. and Nimmo, J. (1994) *Emergent Curriculum*. Washington, DC: NAEYC.
Lave, J. and Wenger, E. (1991) *Situated Learning: Legitimate Peripheral Participation in Communities of Practice*. Cambridge, UK: Cambridge University Press.
NCCA (National Council for Curriculum and Assessment) (2009) *Aistear: The Early Childhood Curriculum Framework* (www.ncca.ie/earlylearning). Dublin: NCCA.
Piaget, J. (1937/1971) *The Construction of Reality in the Child*. New York: Basic Books.
Trevarthen, C. (2004) 'Learning about ourselves from children: why a growing human brain needs interesting companions', *Research and Clinical Centre for Child Development Annual Report 2002–2003*, 9–44. Hokkaido: Graduate School of Education, Hokkaido University <http://eprints.lib.hokudai. ac.jp/dspace/bitstream/2115/25359/1/26_P9-44.pdf> accessed 31 August 2011.
Vygotsky, L. (1933/1976) 'Play and its Role in the Mental Development of the Child' in J. Burner, A. Jolly and K. Sylva (eds) *Play: Its Role in Development and Evolution*. New York: Basic Books.
— (1978) *Mind in Society*. Cambridge, MA: Harvard University Press.

Useful Websites

International Play Association – http://ipaworld.org

Irish Preschool Play Association – www.ippa.ie

Play England – www.playengland.org.uk

Let the Children Play – http://progressiveearlychildhoodeducation.blogspot.com

17

The What, Why and How of Inclusive Early Years Practice

Gerard O'Carroll

Learning Objectives

After studying this chapter the reader should be able to:

- Isolate the knowledge, skills and values that underpin inclusive practice.
- Identify the characteristics of inclusive education.
- Track the evolution from segregation to inclusion via integration.
- Recognise appropriate inclusive pedagogic practices.
- Appreciate the important social and educational value of inclusive early years practice for all children.

INTRODUCTION

The themes of identity and belonging are recognised in both Síolta (CECDE 2006) and Aistear (NCCA 2009) as important principles in the development of the child. In traditional cultures, belonging was often taken for granted as the homogenous nature of society, aligned with geographic proximity, allowed for almost automatic participation in a given community. More recent research considers belonging as a more complex concept. A child develops a sense of belonging, as well as a sense of identity, from a very early age. This knowledge is central to the principles and practice of inclusion.

WHAT IS INCLUSIVE EARLY YEARS EDUCATION?

Inclusion in the educational sense means that all children in an educational environment play, learn and work together at their respective developmental levels, in co-operation with each other, within a shared curriculum. Inclusion means working together in a collective (Feuser 1997).

The early years sector is an ideal, even natural, environment for inclusion to thrive, for a number of reasons. The pre-school environment is a natural progression for the child from an inclusive family situation. Nobody would argue with the child's right to belong to a family, both nuclear and extended. The same right to belong to a community beyond the family, that of the pre-school, is often the first step for the child into the wider social world. This step should also, then, be available as a right to all children.

A criticism sometimes made of inclusive education is that it can be driven by principles and politics rather than by evidence that it works. However, all education is motivated in part by politics and philosophical beliefs, such as the belief that education is good and necessary for the child, that the state has an obligation to provide essential education, that the parent is of prime importance in the equation, etc. Inclusion represents the confluence of several streams of thought, social and political as well as educational (Thomas and Vaughan 2004).

Inclusive practice is underpinned by the belief that all children have certain inherent rights by belonging to the human race. Among these rights is the right to play, learn and work with their peers within local community structures, whatever these may be (Feuser 1997). When considered from a rights perspective, the question is no longer one of whether there should be inclusion, but rather one of how best to achieve inclusion.

Three fundamental elements have been identified as dimensions of inclusion in the educational sense: policies; practices; and cultures. All three are interconnected and dynamic and are based on the principle of school/pre-school improvement. At the base of the dynamic, 'creating inclusive cultures' involves developing a shared vision of what the pre-school can do to support inclusion (Booth and Ainscow 2002). Policies and practices will evolve from this and it is essential that the culture be nurtured and promoted.

Once a vision or culture of inclusion has been embedded, the prospect of producing inclusive policies and evolving inclusive practices is facilitated. This is informed by the shared vision and belief that inclusion is good for the individual child, for all children, for the family, for the professional, for the curriculum and for the wider community.

Inclusive practice goes beyond the confines of the pre-school. Children who feel a sense of belonging and of being included in pre-school benefit from this enriching experience and by transfer and generalisation are more likely to enjoy an enhanced life experience both within education and in the wider social domain. Self-esteem and confidence, essential ingredients for all learning and development, are fostered by inclusive practice and will serve the child well in life.

Inclusion is more than mainstreaming and more than integration. The latter two are in a sense add-ons involving little structural and cultural change. The child is accepted and accommodated in the setting and the emphasis is on adaptation based on the child's perceived needs. In this model, the child is seen as being deficient or defective in some way and the system reacts to fill the gap or fix the problem.

Such an approach, while it moves on from the one-size-fits-all model, concentrates on what the child cannot do and what the child needs support with in order to access the existing curriculum. It is based on needs and the culture of special needs or special educational needs, extra or additional needs developed from this perspective in the medical model, where the deficit is within the child. That deficit may be due to social background, intellectual ability, disability, gender, race, religion, etc.

This concept of need is inadequate on its own as a means of achieving the goals of education (Roaf and Bines 1989). When viewing education from a rights perspective, the whole organisation and structure is considered and the focus shifts to systems and practices that include all children. Inclusive education is not merely more developed integration, but differentiating practice (Thomazet 2009).

The early years sector has obvious advantages that lend it to becoming an exemplary model of inclusion. Traditionally, the weak classification of curriculum, largely free from the requirements of external bodies, used in many pre-schools, allows the flexibility to create an open, humane and individualised learning environment for all children. In the case of Aistear, this approach can be maintained: it is a framework as opposed to a prescribed curriculum which is proposed. The range of developmental stages exhibited by children in the pre-school sector, while varied, is relatively small compared to primary age cohorts. Both Síolta and Aistear, while underpinning the importance of curriculum, recognise the child's individuality and respect for diversity.

From a parental perspective, there is an expectation that the child's holistic development – not only academic issues, which may often take precedence in the mandatory school system – will be addressed. The existence of different approaches, from the more specific (Montessori) to the more generic, allows the sector a diverse offering for a diverse population.

THE HOW OF INCLUSIVE PRACTICE

Inclusive practice involves working with children who are at different development levels and who have reached different degrees of competence in perception, cognition and behaviour (Feuser 1997). It recognises the individuality of each child. The principle of inner differentiation, which allows for individual areas of strength and weakness in the learner profile, ensures that practice provides the appropriate learning steps. This principle of inner differentiation is counterbalanced by the notion of co-operative activity, where each child is responsible not only for his/her own learning but for the learning of the social group within the context of a shared curriculum (Feuser 1997).

The central concept in inclusive practice is that the curriculum becomes individualised to the needs of all learners and can therefore be characterised as child-centred in the true sense of the word (Feuser 1997).

The traditional dialectic between, on the one hand, care and, on the other, education, when describing early years practice, becomes largely redundant in the context of inclusive practice. There can be no education in the true sense without caring and caring has an inherent educational role.

Various models, such as differentiated or multi-level instruction, have been developed to accommodate diverse learners in practice. In this approach, the key concepts used are partial participation, Bloom's taxonomy of cognitive domains, Howard Gardner's model of multiple intelligences and co-operative learning. These involve individualising the learning experience for the child and allowing learning to happen via participation, a form of situated learning. The metric for intensity of instruction will change in that it is no longer the practitioner-led activities which may be the most effective. An alternative measure would be the degree to which children are engaged in meaningful learning activities. Partial participation diminishes the readiness concept, creates a sense of community and recognises that doing part of a task has value. Bloom's cognitive levels, ranging from the simple to the complex, allow learners to participate to different levels in an experience, from knowing and understanding to applying and analysing. Multiple intelligence theory recognises that children may have a preferred learning style and that we can teach to that style or rather vary our teaching to address various learning styles. The above assumes inclusion of all learners in a common programme with individual goals achieved via instructional strategies (Porter 2008).

Product-based pedagogy, multi-learning tasks and phonological skills exercises are beneficial to all children and may be significant in allowing not only children with identified needs but also those who have 'ordinary difficulties' or social difficulties (children at risk) to access learning (Thomazet 2009). The product/content and/or process/methodology may be adapted, resources may vary and the learning environment may be adjusted. Adapting the content may involve moving between the concrete (doing/feeling/experiencing), the symbolic (seeing illustrations/diagrams) and the abstract (thinking/words/ideas) (SESS 2011). Naturalistic instruction which embeds learning opportunities in ongoing classroom activities has a valid place in this philosophy of education as well as teacher-led instructional practices (Odom 2000).

WHY INCLUSIVE PRACTICE?

The bigger question implied by thinking on inclusion is 'What kind of society do we want to develop?' Síolta and Aistear reflect a positive emphasis on diversity where children learn how to challenge bias with other adults in a respectful way. These competencies are developed over time by first working on the child's self concept and sense of self. Only then is the child in a good position to begin to understand the world around him/her.

In keeping with the principle of child-centeredness, inclusive practice is underpinned not by a notion of normality, but by a philosophy of what might be called personal identity. 'This demands that difference not be merely tolerated and accepted but that it is positively valued and celebrated' (Oliver 1995). Difference comes to be seen as a source not of division but of new energy, diversity and variety. The system gives expression to the whole child as a unique person.

Inclusion is the natural order for a child to experience in life. It aims to give children as ordinary an education as possible. If given a choice, it is surely what all would opt for. The fact that it remains a desired, yet sometimes elusive, outcome in contemporary society must, in some way, reflect on a system which in the past and to a certain degree still upholds segregation.

If inclusive education is to become the norm for all children, a rethinking of teacher and pre-school teacher education and training will be required. The knowledge and skills of professionals which have to date been the area of emphasis need to be complemented by attitudes and values. Programmes, not children, have to be ready for inclusion. There is a paradigm shift in action here, in that it is no longer the child who is included but the school and the teaching which are inclusive (Thomazet 2009). 'Inclusion is – first and foremost – a state of mind' (Snow 2001).

CONCLUSION

Inclusive practice is democratic in that all children are exposed to all learning experiences. Access is essential and rather than an external source, either parent or educationalist, selecting a pathway for a child at an early stage, which may lead to separation and segregation, an inclusive approach offers an alternative experience. This chapter concentrated on the 'what, why and how' of inclusive practice and this cannot be achieved without support and resources. However, support and resources without vision and a belief in inclusion as the right of every child will not achieve the desired experience and outcome. There is no way to inclusion without inclusion (Feuser 1997). It is both the means and the end: the goal and the way to achieve this goal.

Key Learning Points

- Belonging and inclusion are important principles in Síolta and Aistear.
- Inclusion is rights-based and is for all children.
- It recognises the individuality of each child.
- Inclusive education uses as strategies, among other things, differentiation, project-based learning, multi-level instruction, co-operative learning and multiple intelligences.

References

Booth, T. and Ainscow, M. (2002) *Index for Inclusion: Developing Learning and Participation in Schools*. Bristol: Centre for Studies on Inclusive Education.

CECDE (Centre for Early Childhood Development and Education) (2006) *Síolta: The National Quality Framework for Early Childhood Education Handbook*. Dublin: CECDE.

Feuser, G. (1997) 'Inclusive Education – Educating all Children and Young People Together in Pre-school Establishments and Schools', thesis, Bremen (online) <http://bidok.uibk.ac.at/library/feuser-thesis-e.html> accessed 20 April 2011.

NCCA (National Council for Curriculum and Assessment) (2009) *Aistear: The Early Childhood Curriculum Framework*. NCCA, Dublin.

Odom, S.L. (2000) 'Pre-school inclusion: what we know and where we go from here', *Topics in Early Childhood Special Education* 20:1, 20–7.

Oliver, M. (1995) 'Does special education have a role to play in the 21st century?' *REACH, Journal of Special Needs Education in Ireland* 8:2, 67–76.

Porter, G. (2008) 'Education for All: On the Road to Inclusion', workshop, Graz <www.e-include.eu>.

Roaf, C. and Bines, H. (1989) 'Needs, Rights and Opportunities in Special Education' in C. Roaf and H. Bines (eds), *Needs, Rights and Opportunities: Developing Approaches to Special Education*. London: Falmer Press.

Snow, K. (2001) *Disability is Natural: Revolutionary Common Sense for Raising Successful Children with Disabilities*. Woodland Park, CO: Braveheart Press.

SESS (Special Education Support Service) 'Differentiation in the Classroom for Students with Special Educational Needs' (online) <www.sess.ie/resources/teaching-methods-and-organisation> accessed 13 June 2011.

Thomas, G. and Vaughan, M. (2004) *Inclusive Education: Readings and Reflections*. Glasgow: OPU.

Thomazet, S. (2009) 'From integration to inclusive education: does changing the terms improve practice?' *International Journal of Inclusive Education* 13:6, September, 553–63.

Further Reading

National Council for Special Education (NCSE) (2010) 'Literature review of the principles and practices relating to inclusive education for children with special educational needs', ICEP Europe.

Thomas, G. and Vaughan, M. (2004) *Inclusive Education: Readings and Reflections*. Glasgow: OPU.

Useful Websites

Centre for Studies on Inclusive Education (UK) – www.csie.org.uk
National Council for Curriculum and Assessment – www.ncca.ie
Síolta – www.siolta.ie
Special Education Support Service – www.sess.ie

18

Early Interventions in Early Childhood Education and Care

Áine de Róiste and Margaret Gilmore

Learning Objectives

After studying this chapter the reader should understand:

- The various ways in which early interventions can be made with children and families, and the relevance of timing, resources and skills.
- The benefits of early intervention in different contexts and its relevance to an early childhood education and care (ECEC) course.
- The importance of family well-being and empowerment.

INTRODUCTION

The concept of 'intervention' can be viewed in many ways. One could think of it as interfering in a family's privacy or, more benignly, as helping them out when assistance is needed. One of the difficulties with intervention is that the family who may benefit most from intervention does not always recognise when intervention would be useful; they may not be aware of difficulties or, at the other end of the spectrum, they may be trying to hide them. When a case such as the 'Roscommon case' (Gibbons 2010) is made public, people ask, 'But why did no one do something?' Often in such cases, many people have tried to intervene at various times and in different ways, but without success. We do not hear so much about the successful interventions, but we have much to learn from examining what works and what does not work.

EARLY INTERVENTION: WHAT DOES IT MEAN?

Early intervention can be defined as 'intervening early and as soon as possible to tackle problems emerging for children, young people and their families or with a population most at risk of developing problems. Effective intervention may occur at any point in a child or young person's life' (C4EO 2010:2). Tackling these problems as early as possible is proactive, leading to their resolution, and therefore less time is lost in relationship building and other vital tasks of early childhood development.

TYPES AND LEVELS OF INTERVENTION

A well-functioning society needs universally available social services to ensure optimum growth and development of its most vulnerable citizens, the very young. Developed societies have decided what standards are acceptable in housing, health and education. Those who need support, material or not, are identified by low income or requests for services. For most families, this base-level support is all they need. A small number, however, will need additional supports (Brady, Dolan and Canavan 2004), which can be categorised (citing Hardiker, Exton and Barker 1991) as follows.

LEVEL ONE – TARGETED SERVICE PROVISION

This includes parent support projects, drop-in centres and specialised pre-school support offered for those families who need additional help. These measures aim to empower and support parents and promote healthy childhood development, and are preventive in nature.

LEVEL TWO – TARGETED EARLY RISKS

Examples of these supports include Springboard and Neighbourhood Youth Projects. These services are aimed at families with identified risks to prevent difficulties from escalating. Again this is preventive, and research has shown it to be very effective; for example, an evaluation in Sligo concluded that 'the Resource House Project offers a crucially important family support service to the families, adults and young people with whom it works' (Forkan 2008:152).

LEVEL THREE – ESTABLISHED DIFFICULTIES AND POSSIBLY SERIOUS RISKS

The family may be in danger of breaking down or is functioning so badly that there are risks to the children. Interventions at this level may involve the social work services and foster care placements, with a focus on specific families and the eventual aim of restoring the family to effective functioning.

LEVEL FOUR – ALTERNATIVE CARE REQUIRED

This is the outcome no one wants to see: the child is removed permanently from their natural family and lives in either long-term foster care or residential childcare. Efforts are still made to retain ties with the family but the focus is on preparing the young person for independent living (Brady, Dolan and Canavan 2004).

As can be seen, the extent or invasiveness of the intervention with individual families increases from level one to level four. It is also worth noting that a shift from targeted towards universal interventions has been contended by Hayes (2008) among others. The former can be contended to work with the implicit assumption that poverty and related problems are derived from individual failures rather than socio-economic factors. Universal interventions (with additional supports where necessary), on the other hand, reach a wider population and see family problems as being caused by a number of factors (Dahlberg and Moss 2006).

EARLY INTERVENTION AND EARLY CHILDHOOD

Early childhood is seen as a very crucial period for intervention as this period is considered a 'critical' or 'sensitive' period for development (National Research Council and Institute for Medicine 2001). The young brain is at this time particularly vulnerable to influences which may be harmful or beneficial. By 4 years of age, half of all intellectual abilities are developed (Young 1999). It is also reported that parts of the brain nearly double in size during the pre-school years (UNICEF 2004). Research, both Irish and international, has identified that low income, poor nutrition, impaired social and emotional stimulation and/or poor health status all impair educational achievement. In addition, where there are greater socio-economic inequalities, there is an increased likelihood of educational inequalities (NESF 2002; Combat Poverty Agency 2005). (See Chapter 6 in this book for an overview of social policy and social justice issues in ECEC.)

Language gives us a particularly good example of the importance of early intervention as the developing brain is particularly sensitive to the acquisition of language. The normal adult–baby or adult–toddler interaction occurs when adults respond with 'baby talk', gestures and facial expressions to gurgling, later babbling and eventually recognisable words. A child who missed out on this is a child already at a disadvantage. A child may be physically well cared for, for example in a group care setting, but yet miss this component. Without being able to communicate verbally, his/her whole world remains difficult to decipher and his/her development is delayed (Taylor and Woods 2005). (See Chapter 21 of this book for an in-depth account of children's language development.)

TARGETING DISADVANTAGE

Internationally, research has established the importance of early intervention in the pre-school years to tackle disadvantage and social exclusion (Shonkoff and Phillips 2000). By the time of school entry, children from disadvantaged areas are already behind their more affluent counterparts on academic, social and physical measurements of development. Consequently, disadvantaged children are less prepared and ready for formal education (Gershoff 2003).

Many early interventions aim to tackle inequality and social exclusion by attempting to give children from disadvantaged circumstances an 'equal chance' (equal to children who are not so disadvantaged) of realising their full potential.

The 1999 White Paper on early education recognised that the benefits of ECEC services are more significant for children who are disadvantaged or those who have additional needs, especially in the 3–6 years age period (Hanlon 2005).

Such interventions, it is suggested, should be integrated services provided by the health, social welfare and education sectors. The active involvement of parents is also noted as crucial for child development and early education, particularly from birth to 3 years old (Hanlon 2005).

Student Exercise
- Do you know what early intervention measures are in place in your local town?
- Try to identify at least one service providing early intervention. What is their mission statement? Do they openly talk about early intervention? What do you think about the idea of early intervention and its value for parent and child?

Next we will look critically at some practical examples of interventions; how they work; and how they are perceived by children, parents and staff.

INTERVENTIONS IN THE HOME

PARENTING PROGRAMMES

Many parenting programmes are available, but we will consider just one, Fás le Cheile ('growing together'), a Health Services Executive (HSE)-funded programme that is widely available. It brings together groups of parents and facilitates discussion on relevant topics over a period of weeks. Benefits include networking, sharing problems, solutions and new ideas to enrich the parenting experience. Facilitators are themselves parents who are trained for this purpose (see www.barnardos.ie). Parents are thus empowering other parents to be more effective and attendance is voluntary, thereby ensuring highly motivated group sessions.

COMMUNITY MOTHERS

This very successful programme has been running since 1988, when it evolved from using public health nurses to visit and support families with newborn babies to training volunteer parents from the local community to undertake this support. Not alone does the immediate family benefit from a visit, but community networks are built, often in situations where communities are fragmented.

Community mothers are volunteers who are trained and supported by family development workers. They support new parents in a selection of HSE Dublin areas for the first two years after the baby's birth. They visit parents once a month, using an empathetic and facilitation approach and with a focus on child development. A community mother typically has a 'case-load' of between five and fifteen families and they usually spend thirteen hours plus per month with each family, with nominal expenses given for visits (Molloy and Harper 2009). In turn, the community mothers are supported by each other and by the family development worker.

Families receiving this intervention report more positive feelings about parenthood, and better parenting skills, nutrition and parental self-esteem. Children are also more likely to be breastfed, to have been immunised and to show better nutrition intake (Johnson *et al.* 2000).

'The approach supports the parents' own ideas and acknowledges they will want to do what is best for their child' (Hosking and Walsh 2010:91). The benefits also extended to subsequent births: children were more likely to complete their primary and MMR immunisation and to be breastfed (Hosking and Walsh 2010).

HOME-START

Home-Start is another good example of a locally based organisation affiliated to a wider network. Home-Start (www.home-start.org.uk) helps to increase families' confidence and independence by:

- visiting families in their own homes to offer support, friendship and practical assistance
- reassuring parents that their childcare problems are not unusual or unique
- encouraging parents' strengths and emotional well-being for the ultimate benefit of their children
- trying to get the fun back into family life.

Parents may be referred, but 25 per cent of clients are self-referrals, which is a strong testimony to the service offered.

In Ireland, the service is mostly based in Dublin. Almost 35 per cent of the families supported by Home-Start, and 15 per cent of volunteers, are from non-Irish national backgrounds.

Student Exercise: Pause for Thought!
The issue of immigrant status is worth considering. What might the difficulties be for non-Irish national families? Put yourself in the situation of being a new parent in a foreign country where you do not have family and friends, and perhaps do not speak the language well enough to access services easily. What supports might you need?

LIFESTART

Another voluntary organisation which has a parenting support programme is the Lifestart Foundation (www.lifestartfoundation.org). 'The Growing Child' is a written resource offered monthly, by trained family visitors who call to the child's home and are available to discuss parenting issues.

This structured monthly curriculum offers information, knowledge and practical tips for the relevant stage of the child, encouraging parent–child interaction and the use of ordinary household equipment for play, music and movement.

The philosophy is that the parent is the primary educator, with Lifestart offering support. Uptake is almost universal for this free (funded by the HSE in Ireland), non-targeted programme which aims not to stigmatise.

Lifestart also offers the Toybox Project, a targeted early intervention, to Traveller children and families who might be reluctant to avail of pre-school, as 'a rights-based service development model which aims to significantly reduce social and education inequalities' (www.early-years.org/toybox/).

Springboard

Springboard is a government-supported family support initiative which has been in operation since 1998. Springboard projects, based in fourteen locations across the country, aim to provide universal services to the community while at the same time targeting the most disadvantaged and vulnerable families, identifying their needs (whether ongoing or in crisis situations), and working with other agencies where possible. This follows the recommendations of the Commission on the Family (DSCFA 1998).

Springboard projects aim to achieve the following goals:

- To identify the needs of parents and children, especially where there are child protection issues, ongoing health and welfare problems or crises.
- To target the most disadvantaged and vulnerable families in the locality, focusing on improving family dynamics.
- To co-work with others in the community in developing family support.
- To provide a definite service of care, intervention, support and counselling to both the targeted families and other families who may seek it (McKeown, Haase and Pratschke 2001).

One of the key features of Springboard is that it provides universal services to all families in the community, together with targeted provision to those in specific situations. This double approach has allowed services to be provided in a way which lessens potential stigma (Forkan 2008).

CLASSROOM-BASED INTERVENTIONS

In Ireland, the Rutland Street Pre-school Project (established in 1969) was one of the first early educational interventions. (See Chapter 1 of this book for a historical overview of ECEC developments in Ireland.)

The Rutland Street Project worked with children aged 3–5 years in an economically disadvantaged area of inner-city Dublin where there was a low level of parent education, high unemployment and where children were scoring below average academically (Kellaghan and Greaney 1993). The project, a two-year programme, was anchored in Piagetian principles and concentrated on developing children's cognitive skills and their readiness for school. It provided half-day pre-school education, with a cooked lunch, for 3–4-year-olds. The evaluation compared the outcomes for programme participants with a control group of others in the same neighbourhood. After two years, the participants had higher IQ scores and higher scores on measures of pre-school readiness; they continued to have higher IQ scores after three years of school (though their scores did fall), but there was no difference in reading performance at age 8. However, by age 16 they were much more likely (two and three times) to take state examinations at secondary school, and just under a tenth took the Leaving Certificate, compared with none of the control group. There were no differences in school absenteeism or social deviance (Waldfogel 2002).

As with other studies, children initially showed educational benefits (scholastic ability, vocabulary, numeracy) but such gains deteriorated over time after the children started primary school (Kellaghan and Greaney 1993). This highlights the role of other variables in the child's home, community and school, such as parental support, cultural features and school resources, which may influence whether the effects of any early intervention persist over time. Education and care *cannot* be separated in evaluating the impact of any educational interventions. As intervention outcomes are sensitive to influences from parallel or successive contexts, such as primary/secondary schooling, these may build on or overshadow competencies developed during early educational interventions (Hayes and O'Flaherty 1997; O'Flaherty 1995).

EARLY START

Over the period 1994–1995 the Department of Education and Science (DES) established Early Start, an early childhood intervention programme run initially in eight primary schools and still offered in forty primary schools throughout the Republic of Ireland. The aims of Early Start were to compensate for background deprivation and to promote children's overall development, but in particular their language and cognitive development, as well as to prevent school failure (Lewis and Archer 2002; O'Toole 2000). In Early Start, unlike infant classes at primary school, the school day is shorter (a morning or an afternoon), class size is limited to fifteen pupils and each teacher is assisted by a full-time child care worker. Particular attention is paid to the:

- identification of 'learning outcomes' for each child
- strategies used by adults (types of adult-directed activity)
- interactional style of the adults (such as questioning, provoking, clarifying)

- 'structure', i.e. how learning activities are organised (time, interactional format and follow-up)
- learning 'contexts' (grouping arrangements and materials) deployed (Lewis and Archer 2002).

A home–school community liaison co-ordinator is involved in each Early Start school and a strong emphasis is placed on parental involvement. Parents are encouraged by the home–school community liaison co-ordinator to become actively involved in the classroom and to further their own personal and educational development. Each parent takes a turn to spend one full session each month with his/her own child in the classroom. Known as their 'Special Day', this is a feature that children really look forward to (Lewis and Archer 2003); and it is in keeping with the White Paper on Early Childhood Education, which highlights involving parents in their children's education.

The child is actively involved in the learning process. Play is integral to learning, often in small group contexts or on a one-to-one basis. High-quality educational play equipment is used, enabling a wide variety of different play contexts such as sand and water play, block/construction play, socio-dramatic and creative play, jigsaws, story, art, games, music and movement. Evaluations were carried out (Educational Research Centre 1998; Kelly and Kellaghan 1999; Lewis and Archer 2003) which led to changes in emphasis on cognitive and language development as well as small group work and profiling pupil achievements. In addition, teachers and parents reported that participation in Early Start led to an earlier identification of speech and language difficulties.

As well as Early Start, after-school programmes, including homework clubs and community-based after-school projects, are also known to potentially provide educational and social advantages as well as wider opportunities not available at home (Hennessy and Donnelly 2005).

THE INCREDIBLE YEARS PROGRAMME

This programme was developed in the 1980s by Carolyn Webster-Stratton, a Canadian educational psychologist with a public health nursing background. It is aimed at parents of children aged 1–10 who have early indications of conduct disorder, or are at high risk of developing conduct disorder (defined as high rates of aggression, defiance, oppositional and impulsive behaviours). It is a behavioural humanistic programme addressing child behaviour and the parent–child relationship. It was used in the US Head Start programme and has been used in various Sure Start initiatives in Wales. The initiative comprises a number of different interventions involving parents, teachers and children:

- *Basic Parent Training Programme*, targeting parenting skills and delivered in the home.
- *Advanced Parent Training Programme*, targeting interpersonal skills for parents, delivered in the home.

- *Education Parent Training Programme*, targeting academic skills for parents, delivered in home and school.
- *Teacher Training Programme*, targeting classroom management skills and delivered in schools.
- *Child Training Programme*, targeting social skills, problem-solving and classroom behaviour, delivered in home and school.

Design of the Incredible Years Programme

This intervention addresses multiple risk factors across settings known to be related to the development of conduct disorders in children. In all three training initiatives, trained facilitators use videotape scenes to encourage group discussion, problem-solving and sharing of ideas. The Basic parent series is 'core' and a necessary component of the prevention programme delivery. The programme has been shown by McGilloway and colleagues (2009) to affect the following risk and protective factors:

Parents:

- Increased positive and nurturing parenting style.
- Decreased harsh, inconsistent and unnecessary parental discipline and increased praise and effective discipline.
- Decreased parental stress and depression.

Teachers:

- Increased proactive and positive classroom management skills and an enhanced classroom atmosphere.
- Decreased harsh and critical classroom management style.

Children:

- Increased positive conflict management skills and social skills with peers.
- Decreased negative behaviours, peer aggression and disruptive behaviours in the classroom and non-compliance with parents at home.
- Increased social competence at school, academic engagement, school readiness and co-operation with teachers.

Student Exercise
- Identify what factors might influence whether or not parents and children engage in such an intervention. How might these factors be taken into consideration?

EARLY INTERVENTIONS WITH CHILDREN WITH AUTISM SPECTRUM DISORDERS (ASDS)

The DES (2006:79) supports the importance of early diagnosis of, and intervention with, children with ASDs. Yet while a diagnosis of ASD is typically made between 3 and 4 years, access to intervention services often does not occur until the child is 4.5–6 years of age (DES 2006), indicating a need for enhanced provision of early intervention services for such children.

There are a wide variety of approaches to educational early interventions with children with ASDs. These may be categorised (DES 2006) as follows.

INTERACTIVE

These focus on developing social and communicative skills. Floortime or the Greenspan approach (Greenspan and Wieder 2006), Social Stories (www.the graycenter.org/) and the NAS EarlyBird programme (Shields 2001) are examples.

COMMUNICATIVE

These concentrate on the promotion and development of communication skills and include augmentative communication programmes. The Picture Exchange Communication System (PECS) (Baker 2001) is an example. Others include the Hanen programme, Makaton signing and symbols and Lámh (Sheehy and Duffy 2009; www.isaacireland.org).

INTEGRATION

Integration approaches use integration with mainstream peers as the primary learning medium. An example of this is the LEAP method (Dawson and Osterling 1997). This method involves training in prompting strategies, parenting, peer-mediated instruction and applied behavioural analysis (ABA).

BEHAVIOURAL

These approaches include ABA, which draws on behavioural learning theory; it is frequently used for treating children with developmental problems, including those with ASDs. ABA's principles and practice are anchored in research on learning and behaviour. As well as being delivered in the classroom it can also be delivered in the home by instructors and/or trained caregivers (Healy, Greer and Barnes-Holmes 2003).

Seven key principles can be construed as being central to ABA-based programmes (Baer, Wolf and Risely (1968) in Healy, Greer and Barnes-Holmes 2009):

1 The focused behaviours have some social significance for the child (the programme is *applied*).
2 Systematic recordings are taken of behavioural and environmental changes, including teacher–pupil interaction (the programme is *behavioural*).
3 A *methodological analysis* of behavioural change is undertaken through the collection of data on the impact of the programme on the behaviour observed.
4 Recordings are taken of the actions of the 'behaviour change agent' (tutor/teacher) in terms of the techniques s/he uses, enabling replication by others (the programme is *technological*).
5 The programme is visibly underpinned by established principles such as those of 'reinforcement', 'generalisation' and 'punishment' from learning theory (the programme is *conceptually systematic*).
6 Target behaviours are identified, which are the focus for the intervention programme, to be altered to a degree significant enough for the individual involved in the programme (the programme is *effective*).
7 The behaviour that is the target of the intervention is altered to a degree that such change is generalised (transferred) across contexts (the programme should display *generality*).

DISCRETE

These are comprehensive approaches to the learning and teaching of children with ASDs. They include the Treatment and Education of Autistic and related Communication-handicapped Children (TEACCH), a programme which originated in the USA and helps children and families to cope with autism. It emphasises structured teaching involving known, predictable routines and environmental adjustments to reduce distractors.

In TEACCH, clear directions, visual and verbal prompts as well as reinforcers are deployed in ways that address the strengths children with ASDs have (specialist interests, strong visual processing skills and rote recall as well as a penchant for routine) (Mesibov, Shea and Schopler 2005). An individualised plan is also formulated for each child, rather than using a standard curriculum.

Addressing the child's difficulty with sequential memory and their organisation of time, while also helping them to reduce their anxiety and to understand what is expected of them, the key elements of TEACCH are:

- physical organisation of the environment, facilitating the child to understand where activities occur
- schedules with visual support that assist the child to understand what activities will take place, at what time and where
- work systems with visual supports which inform the child what to do while learning independently.

OTHER

Various creative and sensory programmes (massage, movement, art, music and drama therapy) have also been developed as well as programmes which focus on, for example, computer-assisted learning, daily life therapy (Drudy 2001; Siegel 2000). Many of these lack rigorous scientific evaluation, though research exploring their effectiveness is ongoing. The Report of the Task Force on Autism (DES 2001) concluded that there was no definitive evidence to support any one intervention as the most effective for all children with ASDs, which is understandable as children with ASDs are a very heterogeneous group. Any given intervention *may* only be effective for a subset of these children.

The DES has emphasised that teachers 'should have access to courses on the various approaches, such as TEACCH, ABA and PECS' (DES 2006:83), suggesting that an 'eclectic' approach in the education of children with ASDs is favoured.

Student Exercise

Many of the projects mentioned above are run by voluntary organisations. Frequently the government supports such voluntary organisations.

Why do statutory services not provide these supports? What is the rationale here? What happens in other countries, e.g. the UK and Denmark?

WHAT MAKES AN EARLY INTERVENTION EFFECTIVE?

Hosking and Walsh's report on the experience of early intervention for children, young people and their families (Hosking and Walsh 2010) included six key messages. These are listed here, with examples of interventions that illustrate each point.

1 Those who prioritise investment in the earliest years secure the best outcomes – Fás le Cheile parenting programme.
2 The quality of parenting/care is the key to a successful society – Lifestart.
3 There could be a major dividend from focused commitment to ensure children arrive at school 'school ready' – Early Start, Toybox.
4 The impact of poor early care can be alleviated by the right experience during school years – Incredible Years.
5 Galvanising the community is the secret of success – Community Mothers.
6 Innovative approaches to social care can provide significant benefits at minimum cost – Springboard.

These examples are merely illustrations, as many of the programmes are beneficial under several headings.

> *Student Exercise*
> Why might some early educational interventions be more effective than others?

1 INTEGRATED PROGRAMMES

In the UK the Effective Provision of Pre-School Education (EPPE) project, which ran from 1997 to 2004, involved high-quality pre-school education for children deemed to be disadvantaged. Enhanced intellectual and social/behavioural development, especially for boys, was reported and it was concluded that such interventions are more effective when they include children from a diversity of socio-economic groups rather than a single homogenous disadvantaged group (Sylva *et al.* 2004). This may be because of a greater sharing of norms, values and expectations between the various socio-economic groups so that 'own group' norms, values and expectations lose some of their dominance.

2 GOOD EARLY CHILDHOOD PRACTITIONER–CHILD RELATIONSHIPS

An important element of effective educational interventions is good teacher–child relationships. This can be extended to good practitioner–child relationships. The EPPE project and a related project, Researching Effective Pedagogy in the Early Years (REPEY) (Siraj-Blatchford *et al.* 2002), showed the importance of the teacher–child relationship. This concurs with an American National Institute of Child Health and Human Development (NICHD) study, which noted the importance of positive staff who were 'more educated' and held more child-centred beliefs about childrearing (NICHD 2000). Frede (1995:123) concluded that:

> Intensity may encompass more than time, also including the concentration that comes from low ratios, home visiting, and coherent curricula.

She stressed that:

> [T]he approaches identified as effective all increased the contact between teachers and children and gave the teachers greater knowledge about the children in their care, permitting the teachers to tailor their teaching styles to meet each child's individual needs. (Frede 1995:123)

The quality of teacher–child interaction, with due cognisance of contextual factors pertinent to the location and culture of where the intervention is placed, is thus crucial for the effectiveness of any intervention (Hayes 2008).

3 Skills (Cognitive and Non-Cognitive) Development

In attempting to explain how 'skills beget skills' through early intervention programmes, Cunha *et al.* (2005) identified two mechanisms: self-productivity; and complementarity. Self-productivity refers to how skills that develop in one period persist into future periods, i.e. skills are self-reinforcing: 'For example, self-control and emotional security may reinforce intellectual curiosity and promote more vigorous learning of cognitive skills' (Cunha *et al.* 2005:5). Skills developed through early interventions may be the building blocks of later skills and competencies. Research on Early Start over the long term has identified improved 'number sense' (i.e. numeracy), possibly moderated by enhanced confidence and the development of a positive attitude in children towards learning, particularly mathematics (Martin 2010).

Complementarity, on the other hand, refers to how early investment needs to be followed up by later investment in order for the early investment to be productive, i.e. facilitating environments have to follow facilitating environments. Cunha *et al.* (2005) also stressed the importance of non-cognitive skills (such as perseverance, motivation, self-control) in academic and other forms of achievement. According to Hayes (2008:25):

> Early interventions impact on aspects of self-regulation, learning dispositions and motivation. A review of the research suggests that child development is enhanced if group sizes are small; settings are child-focused and well organised, with adults playing a facilitative rather than a didactic [role].

Research has shown that poverty is associated with a low level of pre-school ability and 'pre-school ability seems to set the stage for children's transition into the formal school system' (Hayes 2008:22).

This has been well established across the world. Seven types of experience have been identified by Ramey and Ramey (1999) as essential for school readiness and normative development:

1 The encouragement of exploration.
2 Mentoring in basic skills.
3 Celebration of developmental advances.
4 Rehearsal and extension of new skills.
5 Protection from inappropriate disapproval, teasing and punishment.
6 Rich, responsive communication.
7 Behavioural guidance and boundaries.

Ramey and Ramey (2004) contend that these are the mediating variables through which early educational interventions exert a positive effect on school readiness and development.

Student Exercise
Identify examples of the seven experiences listed above in early childhood education contexts.

4 PARENTAL (AND FAMILY) INVOLVEMENT

Parental and wider family involvement has been known to play a key role in contributing to the effectiveness of early school-based interventions and the sustainability of effects over time. This recognises that any classroom-based interventions are not carried out in a 'vacuum' but rather are embedded within the child's family and cultural contexts. As noted by the Centre for Excellence and Outcomes in Children and Young People's Services (C4EO 2010:7), 'Effective intervention with children depends not only on the fact of involving their parents, and sometimes wider family, but also on the way of doing so.'

It is not just the parental involvement per se but rather the *quality* of this involvement which is important for enhancing the effectiveness of any intervention. This was also highlighted by Hayes (2008) as one of the five factors common to effective early childhood care and education, which are:

1 Quality of adult–child verbal interactions.
2 Knowledge and understanding of the curriculum.
3 Knowledge of how children learn.
4 Adults' skill in supporting children in resolving conflicts.
5 Helping parents to support children's learning in the home.

CONCLUSION

We have looked at many examples of early intervention in different contexts. The importance of intervening as early as possible to prevent ongoing difficulties cannot be stressed enough. In order to do this, an early years worker needs to be observant and skilled in dealing with both children and adults. Appropriateness and timing of interventions are very important in the empowerment of parents to become even better in their demanding task. Parents can become overwhelmed by difficult situations and they may need additional support to be able to nurture the whole family and themselves in a complex situation. Ultimately, there is no substitute for parental love, but there are times when parents need professional support to be able to parent successfully and to foster their children's full potential.

Key Learning Points
• Parents may need various levels of support and empowerment in their parenting.
• Interventions based on sound theory, which are integrated in the community, are most effective.

- Early childhood is a crucial time for ensuring that children's development is optimised for their benefit and for society as a whole.

References

Baer, D., Wolf, M.M. and Risely, T.R. (1968) in Healy *et al.* (2009) 'Some current dimensions of applied behaviour analysis', *Journal of Applied Behavior Analysis* 1, 91–7.

Baker, S. (2001) 'The Picture Exchange Communication System' in *National Autistic Society Approaches to Autism*. London: National Autistic Society.

Brady, B., Dolan, P. and Canavan, J. (2004) *Working for Children and Families*. Galway: Western Health Board/Child and Family Research and Policy Unit, NUIG.

C4EO (Centre for Excellence and Outcomes in Children and Young People's Services) (2010) 'Grasping the Nettle: Early Intervention for Children, Families and Communities'. Available at: www.c4eo.org.uk/themes/earlyintervention/files/early_intervention_grasping_the_nettle_full_report.pdf.

Combat Poverty Agency (2005). *Mapping Poverty: National Regional and County Patterns*. Dublin: Combat Poverty Agency.

Cunha, F., Heckman, J.J., Lochner, L. and Masterov, D. (2005). 'Interpreting the evidence on life cycle skill formation', *British Educational Research Journal* 30:5, 713–30.

Dahlberg, G. and Moss, P. (2006) *Ethics and Politics in Early Childhood Education*. London: Routledge Farmer.

Dawson, G. and Osterling, J. (1997) 'Early Intervention in Autism' in M.J. Guralnick (ed.) *The Effectiveness of Early Intervention*. Baltimore: P.H. Brooks, pp. 307–26.

DES (Department of Education and Science) (2006) *An Evaluation of Educational Provision for Children with Autistic Spectrum Disorders*. Dublin: Stationery Office.

Drudy, S. (2001) *Educational Provision and Support for Persons with Autistic Spectrum Disorders: The Report of the Task Force on Autism*. Ireland: Ministry for Education and Science.

DSCFA (Department of Social, Community and Family Affairs) (1998) *Commission on the Family*. Dublin: Stationery Office.

Educational Research Centre (1998). *Early Start Pre-school Programme: Final Evaluation Report*. Dublin: Educational Research Centre.

Forkan, C. (2008) *An Evaluation of the Sligo Springboard Resource House Project*. Galway: Child and Family Research Centre, NUIG.

Frede, E. (1995) 'The role of program quality in producing early childhood program benefits', *The Future of Children* 5:3, 115–32.

Gershoff, E. (2003) *Living at the Edge: Low Income and the Development of America's Kindergartners*, Research Brief No 4. New York: National Center for Children in Poverty, Mailman School of Public Health, Columbia University.

Gibbons, N. (2010) *Roscommon Child Care Case: Report of Inquiry Team to the Health Service Executive*. Available at: www.hse.ie/eng/services/Publications/services/Children/RoscommonChildCareCase.pdf.

Greenspan, S.J. and Wieder, S. (2006) *Engaging Autism: The Floortime Approach to Helping Children Relate, Communicate and Think*. USA: Perseus Books.

Hanlon, L. (2005) *Early Assessment and Intervention in Educational Disadvantage*. Dublin: Centre for Social and Educational Research, DIT. Available at http://arrow.dit.ie/ cserrep/9.

Hardiker, P., Exton K. and Barker, M. (1991) *Policies and Practices in Preventive Child Care*. Aldershot: Avebury.

Hayes, N. (2008) *The Role of Early Childhood Care and Education: An Anti-Poverty Perspective*. Dublin: Combat Poverty Agency.

Hayes, N. and O'Flaherty, J., with Kiernan, M. (1997) *A Window on Early Education in Ireland*. Dublin: DIT.

Healy, O., Greer, D. and Barnes-Holmes, D. (2003) 'The comprehensive application of behaviour analysis to schooling: a school wide approach to teaching', *Irish Psychologist* 30, 21–3.

Hennessy, E. and Donnelly, M. (2005) *After-School Care in Disadvantaged Areas: The Perspectives of Children, Parents and Experts*. Dublin: Combat Poverty Agency.

Hosking, G. and Walsh, I. (2010). *International Experience of Early Intervention for Children, Young People and their Families*. C4EO. Available at: www.c4eo.org.uk/ themes/earlyintervention/files/early_intervention_wave_trust_international_desk _study.pdf

Johnson, Z., Molloy, B., Scallon, E., Fitzpatrick, P., Rooney, B., Keegan, T. and Byrne, P. (2000) 'Community mothers programme: seven year follow-up of a randomised controlled trial of non-professional intervention in parenting', *Journal of Public Health Medicine* 22:3, 337–42.

Kellaghan, T. and Greaney, V. (1993) *The Educational Development of Students following Participation in a Pre-school Programme in a Disadvantaged Area*. Dublin: Educational Research Centre.

Kelly, D. and Kellaghan, T. (1999) *The Literacy and Numeracy Achievements of the First Cohort of Early Start Children (1994–1995) when they were in Second Class (1998–1999)*. Dublin: Educational Research Centre.

Lewis, M. and Archer, P. (2002) *Further Evaluation of Early Start*. Dublin: Educational Research Centre.

— (2003) *Early Start Evaluation: Report on Observation Visits to Schools*. Dublin: Educational Research Centre.

Martin, S. (2010) 'An early childhood intervention programme and the long-term outcomes for students', *Child Care in Practice*, 16:3, 257–74.

McGilloway, S., Bywater, T., NiMhaille, G., Furlong, M., O'Neill, D., Comiskey, C., Leckey, Y., Kelly, P. and Donnelly, M. (2009) *Proving the Power of Positive Parenting: A Randomised Controlled Trial to Investigate the Effectiveness of the Incredible Years BASIC Parent Training Programme in an Irish Context (Short-Term Outcomes)*. Report prepared for Archways.

McKeown, K., Haase, T. and Pratschke, J. (2001) *Springboard: Promoting Family Well-Being through Family Support Services. Final Evaluation*. Dublin: Department of Health and Children.

Mesibov, G.B., Shea, V. and Schopler, E. (2005) *The TEACCH Approach to Autism Spectrum Disorders*. Springer.

Molloy, B. and Harper, G. (2009) *Community Mothers Programme Annual Report*. Lenus, Irish Health Repository. Available at: www.lenus.ie/hse /handle/10147/ 110453

National Research Council and Institute for Medicine (2001). 'From Neurons to Neighborhoods: The Science of Early Childhood Development' in J. Shonkoff and D. Phillips (eds) *Board on Children, Youth and Families: Commission on Behavior and Social Sciences and Education*. Washington, DC: National Academy Press.

NESF (National Economic and Social Forum) (2002) *A Strategic Policy Framework for Equality Issues*, Report no. 23. Dublin: NESF.

NICHD (National Institute of Child Health and Human Development) (2000) 'The relation of child care to cognitive and language development', *Child Development* 71:4.

O'Flaherty, J. (1995) *Intervention in the Early Years: An Evaluation of the High/Scope Curriculum*. Dublin: Barnardos.

O'Toole, J. (2000) 'Early childhood care and education in Ireland and the challenge to educational disadvantage', *Irish Journal of Applied Social Studies* 2:2, 125–48.

Ramey, C.T. and Ramey, S.L. (1999). *Right from Birth: Building your Child's Foundation for Life*. New York: Goddard Press.

— (2004). 'Early learning and school readiness: can early intervention make a difference?' *Merrill-Palmer Quarterly* 50:4, 471–91.

Sheehy, K. and Duffy, H. (2009) 'Attitudes to Makaton in the ages of integration and inclusion', *International Journal of Special Education* 24:2, 91–102.

Shields, J. (2001) 'The NAS EarlyBird programme: partnerships with parents in early intervention', *Autism* 5:1, 49–56.

Shonkoff, J. and Phillips, D. (eds) (2000) *From Neurons to Neighbourhoods: The Science of Early Childhood Development*. Washington, DC: National Academy Press.

Siegel, B. (2000) 'Behavioural and educational treatments for autistic spectrum disorders', *Advocate: Autism Society of America*, 33:6, 22–31.

Siraj-Blatchford, I., Sylva, K., Muttock, S., Gilden, R. and Bell, D. (2002) *Researching Effective Pedagogy in the Early Years* (REPEY), DfES Research Report 356. Available at: www.dfes.gov.uk/research/data/uploadfiles/RR356.pdf.

Sylva, K., Melhuish, E., Sammons, P., Siraj-Blatchford, I. and Taggart, B. (2004) *The Effective Provision of Pre-School Education (EPPE) Project: Final Report*. London: Institute of Education/Sure Start.

Taylor, J. and Woods, M. (eds) (2005) *Early Childhood Studies: An Holistic Introduction* (2nd edn). London, Hodder Arnold.

UNICEF (2004) *Fast Facts for Children: Early Childhood*. Available at: www.unicef.org/media/media_9475.html.

Waldfogel, J. (2002) 'Child care, women's employment, and child outcomes', *Journal of Population Economics* 15, 527–48.

Webster-Stratton, C. (2001) *The Incredible Years Parent*, Book 11, Teacher and Child Training Series. Seattle, WA: Incredible Years.

Young, M.E. (1999) *Early Child Development: Investing in the Future*. Washington, DC: World Bank.

Useful Websites

Fás le Cheile – www.barnardos.ie

Home-Start – www.home-start.org.uk

Home-Start Ireland – www.homestartireland.ie

ISAAC (International Society for Augmentative and Alternative Communication) – www.isaacireland.org

Lifestart Foundation – www.lifestartfoundation.org/

Social Stories – www.thegraycenter.org/

TEACCH – www.teacch.com

Toybox project – www.early-years.org/toybox/

19

Early Childhood Education in the Primary School Curriculum

Joan Kiely

> *Learning Objectives*
> After studying this chapter the reader will be able to:
> - Define curriculum.
> - Describe the view of the child as articulated in the primary school curriculum.
> - Understand the structure of the curriculum and how it is mediated in an early childhood context.
> - Evaluate how the primary school curriculum supports the teacher in working with the young child aged 4–6 years.

INTRODUCTION

One of the key issues in primary education is 'the crucial role of early childhood education' (NCCA 1999). This chapter will examine how that is borne out in the Irish Primary School Curriculum 1999.

As an introduction to this exploration, curriculum will be defined, and there will be a consideration of the ideological origins of the curriculum. This will clarify for the student the view of the child and how he/she learns as described in the primary school curriculum.

DEFINING CURRICULUM

To put it in its simplest terms, a curriculum is a plan. What goes into the plan defines what type of curriculum it is.

The word curriculum comes from ancient Greece. Its original meaning is 'a course' and it refers to running tracks or chariot tracks. The activities on these Ancient Greek courses varied; there may have been sprints, hurdle races, long-distance races, chariot races. The course was laid out and used in different ways. Similarly the curriculum is a course that is used or written in different ways depending on the intentions of the user or writer.

Modern foci on curriculum assert that there are three types of curriculum:

1 curriculum as content
2 curriculum as product
3 curriculum as process.

Curriculum as *content* is when the plan dictates what is to be taught. The curriculum is a syllabus in this context and the emphasis is on the transmission of knowledge. Curriculum as *product* focuses on learning outcomes, on the competencies that will be attained by the learner rather than on how the learner will negotiate the learning path. Curriculum as *process* is when the plan focuses on how learning will take place as well as what will be taught. The Primary School Curriculum 1999 comes predominantly under the category of curriculum as process.

The curriculum as process approach is a child-centred approach. The content of the curriculum is chosen on the basis of how it will contribute to the child's development rather than for the intrinsic value of the knowledge itself. Curriculum as process focuses on assisting the child to 'learn how to learn' rather than learning pre-packaged knowledge (Murphy 2006). An example of this is a trial and error approach or a problem-solving approach to learning. The child tries out an idea and persists with it in different ways until s/he comes up with a solution. Errors are not equated with failure but with a narrowing down of possible solutions. Concepts of floating and sinking, for example, are actively explored using real objects and water.

A curriculum as process approach is nearer to a democratic model of curriculum than is curriculum as content or curriculum as product because it is not authoritarian. The teacher is facilitative rather than didactic. The learner is empowered to take action. S/he makes decisions and works with other learners to construct and negotiate knowledge. Curriculum as process 'sees education as the process by which human animals are assisted to become human beings' (Kelly 1999). This understanding of curriculum provides us with a context for how the child is viewed in the primary school curriculum.

THE VIEW OF THE CHILD IN THE PRIMARY SCHOOL CURRICULUM 1999

There are three general aims of primary education:

1 To enable the child to live a full life as a child and to realise his or her potential as a unique individual.
2 To enable the child to develop as a social being through living and co-operating with others and so contribute to the good of society.
3 To prepare the child for further education and lifelong learning. (NCCA 1999:34)

From this we can see that the child is celebrated in the primary school curriculum; it is not focused simply on the future adult.

The view of the child in the primary school curriculum is encapsulated in its principles of learning (NCCA 1999). Three sample principles are outlined here.

1 The child is an active, not passive, agent in his/her own learning. Perhaps s/he works with a peer to determine how a magnet works or s/he might problem solve in mathematics using real materials and real-life problems.
2 Language is central to the learning process. The curriculum considers talk and discussion as a core learning methodology. Bruner (1960) claims that talk shapes thinking. If this is the case, talk is vital as a learning tool.
3 Learning is developmental, but development does not necessarily occur in distinct phases. Learning is layered rather than linear. Therefore the child learns best by revisiting topics at increasingly complex levels as s/he matures. New knowledge is accommodated by reorganising and amending older understandings.

EARLY CHILDHOOD EDUCATION IN THE PRIMARY SCHOOL CURRICULUM

In Ireland, compulsory primary schooling does not commence until children are aged 6 years. However, it is common practice for children to begin school at the age of 4 years. Parents have traditionally opted to enrol their children in school between the ages of 4 and 5 instead of choosing private childcare provision. Therefore, for many children early childhood education will take place in a formal school setting. Since January 2010, the Irish state has provided a free pre-school year for children aged between 3 years and 3 months and 4 years and 6 months. It remains to be seen if this has any effect on the age at which children begin their primary school education.

A new curriculum framework for children aged from birth to 6 years, Aistear, was published in 2009. This framework, which is play-based and child-centred, is for use in the first two years of primary school. Whereas the primary school curriculum covers childhood from 4 to 12 years, Aistear is focused specifically on the needs of children in their early childhood years. (See Chapter 8 for more about this curriculum framework.)

THE STRUCTURE OF THE PRIMARY SCHOOL CURRICULUM AND HOW IT IS MEDIATED

There are six curricular areas in the primary school curriculum: Language (Irish and English); Mathematics; Social, Environmental and Scientific Education (SESE), which incorporates History, Geography and Science; Arts Education, incorporating Drama, Music and the Visual Arts; Physical Education; and Social, Personal and Health Education. All of these curricular areas are introduced at early childhood level and continue through to sixth class when children are approximately 12 years old. All are mediated through an integrated approach.

The integrated approach can be best illustrated by the following example: The child, let us call her Sarah, might be exploring the concept of capacity during water play and is developing her language around the topic at the same time. Later in the day Sarah makes lemonade with her classmates as part of an exploration in SESE and uses her knowledge of measurement practised earlier in the water play activity. Story time features a narrative about sharing which focuses on the problem of dividing a bucket of milk in equal amounts to feed pet animals. During her 'rang Gaeilge', Sarah is busy 'ag ól uisce, bainne agus líomanáide'. The children's learning for the day is connected and meaningful rather than divided into unconnected subjects. Children's learning is integrated because children do not learn in a linear fashion. Children build on their experience and knowledge base and new knowledge is integrated with that which is already held. The same ideas are continually revisited at varying levels of difficulty. This makes learning spiral rather than linear (Bruner 1960). Sarah is encouraged to learn through exploration rather than the absorption of facts. This exploration is supported by the teacher as necessary. Higher-order thinking and problem-solving skills are nurtured. The aim is that Sarah learns how to learn in order that she may become an independent learner.

In the primary school curriculum each subject is accompanied by two books: a *Curriculum Statement* and a book of *Teacher Guidelines*. A curriculum statement includes aims and objectives for the subject, a focus on content and also on skills and content development. It details what the child should be enabled to do in each subject at particular stages of their learning. The teacher guidelines explore the content of the subject and advise with regard to planning and teaching methodologies.

The primary school curriculum espouses a holistic approach to learning: the social, emotional, physical and spiritual as well as the intellectual dimensions of learning are valued. Thus the teacher's role is that of nurturer and carer as well as stimulator and facilitator of learning.

The importance of assessment, planning and organising for learning is also recognised in the primary school curriculum.

Assessment is used to identify children's needs as much as it is to monitor learning.

Using the relevant curriculum statement and teacher guidelines, let us now look at an example of how teacher Anna prepares for an exploration of the past with her junior infant class. These children are aged between 4 and 5 years old.

Exploring and Recording Significant Personal Events and Dates with a Junior Infant Class
The skills that a junior infant child might develop in a history lesson, according to the curriculum, are:

- time and chronology
- using evidence
- communication.

The content objectives are as follows.

The child should be enabled to:

- explore and record significant personal events and dates: my age, when I was born, when I took my first steps, as I grew up, first day at school, places where I have lived
- collect and examine simple evidence: photographs of oneself when younger, first toys
- compare photographs, clothes worn or toys used at different ages, noting development and things which have stayed the same.

Anna, the teacher, contacts parents to let them know that she will be asking the children to bring to school artefacts from their early childhood.

Anna will use any or all of the following teaching methodologies to support children's learning:

- talk and discussion
- active learning
- collaborative learning
- problem solving
- use of the environment
- developing skills through content.

The children in Anna's class will be actively engaged in putting photographs of themselves in chronological order according to stages of growth, or classifying toys they played with according to the age at which they were used, or comparing what games they liked to play as a toddler with games they like to play nowadays. They will talk with one another and with Anna about the process in which they are engaged.

The sample activity outlined above demonstrates how the teacher, Anna, organises and *scaffolds* (Bruner's term for supporting learning and removing the support when it is no longer needed) the activity as necessary and the children collaboratively explore and manipulate the historical artefacts as part of the learning process. Anna is focused on history skills in her approach. Her role is not didactic. She facilitates and supports learning. Her aim is to support children in learning how to learn so that they will develop into independent learners and independent thinkers. Children will progress at a pace suited to their learning needs rather than at a pace dictated by the teacher and they will be supported by a teacher who practises a differentiated approach; that is, she supports each child in a way that meets the child's particular learning needs.

CONCLUSION

Research demonstrates that children learn best through a play-based approach (see, for example, Walsh *et al.* 2006), but primary school teachers in Ireland have over the years been criticised for overly didactic teaching methods (OECD 2004). While much of this criticism is substantiated in the research, many factors, including the following, militate against teachers implementing a play-based approach in what have traditionally been described as the infant classes.

* Class sizes are too large.
* The teacher operates without the support of another adult.
* There is a lack of classroom space.
* There is a lack of teaching resources and a lack of funding for resources.
* There is insufficient provision for continuing professional development for teachers.
* There is insufficient curriculum guidance on play-based learning.

With regard to the final point above, the primary school curriculum endorses active learning and a play-based approach to learning, but it needs to provide teachers with more examples of how this might be implemented. There are some exemplars on play in the curriculum but they are insufficient in number. The primary school curriculum is currently being reviewed by the National Council for Curriculum and Assessment (NCCA) and this is one of the areas that have been highlighted for attention. The introduction of Aistear, the early childhood curriculum framework, will assist teachers with play-based practice, but the constraints mentioned above must be addressed if we are serious about quality early years practice.

Many people would agree that school is a happier place nowadays than it was thirty years ago. One of the main factors contributing to this is a child-centred primary school curriculum that is mediated by highly skilled personnel whose interests are the security, happiness and development of the primary school-going child.

References
Bruce, T. (2001) *Time to Play in Early Childhood Education*. UK: Hodder & Stoughton.
Bruner, J. (1960) *The Process of Education: A Landmark in Educational Theory*. Cambridge, MA: Harvard University Press.
Kelly, A.V. (1999) *The Curriculum: Theory and Practice*. London: Paul Chapman.
Murphy, B. (2006) 'Child-centred practice in Irish infant classrooms – a case of imaginary play?', *International Journal of Early Childhood* 38:1, 112–16.
NCCA (National Council for Curriculum and Assessment) (1999) *Primary School Curriculum: Introduction*. Dublin: Stationery Office.
OECD (Organisation for Economic Co-operation and Development (2004). *Country Note for Ireland: Early Childhood Education and Care Policy*. OECD.

Walsh, G., Sproule, L., McGuinness, C., Trew, K., Rafferty, H. and Sheehy, N. (2006) 'An appropriate curriculum for 4–5-year-old children in Northern Ireland: comparing play-based and formal approaches', *Early Years: An International Journal of Research and Development*, 26:2, 201–22.

Useful Websites

National Council for Curriculum and Assessment: Aistear can be viewed here as well as matters relating to curriculum development – www.ncca.ie.

Primary school curriculum – www.curriculumonline.ie

Professional Development Service for Teachers (PDST) – www.pdst.ie

Scoilnet: support for teachers in the form of strategies and ideas – www.scoilnet.ie

PART 3
PEDAGOGY AND LEARNING

20

Perspectives on Early Learning

Elizabeth Dunphy

Learning Objectives

After studying this chapter (and related literature) the reader will be able to discuss:

- Socio-cultural perspectives on early learning.
- The role of the educator in promoting early learning.
- The importance of collaboration between the educator and the learner.
- The terms *ZPD* and *scaffolding*.

INTRODUCTION

This chapter outlines some key ideas regarding current theoretical approaches to understanding early learning. It draws on Vygotsky's work (e.g. Vygotsky 1978, 1986) but also on that of a number of early education theorists who also take a cultural historical perspective on learning and development (i.e. an approach in which both culture and experience is seen as important in explaining development and learning).

WHAT IS LEARNING?

In this chapter the definition of learning is drawn from Rogoff (1998). Learning is seen as the process by which children change, as a result of taking part in activity. They become more able, and they participate with increasing confidence in similar activities. Children change both in terms of their understanding of the activity and in terms of their role in the activity, moving from an initial peripheral role to a more central role as they gain confidence. Also in keeping with Rogoff, in this chapter the terms *learning* and *development* are used interchangeably.

HOW DO WE UNDERSTAND EARLY LEARNING?

Learning at any age or stage of life is generally considered to be a complex process not easily explained by a single theory or perspective. Modern constructivist theories emphasise the active, constructivist nature of human learning and development and the idea that we each construct our own learning. Social constructivist theories take account of the central role of social interaction in shaping learning. Theories which consider culture and cultural influences, in addition to the social aspect, as centrally important to learning are generally referred to as socio-cultural theories of learning. In recent times socio-cultural theories have also come to be referred to as cultural-historical theories of learning and development, in order to explain the role that the past is seen to play in present culture and in social interactions. Cultural-historical theories are increasingly the dominant framework used in the early childhood education community to think about and discuss practice in early childhood education (e.g. Anning, Cullen and Fleer 2009).

The roots of cultural-historical perspectives on learning and development are to be found in the writings of the Russian psychologist Lev Vygotsky (1978, 1986). He argued that children are cultural beings, living in particular communities at particular times, and living and constructing a particular history. From a cultural-historical perspective, adult and child learners are seen as situated in particular social, cultural and historical contexts. Learning is constrained (i.e. limited) by the beliefs, artefacts and practices of the particular context in which learning is taking place.

WHAT IS THE EDUCATOR'S ROLE IN EARLY LEARNING?

From a cultural-historical perspective the educator adopts a proactive approach to promoting learning through active engagement with the learner; interactions that occur between learners are seen as critically important for learning; knowledge is understood to be co-constructed between learners; and the context in which learning is taking place is central (Anning, Cullen and Fleer 2009).

The relationships that mediate learning are seen as an important focus for the evaluation of quality. Collaboration between the child and peers is valued, as well as that which occurs between the child and adults. Conversations with and between children are viewed as occurring in joint activity contexts that promote dialogic enquiry and knowledge building (e.g. when children play together and/or with the educator).

The role adopted by the educator is seen as central for children's learning and development since it is the educator who enables the learning to take place by actively engaging with the child, the curriculum and the learning context. The pedagogy required is both proactive and interactive, and the child is seen as an equal partner in any transaction. Pedagogical strategies include ensuring a balance between learning that is controlled by the child and learning that is controlled by the educator. Ensuring opportunities for children to interact with each other in appropriate and mutually beneficial ways is also seen as essential (e.g. Bowman, Donovan and Burns 2001; Siraj-Blatchford et al. 2002).

WHAT IS IT WE WANT YOUNG CHILDREN TO LEARN?

General goals for early learning are articulated in *Aistear: The Early Childhood Curriculum Framework* (NCCA 2009). In the framework, attention is drawn to the fact that the development of general learning dispositions in early childhood is now seen as a high priority (e.g. Dweck and Leggett 1988). Dispositions to learn are defined as learning (or coping) strategies that have become habits of mind, tendencies to respond to, edit and select from situations in certain ways (Carr 2000). Desirable dispositions might include perseverance, risk-taking and curiosity. Undesirable ones might include helplessness. The educator's role is to recognise and foster desirable dispositions for learning. Dispositions develop over time with the child's active involvement (Bertram and Pascal 2002). For instance, children play an active role in the development of a disposition towards mathematics by participating and collaborating in mathematics-related activity. Children's eagerness to learn is what drives their learning.

Curricula for early childhood generally address the *what* of early learning and often specify more specific goals than general ones. The curriculum, whether selected, recommended or mandated, should attend to all aspects of children's development. It should develop a range of cognitive abilities in ways that develop and extend children's interests in all aspects of the world around them (e.g. Bowman, Donovan and Burns 2001).

One key aspect of the world for all of us is the way in which we use literacy and mathematics to communicate. A key concern of government is the improvement of literacy and numeracy for all of our young people (DES 2010). Increasingly, in early childhood education mathematics and literacy are explicitly included as part of curriculum content (OECD 2010). Some (e.g. Bowman, Donovan and Burns 2001) would also include scientific understanding since it can be argued that this is a domain of natural interest to children (i.e. how we explain and understand the world around us). We know from research that young children's understandings of literacy and mathematics develop very early in childhood (e.g. Spodek and Saracho 2006). There is now a growing recognition that in relation to the central processes of communication such as literacy and mathematics, early childhood is as much concerned with understanding literacy and mathematics in a general sense as it is about learning the skills that contribute to literacy and mathematics. These are the years when children's *metacognitive frameworks* are developed (Munn 1994), i.e. their general understandings of what these processes are all about.

It is essential that children develop in early childhood the key concepts related to mathematics and literacy (i.e. the big ideas) as well as skills and information. Literacy learning begins with language learning and is developed by children's interactions with others, especially adults, and by participation in social make-believe play. It is further supported by educators engaging children in listening to and discussing stories, and other literacy-based activities (e.g. Dickenson and Tabors 2001). Mathematical understanding grows with participation in everyday tasks as well as in learning experiences specially designed by educators to introduce mathematical ideas (e.g. in different types of play, music, story). The intentions for such learning experiences are that children come to recognise mathematics as a powerful means of communication (e.g. Pound 1999).

HOW CAN WE BEST CHARACTERISE THE ROLE THAT CHILDREN PLAY IN THEIR OWN LEARNING?

A crucial aspect of identity and self-esteem is that children see themselves as agents in control of their own actions. In the context of learning, agency is seen as 'taking more control of your own mental activity' (Bruner 1996:87). Children's agency is particularly visible in their play and it is argued that one meaning of play for children is related to the fact that it engenders in them feelings of agency, power and control (e.g. Wood 2010). Bruner argues that 'the agentive mind is not only active in nature but it seeks out dialogue and discourse with other active minds' (Bruner 1996:93). This is based on the belief that children are able to reason; to make sense (both alone and in discourse with others); to reflect; and to hold theories about self and about the world. Rogoff (1998) has illustrated how children make an important contribution in collaborating in the process of establishing joint understanding or *intersubjectivity*. For example, she points out that the child, in seeking to help the adult in everyday chores, very often initiates such activity. Older toddlers and young children will often seek to assert their independence in doing a particular task themselves, but Rogoff's analysis of the research suggests that they will also actively seek assistance when they are stuck. Children, including infants in the first year of life, can sometimes be observed to be deliberately taking the lead in collaborative activities by seeking information or by directing activities. Rogoff's analysis, consistent with Vygotsky, suggests that the intersubjectivity achieved by adults and babies will differ from that achieved by children who can use linguistic (verbal and gestural) communication to achieve mutual understandings.

HOW DO CHILDREN AND EDUCATORS COLLABORATE IN LEARNING?

In considering this question there are two important concepts that educators need to understand: the *zone of proximal development* (ZPD) and *scaffolding*.

THE ZONE OF PROXIMAL DEVELOPMENT

Vygotsky's theory of learning (1978, 1986) has been highly influential in helping to explain the processes of learning in early childhood. Berk and Winsler (1995:26) describe Vygotsky's ZPD as:

> . . . a dynamic zone of sensitivity in which learning and cognitive development occur. Tasks that children cannot do individually but they can do with help from others invoke mental functions that are currently in the process of developing, rather than those that have already matured.

For example, working in the ZPD with a toddler will include the adult focusing the child's attention on a particular object or process, or perhaps attending to the child's focus of attention. The educator may then engage in activity with the child, demonstrating, for example, how the object works. This may be extended by engaging with the child in collaborative activity with the object (e.g. play).

SCAFFOLDING

Scaffolding means that the educator provides guidance and support as the learner engages with a task. Effective scaffolding, where the adult guides the child's learning in the ZPD, is an important feature of the engagement of the child in joint problem solving. When the opportunity to guide the child's learning arises, an educator has a number of judgements to make:

- The level of challenge to be introduced.
- The point at which to offer help.
- The type of help to offer.
- When to pull back in order that the child can take responsibility for the learning (e.g. Wood 1998).

During the encounter the child and educator interact while they try to reach a particular goal. This results in the establishment of a shared understanding between them whilst they undertake the task that they had each approached from different perspectives. The objective of scaffolding is to ensure that the learner takes increasing responsibility for the task as proficiency and confidence grow.

When scaffolding, the educator's interactions with the learner are always contingent on the learner's responses. The success with which the educator works is dependent, then, on understanding the learner's perspective on the task. As Rogoff explains, working in the ZPD involves scaffolding learning (as above), but focusing especially on the processes of communication that build a continually evolving mutual perspective. Rogoff sees mutual contribution (i.e. that of both child and adult) as an essential consideration. For her, interactions, communicative and collaborative processes all form part of the picture.

CHILDREN AS CO-CONSTRUCTORS OF KNOWLEDGE

In recent times the term *co-construction* has featured prominently in influential early childhood publications, although it was implicit in the last century in the work of Dewey, who emphasised the ways in which children construct their learning by actively engaging in, and shaping, their experiences and environments.

For instance, Jordan (2009) discusses the term *scaffolding* and compares it with *co-construction*. The specific pattern of interaction that characterised early accounts of scaffolding, according to Jordan, generally vested power and control in the adult.

She argues that the term co-construction emphasises the child as a powerful player in his/her own learning, and in this respect her view of how best to guide children's learning within the ZPD is very much in keeping with that of Rogoff. An example of how this process of co-construction works in practice is illustrated in discussions of the Reggio Emilia approach to early childhood education (Edwards, Gandini and Forman 1998). Co-construction refers to staff and children making meaning and knowledge together (MacNaughton and Williams 2004). Co-construction recognises the child's expertise, and in order to understand the extent of the expertise, the educator needs to interact in specific ways with the child. The educator seeks to become aware of and understand the child's thoughts and thereby to establish intersubjectivity (i.e. joint understanding). Research by Siraj-Blatchford *et al.* (2002) also highlighted the process of co-construction and found it to be a key factor in terms of promoting children's learning. Essentially, a co-construction perspective emphasises understanding and meaning on the part of both child and adult, rather than the acquisition of facts by the child. Jordan concludes that the two concepts, scaffolding and co-construction, have different applicability depending on whether the goal of the practitioner is the exploration of thinking or the achievement of pre-specified learning goals.

Jordan (2009) further argues that when educators constantly scaffold children's learning, as opposed to co-constructing meaning with them, they are supporting ongoing dependence on the part of the child but also a disposition towards praise and performance. Smiley and Dweck (1994) found that young children (under 5 years of age) were already displaying learning dispositions which in some cases would support optimum learning and development (they displayed an orientation towards learning goals and a consequent tendency towards persisting and having a go). However, in other cases children displayed dispositions which would serve as obstacles in learning situations (e.g. an orientation towards performance goals and a consequent tendency to avoid taking a risk or getting it 'wrong').

WHAT ABOUT THE CONTEXT FOR EARLY LEARNING?

In early learning settings adults structure the environment to promote optimal learning. They do this by providing meaningful and challenging experiences and activities that make sense to children. These include opportunities for extended talk and discussion; rich imaginative experiences; and first-hand learning (Adams *et al.* 2004).

EXTENDED TALK AND DISCUSSION

Out-of-home settings can be challenging for many children in terms of their willingness or ability to participate in extended discussion with educators. The size of the group, the focus for conversation, the type of questioning and discussion engaged in by the adult, and the sharing of the educator's attention with other children are all possible issues for young children. It can be challenging for educators to provide regular opportunities for engagement with children in extended conversations (e.g. Wood 1998). Nevertheless, it is essential that they do so because children use talk to learn (e.g. Vygotsky 1978; Wells 1992). Educators intentionally develop children's thinking through talk and discussion. The thinking skills of reporting and describing, but also the higher-order skills such as hypothesising (what if?) and projecting, can be developed through the deliberate use, by the educator, of particular conversational strategies in discussion with children. Supportive strategies include supporting children's efforts to convey meaning, wondering with children, sharing meaning through discussion, questioning, and responding thoughtfully to children's questions.

RICH IMAGINATIVE EXPERIENCES

When Vygotsky suggested play as a leading activity in young children's learning and development, he was following in the tradition of many early educators such as Rousseau and Froebel. A pedagogy of play is now generally regarded as appropriate for children in the early years (e.g. Bowman, Donovan and Burns 2001). Much of the current literature on play pedagogy seeks to illustrate how and why play is appropriate for young learners. For instance, it is seen as fitting with the lively, inquisitive and exploratory nature of young learners (Moyles, Adams and Musgrove 2002). It is also seen as providing scope for children to develop and test theories about the world and to try to make sense of the world. Play is recognised as an important context in which children can practise new and complex language, and we also know that both language and play can be enhanced by educator involvement (e.g. Cohen de Lara 2008). It is important for the educator to be able to articulate an understanding of the relationship between play and learning and also to show clearly how different types of play support different types of learning. Recent years have also seen increasingly compelling arguments that seek to articulate the importance of play for young children's learning across the curriculum in areas such as literacy (e.g. Roskos and Christie 2001, 2007).

Engaging with story, listening and responding to music and song, dance, and exploring different creative and expressive media, including digital technologies, are all ways in which educators can ensure that children have extensive scope for rich imaginative experiences.

FIRST-HAND LEARNING

Children's learning is stimulated by high-quality first-hand experiences (Rich *et al.* 2005). The educator's task is to provide opportunities for children to experience at first hand aspects of the real world outside the early education setting. Accounts of the projects undertaken by children and educators in Reggio Emilia provide many examples of how, in their pre-schools, first-hand experiences supported children's learning (e.g. Edwards, Gandini and Forman 1998). Rich and her colleagues suggest that when seeking to provide first-hand learning experiences for the children in their settings, educators should focus on engaging children in experiences which are meaningful for them. In the course of these experiences children should be offered frequent opportunities to handle and use authentic objects (e.g. tools, cooking utensils, the digital camera); to go to places and to meet people (the baby clinic, the fire station, the supermarket); to explore the outdoors (the leaves in the park, the seashore, climbing on rocks). They strongly argue that unless children engage in first-hand experiences they have very little to draw on in their make-believe play, their storying, their painting and drawing or their modelling.

Key Learning Points Related to this Chapter

- The educator must be proactive in promoting children's learning and development.
- Priorities for early learning must include the development of positive learning dispositions and the development of children's ideas of what literacy and mathematics are all about.
- The educator seeks a shared perspective with children in order to anticipate their needs in terms of assistance and to guide and challenge them in their learning.
- The child is a powerful agent in his/her own learning and in co-constructing meaning with others s/he displays his/her ability to exercise that agency.
- It is the educators' responsibility to plan appropriate and challenging learning experiences that incorporate extended talk and discussion, rich imaginary experiences *and* first-hand learning.

Student Exercise

This activity is related to *Rosie's Walk* by Pat Hutchins, published by Aladdin (ISBN 0020437501).

Examine this children's picture book, which tells the story of Rosie the little hen, who takes a walk across the farmyard. Besides offering opportunities to engage in talk and discussion about the story itself, the book also encapsulates a range of language related to spatial concepts.

The use of locational language (e.g. over, across, around) in meaningful contexts, such as in this story, helps to promote children's language development and their spatial awareness. Spatial awareness is now considered a key thinking tool for young children across all areas of learning (Goswami and Bryant 2010). Promoting children's vocabulary development is also a key concern in early literacy development. There is also scope here for the educator to plan play experiences in which children make sense of the story through, for instance, building the farmyard and the various elements featured in the story and then walking Rosie through the yard. Children will also benefit from opportunities to use the spatial language in other contexts besides the story context. A visit to the playground would provide such a context; so too would a walk in the locality. During the walk children might use digital cameras to record the events. These photos will provide an essential prop as children later recall their adventure using the appropriate spatial/locational language which the educator seeks to develop.

The task

For a specified group of toddlers or young children, plan appropriate learning experiences and activities that encompass extended talk and discussion about the story, rich imaginative experiences based on the story and first-hand experiences related to aspects of the story. List the resources you would use to support children's learning during repeated encounters with the story; how you would recognise learning in relation to spatial awareness and language; and how you might document that learning.

CONCLUSION

It is important for the educator to be aware of recent theoretical perspectives on early learning. These serve to assist the educator in developing effective approaches to supporting early learning and to actively engaging with babies, toddlers and young children in ways that promote learning.

Key Learning Points in this Chapter

- The educator must play a proactive role in enabling learning in early childhood.
- Children are active participants in learning.
- Key contexts for early learning include talk and discussion; rich imaginative experiences; and first-hand learning.

References

Adams, S., Alexander, E., Drummond, M. and Moyles, J. (2004) *Inside the Foundation Stage: Recreating the Reception Year*. UK: Association of Teachers and Lecturers.

Anning, A., Cullen, J. and Fleer, M. (eds) (2009) *Early Childhood Education: Society and Culture* (2nd edn). UK: Sage.

Berk, L. and Winsler, A. (1995) *Scaffolding Children's Learning: Vygotsky and Early Childhood Education*. USA: National Association for the Education of Young Children.

Bertram, T. and Pascal, C. (2002) 'Assessing what Matters in the Early Years' in J. Fisher (ed.) *The Foundations of Learning*. UK: Open University Press, pp. 86–101.

Bowman, B., Donovan, S. and Burns, S. (eds) (2001) *Eager to Learn: Educating our Preschoolers. Report of Committee on Early Childhood Pedagogy*. USA: National Academy Press.

Bruner, J. (1996) *The Culture of Education*. Cambridge, MA: Harvard University Press.

Carr, M. (2000) 'Seeking Children's Perspectives about their Learning' in A. Smith, N. Taylor and M. Gollop (eds) *Children's Voices: Research, Policy and Practice*. New Zealand: Pearson Education, pp. 37–55.

Cohen de Lara, H. (2008) *The Basis: Theory and Practice of Early Childhood Education*. Available at: www.cohendelara.com/pdf/ECEC.pdf

DES (Department of Education and Skills) (2010) *Better Literacy and Numeracy for Children and Young People: A Draft National Plan to Improve Literacy and Numeracy in Schools*. Dublin: DES.

Dickenson, D. and Tabors, O. (2001) *Beginning Literacy with Language*. USA: Brooks.

Dweck, C.S. and Leggett, E.L. (1988) 'A social-cognitive approach to motivation and personality', *Psychological Review* 95, 256–73.

Edwards, C., Gandini, L. and Forman, G. (eds) (1998) *The Hundred Languages of Children: The Reggio Emilia Approach – Advanced Reflections* (2nd edn). USA: Ablex.

Goswami, U. and Bryant, P. (2010) 'Children's Cognitive Development and Learning' in R. Alexander (ed.) *The Cambridge Primary Review Research Surveys*. London: Routledge, pp. 141–69.

Jordan, B. (2009) 'Scaffolding Learning and Co-Constructing Understandings' in A. Anning, J. Cullen and M. Fleer (eds) *Early Childhood Education: Society and Culture*. London: Sage, pp. 31–42.

Katz, L. (2003) 'The right of the child to develop and learn in quality environments', *International Journal of Early Childhood* 35:1, 13–22.

MacNaughton, G. and Williams, G. (2004) *Techniques for Teaching Young Children: Choices in Theory and Practice* (2nd edn). Australia: Pearson Education.

Moyles, J., Adams, S. and Musgrove, A. (2002) *SPEEL: Study of Pedagogical Effectiveness in Early Learning*. Research Report No. 363. UK: DfE.

Munn, P. (1994) 'The early development of literacy and numeracy skills', *European Early Childhood Education Research Journal* 2:1, 5–18.

NCCA (National Council for Curriculum and Assessment) (2009). *Aistear: The Early Childhood Curriculum Framework*. Dublin: NCCA.

OECD (Organisation for Economic Co-operation and Development) (2010) *Revised Literature Overview for the 7th Meeting of the Network on Early Childhood Education and Care*. Available at: www.oecd.org/officialdocuments/publicdisplaydocument pdf/?cote=EDU/EDPC/ECEC(2010)3/REV1&docLa.

Pound, L. (1999) *Supporting Mathematical Development in the Early Years*. UK: Open University Press.

Rich, D., Casanova, D., Dixon, A., Drummond, M., Durrant, A. and Myer, C. (2005) *First Hand Experiences: What Matters to Children*. UK: Rich Learning Opportunities.

Rogoff, B. (1998) 'Cognition as a Collaborative Process' in W. Damon (ed.) *Handbook of Child Psychology* (5th edn). USA: John Wylie, pp.679–744.

Roskos, K. and Christie, J. (2001) 'Examining the play–literacy interface: a critical review and future directions', *Journal of Early Childhood Literacy* 1:1, 59–89.

— (eds) (2007) *Play and Literacy in Early Childhood: Research from Multiple Perspectives* (2nd edn). New York: Lawrence Erlbaum Associates.

Siraj-Blatchford, I., Sylva, K., Muttock, S., Gilden, R. and Bell, D. (2002). *Researching Effective Pedagogy in the Early Years* (REPEY), DfES Research Report 356. UK: HMSO.

Smiley, P. and Dweck, C. (1994) 'Individual differences in achievement goals among young children', *Child Development* 65, 1723–43.

Spodek, B. and Saracho, O. (eds) (2006) *Handbook of Research on the Education of Young Children* (2nd edn). USA: Lawrence Erlbaum Associates.

Vygotsky, L. (1978) *Mind in Society*. Cambridge, MA: Harvard University Press.

— (1986) *Thought and Language*. Cambridge, MA: MIT Press.

Wells, C. G. (1992) 'The Centrality of Talk in Education' in K. Norman (ed.) *Thinking Voices*. UK: Hodder & Stoughton.

Wood, D. (1998) *How Children Think and Learn* (2nd edn). UK: Blackwell.

Wood, E. (2010) 'Developing Integrated Pedagogical Approaches to Play and Learning' in P. Broadhead, J. Howard and E. Wood (eds) *Play and Learning in the Early Years*. UK: Sage.

21

Child Language in the Early Years

Máire Mhic Mhathúna

Learning Objectives
After studying this chapter the reader should be able to:
- Describe how children acquire their first language in the early years.
- Describe how children learn a second language in early years settings.
- Outline the main theories of first and second language acquisition.
- Examine a number of adult support strategies for first and second language acquisition and for children with language delay.

INTRODUCTION

Language is something we use all the time, but we may never reflect on how we learned the languages we know or how we can help children acquire language(s). Language is a powerful tool for thinking, expressing feelings and emotions, communicating and learning. It appears effortless but the process is neither simple nor automatic. It requires a great deal of effort from children and supporting adults/other children to accomplish this complex task, and practitioners in early years settings can play a significant role in developing child language.

Language acquisition is the term used to describe the process by which children learn languages subconsciously. The views of several theorists will be discussed later in the chapter, but we take the general stance that children construct linguistic knowledge from the talk they hear in their natural environment and that they are active contributing partners in this process (Owens 2011).

Children are born with a natural disposition to communicate and this disposition takes the form of the languages used in their language community. Children can tune in to the sounds of all languages but gradually narrow down the focus of what they perceive to the sounds that are dominant in the languages they hear. Language development is intrinsically connected to physical, neurological and cognitive development (Buckley 2003). Environmental factors also play an important role in language development. Secure, warm, responsive relationships with caregivers are necessary to maintain motivation and to provide feedback. Children need interaction with familiar and non-familiar adults and children. Familiar people and events provide security and the necessary repetition to enable acquisition, while new people and new events stimulate growth of experience, vocabulary and language structures (Owens 2011).

Play is one of the most facilitative ways of trying out new roles and experiences and through them acquiring new language. As play is not goal-oriented (Hayes 2010), there is no pressure to achieve a definite outcome, so children are free to experiment with ideas and with language. The other children who are playing with them are by definition also involved in the game, so they are sharing ideas and plans for the game, a shared focus of attention. Child-led games generally involve some turn-taking and sharing of roles, so turn-taking in play is providing practice for turn-taking in conversations. Play and language develop interdependently based on underlying cognitive development. This development moves from play with concrete objects, and associated vocabulary, to more complex and abstract ideas and language. Children are free to experiment, to play with language and with ideas (Owens 2011).

Sammons (2010) found that attendance at a high-quality early years setting significantly improved young children's language abilities in comparison to children who stayed at home and that duration – the length of time children spent at pre-school – was significant. The positive effect of duration was likely to reflect the benefits of mixing with a wide range of children and adults that exposed them to a broader and richer range of language experiences. This positive effect was even more marked in relation to children learning English as an additional language as these children showed particularly strong improvement in English language development over the pre-school period (Sammons 2010). Siraj-Blatchford (2010), in the same study, also found that highly trained staff played a significant role in developing children's language skills, especially through engaging children in sustained, shared thinking and collaborative play.

AISTEAR: THE EARLY CHILDHOOD CURRICULUM FRAMEWORK

Communication is one of the four main themes in Aistear, the Early Childhood Curriculum Framework (NCCA 2009). The theme of communicating is about 'children sharing their experiences, thoughts, ideas and feelings with others with growing confidence and competence in a variety of ways and for a variety of purposes'. Language is one of these modes of communicating. Aistear stresses the importance of adults empowering children to be good communicators by listening to them, interpreting what they are saying, responding and by modelling good communication skills within a stimulating and supportive environment. The aims and learning goals for child language in Aistear's 'Communication' strand include the aim that children will use language to:

1 Interact with other children and adults by listening, discussing and taking turns in conversations.
2 Explore sound, pattern, rhythm and repetition in language.

3 Use an expanding vocabulary and show a growing understanding of syntax and meaning.
4 Use language with confidence and competence for a range of language functions.
5 Become proficient in one language and have an awareness and appreciation of other languages.
6 Be positive about their home language and know that they can use other languages in different contexts (NCCA 2009).

Aistear provides guidance with regard to language development through sample learning opportunities. In order to assist students in supporting child language development, it is necessary to understand the process of learning first and second languages.

PROCESS OF FIRST LANGUAGE DEVELOPMENT

Young babies cry in response to physical states such as hunger or tiredness. The production of sound is dependent upon physical growth and babies are physically capable of making some, but not all, sounds of their native language. Babies gradually become interested in other people and linguists think that they can communicate intentionally by the age of at least 6 months (Owens 2011). Babbling is the typical pattern or sound that we associate with 6-month-old babies and this pattern gradually develops into more meaningful sounds. Adults respond to a child's babbling as though it has meaning and, through this process, meaning is attached to sounds in the child's mind and becomes fixed. Babies gradually understand tones of voice, their own name and the names of toys and objects that are used often. They begin to vocalise when talked to and start to learn the rules of turn-taking in conversations (Buckley 2003). By 1 year of age, they can use gestures to wave goodbye, they can point and use eye gaze to direct attention to something they are interested in and they can play briefly with toys and objects.

AGE 1–2 YEARS

Joint attention between a child and an adult or other child is the basis of much development in the second year of life. This is when both people are focusing on the same object, event or action. Young children can focus on only one aspect of a situation or one quality of an object, e.g. the shape of a block, rather than the way it can be moved. Adults can tune in to a child's focus of attention and use the child's interest as a language-learning opportunity. The child is most receptive to language when the adult's language follows his/her interest.

Children begin to categorise their own experiences and feelings. They start with broad concepts and begin to name categories such as animals. The categorisation usually needs some fine-tuning as the categories may be too broad (over-extension), when all animals are called 'horsies' or too narrow (under-extension) when 'dog' refers only to the family pet. At this stage children also begin to play with objects in line with their original purpose, e.g. brushing their hair with a toy hairbrush, pretend eating/drinking with tea sets. This early playful behaviour is laying down the foundation for future development. Children of this age are usually context-bound; that is, they can recognise or relate to objects and experiences only in their original context. If they see a picture of a banana, for example, they may not recognise it as a type of food they eat.

AGE 2–3 YEARS

Children of this age begin to develop their sense of being *communicators* and are fast acquiring the words and structures with which to talk about their interests and feelings. They begin to broaden their understanding of concepts between 2 and 3 years of age. In addition to broad categories, they begin to understand opposites such as hot/cold and big/small. They also begin to understand spatial concepts, that is how one object is situated in relation to another. We use prepositions to show this relationship: the sand is *in* the bucket; the doll is sitting *on* the chair; and the teddy is *under* that table. The child has begun to understand the concept of colours and begins to use colour words for items and objects that s/he uses often. Children of this age develop their sense of being communicators and are fast acquiring the words and structures in which to do the telling.

Cognitive development precedes the child's ability to name the object or concept (Owens 2011). This is also true in relation to understanding and then asking questions. Children first understand questions and during the third year of life, age 2 to 3, they themselves begin to ask questions by using intonation. They might ask where their father put the buggy by saying 'Dada buggy?' with a rising intonation. Children then develop the ability to ask simple questions and finally can ask more complex questions. Questions using the words 'What', 'Where' and 'Who' are simpler to understand than 'Why' and tend to be acquired in that order. It takes a little longer for children to understand perspective, the view of the speaker or listener. This is shown in the difference between 'here' and 'there', 'come' and 'go' as the perspective of the speaker and listener could be quite different. Children also begin to express feelings and emotions and can use phrases that adults use with them in an appropriate way, e.g. 'I'm very cross with you.'

AGE 3–5 YEARS

By 4 years most children can understand and use all basic grammatical structures. Their *vocabulary* continues to expand in line with their experience and by 5 years of age children can use up to five thousand words. They can understand many more, but in the case of new or complicated words, the context is very important in aiding comprehension. Children of this age begin to express their thoughts in more elaborate ways by using more elaborate sentence structures. They can understand simple passive sentences and can use the active construction, 'The boy kicked the ball,' but still find it more difficult to use the passive construction, 'The ball was kicked by the boy.' They are also able to take part in longer conversations and to keep on topic for longer. Their sentences are increasingly longer because they have increased cognitive understanding and have acquired words such as 'and', 'because', 'that', 'if' and 'is' to express connections and consequences. Developmental errors may continue for some time as children have begun to think about the rules of language and are trying to make irregular forms of verbs and nouns conform to a regular pattern. Examples could be 'Yesterday I *runned* very fast,' 'The *mices* in the story were tiny,' 'Susan *taked* my biscuit.' These are called developmental errors because they are part and parcel of the process of language learning. They are best corrected by adults modelling the correct form in a later turn in the conversation as young children cannot yet learn grammar intentionally (Saville-Troike 2006).

Children have acquired most sounds in their native language by 4½ years, including consonant clusters such as 'tr', 'cl' and 'gr', but a minority will continue to substitute sounds that they can say for those they cannot. 'Train' might be said as 'twain', 'cloud' is 'loud', 'green' is 'geen'. More complex sounds such as 'sch', 'j' and 'sh' may appear a little later. When children are acquiring new grammatical structures, sometimes their thoughts run ahead of their ability to articulate coherently and stuttering may appear for a time. This is usually a passing phase until the grammar becomes stabilised, and unless a child becomes anxious, it is likely to pass without any additional problems.

PERSONAL NARRATIVES

Children can also use language to do more elaborate things such as tell stories. They begin to tell stories in a very simple way, sometimes with one or two words, and the stories can be about their own personal experiences. These are called *personal narratives* and often reveal a great deal about their understanding of the world, attitudes and feelings (Hudson and Shapiro 1991). Two-year old children rely heavily on cues and prompts from adults to recall a particular event and 3-year-old children can report details of past events without much adult help. As children reach 4–6 years, they are able to tell stories independently, leaving them free to focus on aspects of experience that are important to them. They gradually begin to report more information and give more elaborate description when asked to remember specific events. They increasingly add more orientation information as they have begun to understand that the listener may not know the details of the participants/events and the number of the complicating events or details of the story also increase with age. Three-year olds tend to evaluate their experiences by comparison with similar events: 'like I do at home'. Four-year-olds use emotional reactions, e.g. 'I was really scared,' while 5-year-olds use intensity/quantity markers in addition to comparisons and emotional reactions (Hudson and Shapiro 1991). Very often children tell more elaborate stories in the course of a conversation than when asked to tell a story. This is also true of the imaginary scenarios they create in their play. They also revel in the enjoyment of listening to other people's stories and to storybooks (see Chapter 22).

LANGUAGE DELAY

Most children become capable and confident users of language, especially when helped by competent adults. However, some children may *progress at a different rate* due to biological or environmental factors. Problems can arise in relation to a child's capacity to articulate words or to process meaning. This could be due to a language-specific impairment or to causes such as hearing loss, neurological impairment or emotional and behavioural difficulties. The term *language delay* is used to describe these cases in general. Children who are difficult to understand or show signs of being at a level of language development appropriate to a much younger child should be referred to a speech and language therapist for assessment (see Chapter 17).

SECOND LANGUAGE ACQUISITION

Second language acquisition is the term used to describe the process of *acquiring a second language* in addition to a person's first language (Baker 2011). The second language can be acquired at the same time as the first (simultaneous acquisition), or it can be acquired at a later stage (sequential acquisition). In Ireland, some children acquire English and Irish at home simultaneously. Other children speak Irish or Polish at home and learn English sequentially when they attend an early years centre or go to school. Based on current understanding of socio-cultural theories (Lantolf 2000), the context in which language learning takes place and the affordances and opportunities provided are of great significance in providing input and support to young children acquiring a second language.

Most children who are learning a second language have age-appropriate competency in their first language and know how to use language in a variety of ways, e.g. to make requests, describe events and express their feelings. It is of the utmost importance that they maintain and continue to develop their first language as this may be their main means of thinking, forming relationships with key people in their lives and expressing their emotions.

Bilingual babies follow the same basic pattern in each of their languages as monolingual babies in theirs. Both languages tend to be kept fairly separate with regard to grammar and sentence construction, but some mixing of words will be likely to occur. Mixing tends to follow the same pattern of language mixing that people around them use. By age three most bilingual children realise that they have two ways of speaking at their command and can move freely between the two languages. They can also judge which language to speak to which person and adjust their language accordingly.

Children who acquire a second language in addition to the first can use that language-learning experience to good effect. They can already communicate through language in an age-appropriate way and can transfer this knowledge to the new language. Where their first language is recognised and valued, the second language is regarded as an additional bonus (additive bilingualism). Children who speak a major European language at home, French or German for example, would be in this category. Children who speak a less highly valued language, such as a minority or regional language, could be in a subtractive situation, struggling to learn English, if society appears to place little value on their home language (subtractive bilingualism). This negative situation can have major implications for the child's and the family's self-image and self-esteem. The transmission of family values and culture may be lost as the parents may not have sufficient English to pass on their beliefs and understandings in the new language. It may lessen the bonds with the extended family in their home country as the children may not be able to communicate with their grandparents and other family members in their native language.

PATTERN OF SECOND LANGUAGE ACQUISITION

Many children acquiring English as a second language in an early years centre will go through a *silent period*. This is the time in which they pay attention to the sounds and meanings of the new language and try to work out the patterns for themselves. They may try to speak in their first language and, depending on how this is received, may continue to speak that language (English in a Naíonra or Gaelscoil, for example) or stop speaking Polish or Yoruba in the early years setting (Tabors 2008). This should not be confused with developmental delay as it is the natural path of progression in learning a second language. Children will continue to communicate through non-verbal means: gesture, signing, pointing, facial expression, etc. They will observe what the other children are doing and imitate them, giving the impression that they know more than they actually do. Gradually they will begin to use *single words and rote phrases*, very often useful words and phrases to gain attention, request toys or express wishes. They may also use advertising slogans and jingles as they feature very often on children's TV. Rote phrases that they have learned as a unit might include 'My turn,' 'Sharing is caring,' 'Can't do it.' Other phrases that could be useful are sentences that have slots that can be filled with different words, such as 'I want . . .' These phrases are immediately useful and grammatically correct. When the child has built up a sufficient stock of these words and phrases, s/he can begin to speak more creatively, but as s/he is now processing the language independently, s/he may appear to be making more mistakes than before. Over time s/he will acquire an age-appropriate level of competency in English. It is estimated that children can build up communicative competency in about three years but that it takes older learners five to seven years to gain more academic competencies in a new language.

THEORIES OF FIRST LANGUAGE ACQUISITION

Many theories have been proposed to help our understanding of how children acquire their first and second languages. Some of these theories are closely related to theories in psychology and others are more focused on language learning itself. The theories range along a continuum, moving from an emphasis on correct form or grammar to appropriate language use in context.

According to B. F. Skinner, all *behaviour*, including verbal behaviour, is learned and is changed or modified by the consequences of that behaviour. When an adult responds to certain sounds in a child's vocalisations, the child learns that this produces the desired effect and continues to use these sounds. A child hears a word in the presence of a certain object, learns to associate the sound with the meaning and continues to use the word because it works. More complex words and phrases are learned through approximations or good guesses. Language is, according to Skinner, learned by modelling, imitation, practice and selective reinforcement (Owens 2011).

Skinner's behaviourist theory was heavily criticised by Noam Chomsky, who found no evidence by which the behaviourist theory could adequately explain the 'logical problem of language', i.e. how children learned to say novel utterances. His main argument was that young children produce many novel and innovative sentences that they have not heard before, including many that adults would not use. In more recent times the role of input and the linguistic environment has been reassessed and valued. Chomsky proposed a psycholinguistic theory for language acquisition, looking at how the brain processes language. He held that the human brain is hardwired for language and that it has a separate facility for language processing, which he called the *language acquisition device* (LAD). Chomsky thought that all human languages differ only superficially and that there is a common underlying deep structure beneath them. He called this structure *universal grammar*. A child must hear the language spoken and then work out the rules of his/her native tongue by applying the general principles of universal grammar to the particular language. However, this theory does not adequately account for the understanding of the meaning of words and sentences (semantics), nor does it explain the consistent pattern of child language development across languages. Chomsky did, however, provide a new model of describing language and language development that shows how the human brain is actively processing language in novel and creative ways (Owens 2011).

Socio-linguistic models of language acquisition emphasise the larger units of language, the communication units required to convey information, and places language acquisition in its *social and cultural context*. Children acquire language in the everyday contexts in which they use it; that is, learning by doing. The role of the child's communication partners, adults or children, is crucial as they provide the input and support to the child learner. Not only does the child learn the rules of speech, s/he also learns the rules of language interaction. Lev Vygotsky and other socio-cultural writers prioritise the role of the social environment in language learning. They state that language is learned through social interaction and is then internalised by the child. Children continue to learn language that meets their language needs, i.e. they learn language through their interactions with other people and language learning is embedded in its social context. This model explains the social nature of language learning and language use, but does not explain the link between the child's intentions and the process by which they acquire means to express those intentions.

Muriel Saville-Troike and other theorists hold that the first language must be learned by a certain period in life. The *critical period* hypothesis states that the basic structures of a child's native language must be acquired by the onset of puberty as the brain's plasticity changes after that time. While difficult to prove, tragic examples of linguistic deprivation, such as the French boy Victor, the American girl Genie and abandoned children, show that without appropriate linguistic input in early and middle childhood, the full system of first language acquisition is unlikely to develop. Linguists now believe that the brain's plasticity begins to decline earlier than previously thought, at about 5 years of age, but that a great deal depends on individual differences and context.

The next section in this chapter outlines some useful strategies for putting into practice the understanding of child language and the principles of Aistear.

STRATEGIES FOR SUPPORTING FIRST LANGUAGE DEVELOPMENT

Children must participate in language interactions in order to acquire language(s). The more experience they have, the more proficient they become. Some of the following strategies apply to first and second language learners but it should be borne in mind that interaction and input with children should suit the individual child/group of children and should be age-appropriate.

The process of treating babies and young children as *conversation partners* in their first language begins with very young babies, through gaining their attention, by talking about things that interest them and by regarding any vocalisations as their turn in the conversation. Adults in our culture typically use a higher pitch of voice when talking to young babies and this tone indicates for the child that the conversation is directed at him/her. Adults slow down the pace of the conversation and adapt their language by simplifying the vocabulary, using short sentences and exaggerated intonation, emphasising key words and using a great deal of repetition. This style of talking to babies and young children is called 'child-directed speech' or 'motherese' and is used in many Western cultures but not universally (Lightbrown and Spada 2006).

Action songs and games, such as peek-a-boo and tickling games, are important because it is through repeated experiences that the child can learn what is expected of him/her regarding actions and speech. Through playing games and routines with a child or adult, s/he will learn to participate and then to take the lead.

As children develop their language, the adult's language also changes and less use is made of the child-directed style of talking. The adult can use the proper names of objects instead of baby words, but children still love to hear and use onomatopoeia and fun words. Adults can expand on children's one- or two-word utterances (age 1–2 years) and extend the topic by giving more information. Explanations can help children understand cause and effect and we can help children verbalise their feelings by giving simple descriptions for happy events, upsets and distress. Weitzman and Greenberg (2002) also suggest using questions to include the child in the conversation. They advise asking open questions, when possible, that show your interest because children can spot 'test' or closed questions easily and become bored. Closed questions are those which require a 'Yes' or 'No' an answer, while open questions are real questions to which we don't know the answer. As they get older, children can participate more fully in conversations and learn to become clearer communicators. They realise how much background information it is necessary to give about people and events to enable the listener to understand and they learn how to add information that is relevant to the topic of the conversation. In this way children can be supported to go beyond the here and now and use language to play, learn, predict, imagine and reflect on their experience.

THEORIES OF SECOND LANGUAGE ACQUISITION

Cognitive theories include Skinner's behaviourist theory, discussed above, and Krashen's *monitor* model. Krashen (Lightbrown and Spada 2006) held that there is a natural order of language acquisition, that understanding input is important and that learners monitor their own speech to see if it is correct. He also held that motives, attitudes and emotions play a significant role in second language learning. While both these theories have been critiqued, it is also true that repetition plays a large role in language learning and that learners do self-correct. Michael Long went on to state that *comprehensible input* is critical to successful language learning and therefore that the modifications made by adults/native speakers to aid understanding are crucial (Lightbrown and Spada 2006). The relationship between the learner and the native speaker is considered important and the role of the wider social environment in determining contexts and opportunities for language learning is significant. Children learn languages through the interaction of their own cognitive processes and through interactions in the social environment.

James Lantolf (2000) holds that the *social, economic and political environment* provides the opportunities for language learning and for benefiting from knowing a second language. The situation of newcomer children learning English in Irish early years settings illustrates this theory well. Many of their parents came to Ireland to work during the Celtic Tiger years and settled down here. Now their children are growing up in Ireland. The children are learning English in early years settings, they will be able to benefit from the Irish education system and contribute socially and, in time, economically to Irish society, just as their parents are doing. However, the full benefits of bilingualism are only available to those who attain a high level of competency in their two languages.

STRATEGIES FOR SUPPORTING SECOND LANGUAGE DEVELOPMENT

Adults can support second language learners through a range of *scaffolding strategies*. Children who are learning English as an additional language already speak the first language and should not be treated as though they were younger. Most talk with young children is about the immediate context. This makes it natural and authentic to speak about the current task, game or event with a child and to use the ongoing actions as the focus of talk, a form of running commentary that is self-explanatory. The adult can speak at a slightly slower pace than usual and emphasise key words in the sentence. S/he can repeat what has been said and demonstration can be used to show what is meant. The adults can expand the one-word utterances of the child, thus showing acceptance of the child's comment and giving more input in an incremental way. A child may talk about a car. The adult can expand this first to a phrase such as, 'Yes, that's a red car' and then proceed to mimic car noises. As the children become familiar with one set of words and phrases, the adult can provide input for the next stage and praise the new effort being made by the child. This changing focus of support, moving on from something that is known to a new item, is termed *dynamic scaffolding* and it supports a child in making progress (Owens 2011). It is also important to give a child enough time to process the language and to think. Mistakes should be corrected through modelling the correct form rather than correcting the mistake directly, as young children are not yet capable of learning directly about correct forms of grammar (Saville-Troike 2006).

ENVIRONMENTAL SCAFFOLDING IN EARLY YEARS SETTINGS

Weitzman and Greenberg (2002) and Tabors (2008) offer practical advice on how language learning opportunities can be facilitated within early years settings. Strategies should be tailored to the individual needs of the children/whole group and the particular environment.

Children will be more inclined to listen and talk in an interesting, calm and well-organised physical environment and in an affective atmosphere that accepts, respects and supports them. By showing a real interest in what children have to say as well as how they say it, adults show that they value children as communicators. Weitzman and Greenberg (2002) advise practitioners to wait for children's initiatives at the beginning of an activity and to follow the child's lead by commenting on children's initiatives and joining in with their make-believe. They advise adapting daily routines to make time for talk, by planning in advance and organising staff and space. Practitioners should consider how best to manage staff resources, the number of children in the group for particular activities/routines and the daily schedule or timetable. Perhaps groups could be split if the number of children is large, as children rarely have to do the same thing all at the same time. Smaller groups are easier to manage and time to talk can be built into the routine. Equipment can be stored near where it is used or placed on a trolley that can be moved when needed.

Tabors (2008) refers to a range of scaffolding strategies for second language children. As is the case in all aspects of working with young children, she advises starting with the child and gathering basic demographic information about their family background, including the languages that they know. Early years settings use a range of methods for giving information to the parents, such as meetings, booklets in English and translated into the most common languages required. The practitioners in a small-scale study by Mhic Mhathúna and Hill (2007) said that they felt the strategies they used with English-as-additional-language children were an extension of those they used with Irish children. They named what the newcomer children were doing and described the ongoing action. This provided the opportunity to describe the activity that the child was currently involved in. The staff could also encourage the child to observe what other children nearby were doing. Some staff learned basic words in the children's language and found that this was very useful when new children were settling into the nursery. They sandwiched the foreign language word between two English words when talking to the new children and this helped to build communication quickly. One of the most useful tools they found was photography, which they used as part of the HighScope plan–do–review routine. It facilitated independent choice and play and could be used to document many forms of play and learning. The photographs could also be shown to the parents to explain what the children had been doing and to show that they were happy in the setting. One setting also used the photographs to make books about the centre and asked the parents to provide translations of the English captions in their native languages.

Tabors recognises the language opportunities in the physical environment and suggests that physical/manipulative play is particularly suitable for newcomer children as it is age-appropriate but not language-dependent to the same degree as other types of play. This type of play includes block play, dressing up, sand and water play, jigsaws, Lego, etc. The 'safe haven' of physical play may also develop into parallel play and so provide the opportunity for social contact and language input from other children.

Consistent routines allow all children to work out what to do by observation and by following other children. Some second language children may in fact appear more competent than they actually are by observing the other children closely and by imitating them. Small group activities, which at times include both first and second language children, offer many language opportunities for peer-assisted scaffolding as children can be very understanding of the language needs of their peers. Lunchtimes can also provide a lot of context-embedded talk about food, likes and dislikes and other topics. Staff can encourage children to participate in circle time by keeping to a stable and predictable routine within the structure, by singing action songs and rhymes and by giving other children the opportunity to respond before asking second language children for their turn. This practice gives the second language children the opportunity to hear the question and response several times before they are called on to participate.

STRATEGIES FOR SUPPORTING CHILDREN WITH LANGUAGE DELAY

Due to complex factors, some children may be delayed in their language development and may require *differentiated support* from early years practitioners. Practitioners should make every effort to communicate with the child and treat his/her responses as communication. They can gain the child's attention through gestures and animated play and maintain it though eye contact. They should encourage turn-taking and questions. By focusing on the child's interests, they can develop joint attention with the child and use toys or items that interest him/her to play one-to-one games. This will help to develop turn-taking in concrete ways. Social routines are very useful to build up predictable sequences for the child, and repeated, predictable routines around greetings, mealtimes, games, tabletop activities, moving from one room to another or outside are very useful strategies. Songs, nursery rhymes and games offer stability and predictability as the child receives cues as to what is expected of him/her in relation to participation, turn-taking, actions and gradually through words. Speech and language therapists will be able to advise on specific strategies for the individual child and on ways to adapt the daily routine to suit the language delayed child.

CONCLUSION

Language is an essential tool for thinking, communicating and learning. Every child is unique, but the general process of language acquisition offers a useful guide to language development. Early years practitioners can play a significant role in supporting young children in their language learning through understanding the process of first and second language learning and by using this knowledge to devise language support strategies for all children.

Many theorists have sought to explain the process of language acquisition and while the emphasis placed on theories changes over time, current thinking favours acknowledging that language is a complex match between cognitive processing and a supportive environment. This involves a strong bond between children and caregivers, and regular interaction with a small number of key practitioners, and it takes place in a social and cultural context.

Language is one of the most rule-governed systems we use and at the same time it is one of the most creative and imaginative ways of communicating. We should try to bring the resultant sense of fun and endless possibilities to our work with young children.

Key Learning Points
- There is a general process of language development, moving from simple one-word utterances to complex sentences.
- Children learn language by participating in language interactions in age- and development-appropriate ways.

- Theories of first and second language acquisition help our understanding of aspects of the process of language acquisition.
- Regular contact by the child with a small number of key people provides a stable base for routines and interactions that support language development.
- Children with language impairment need differentiated support and predictable routines and activities.
- The management of time and space can be organised to support language interactions.

References

Baker, C. (2011) *Foundations of Bilingual Education and Bilingualism* (5th edn). Bristol: Multilingual Matters.

Buckley, B. (2003) *Children's Communication Skills from Birth to Five Years*. London: Routledge.

Hayes, N. (2010) *Early Childhood: An Introductory Text* (4th edn). Dublin: Gill & Macmillan.

Hudson, J. and Shapiro, L. (1991) 'From Knowing to Telling: The Development of Children's Scripts, Stories and Personal Narratives' in A. McCabe and C. Peterson (eds) *Developing Narrative Structure*. Hillsdale NJ: Lawrence Erlbaum, pp. 89–136.

Lantolf, J. (2000) *Sociocultural Theory and Second Language Learning*. Oxford: Oxford University Press.

Lightbrown, P. and Spada, N. (2006) *How Languages are Learned* (3rd edn). Oxford: Oxford University Press.

Mhic Mhathúna, M. and Hill, Ú. (2007) 'Strategies in working with children learning English as a second language', *An Leanbh Óg* 1, 113–25.

NCCA (National Council for Curriculum and Assessment) (2009) *Aistear: The Early Childhood Curriculum Framework*. Dublin: NCCA.

Owens, R. (2011) *Language Development: An Introduction* (8th edn). Boston and London: Pearson.

Sammons, P. (2010) 'Does Pre-school Make a Difference? Identifying the Impact of Pre-school on Children's Cognitive and Social Behavioural Development at Different Ages' in K. Sylva, E. Melhuish, P. Sammons, I. Siraj-Blatchford, and B. Taggart, *Early Childhood Matters: Evidence from the Effective Pre-School and Primary Education Project*. London: Routledge, pp. 92–113.

Saville-Troike, M. (2006) *Introducing Second Language Acquisition*. Cambridge: Cambridge University Press.

Siraj-Blatchford, I. (2010) 'A Focus on Pedagogy: Case Studies of Effective Practice' in K. Sylva, E. Melhuish, P. Sammons, I. Siraj-Blatchford, and B. Taggart, *Early Childhood Matters: Evidence from the Effective Pre-School and Primary Education Project*. London: Routledge, pp. 149–65.

Tabors, P. (2008) *One Child, Two Languages* (2nd edn). Baltimore: Paul Brookes.

Weitzman, E. and Greenberg, S. (2002) *Learning Language and Loving It* (2nd edn). Toronto: Hannen.

Further Reading

Barron-Hauwaert, S. (2004) *Language Strategies in Bilingual Families*. Clevedon: Multilingual Matters.

Harding-Esch, E. and Riley, P. (2003) *The Bilingual Family: A Handbook for Parents*. Cambridge: Cambridge University Press.

Kersner, M. and Wright, J. (1996) *How to Manage Communication Problems in Young Children*. London: David Fulton.

Law, J. and Elias, J. (1996) *Trouble Talking*. London: Jessica Kingsley.

Useful Websites

University of Birmingham bilingualism database – www.education.bham.ac.uk/research/projects1/bilingualism_database.shtml

Centre for Information on Language Teaching and Research (CILT) – www.nacell.org.uk/ideas/index.htm

I Can: an information portal with information on supporting children's speech and language development – www.ican.org.uk

Talking Point: an information portal with information on supporting children's speech, language and communication development – www.talkingpoint.org.uk

22

Children's Literature and Early Literacy

Joe Moynihan

Learning Objectives

After studying this chapter the reader will be able to:

- Recognise the importance of children's literature.
- Describe what type of literature is most suitable for children at various developmental stages.
- Understand the role that early literacy plays in pre-school education.
- Realise the implications that multiliteracy has for early education.
- Implement pedagogical strategies that will help to promote the development of early literacy in an early education environment.

CHILDREN'S LITERATURE

This chapter will discuss children's literature and early literacy in relation to early education contexts. What constitutes children's literature is subject to continuous debate, but children's literature can be broadly defined in four different ways:

1 books written by children
2 books written for children
3 books chosen for children
4 books chosen by children.

Children's books can also be categorised by genre. Anderson (2006) has detailed six main genre classifications:

1 picture books
2 traditional literature
3 fiction
4 non-fiction
5 biography
6 poetry and verse.

Literature for pre-school children almost always comes replete with illustrations, since artwork plays a much larger role in the education of pre-literate children.

Children's literature is a useful tool for achieving the aims of early childhood education. It aspires to develop in young children necessary social, emotional, cognitive, linguistic and physical life skills. This is early education in its most holistic sense: where a child is supported in their development as a whole through a variety of activities while simultaneously developing their personality and their learning. Towards this objective, children's literature allows educators the opportunity to access a range of experiences that empower children to discover a love of language, to give expression to their own stories and to communicate their own ideas. Children often see stories from their own life mirrored in the stories found in books. Consequently, children's literature can prove to be an important vehicle for the teaching of various skills and life lessons in early education programmes.

BOOKS SUITABLE FOR THE EARLY YEARS

Just as children's minds and bodies change and develop, so do their interests and appreciation of different types of literature. In this section, I will examine the various types of books and general topics that are most relevant to children aged 0–6 years. By matching this generic age-related advice with the unique interests of the child, the early educator can favourably match titles of books with children from specific age groups. Various types of book suitable for the early years are listed below under the key age ranges: 0–2 years; 2–4 years; and 4–6 years. Up-to-date examples will be given for each type of children's book.

AGES 0–2 YEARS

In selecting books for infants, one should bear in mind the following practical considerations:

- How well they can see the drawings in the book.
- The length of time they can sit still for the experience.

The best books for this age group tend to be those that advance oral language development. These books do not necessarily have to have text, but should promote conversation and dialogue.

CONCEPT BOOKS

Books for babies usually fall under the category of concept books. These are short, plotless books that deal with everyday routines and familiar objects related to the infant's experience. The content is presented primarily through illustrations. The illustrations contained in these books consist of easily recognisable, vividly coloured pictures, preferably positioned on a plain background. The materials used to manufacture this type of book tend to be very durable, and include board, vinyl and cloth.

Examples

- *Go, Dog, Go!* – P. D. Eastman.
- *White on Black* – Tana Hoban.

NURSERY RHYMES

Infants tend to have very positive reactions to easily recognised and imitated patterns in sound and movement. The exaggerated rhythms and rhymes that can be found in nursery rhymes tend to fall into this category. These types of book work exceptionally well with groups of young children during read-aloud sessions, where both words and movement can be integrated into the telling of the story. Nursery rhymes are part of our literary inheritance and tend to be passed down from generation to generation. There are countless numbers of these nursery rhymes, and sometimes it may be difficult to put your hands on the one you really want; however, the better-quality nursery rhyme collections come usefully organised around topics or themes and include an index of titles or first names.

Examples

- *Mother Goose: One Hundred Best-Loved Verses* – Mary Engelbreit.
- *Mother Goose Flies Again* – Tomie dePaola.

INTERACTIVE BOOKS

Interactive books are an extension of the experience of play. These are books that engage children's verbal and physical skills through asking children questions, getting them to recite rhymes or lines in unison, inviting them to clap, dance or do actions to the cadence of the words or sentences; or the book may have a tactile quality so that a child can touch various textures in the book or manipulate the story by opening doors, pulling paper tabs or scratching and sniffing.

Examples

- *Pat the Bunny* – Dorothy Kunhardt.
- *Tails* – Matthew VanFleet.
- *I Love You Every Little Bit: A Pop Up Book* – Margaret Wang.
- *Pat Them Gently* – Melanie O'Brien.

A recent innovation in interactive stories for children is in children's online storybooks, where technology and literature merge. Examples of online storybooks can be found at www.magickeys.com/books/ and there are already numerous children's stories, such as the Dr Seuss books, that can be downloaded onto various interactive media.

AGES 2–4 YEARS

There are many similarities between the books recommended for infants and those suitable for toddlers. Topics of relevance for toddlers include daily routines and familiar objects. See below for suitable books for the age group 2–4 years.

PICTURE BOOKS

Picture books give children a vicarious enjoyment of literature from their early years because they can 'read' the illustrations and thus follow the story's narrative, name the characters and objects in the drawings and discuss these with adults or other children. Picture books are an excellent pedagogical tool for early education because:

- Children begin to understand the value of reading and are motivated to learn to read by hearing picture books frequently read to them.
- The visual cues in picture books allow non-readers and those beginning to read to take pleasure in 'reading' independently. Once a picture book has been read to a child, they can choose to go back to the book and use the visual cues to remember enough of the text to enjoy the experience on their own.
- Encouraging children to engage with picture books aids language development. It also enables them to gain access to new ideas, nurtures imagination and encourages them to question the world around them.
- Picture books can provide children with the opportunity to appreciate art. This is especially true at present since there are many talented artists illustrating children's books.

Examples

- *Blueberries for Sal* – Robert McCloskey.
- *The Boy who was Raised by Librarians* – Elizabeth Kennedy.
- *The Carrot Seed* – Ruth Kraus.

CONCEPT BOOKS

Concept books for toddlers tend to be more complex than those for infants. These concept books can now include letters (alphabet books), numbers (counting books), opposites, language development, objects (e.g. tractors), activities (e.g. gardening), and naming things (naming books).

ALPHABET BOOKS

This type of book introduces the child to the ABC letter by letter. The objective behind this is to allow young children to become familiar with the shapes, names and, in the more modern versions, the sounds of each letter. Alphabet books are usually built around a given theme (fruit, vegetables, animals, fairies, etc.) or a linking device (C is for Cow) where the objects denoted by the selected letter are found on the same page. Three important points to bear in mind when selecting an alphabet book are:

1 Is the theme or linking device appropriate for the age group under consideration?
2 Are capital letters or lower-case letters used?
3 What style of print is used? (Alphabet books done in the style of the Book of Kells tend to be too complicated for this age group.)

Examples

- *Chicka Chicka Boom Boom* (book and CD) – Bill Martin.
- *Alphabet City* – Stephen Johnson.

COUNTING BOOKS

The object of counting books is to introduce children to numerals and their shapes (1, 2, 3, 4 . . .), the names of each number (one, two, three, four . . .), the counting sequence and what number each numeral stands for. In a similar vein to alphabet books, counting books use various themes and methods to make them more enjoyable for young children. The illustration content in these books must be taken into account when choosing a particular title. The best counting books employ certain themes and objects in order to give children a coherent conceptualisation of number.

Examples

- *One to Ten . . . and Back Again: An Amazing Pull-the-Ribbon Book* – Betty Ann Schwartz and Susie Shakir.
- *The Ants Go Marching* – Dan Crisp.

NURSERY RHYMES AND FAIRYTALES

Children in this age range tend to fall more in love with nursery rhymes than when they were infants, and their enjoyment is enhanced even further when they memorise favourite rhymes and are able to recite them to others. At this stage, the literary heritage afforded by fairytales becomes accessible to children. Children in this age group tend to gravitate towards those fairytales that have repetitive elements.

Examples

- *Mixed Up Fairy Tales* – Hilary Robinson.
- *Irish Legends for the Very Young* – Niamh Sharkey.
- *A Child's Treasury of Irish Rhymes* – Alice Taylor and Nicola Emoe.

AGES 4–6 YEARS

It is around this stage that children begin 'play-reading': they have memorised their favourite picture storybook and are able to enjoy the book on their own. Most books listed here should be read aloud to children by a fluent reader, but it is not unusual for young children to acquire the fundamentals of reading at this stage. Even at this early stage young children can understand the following basic concepts associated with literacy:

- that stories and the words presented alongside the pictures have meaning
- certain words can be recognised and can be said on sight
- the left-to-right and top-to-bottom progression of print in texts.

PICTURE STORYBOOKS

Picture storybooks are still very attractive to this age group. To make things even more enjoyable, try to choose picture books with humorous content suitable for this age range. At ages 4–6 years, children's humour tends to reflect the developmental stage they are at, which usually involves a new-found appreciation of absurdity and wordplay.

Examples

- *Boomer Goes to School* – Constance McGeorge.
- *Skin Again* – bell hooks.
- *Not All Princesses Dress in Pink* – Jane Yolen and Heidi E. Y. Stemple.

EASY-TO-READ BOOKS

These books help to stimulate a child's appetite for reading by using descriptive illustrations, familiar words, word patterns and, in some cases, rhyme to aid in the predictability of the text.

Examples

- *I Saw an Ant in a Parking Lot* – Joshua Prince.
- *Hip Hop Dog* – Chris Raschka.

INFORMATIONAL BOOKS

Children are very curious at this age and tend to display an almost boundless relish for finding out about the world and its many facets. Early educators can use this enthusiasm constructively by introducing children to informational books suitable for this age range.

Examples

- *The Milk Makers* – Gail Gibbons.
- *When My Parents Forgot How to Be Friends* – Jennifer Moore-Mallinos and Marta Fabrega.
- *Too Small for Honey Cake* – Gillian Lobel.

EARLY LITERACY

Inherently linked to children's literature is the area of early literacy. Early language and literacy development begins during a child's first three years and parallels a child's earliest experiences with books and stories. The whole area of early literacy has gone through a renaissance in recent years, with the area of early literacy being extended to the emotional, social and technological spheres (Justice *et al.* 2009; Makin, Jones Diaz and McLachlan 2007; Mortlock 2005).

Yet the recent advances in this area do not take away from the fact that interaction is the single most important factor in the development of literacy skills. There are two areas of interaction when it comes to early literacy: material and social. *Material interactions* are interactions that young children have with various literacy materials, which have traditionally included books, paper and crayons, but have now been extended to technological media, such as e-books (electronic books) and interactive digital story telling. *Social interaction* refers to a child's observations of and interactions with adults and older children in their relationships with literary materials.

There are two areas in which social interaction plays an important role in early literacy:

1 early educators and children
2 parents and children.

Early literacy research has repeatedly shown that these areas of interaction provide fertile soil for language, reading and writing development, as well as future academic success and social skills (Ard and Beverly 2004).

MULTILITERACIES

A cultural shift has occurred in the area of literacy and this shift has been primarily brought about by technological evolution. The ubiquitous presence of computers and other interactive media in Irish people's homes, coupled with the globalised nature of children's entertainment, has meant that Irish children are currently exposed to an enormous diversity of literacy experiences that have advanced beyond traditional 'texts', such as books and stationary illustrations. The term for these new types of literacy is 'multiliteracies' or 'multi-modal literacies' (Iyer and Luke 2009). This calls into question the traditional view of literacy as being a restrictive skill-based model of learning to read and write in preparation for the primary school curriculum.

The wind of this cultural change is also being felt in the pre-school classroom, as multiliteracy affords a unique challenge to teaching practice. By acknowledging the existence of multiliteracy, pre-school pedagogues need to open their eyes to the relevance of children's individual cultural and social skills, educate themselves in the new literacy and integrate their new insights into the classroom. The wider ramifications of this are enormous as the long-established practices of early literacy were product-based and individualised (the individual child reading and writing), whereas the practices of multiliteracy are process-based and interactive (the child communicating to an audience using multimedia tools).

Multiliteracy practices acknowledge that the attitudes, feelings, expectations, values and beliefs of children, their families and teachers, and members of the wider community are integral to the literacy process (Colbert 2006). The objective behind this new evaluation of early literacy involves an increased appreciation of other ways of experiencing and communicating information, and the tools that children make use of to learn about their world.

PEDAGOGICAL STRATEGIES FOR THE DEVELOPMENT OF EARLY LITERACY

This section consists of two parts. The first part looks at how to use books in an early education setting. The second looks at how to integrate multiliteracies into the curriculum using information and communication technology (ICT).

1 USING BOOKS IN EARLY EDUCATION

Books give children the opportunity to profoundly engage with and learn about not only the world around them, but also the world of the imagination. The sharing of books both at home and in the classroom fosters the development of children's literacy and literacy skills. Reading books to children cultivates curiosity, ignites the imagination and nourishes new understanding. Although, one presumes, early educators can read, when using books with children *how* and *what* you read is of the utmost importance.

Choosing Books for Children

There are some considerations that you have to bear in mind when choosing books for children.

- *Genre:* What type of book is it? Is it suitable for the age group you are teaching? Will it hold the children's' attention?
- *Topic:* What is the book about? Your library should include books on a diverse range of topics so as to attract the interest of every child.
- *Illustrations:* What type of illustrations are used? Good illustrations complement the words on the page and can elicit an emotional response (laughter, curiosity, etc.) from your audience.
- *Language:* What type of language is used to tell the story? Each book tells a story in a different way. Will your audience understand the words used? Does it introduce any new words? Is there word play, such as rhyme, rhythm, repetition, onomatopoeia or alliteration, that will engage the children?

Reading Aloud to Children

When reading aloud to children, the act of reading needs to become a performance, the reader acting out each character for the benefit of the audience. Here are some suggestions on how to do this.

- *Pitch and tone:* The pitch and tone of the reader's voice can be used to give definition to the characters or to highlight important elements in the book. A high and varied pitch of voice (called 'motherese' or 'parentese') is especially good for attracting the attention of infants.
- *Rhythm and tempo:* This can be used to create suspense and drama. Your voice should speed up or slow down depending on the amount of action unfolding.
- *Facial expressions:* Change your facial expressions or use props (such as a wig or mask) to further enliven a reading session.
- *Can all the children see the book?* Make sure everyone can see the book the right way up and that the pictures are big enough so that those at the back of the class can see.

Discussing Books with Children

Reading a book with children is all about stimulating interest and getting children to talk about the book. Here are some strategies for doing this.

- Elaborate on and explain the story at key moments.
- Let the children decide when the page should be turned.
- Ask the children to make predictions about the story: 'What's going to happen when I turn the page?'

- 'Pause for thought' when reading, so that both children and adults can give opinions on the words, story or illustrations.
- Respond to children's one-word labels with full sentences: For example, when a child points to a picture and says, 'Frog', you could say, 'Yes, the frog is dancing down the road.'
- Talk about the language used. For example, draw attention to the fact that some words rhyme or that some words start with the same sound.
- Reading and re-reading. Be prepared to re-read a book again and again. Each time you do this children gain something different from the story, the illustrations or the information. This also enables them to become accustomed to the words in the text as well as the book's structure.

2 ENABLING MULTILITERACIES

There is a growing acceptance that literacy and what is understood as 'literature' is evolving far beyond physical printed media. In the twenty-first century, literacy approaches for young children are increasingly embracing the idea that ICT can complement, and indeed enhance, the learning experience (Makin, Jones Diaz and McLachlan 2007). Examples of ICTs include computers, digital recorders and cameras, interactive whiteboards and the internet. When used for educational purposes, ICTs can enrich young learners' oral language and literacy development. This is still very much an evolving area and the potential inherent in applying ICT to early learning contexts has yet to be realised.

Historically, society has held the ability to communicate through print-based media to be the gold standard of literacy; however, a shift has occurred towards an acceptance of digital forms of literacy (Jewitt and Kress 2003). Currently Irish children are more likely to be exposed to communication devices and interactive situations that not only entail an exposure to print and numbers, but also include photographs, animations, film, hypertext, symbols, music, voice recognition, virtual and internet environments. We are witnessing an enormous cultural shift in communicative media from print media to digital media that marry the written word with visual images and sound effects. In early learning environments, the creation of e-books is one response to this trend. Simple e-books are useful vehicles for capturing the imaginations of both children and teachers by immersing them in new literacy experiences and creating an ideal marriage between reading and ICT. And the best part is that it is so easy to do! See the exercise below.

Student Exercise: Make Your Own E-book for Use in an Early Education Setting

A simple e-book can be made using common presentation software applications, such as Powerpoint or Impress/Sun StarOffice. Creating an e-book on a computer has many advantages over traditional children's literature as you can incorporate other types of media alongside text. Examples include music, voice recordings, sound effects, photos, images, animations, interactive graphics, video, interactive buttons and internet links. By using a mixture of these elements the story-telling experience or factual presentation is remarkably enhanced. Unlike traditional books, e-books can be modified over time. They can also be printed out and laminated so as to become part of your library. If you are sharing e-books with parents or colleagues, bear in mind that copyright laws apply to e-books if they are used outside an educational setting. See the Copyright Association of Ireland's website for further details.

How to make an e-book

1 Pick an age group and choose a suitable theme or topic.
2 Plan the e-book so that it has a beginning, middle and end. What happens in each section?
3 Write out the story. Try to use language that is suitable for the age group you have chosen.
4 Think about the visuals and match them with the text. Draw your own pictures, or get the children to draw the relevant pictures. You could also use photographs.
5 Include voice/sound recordings, videos related to your topic/theme, or interactive games that the children can play.
6 Have fun – it's contagious!

References

Anderson, N. (2006) *Elementary Children's Literature*. Boston: Pearson Education.

Ard, L.M. and Beverly, B. (2004) 'Preschool word learning during joint book reading: effect of adult questions', *Communication Disorders Quarterly* 26:1 17–28.

Clay, M. (1998) 'From acts to awareness in early literacy', *Childrenz Issues* 2:1, 12–20.

Colbert, J. (2006) 'New forms of old art: children's storytelling and ICT', *Early Childhood Folio* 10, 2–5.

Iyer, R. and Luke, C. (2009) 'Multimodal, Multiliteracies: Texts and Literacies for the 21st Century' in D.L. Pullen and D.R. Cole (eds) *Multiliteracies and Technology Enhanced Education: Social Practice and the Global Classroom*. Hershey, NY: Information Science Reference.

Jalongo, M.R. (1988) *Young Children and Picture Books: Literature from Infancy to Six*. Washington, DC: National Association for the Education of Young Children.

Jewitt, C. and Kress, G. (2003) *Multimodal Literacy*. New York: Peter Lang.

Justice, L.M., Kaderavek, J.N., Xitao, F., Sofka, A. and Hunt, A. (2009) 'Accelerating preschoolers' early literacy development through classroom-based teacher–child storybook reading and explicit print referencing', *Language, Speech and Hearing Services in Schools* 40:1, 67–85.

Lurie, A. (1990) *Don't Tell the Grown-Ups: Subversive Children's Literature*. Little, Brown: Boston.

Makin, L., Jones Diaz, C. and McLachlan, C. (2007) *Literacies in Childhood: Changing Views, Challenging Practice* (2nd edn). Sydney: MacLennan and Petty.

Mawson, B. (2002) 'Developing technology in early childhood settings', *Early Education* 29, 11–16.

Mortlock, A. (2005). 'The technologist–toddler and "intentionality"', *The First Years: Ng Tuatahi* 7:2, 30–2.

Mortlock, A., Higgins, A., Boniface, S., Easter, H., Gibbins, C.A., Hunter, S., Reid, A. and Tugaga, A. (2005) 'Technology and identity formation of infants and toddlers', *The First Years: Nga Tuatahi* 7:2, 32–4.

Rinaldi, C. (2001) *Making Learning Visible: Children as Individual and Group Learners*. Reggio Emilia: Reggio Children.

Soundy, C.S. (1997) 'Nurturing literacy with infants and toddlers in group settings', *Childhood Education* 73:3, 149–53.

Wright, S. (2007) 'Young children's meaning-making through drawing and "telling": analogies to filmic textual features', *Australian Journal of Early Childhood* 32:4, 37–48.

Useful Websites

Copyright Association of Ireland – www.cai.ie/index.htm

Children's storybooks online – www.magickeys.com/books/links.html

Interactive storybooks online – www.woodlands-junior.kent.sch.uk/.../onlinestory.htm

Literacy Center Education Network: Play and Learn English – www.literacycenter.net/lessonview_en.php

Literacy websites for pre-schoolers at the Literacy Web – www.literacy.uconn.edu/pksites.htm

ShelSilverstein.com: the 'Official Site for Kids' – www.shelsilverstein.com/indexSite.html

23

Numeracy through Play and Real-Life Experiences

Patsy Stafford

Learning Objectives

After studying this chapter the reader should have an understanding of:

- How young children develop numeracy.
- The mathematical learning that naturally occurs while young children are playing.
- How everyday routines and experiences can be used to provide mathematical opportunities for young children.
- The role of the practitioner in developing numeracy through play and everyday routines and experiences.

INTRODUCTION

The Department of Education and Skills defines numeracy as 'the ability to use mathematics to solve problems and meet the demands of day to day living' (DES 2011:8).

Young children experience a wide range of mathematical concepts in their everyday lives. They are told that their clothes are too short or their hair too long. They observe adults measuring out medicine or baby formula, and weighing vegetables at the supermarket. They have their feet measured for new shoes or their height measured against the wall. They proudly tell you that they are three and a half or that their birthday is in the summer. They see numbers all around them, on the doors of houses, buses, clocks, phones, calendars and birthday cards. From an early age they learn to ask for 'more' and to share with their siblings or friends. Mathematics is all around us and children engage with mathematical ideas from a very young age.

HOW DO YOUNG CHILDREN DEVELOP NUMERACY?

Aistear gives six principles of how children learn and develop:

1 holistic learning and development
2 active learning
3 play and hands-on experiences
4 relevant and meaningful experiences
5 communication and language
6 the learning environment (NCCA 2009:7).

These principles are based on a socio-cultural understanding of learning and are influenced by the theories of Piaget, Vygotsky, Bruner, Rogoff, Bronfenbrenner and others. These theories help us understand how best to help children develop numeracy by providing opportunities to play and explore, to learn from real-life experiences and interactions with others.

Of course mathematical learning does not occur at a given time of the day or in a certain area of an early childhood setting: it can occur at any time during the day and in any area of the indoor or outdoor environment, from everyday routines to rhymes and songs, to play areas and the outdoors, as well as in the home, neighbourhood and society at large.

Children come to early years settings with some mathematical understanding and knowledge, which practitioners can help to build on and develop. Play experiences in early years settings provide rich mathematical context that mirror everyday life situations. Engaging with mathematical concepts through play helps children to foster a positive attitude to mathematics, which has been recognised as one of the reasons why children succeed at mathematics.

> Research suggests that children's early mathematical experiences play an enormous role in the development of their understanding of mathematics, serve as a foundation for their cognitive development, and can predict mathematics success in the high school years. (Shaklee, O'Hara and Demarest 2008:1)

The US National Association for the Education of Young Children states: 'Play does not guarantee mathematical development, but it offers rich possibilities' (NAEYC/NCTM 2002:8).

What is the mathematical learning that naturally occurs while young children are playing?

> *Case Study*
> Ellen and Jane are playing in the home corner, where they are tending to a sick baby (doll).
> Jane (the doctor) puts a lollipop stick in the doll's mouth and pretends to take her temperature.
> *Jane:* She's burning, five-o-two. You have to give her two spoons of Calpol.
> *Ellen (mother):* What time?
> *Jane:* Five thirty o'clock.
> *Ellen:* Pretend that we have to call the ambulance.
> Ellen runs to the phone and starts pushing buttons.
> *Ellen:* Three, two, six. Please send an ambulance quick.

The children in the case study above are developing numeracy through play as they make sense of time, temperature, numbers and quantity concepts they have experienced in their everyday lives. Here are more ideas of how mathematical learning happens when children are engaged in play.

Table 23.1 Numeracy opportunities through play in early years settings

Type of play	Mathematical concept	Activity	Language	Resources
Pretend/socio-dramatic play	Matching	Setting table – one cup to one saucer at each chair	'One for you and one for me'	Furniture and equipment that reflect home, shop, doctor's office
	One-to-one correspondence	Buttoning dress on doll's clothes		Large hollow blocks for children to create props for their play (e.g. spaceship, aeroplane, etc.). Old clothes for dress-up, dolls and clothes, buggy, tape measures, telephones, clocks, calendars, calculators, etc.
	Classifying	Putting away resources at tidy-up time	'Put all the clothes in the basket'	

Type of play	Mathematical concept	Activity	Language	Resources
Pretend/socio-dramatic play	**Number**			As above
	Number recognition	Using telephone/calculator/cash register	Calling out telephone numbers	
	Writing numbers	Make sign to indicate opening time for shop/doctor's office		
	Sharing	Sharing out resources	'Do we have enough? How many do we have? How many do we need?'	
	Counting		'Do we have enough? How many do we have? How many do we need?'	
Pretend/socio-dramatic play	**Measures**			As above
	Length/height/width	Measuring with tape measure	'It's three long'	
	Money	Pricing goods in shop Paying for goods Serving in shop	'How much?' 'Five cent, please'	
	Time	Make sign to indicate opening time for shop/doctor's office	Five o'clock Morning Monday, Friday, tomorrow	

Type of play	Mathematical concept	Activity	Language	Resources
Pretend/socio-dramatic play	**Algebra** Patterns	Routines of everyday home life	'It's morning time: we need to get up and get dressed and get our breakfast'	As above
Pretend/socio-dramatic play	**Shape and space** Spatial awareness	Moving the buggy around the area Putting the cake in the oven, etc.	On the shelf, under the table, beside the cupboard	As above
	3-D shape	Making food for shop/home from playdough		
Block play	2-D shape 3-D shape Spatial awareness Size, order Length, height Fractions Symmetry Tessellations Counting Problem solving Classification/ sorting/ matching	Creating buildings, towns, environments Using creations for pretend play Putting away blocks Matching to shape on shelf	Tall, taller, tallest Long, longer, longest On top of, beside, over, under More Same, different, more, less, small, large 'We need two more of the long ones'	Wooden unit blocks and hollow blocks, vehicles, toy animals and people, fabric or bits of carpet to represent rivers, fields, etc.
Art centre	One-to-one correspondence	One brush for each paint pot	More, less	Art materials and junk for painting, drawing, 3-D construction, collage
	Area	Covering table with sheets of newspaper	'How many do we need to cover the table? Do we have enough?'	

Type of play	Mathematical concept	Activity	Language	Resources
Art centre	3-D shapes	Clay/playdough 3-D construction with junk		
	Spatial awareness	Discussion of construction	Cylinder, cube, cuboid, sphere	
	2-D shapes	Drawing, painting, collage	On top of, beside, over, under	
Manipulative play	Patterns	Threading beads in patterns	Red, blue, red, blue	Pattern blocks, beads and string, peg boards, button/key collections, junk collections, etc.
	Combine and tessellate shapes	Building patterns with pattern blocks		
	Fractions	Using pattern block shapes to create other shapes/fractional parts		
	2-D shapes Sorting Matching Counting	Classifying pattern blocks and collections and counting and matching sets		
Games	Counting One-to-one correspondence Number recognition Substituting Addition Counting all, counting on	Playing board games and card games	Numbers: 'I have to get two more' Number sequence: 'Three, four, five'	Board games and card games

Type of play	Mathematical concept	Activity	Language	Resources
Small world play	Comparing Ordering Length, height	Putting animals in order from biggest to smallest Putting animals beside each other to compare size	Big, bigger Tall, taller, tallest Long, longer, longest	Dinosaurs, farm animals, dolls' house, etc.
Water and sand play (indoors or outdoors)	Capacity	Filling one container with another	Full, empty	Water/sand table or large tub, beach toys, funnels, colander, tubing, pipes, plastic bottles and containers, spoons, scoops, etc.
	Time and speed	How long will it take for each container to empty?		
	Counting	How many cups will fill the bowl?	'Five cups fill this bowl'	
	Classifying and ordering	This bottle holds more than that one One spoon in each cup	Holds more than, holds less than	
	Conservation	Counting each spoon as it is poured		
Outdoor play	Counting One-to-one correspondence	Ball games, countdown for rocket	One, two, three Three, two, one, blast-off	Small balls, tricycles, dolls' buggies, natural materials, large hollow blocks for children to create props for their play, e.g. spaceship, aeroplane, etc.
	Spatial awareness	Moving the buggy/tricycles around the area, running around		
	Numeral writing	Chalk		
	Sorting, counting, ordering	Natural materials – leaves, stones, seeds		

How can everyday routines and experiences be used to provide mathematical opportunities for young children?

Just as children are exposed to mathematical concepts in their everyday lives with their families, they also encounter many mathematical concepts in the day-to-day routines and experiences of early years settings. Children have opportunities to put their mathematical knowledge to use in real-life situations similar to those found at home.

Case Study

Tom and Leah are helping set up snack time at their crèche. Tom first puts one cup at each place and then one plate. Leah puts two crackers on each plate. They then collect information on how many children want milk and how many children want water by checking the chart on the wall where the children in the group have put a picture of a glass of milk or a glass of water beside their photograph to indicate their choice. Tom and Leah carefully pour milk or water from a jug into each cup.

The children in the case study above are learning about quantity, one-to-one correspondence, data collection and capacity as they help to prepare snack time. Table 23.2 gives some more ideas for how everyday routines and experiences can be used to provide mathematical opportunities for young children.

Table 23.2 Numeracy opportunities in everyday routines and experiences in early years settings

Routines/experiences	Mathematical concepts	Language
Morning circle time		
Daily schedule	Time, sequencing	Snack time, playtime, later, etc.
Centres chart	Counting, one-to-one correspondence	Only five children are allowed in blocks
Lining up		
Going outside/coming in from outside, etc.	Positional numbers Spatial awareness Counting	1st, 2nd, 3rd In front of, behind, beside

Routines/experiences	Mathematical concepts	Language
Setting up art centre		
Covering table with newspaper	Area	Cover the whole area
Putting one brush in each paint pot	One-to-one correspondence	One brush for each pot
Wiping the table	Spatial awareness	Make sure to clean the edges
Literacy time		
Create sequencing photographs/ books/cards of the children's daily and weekly activities Encourage children to put the cards in sequence and tell about their day/week	Sequencing, patterns Time Days of the week	After lunch we have story time On Mondays we have dance Before, after, yesterday, today, tomorrow, next, days of the week
Story time		
Retelling stories, stories with mathematical ideas, e.g. *The Very Hungry Caterpillar* (Eric Carle), Goldilocks and the Three Bears	Sequencing, counting, patterns, matching, size, days of the week, etc.	First, then, next What happened next? Which chair belongs to Daddy Bear?
Transition times		
Number rhymes, songs, poems, mental maths, finger play, numbers in the environment	Counting, numeration, pattern, sequencing	Counting songs Let's see how many numbers we can find around the room
Mealtimes		
Having children involved in the preparation and cleaning up at mealtimes provides many opportunities for mathematical experiences	One-to-one correspondence, counting, capacity, matching, fractions	One cup at each place One spoon with one fork Two crackers each Quarter of an apple each Half a cup each

Routines/experiences	Mathematical concepts	Language
Cooking		
Cook using simple picture recipes with a small group of children using everyday cooking utensils	Quantity, numeration, counting, measuring, temperature, shape, etc.	Two cups of flour One more egg Full, empty Hot oven, cold fridge Square, circle, etc.
Clean-up time		
Clean-up time can be an opportunity to use classification and spatial awareness and rich mathematical language	Sorting/classifying	Put all the long block together
	Matching	Find the shelf with a picture of Lego on it
	Position words	Put it behind the easel

What is the role of the practitioner in developing numeracy through play and everyday routines and experiences?

- Create a play environment (indoor and outdoor) that is rich in mathematical experiences. Make sure to display numbers used in real-life situations, for example clocks, calendars, charts with recipes, signs with the number of children allowed in an area, etc.
- Be aware of the opportunities for children to develop numeracy through their play and everyday routines and experiences.
- Build on children's prior knowledge and experience and encourage children's natural interest in mathematics.
- Help children make connections between the mathematics they encounter in their everyday lives and the mathematics they encounter in the early years setting.
- Model the use of mathematical language and discussion of mathematical ideas. Use every opportunity to use mathematical language and to talk about your mathematical thinking, and encourage children to do the same.
- Observe, document/record, reflect on and use information about children's mathematical understanding to plan future play experiences that are mathematically rich.
- Communicate with parents and families about children's mathematical development through play and everyday routines and experiences. Give examples of how you use play and everyday routines and experiences to help develop numeracy, and encourage parents to provide similar opportunities in their homes. (Developed from Stafford 2011.)

CONCLUSION

Play and everyday routines and experiences can provide many opportunities for young children to investigate mathematical ideas, use mathematical vocabulary and reinforce existing mathematical knowledge. Engaging with mathematical concepts through play and everyday routines and experiences helps children to develop a positive attitude to mathematics, which is recognised in *The 2009 National Assessments of Mathematics and English Reading* research as one of the characteristics of children who succeed at mathematics (Eivers *et al.* 2010). Practitioners should be aware of and develop every opportunity that play and everyday routines and experiences offer for mathematical learning in the early years.

Key Learning Points
- Important mathematical learning happens when children play in carefully created mathematical environments.
- Young children learn best when experiences are relevant to their everyday lives.
- Practitioners need to be aware of the opportunities for mathematical learning that occur both indoors and outdoors in early learning settings.
- Practitioners need to model mathematical language and thinking for young children.

References

DES (Department of Education and Skills) (2011) *Literacy and Numeracy for Learning and Life – The National Strategy to Improve Literacy and Numeracy among Children and Young People 2011–2020*. Dublin: DES. Available at: www.education.ie/admin/servlet/blobservlet/lit_num_strat.pdf?language=EN&igstat=true

Eivers, E., Close, S., Shiel, G., Millar, D., Clerkin, A., Gilleece, L. and Kiniry, J. (2010) *The 2009 National Assessments of Mathematics and English Reading*. Dublin: Educational Research Centre.

NAEYC/NCTM (National Association for the Education of Young Children/National Council of Teachers of Mathematics) (2002) *Early Childhood Mathematics: Promoting Good Beginnings. A Joint Position Statement of NAEYC and NCTM*. Available at: www.naeyc.org/positionstatements/mathematics.

NCCA (National Council for Curriculum and Assessment) (2009) *Aistear: The Early Childhood Curriculum Framework*. Dublin: NCCA. Available at: www.ncca.ie/earlylearning.

Shaklee, H., O'Hara, P. and Demarest, D. (2008) *Early Math Skills – Building Blocks for the Future*. Idaho: University of Idaho. Available at: www.scribd.com/doc/34328921/Research-Brief-Early-Math-Skills-Building-Blocks-for-the-Future.

Stafford, P. (2011) 'Numeracy through play in infant classes – how play helps numeracy development', *In Touch*, March.

Further Reading

Copley, J.V. (ed.) (2000) *The Young Child and Mathematics*. Washington, DC: NAEYC.

Fleer, M. and Raban, B. (2007) *Early Childhood Literacy and Numeracy: Building Good Practice*. Australia: Department of Education, Employment and Workplace Relations. Available at: www.dest.gov.au/NR/rdonlyres/072400D9-3172-460A-910B-C190C3C21FDA/18862/ecl_buildinggoodpractice.pdf.

Montague-Smith, A. (2002) *Mathematics in Nursery Education*. London: David Fulton.

Tucker, K. (2005) *Mathematics through Play in the Early Years*. London: Paul Chapman.

Uppal, H. (2004) *Play Activities for the Early Years*. Bedfordshire: Brilliant Publications.

Worthington, M. and Carruthers, E. (2003) *Children's Mathematics: Making Marks, Making Meaning*. London: Paul Chapman.

Children's Books Rich in Mathematical Ideas

Allen, P. (1990) *Who Sank the Boat?* London: Picture Puffin Books.

— (1994) *Mr Archimedes' Bath*. London: Picture Puffin Books.

Beck, I. (2007) *Five Little Ducks*. London: Orchard Books.

Binder Scott, L. (2000) *Ten Little Fingers: 100 Number Rhymes for Young Children*. London: LDA.

Browne, E. (1994) *Handa's Surprise*. London: Walker Books.

— (2002) *Handa's Hen*. London: Walker Books.

Burningham, J. (2001) *Mr Grumpy's Outing*. London: Random House Children's Books.

Carle, E. (1970) *The Very Hungry Caterpillar*. New York: Philomel Books.

— (2009) *The Tiny Seed*. London: Simon & Schuster.

Donaldson, J. (2001) *Room on the Broom*. London: Macmillan Children's Books.

Donaldson, J. and Scheffler, A. (2003) *A Squash and a Squeeze*. London: Macmillan Children's Books.

Finch, M. (2001) *The Three Billy Goats Gruff*. Cambridge, MA: Barefoot Books.

Freeman, T. *Ten Little Monkeys Jumping on the Bed*. UK: Child's Play.

Hillman, J. (2003) *Goldilocks* Big Book. Kingscourt.

Hornsby, D. (2002) *The Three Little Pigs* Big Book. Kingscourt.

Hutchins, P. (1986) *The Doorbell Rang*. UK: Bodley Head.

— (1968) *Rosie's Walk*. New York: Simon & Schuster Children's Publishing.

— (1972) *Titch*. UK: Bodley Head.

Macgregor, H., Evans, M. and Sanderson, A. (2005) *Tom Thumb's Musical Maths: Developing Maths Skills with Simple Songs*. London: A&C Black.

Moore, I. (1990) *Six Dinner Sid*. London: Hodder Children's Books.

Umansky, K., Pierce, M., Sanderson, A. and Roberts, S. (2005) *Three Tapping Teddies: Musical Stories and Chants for the Very Young*. London: A&C Black.

Waddell, M. and Benson, P. (1994) *Owl Babies*. London: Walker Books.

Waddell, M. and Barton, J. (1992) *The Pig in the Pond*. London: Walker Books.
Waddell, M. and Firth, B. (2006) *Sleep Tight Little Bear*. London: Walker Books.

Useful Websites

National Association for the Education of Young Children – www.naeyc.org
National Council for Curriculum and Assessment – www.ncca.ie/earlylearning
National Council of Teachers of Mathematics – www.nctm.org
New Zealand Ministry of Education: Mathematics – www.nzmaths.co.nz

24

Learning Outdoors

Jan Pettersen

Learning Objectives

After studying this chapter the reader should:

- Understand the key issues in relation to young children and the outdoors from multidisciplinary perspectives including sociology, psychology, health, geography and early childhood education.
- Appreciate the historical developments which have influenced the use of the outdoors in early childhood education settings.
- Have an appreciation of children's right to play outdoors and be aware of the relevant legislation and policies in this regard.
- Be able to identify important features of early years outdoor environments.

INTRODUCTION

The outdoors is an environment that provides boundless opportunities for children to learn and develop, and it is a widely held view that early childhood services should provide an opportunity for outdoor experiences to take place (NCCA 2009; CECDE 2006; DoHC 2006). This chapter explores some of the key issues of outdoor play, and provides an introduction to the range of experiences that make the outdoors such an exceptional environment for young children.

Traditionally, the outdoor play areas of Irish early childhood services have been used to facilitate free play. The space is more generous and less restricted than indoor areas, which means that children's activity can occur more spontaneously.

The open air is also more conducive to higher noise levels and adult supervision is more relaxed than it is indoors (Bilton 2010), so children have the freedom to scream and run and they are encouraged to be more enthusiastic and energetic.

But outdoor play provides a lot more than free play and motor skill development in children. It also allows them to experience the world in which they live through sensory, hands-on interaction, and there is rich evidence in the literature (Morsdal 2010; Bilton 2010; Ericsson 2003; Stephenson 2003) to support the view that outdoor play can enhance both the psychological and emotional well-being of children as they expend energy, exercise their bodies, use their senses, learn, grow and develop.

PLANNING FOR OUTDOOR PLAY

In Ireland, outdoor activity in early childhood services is regulated by the pre-school (services) regulations (DoHC 2006), which states that pre-school services must ensure that 'Children in part-time or full day care services should have access to the outdoors on a daily basis, weather permitting.'

As most early years services have access to an outdoor area, it is critical that the use of this space is planned and laid out in a way that will stimulate the innate ability of the child to explore and apply itself in the space provided. In the same way as we can affect the development of the child and encourage particular interests in the child by carefully planning the indoor space, the outdoor area should also be planned and actively used in this way in order to achieve successful outcomes.

Issues that will affect the planning stage include access and size. Other issues to consider are fixed equipment; the weather, which can affect play; surfaces; seating; the look of the area; storage.

ACCESS

When discussing the issue of access, it is perhaps more important to focus on our ability to provide a high frequency of access. For example, children should have the opportunity to choose the outdoors as an activity in the same way as they choose to be at the water/sand table, in the dress-up area, or in the home corner.

SIZE

The outdoor area should be planned according to the space that is available, incorporating an appropriate amount of varied learning experiences. If the space is generous, the children should be able to access a variety of natural materials, equipment, surfaces, spatial variations and challenges.

OUTDOOR ENVIRONMENTS

White and Stoecklin (1998) maintain that natural outdoor environments have three qualities that are unique and appealing to children as play environments:

1 their unending diversity
2 the fact that they are not created by adults
3 their feeling of timelessness – the landscapes, trees and rivers described in fairy tales and myths still exist today.

Furthermore, they argue that children experience the natural environment differently from adults. While adults typically see nature as the background for what they are doing, children experience nature, not as the background for events, but rather as a stimulator of their senses and experiential component of their activities. So if we must strive to provide the child with experiences that are sensory rich (Morsdal 2010), outdoor play should provide a range of different environments. Natural habitats with plants, soil, rock, sand and water provide learning situations that are 'open-ended', allowing the child free range to manipulate, explore and experience in a way that is qualitatively different from their use of indoor play equipment. Children can use their senses to touch, smell, see, listen, and in some cases also taste what is around them. For example, they can build a trench in the sand and dirt, or a rock dam over a stream.

The varying levels of complexity that nature offers invites longer and more varied play because of the interactive properties found in nature: think of the beach with its sand, reeds, pebbles and water; the forest with its rough and smooth surfaces and variety of plants and trees; and the field with its multitude of grasses and flowers.

Depending on our motivation as adults, it not always possible to bring children to these natural habitats, so instead we try to create an outdoor space where children are presented with the opportunity to sample some or all of these.

For example, it is seen as best practice to incorporate a garden patch where plants can help to stimulate discovery, dramatic pretend play and imagination. White and Stoecklin (1998) states that plants speak to all of the senses, so it's not surprising that children are closely attuned to environments that contain vegetation. Plants, in a pleasant environment with a mixture of sun, shade, colour, texture, fragrance and softness, also engender a sense of peacefulness.

Natural settings offer opportunities for children to be able to explore wildlife at close hand. They can observe insects through special observation containers, which are readily available in any hobby or toy store. Or they can help build bird boxes and share the excitement of the busy life of the nesting bird family.

In addition to the above, the Irish Preschool Play Association (IPPA) recommends the following for consideration in outdoor areas:

- sand and water
- construction
- dens and private spaces
- area for wheeled vehicles
- grassed area/open space for ball games and picnics
- imaginative and pretend play area
- storage area. (IPPA 2006)

If the space is limited, it may be necessary to rotate the experiences available to the child by using removable nets, or bags filled with material and equipment that can be provided based on the interests of the child or what is appropriate at the time of the year. Alternatively, you may also need to consider the possibility of bringing the outdoors indoors.

Regardless of the space available, outdoor play experiences for children can be extended through incorporating the use of a 'reference area', which Morsdal (2010:8) defines as 'a specified nature area where children can develop learning and improve their sensory motor ability through varied and holistic activity'.

A reference area can be a site in a park, on a beach, on a hill or in a nearby field, where the teacher and children return at regular intervals to observe changes in nature. One important quality of the reference area is that it allows children to play in an area that provides interesting challenges and opportunities. This approach, which has been developed and spearheaded by the Scandinavian countries, is increasing in popularity throughout Europe because of the obvious benefits implied, such as the development of imagination and the sense of wonder. Wonder is important as it a motivator for lifelong learning (Bilton *et al.* 2005). However, it does perhaps constitute a conceptual change from the daily running of the service, as it does involve, for example, a different distribution of staff and a change in curricular focus.

LEARNING BENEFITS

At present in Ireland, it is the norm rather than the exception that in early years services both the indoors and the outdoors are carefully planned to be hazard free, and risk management strategies are implemented so that the setting is a safe place for young children to play and learn. However, as risk management is put in place, the naturally occurring opportunities for children to learn risk management first hand and to develop self-control and awareness are also removed. In a misconstrued attempt to do what is right for the child, society is developing in the child what the American psychologist Martin Seligman termed 'learned helplessness' (Peterson and Park 1998). Although the context is different from that of Seligman's research, the outcome is the same. Children are being instructed to abstain from environments that are in any way 'unpredictable' and challenging and with few exceptions they will retain this position throughout their lives.

However, two different factors are contributing to a change in this state of affairs. First, current literature (French and Murphy 2005; IPPA 2006; Bilton 2010) is helping to raise awareness of the important learning experiences associated with outdoor play. Second, as stated in the opening paragraph of this chapter, recent policy documents support the views upheld in the literature, ensuring that early education providers are becoming keener to implement holistic outdoor experiences, and a wider variety of experiences, in their curriculum.

Two highly desirable outcomes in early childhood education are to instil in the child body control and self-esteem. Through their interaction with the natural environment children can become aware of the hazards of certain actions such as climbing and jumping (Sandseter 2009). It is often the case that children learn valuable lessons through the mistakes they make, but through guidance by other expert children and supportive adults in the outdoors they can be allowed to persist and perfect their skills and to succeed.

When talking about sensory development in the context of outdoor play, Morsdal (2010) argues that we should particularly highlight the potential for sensorimotor development. The reason for this, he maintains, is that the outdoors can stimulate this kind of development to a much greater extent than any indoor environment can replicate.

Sensorimotor foundation skills rely on the interaction of sensation and movement, and the skill increases with the complexity of the environment that the child is exposed to and interacts with. For instance, a child who on a daily basis is exposed to a rugged or undulating surface will develop his/her balance and co-ordination to a greater extent than the child who always plays on a flat surface. Early childhood experts such as Kurt Morsdal and Thomas Moser (Sandseter 2009) strongly argue that this correlation means that children should be provided with access to areas that would challenge their current development of the following three primary senses.

1 The *tactile* sense: recognised by the organs of touch, which are found mainly in the skin. Natural environments provide boundless opportunity for the child to develop this sense through handling and exploring different kinds of material.
2 The *kinesthetic* sense: the awareness of movement or activity in muscles or joints.
3 The *vestibular* (inner ear) sense: relates to our ability to sense the position and location, and orientation and movement (balance) of the body and its parts.

In recent years, we have also become aware of the potential benefits that play and regular activity in the outdoors can have on a child's intellectual and cognitive development. This has been documented through the Bunkeflo Educational Project in Sweden (Ericsson 2003), a longitudinal research project whose research outcomes showed that children who grow up and develop in an environment rich in sensorimotor experiences, where they can climb, hang, crawl, balance, etc., achieve a higher level of disposition for learning than the control group. The researchers also documented that myelin is produced increasingly dramatically during activity and movement during the first eleven to twelve years of our lives. Myelin aids our cognitive responses through quick and accurate transmission of electrical currents carrying data from one nerve cell to the next.

As society becomes more geared towards a sustainable future, the outdoors can also provide endless prospects for exploration and discovery. Children are able to make connections between plants, animals, insects and the environment in general and see how they depend on each other in order to survive. Perhaps they will have the chance to see a bird building a nest or watching a garden grow. The possibilities for learning in an outdoor setting are only limited by our desire to explore.

Social development and interaction are key aspects of outdoor play in early childhood. Children learn to differentiate between behaviours that are appropriate outdoors and those that are appropriate indoors. Sharing, negotiating and communication are all important skills that children learn while playing with other children. In addition, children can begin to experience independence, as the outdoors will provide opportunities for them to co-operate and to start developing relationships that are built on trust. They can begin to assess who they are in relation to others and who they are independently. This is important in the development of friendships and it also helps the child to build confidence in their own abilities.

This is often done through engaging in what Stephenson (2003) refers to as 'risky play': activities that are not normally possible or even acceptable indoors. These kinds of experience often give young children what can be described as a thrill or a 'rush' in activities that would be seen as totally normal to a bigger child or an adult. The purpose of the activities is also to generate excitement and positive, shared experiences and the focus for the adult is always to teach the child: how to relate to these situations in a positive way; how the child should act to stay safe; and to highlight what could happen unless the child behaves appropriately in each situation. Examples of these experiences are:

- Play with 'great' *heights* – where the child can sense danger of injury from falling. Examples: climbing (in all forms), jumping from heights, hanging/dangling from heights, balancing from heights.
- Play with high *speed* – uncontrolled speed and pace that can lead to collision with something (or someone). Examples: bicycling at high speed, sledging (winter), sliding, running (uncontrollably), ball games such as soccer, tag rugby, Gaelic football and hurling.
- Play with dangerous *tools* – tools that can (potentially) lead to injuries. Examples: axe, saw, knife, hammer, ropes, pliers, screwdriver.
- Play near dangerous *elements* – where you can fall into or from something. Examples: lakes, the sea, fire pits, cliffs.
- *Rough-and-tumble* play – in which children can harm each other. Examples: wrestling, fighting, fencing with sticks, etc.
- Play in which children can *disappear or get lost*. Examples: where the children have a sense that they are without supervision and where there are no 'fences', e.g. in the woods.

It must again be emphasised that none of the above activities implies any actual risk to the child as they are carried out in a controlled environment and always supervised.

THE ADULT ROLE

In years past, outdoor play was often seen as a time when children engaged in free play (Bilton *et al.* 2005) and therefore the adults would regard it as a period when they could catch up with each other, relax and have a chat. However, the reality is of course that the role of the adult in outdoor play is no less important than their role in indoor activities in terms of facilitating a meaningful learning process.

If the adult's main role is that of facilitator, he or she should seek to provide a climate of encouragement for the children, who are given the opportunity to make hypotheses and take risks on their learning paths. This does not mean giving children complete free rein but rather creating an ordered environment in which children are free to explore and learn through purposeful, well-planned play.

The early years practitioner must maintain high expectations for children's learning and find ways of demonstrating to them that they take the work of children seriously, and we know that there are strong links between adult expectations and children's aspirations and performance (Morsdal 2010; Sandseter 2009). Children very quickly sense what adults hold to be of real importance. Talking *with* children rather than *to* them about their work is fundamental and it is important that adults engage with children throughout the activity, and avoid abruptly interrupting with stern commands if they mistakenly perceive that the activity is getting out of hand.

One best practice strategy in this regard comes from the Reggio Emilia approach to early education (Edwards, Gandini and Foreman 1998), where it is the belief that being confused is a fundamental part of the learning process. The practitioner may therefore choose, when they feel it is appropriate, to allow children to go down the wrong path and to let them make 'mistakes' without intervening. Some educators find this to be an unnecessarily lengthy process and others feel it may even be unfair to the children. We must reflect upon how such ideas correspond with our own way of thinking.

References

Apter, M.J. (1992) *The Dangerous Edge: The Psychology of Exitement*. New York: Free Press/Macmillan.

Bilton, H. (2010) *Outdoor Learning in the Early Years: Management and Innovation*. Oxon, UK: Routledge.

Bilton, H., James, K., Wilson, A. and Woonton, M. (2005) *Learning Outdoors: Improving the Quality of Young Children's Play Outdoors*. Oxon, UK: David Fulton.

CECDE (Centre for Early Childhood Development and Education) (2006) *Síolta: The National Quality Framework for Early Childhood Education*. Dublin: CECDE.

DoHC (Department of Health and Children) (2006) *Child Care (Pre-School Services) Regulations*. Dublin: DoHC.

Edwards, C., Gandini, L. and Foreman, G. (eds) (1998) *The Hundred Languages of Children* (2nd edn). New York: Ablex.

Ericsson, I. (2003) *Motorik, Koncentrationsförmåga och Skolprestationer*, PhD thesis, Malmö Medical University, Sweden.

French, G. and Murphy, P. (2005) *Once in a Lifetime: Early Childhood Education from Birth to Three*. Dublin: Barnardos.

Harriman, H. (2008) *The Outdoor Classroom: A Place to Learn*. UK: Red Robin Books.

IPPA (Irish Preschool Play Association) (2006) *Nurture through Nature; Promoting Outdoor Play for Young Children*. Dublin: IPPA.

Karlsson, M. (2002) *Does Exercise Reduce the Burden of Fractures? A Review*. Malmö: Acta.

Knight, S. (2009) *Forest Schools and Outdoor Learning in the Early Years*. UK: Sage.

Morsdal, K. (2010) *Referanseområder som vi har etablert og bruker*. Bodø, Norway: Lille Frøbel <http://lillefrobel.barnehage.no/> accessed 20 May 2011.

NCCA (National Council for Curriculum and Assessment) (2009) *Aistear: The Early Childhood Curriculum Framework*. Dublin: NCCA.

Peterson, C. and Park, C. (1998) 'Learned Helplessness and Explanatory Style' in D.F. Barone, M. Hersen and V.B. VanHasselt (eds), *Advanced Personality*. New York: Plenum Press, pp. 287–308.

Sandseter, E.B.H. (2009) 'Affordances for risky play in preschool: the importance of features in the play environment', *Early Childhood Education Journal* 36:5, 439–46.

Stephenson, A. (2003) 'Physical risk-taking: dangerous or endangered?', *Early Years* 23:1, 35–43.

White, R. and Stoecklin, V. (1998) *Children's Outdoor Play and Learning Environments: Returning to Nature* <www.childrennatureandyou.org/Children's%20Outdoor%20Play%20White%20&%20Stoecklin.pdf> accessed 1 May 2011.

25

Working with Parents in Early Years Services

Anne Fitzpatrick

Learning Objectives

After studying this chapter the reader will be able to:

- Discuss the concept of partnership with parents in early years services.
- Explain why partnership with parents in early years services is important.
- Outline the Irish legal and policy context for partnership in early years services.
- Demonstrate a range of practical ways to promote partnership.
- Evaluate the benefits and challenges of working in partnership with parents.

INTRODUCTION

The case for partnership between parents and early educators is now well established and a partnership approach is widely agreed to ensure best outcomes for children (Wheeler and Connor 2009). The case for partnership is based on the following factors:

- Parents have a right and a desire to play a key role in their child's life in the early childhood education and care (ECEC) service.
- Research evidence shows that the best outcomes for children are achieved when parents and educators work in partnership.

PARENTS' RIGHT AND DESIRE TO PLAY A KEY ROLE

A child's most important relationship is the one the child has with its parents ('parent' denotes anyone who is the primary carer of a child) (NCCA 2009). Belonging to a family is critically important to a child's development and well-being. Parents are experts on their own child while educators are experts on children's learning and development. The child benefits when both sets of experts work together.

Research has shown that most parents want to be listened to and have their views taken into account by educators (Moran, Ghate and van der Merwe 2004; Quinton 2004; Tunstill *et al.* 2005).

A UK study in 2007 found that 67 per cent of parents surveyed wanted to be more involved in the life of their child in the ECEC service. Parents living with socio-economic disadvantage felt strongly about having more involvement (Peters *et al.* 2007). At Pen Green, an early education centre of excellence in the UK that has for many years focused on working with parents, 84 per cent of parents were involved in their children's learning when a variety of types and levels of involvement were offered (Whalley and the Pen Green Centre Team 2001).

The Reggio Emilia approach believes that parents entrust their children to the public institution, so it strongly supports the right of parents to participate actively in the care and development of their children in ECEC services.

The educator should begin with the firm belief that parents are interested in the development and progress of their own children.

RESEARCH EVIDENCE ON BEST OUTCOMES FOR CHILDREN

Parents are the child's first and most influential educators. The learning environment that parents provide, which begins before birth, has a lasting impact on emotional, social and intellectual development. Evidence from research on the development of the baby's brain shows that early childhood experiences can positively or negatively affect how the brain develops (Perry 2002).

Children experiencing socio-economic disadvantage show less ability at 22 months in language and cognitive development and this link continues over time (Feinstein 1999). However, it is possible both to involve parents living with disadvantage in their child's learning and to support them in enhancing the home learning environment (Seaman *et al.* 2006; Evangelou *et al.* 2008).

Research from the Effective Provision of Pre-School Education (EPPE) study in the UK found that for all children, the quality of the home learning environment is more important for intellectual and social development than parental occupation, education or income. A key conclusion of the study was that what parents do is more important than who parents are. Parents who regularly undertake activities that 'stretch a child's mind' positively impact on the child's development. Activities found to be particularly useful include reading with children, going to the library, singing songs and rhymes, drawing and painting, facilitating play with friends and playing with numbers and letters (Siraj-Blatchford 2011). The EPPE research confirmed that the quality of the home learning environment provided by parents can act as a significant modifying factor, giving children an advantage in both social and intellectual development (Sylva *et al.* 2004; Evangelou *et al.* 2005; Siraj-Blatchford 2011).

Therefore, when parents and educators work in partnership in early years services, children's long-term development and learning can be enhanced (Schweinhart,

Barnes and Weikart 1993; Desforges 2003; Sammons *et al.* 2008; Evangelou and Sylva 2003; Lopez, Kreider and Caspe 2004; Siraj-Blatchford 2011).

WHAT IS PARTNERSHIP WITH PARENTS?

The term 'partnership with parents' is often used interchangeably with the term 'parental involvement' when in fact they are quite different. Early years services have a long and respected tradition of parental involvement. Parental involvement might include activities ranging from a conversation at going-home time, fundraising or parents helping out in the service to participation in the management of the service. Partnership goes far beyond involvement, though some types of involvement may also constitute elements of partnership.

The key characteristics of partnership are:

- mutual respect and trust
- commitment to working together
- a common goal
- complementary expertise
- appreciation of different perspectives
- open communication
- willingness to negotiate
- power-sharing and joint decision-making.

'Partnership involves parents, families and educators *working together* to benefit children. Each *recognises, respects and values* what the other does and says. Partnership involves *responsibility* on both sides' (NCCA 2009:7, emphasis in original).

WHY WORK WITH PARENTS?

In this section, the rationale for adopting a partnership approach will be reviewed under the following headings: Irish legal and policy context; child protection; best practice guidelines and early education curricula; and views of early education theorists.

IRISH LEGAL AND POLICY CONTEXT

The Irish state recognises the primary role that parents play in their children's education, which flows from the Constitution. The United Nations Convention on the Rights of the Child, which Ireland ratified in 1992, and more recent public policy (e.g. Síolta and Aistear) have also reflected this right. Article 42.1 of the Irish Constitution states that:

[The] primary and natural educator of the child is the Family and [the Constitution] guarantees to respect the inalienable right and duty of parents to provide, according to their means, for the religious and moral, intellectual, physical and social education of their children. (Bunreacht na hÉireann 1937)

The right and duty of parents to provide for their child's education confers on them the right to active participation with the educator.

Article 18 of the UN Convention on the Rights of the Child (1989) provides that:

State parties shall render appropriate assistance to parents and legal guardians in the performance of their childrearing responsibilities.

Síolta, the National Quality Framework for Early Childhood Education, identifies parents as the primary educators of the child, and that they have a pre-eminent role in promoting the child's well-being, learning and development. Standard 3 states:

Valuing and involving parents and families requires a proactive partnership approach evidenced by a range of clearly stated, accessible and implemented processes, policies and procedures. (CECDE 2006)

Aistear, the Early Childhood Curriculum Framework, emphasises the role of parents in its twelve principles of early learning and development. The following principles are particularly important in relation to partnership with parents:

- the child's uniqueness
- equality and diversity
- relationships
- parents, family and community.

The Guidelines for Good Practice focus on four ways in which parents and practitioners can work together.

1 Supporting learning and development.
2 Sharing information.
3 Contributing to the setting.
4 Making decisions and advocating different approaches and courses of action. (NCCA, 2009)

CHILD PROTECTION

Practitioners in ECEC services play a key role in the prevention of child abuse through their work in promoting children's development and supporting parents. *Children First*, the national guidelines for children's protection and welfare, states that partnership with parents is a principle of best practice in child protection. Good practice in preventive work with parents would include building respectful and trusting relationships, developing honest and regular two-way communication, focusing on families' strengths and collaborating with other professionals in the community. *Children First* highlights the importance of early intervention and support in promoting the welfare of children and families and as a way of minimising risk (DCYA 2011).

BEST PRACTICE GUIDELINES AND EARLY EDUCATION CURRICULA

Many international guidelines for best practice and curricula emphasise the role of partnership as an indicator of quality in early years services. These include, for example:

- Anti-bias/discriminatory practice guidelines: Derman-Sparks 1989; OMC 2006.
- Codes of ethics for early educators: NAEYC 2005.
- Early education curricula and programmes recognised internationally: HighScope, Te Whariki, Reggio Emilia, Pen Green.

VIEWS OF EARLY EDUCATION THEORISTS

Influential theorists in the history of early education have recognised the important role of parents in young children's learning.

- *Comenius* (1592–1670), who influenced the formulation of the general theory of education, spoke about the school of the mother's lap.
- *Pestalozzi* (1747–1827) believed that for children the teaching of their parents will always be core and that the teacher's role is to provide a decent shell around the core.
- *Montessori* (1869–1952) emphasised the importance of the mother's role before the child goes to school.
- *Froebel* (1782–1852) believed that the mother is the child's first educator.
- *Margaret McMillan* (1860–1931) educated mothers in her London nurseries so that they could take control of early years services and their lives. She encouraged every nursery to have its mothers' club to empower mothers both as women and as parents.
- *Vygotsky* (1896–1934), in his development of socio-cultural theory, identified the important role more knowledgeable others (including parents) play in supporting and scaffolding children's learning.
- *Bronfenbrenner* (1917–2005) explained different spheres of influence on the child's life and elevated the role of parents through his belief that the parent/child/educator triangle builds the strongest structure and that home and school should be brought together.

WHO BENEFITS WHEN ECEC PRACTITIONERS AND PARENTS WORK IN PARTNERSHIP?

CHILDREN

- Feel more secure in the service. A trusting relationship with the educator and a safe emotional environment are essential for children's development and learning.
- Feel respected when their family's values, language, culture, diet and traditions are reflected in the service.
- Achieve greater success in their social, emotional and cognitive development.
- Learn from modelling how to develop respectful relationships with other people.
- Have a more meaningful and appropriate experience when there is continuity between home and service.

PARENTS

- Feel more comfortable in the service through knowing educators better.
- Feel valued and respected.
- Will know their child better and have access to information/advice about their child's interests/development.
- Feel confident about contributing to their child's development and learning, both in the service and at home.
- May confide in the educator if they are experiencing difficulties.
- May have higher aspirations for their child and become involved in their later education.
- May get to know other parents better, which may lead to developing support networks.

ECEC PRACTITIONERS

- Can enhance children's sense of emotional well-being, identity and belonging in the service by building on their knowledge of each child's family.
- Can draw on this knowledge in planning for children's learning.
- Can support the parents in their overall parenting role.
- Can benefit from parents' expertise and skills.
- Feel parents value them more in their role.
- Find their roles more varied and interesting.

WHAT IS NEEDED TO DEVELOP A PARTNERSHIP APPROACH?

Partnership will be evident in ECEC services where there is mutual respect between practitioners and parents, where connecting with parents is a priority and where specific strategies to promote partnership are implemented. To develop a partnership approach, the ECEC practitioner should have:

- respect for parents' right to be involved in their children's lives in the ECEC service
- a belief that all families have strengths and want to do the best for their children
- positive, non-judgemental attitudes to parents
- knowledge about each family's values, structures and traditions
- knowledge of the research evidence on the effectiveness of partnership
- good communication skills, including good listening, negotiation and conflict-resolution skills
- knowledge of a wide range of strategies to promote partnership.

GUIDELINES FOR GOOD PRACTICE IN BUILDING PARTNERSHIPS BETWEEN PARENTS AND ECEC PRACTITIONERS

MAKE ALL FAMILIES FEEL WELCOME

- Talk to, listen to and get to know parents.
- Offer an induction programme (visit to centre, home visit, settling-in plan).
- Establish an open-door policy.
- Ensure that the building is accessible for all families.
- Develop good signage for the building.
- Develop a diverse family-friendly environment (adult furniture; tea/coffee facilities; family/language wall; parents' noticeboard; multilingual documentation; pictures and other resources promoting positive views of disability and ethnic, cultural, family and social diversity; staff photos and job titles; family room).
- Arrange social events to help parents develop support networks with other parents and with educators.
- Undertake an audit of the physical environment from a family viewpoint (consider mothers, fathers, grandparents, families from different cultures).

Student Exercise
Arising from the ideas above, how could you make families feel more 'at home' in your service?

PROMOTE RESPECTFUL, EQUAL RELATIONSHIPS BETWEEN PARENTS AND ECEC PRACTITIONERS

- Make building trust and confidence core values and practices in all work with parents.
- Consider a key worker system.
- Review the balance of power between parents and educators.

- Ensure that parents are central in decision-making about their child.
- Encourage parents to act as advocates for their child.

> **Student Exercise**
> Evie is 20 years old and mother to Jamie, 18 months, who attends your service. Evie is in her second year at college and she and Jamie live in a one-bedroom apartment. Consider the challenges for Evie and how the early years service might support her and Jamie.

ESTABLISH AND COMMUNICATE SERVICE POLICIES AND PROCEDURES

- Develop an accessible 'partnership with parents' policy in consultation with all stakeholders (clear language, in children's home language).
- Make the educational aims of the service accessible to parents.
- Develop a parents' handbook (include mission statement, overview of policies, child protection policy, curriculum offered, information on staff qualifications, complaints procedures, opening times, payment of fees).
- Set up a parents' committee or ensure parent representation on any existing committees.

> **Student Exercise**
> Plan a parents' handbook for an ECEC service.

DEVELOP GOOD PRACTICE IN TWO-WAY COMMUNICATIONS

- Promote regular, informal opportunities for parents to talk to educators (consider the needs of parents working full-time).
- Make a regular time for educators to be available to talk to parents.
- Offer written, oral and visual communication opportunities (phone, text, email, daily notebook, photos).
- Share information with parents (e.g. child and family information forms; newsletters; noticeboards; information sessions; workshops; websites; open mornings; home visits; special events).
- Provide a crèche facility to enable parents to attend meetings and events.

> **Student Exercises**
> 1 Consider all of the above issues for parents who do not live together or are separated/divorced.
> 2 Plan a monthly newsletter for parents.

COMMUNICATE ABOUT CHILDREN'S LEARNING

- Share regular two-way observations about the child's learning (e.g. interactive family diary/observations; reviewing children's records; examples of children's work; photos; video footage; curriculum workshops).
- Parent and educator jointly plan for and support the child's learning (see Aistear's 'Building partnerships between Parents and Educators' guidelines for working with parents to support learning and development).
- Use coming and going times to exchange information about children's development.
- Invite parents to participate in the daily life of the service and share in learning activities (read a story; talk about their home culture; demonstrate a skill; play a game; go on an outing; help with cooking; run a book/toy library).
- Support learning in the home through sharing ideas with parents, loaning materials, home visits.

Student Exercise

Plan a 'Learning Story' for one child in your service and outline how you would present the Learning Story to the parent(s).

RESPECT DIVERSITY

- Acknowledge and celebrate difference as an underpinning principle of good practice.
- Develop an understanding of the culture, value systems, child-rearing practices, religion, abilities, disabilities and additional educational needs of the families you serve.
- Ask parents how they would like their culture to be depicted and celebrated.
- Consider the extra challenges of the settling-in process.

Student Exercise

Develop a profile of a family in your service. Consider their values and beliefs, culture, family structure, living accommodation, language and communication style, childcare routines, types of ability/disability, views on curriculum, child management, food preferences.

MAKE FATHERS FEEL WELCOME

- Explore educators' attitudes to father involvement.
- Ensure that the environment is father-friendly.
- Consult with fathers about how they would like to be involved (consider also outings, sport, ICT, practical skills, fathers-only sessions).
- Support fathers in their involvement.

- Arrange flexible timings to suit work schedules.
- Consider non-resident fathers.

Student Exercise
Plan a 'Dads' Week' for your service.

OFFER A VARIETY OF TYPES AND LEVELS OF INVOLVEMENT TO PARENTS

- Parents can contribute to the work of the service without being present in the service (parents might make a Storysack (see www.storysack.com); develop a newsletter/website; fundraise; suggest ideas for activities or outings).
- Parents could become involved in the management of the service (policy development; recruitment of staff).
- Parents could give feedback on their satisfaction with service.
- Practitioner might offer links to other agencies and services (parent and toddler groups; counselling services; adult education classes; parent education courses).

Student Exercise
What opportunities for involvement exist in your service?
Prepare a presentation you will give to parents outlining the possibilities for becoming involved in their child's service.

CHALLENGES OF PARTNERSHIP WITH PARENTS

Why might partnership be difficult for educators and parents?

Educators may experience some of the following:

- Negative attitudes towards parents: not valuing parents' views; resistant attitudes to partnership with parents.
- Lack of training/confidence for working with all or some parents, e.g. fathers, vulnerable or 'different' parents.
- Lack of time and/or funding to work with parents.
- Difficulty in balancing parents' and children's needs and rights.
- Lack of a shared language (literally and metaphorically).
- Lack of time to develop relationships due to constant turnover of children.

Parents may experience some of the above issues and others, such as:

- Negative memories of the education system.
- Not feeling welcome.
- Lack of knowledge/confidence of possible role.

- Fear of being judged.
- Suspicion of professionals.
- Lack of childcare for other children.
- Cost of travel and distance to travel.
- Other personal and social pressures.

CONCLUSION

Research has shown that parents and home play a powerful role in young children's learning and development. This role should be understood, respected and supported by ECEC practitioners. Furthermore, parents have a right to be fully involved in all aspects of their child's life in an early years service. Early years services that develop strong partnerships with parents promote the best long-term outcomes for every child.

Key Learning Points

- Parents and home are the most powerful influence on children's learning and development.
- Parents have a right to active involvement in their child's life in the service.
- When parents and educators work in partnership in early years services, children's long-term development and learning is enhanced.
- Partnership works best when built on respectful relationships, clear communication and commitment to power-sharing between educators and parents.
- Parents should be offered a choice about types and levels of involvement.

References

Bunreacht na hÉireann (1937). Dublin: Stationery Office.

Castagnetti, M., Rubizzi, L. and Vecchi, V. (eds) (1995) *A Journey into the Rights of Children*, Unheard Voice of Children series. Reggio Emilia: Reggio Children.

CECDE (Centre for Early Childhood Development and Education) (2006) *Síolta: The National Quality Framework for Early Childhood Education*. Dublin: CECDE.

Derman-Sparks, L. and ABC Task Force (1989) *Anti-Bias Curriculum: Tools for Empowering Young Children*. Washington, DC: NAEYC.

Desforges, C., with Abouchaar, A. (2003) *The Impact of Parental Involvement, Parental Support and Family Education on Pupils' Achievements and Adjustment: A Literature Review*, Research Report 433. London: DfES.

DCYA (Department of Children and Youth Affairs) (2011) *Children First: National Guidelines for the Protection and Welfare of Children*. Dublin: Stationery Office.

Evangelou, M., Brookes, G., Smith, S., Jennings, D. and Roberts, F. (2005) *The Birth to School Study: A Longitudinal Evaluation of the Peers Early Education Partnership (PEEP) 1998–2005*, Research Report SSU/2005/FR/017) London: DfES.

Evangelou, M. and Sylva, K. (2003) *The Effects of the Peers Early Education Partnership (PEEP) on Children's Developmental Progress*, Research Brief No. RB489. London: DfES.

Evangelou, M., Sylva, K., Edwards, A. and Smith, T. (2008) *Supporting Parents in Promoting Early Learning. The Evaluation of the Early Learning Partnership Project.* London: DCSF.

Feinstein, L. (1999) *Pre-School Inequality? British Children in the 1970 Cohort.* London: Centre for Economic Performance, University College London.

Lopez, M.E., Kreider, H. and Caspe, M. (2004) 'Co-constructing family involvement', *Evaluation Exchange* X:4, 2–3.

Moran, P., Ghate, D. and van der Merwe, A. (2004) *What Works in Parenting Support? A Review of the International Evidence.* Research Report 574. London: DfES.

NAEYC (National Association for the Education of Young Children) (2005) *Code of Ethics.* NAEYC.

NCCA (National Council for Curriculum and Assessment) (2009) *Aistear: The Early Childhood Curriculum Framework.* Dublin: NCCA.

OMC (Office of the Minister for Children) (2006) *Diversity and Equality Guidelines for Childcare Providers.* Dublin: OMC.

Perry, B.D. (2002) 'Childhood experience and the expression of genetic potential: what childhood neglect tells us about nature and nurture', *Brain and Mind* 3, 79–100.

Peters, M., Seeds, K., Goldstein, A. and Coleman, N. (2007) *Parental Involvement in Children's Education Survey.* Research Report 034. London: DCSF.

Quinton, D. (2004) *Supporting Parents: Messages from Research.* London: Jessica Kingsley.

Sammons, P., Sylva, K., Melhuish, E., Siraj-Blatchford, I., Taggart, B., Barreau, S. and Grabbe, Y. (2008) *The Influence of School and Teaching Quality in Children's Progress in Primary School. Effective Pre-School and Primary Education 3–11 (EPPE 3–11).* London: Institute of Education, University of London/DCSF.

Schweinhart, L.J., Barnes, H.V. and Weikart, D.P. (1993) *Significant Benefits: The High/Scope Perry Preschool Study through Age 27*, Monographs of the High/Scope Educational Research Foundation, 10. Ypsilanti: High/Scope Press.

Seaman, P., Turner, K., Hill, M., Stafford, A. and Walker, M. (2006) *Parenting and Children's Resilience in Disadvantaged Communities.* London: National Children's Bureau.

Siraj-Blatchford, I. (2011) 'The Power of Pre-school: Lessons from Research on the Long-Term Impact of Quality Pre-school Provision', DIT/CSER seminar, DIT, Mountjoy Square, Dublin, 8 April.

Sylva, K., Melhuish, E.C., Sammons, P., Siraj-Blatchford, I. and Taggart, B. (2004) *The Effective Provision of Pre-School Education (EPPE) Project: Final Report.* London: DfES/Institute of Education, University of London.

Tunstill, J., Meadows, P., Allknock, D., Akhurst, S. and Garbers, C. (2005) *Implementing Sure Start Local Programmes: An Integrated Overview of the First Four Years*, NESS Summary SF010. London: DfES.

UN (United Nations) (1989) *Convention on the Rights of the Child*. Geneva: UN.

Whalley, M. and the Pen Green Centre Team (2001) *Involving Parents in their Children's Learning*. London: Paul Chapman.

Wheeler, H. and Connor, J. (2009) *Parents, Early Years and Learning (PEAL). Parents as Partners in the Early Years Foundation Stage. Principles into Practice*. London: National Children's Bureau.

Further Reading

Family and Parenting Institute (2007) *Listening to Parents: A Short Guide*. London: FPI.

Keyser, J. (2006) *From Parents to Partners. Building a Family-Centred Early Childhood Program*. St Paul, MN: Redleaf Press.

McDermott, M. (2010) *Partners in Learning: A Parent's Guide to Partnership in Childcare*. Dublin: Barnardos.

McNaughton, G. and Hughes, P. (2011) *Parents and Professionals in Early Childhood Settings*. Maidenhead: Open University Press.

Whalley, M. (2007) *Involving Parents in their Children's Learning* (2nd edn). London: Paul Chapman.

Useful Websites

Aistear – www.ncca.ie

Effective Provision of Pre-School Education (EPPE) Project – www.eppe.ioe.ac.uk

Family and Parenting Institute (UK) – www.familyandparenting.org

Fatherhood Institute – www.fatherhoodinstitute.org

Office of the Minister of Children and Youth Affairs – www.omcya.ie

Parents, Early Years and Learning (PEAL) – www.peal.org.uk

Síolta – www.cecde.ie

PART 4
STRUCTURES AND ISSUES

26

Why Working with Diversity and Equality in Early Childhood Education and Care Matters

Colette Murray

Learning Objectives

After studying this chapter the reader should be able to:

- Understand equality and diversity concepts and their relationship to early childhood education and care (ECEC) and society.
- Recognise that children are aware of diversity and are affected by societal prejudice and discrimination.
- Identify different approaches to diversity education.
- Understand the benefits of personal reflection on assumptions and values.
- Recognise the potential in using a transformative approach in ECEC.

INTRODUCTION

This chapter examines how to work from a diversity and equality perspective in ECEC in the Irish context. The perspective outlined here rests on the belief that the professional in the ECEC sector can work with children and their families to create positive change within communities.

By embracing a diversity and equality perspective, the ECEC sector can:

- address issues of social justice, recognising the influence of the political, social, cultural and economic context
- empower individuals to have pride in and transform their lives
- support adults and children to recognise and confront injustice and to resist oppressive ways
- understand the relationship between racism and oppression and child development.

WHAT DO WE MEAN BY EQUALITY AND DIVERSITY?

Concepts such as diversity and equality are complex and their meanings vary depending on the social conditions and academic or political understandings at a given time. At the same time, our beliefs about diversity and equality do matter: they inform our approach to working with young children and their families. The perspectives on equality and diversity outlined below reflect some of the views of those advocating for social and economic justice in Ireland.

DIVERSITY

Diversity considers the kaleidoscopic nature of a society. Diversity is about all the ways in which people differ and the different ways in which they live their lives as individuals, within groups and as part of a wider social group. For example, a person can be classified – or classify themselves – by their social class, gender, disability, family structure, sexuality (e.g. lesbian, gay, bisexual, transgender (LGBT)), or family status (e.g. lone parent). They can be seen – or see themselves – as part of a minority group, a minority ethnic group (including Roma and Travellers), or as part of the majority/dominant group.

Differences are a natural part of life. No two people are the same and this means that many different elements make up the communities you belong to, and in which you work, learn and live. Diversity is something which should be recognised, accepted and respected and many elements can be celebrated. There is a 'shadow side' to diversity: stereotyping, prejudice, discrimination and racism, sexism, classism, etc. Diversity has a partner: equality.

EQUALITY

Equality is closely linked to recognising, accepting and respecting diversity and to supporting individual and group needs. Inequalities can be instigated by an individual or through policies at an institutional level. Equality can be defined in terms of access, participation or outcomes for all children and their families. Equality of participation is particularly relevant when working with children and parents. This means that the practitioner actively acknowledges and respects the child in the ECEC setting and also works in solidarity with the family. Equality is *not* about treating people the same: it is about meeting needs in different ways. Equality is also not about political correctness. It is about making sure that people are treated without discrimination and that power relations are addressed.

Equality of care is an important component of equality and is a basic human need. Equality of care means that each person can feel a basic sense of value, importance and belonging – of being appreciated and cared for. The components of equality should support all people to live lives of dignity and worth (Baker *et al.* 2004).

HISTORICAL, POLITICAL, CULTURAL, ECONOMIC AND AFFECTIVE CONTEXT

Societies are made up of political, economic, cultural and affective systems which sustain inequality or promote equality. Beliefs and assumptions about these systems influence, among others, government decisions which impinge on the ECEC system and, in consequence, on young children. For example:

- *Political:* Decisions made to prioritise children in ECEC are made at government level.
- *Economic:* Providing quality services for children and families is linked to the allocation of funding.
- *Cultural:* Who is recognised, respected and made visible in ECEC training programmes and decisions about curriculum development made at state level.
- *Affective:* How are carers and care valued in society?

This short list shows how the systems are interlinked. It is useful to have an awareness of the effects of societal structures and systems that affect the daily lives of families. This knowledge helps build empathy, solidarity and mindfulness around the needs of both minority and majority children who enter an ECEC service.

There is a tendency to think of Ireland as having only recently become demographically and culturally diverse, with some considering diversity to be a new phenomenon in our country. In fact, coming to terms with diversity has been an ongoing challenge since Irish independence (Crowley 2006), not least in terms of developing appropriate and effective social policies for children (Deegan, Devine and Lodge 2004; Lodge and Lynch 2004).

Ireland has tended to approach policy development from a homogeneous point of view: 'one size fits all'. Addressing equality and diversity is a relatively recent occurrence in the national and international ECEC contexts (OECD 2006; NESF 2005; CECDE 2006).

For example, only recently have the concepts of equality and diversity been included in any substantive way in Irish ECEC policy documents. The principles of Aistear and Síolta recognise that equality is about both *individual* and *structural* or institutional injustice: 'about creating a fairer society' (NCCA 2009); 'a critical prerequisite for supporting the optimal development of all children in Ireland' (CECDE 2006).

CHILDREN AND DIVERSITY AND EQUALITY

International research evidence confirms the importance of addressing the issues of diversity and equality in ECEC (Woodhead and Brooker 2008; Mac Naughton 2003). How children learn about diversity and equality issues is closely bound up with the development of their identities and attitudes. Within their sphere children learn and come to internalise the types of relations and attitudes to diversity from their immediate environment, local communities and the media. What children learn about diversity varies from one context to another. However, all children learn attitudes, both positive and negative, associated with diversity.

Prejudice, discrimination and racism, sexism, etc. affect everyone; these attitudes are harmful both to those who exhibit them and those who are targeted (Murray and O'Doherty 2001). Very young children (2+ years) are aware of and are affected by racism and other forms of discrimination (Van Ausdale and Feagin 2001; Connolly, Smith and Kelly 2002). For example:

> *Mother:* 'Why are you washing your hands so much?'
> *Child:* 'I have to wash the brown off, they are dirty.'
> (Three-year-old mixed race child who had just started pre-school. Source: the child's aunt.)

> Catholics are different to ordinary human beings because they are badder. (Six-year-old Protestant child in Northern Ireland, quoted in Connolly, Smith and Kelly (2002))

Much of the research highlights that by the time children enter primary school their perceptions largely reflect the dominant stereotypes and prejudices around race, gender, sexual orientation, class and body image that prevail in the broader society. It also demonstrates that children play a 'critical and active role' in the construction and perpetuation of social inequalities through their learned perceptions of the world and everyday interactions with each other and with adults (Robinson and Jones Diaz 2007).

Research affirms that as professionals it is time to go beyond the dolls and festivals approach and embrace children's right to their 'individual and group identity' (Derman-Sparks/ABC 1998), their right to non-discrimination (UN 1989) and their right to equality of 'respect, recognition and love, care and solidarity' (Baker *et al.* 2004).

APPROACHES TO DIVERSITY

Different approaches to addressing integration, inclusion and equitable practice have been developed over time. Having a critically reflective view of these approaches will help you look at and challenge your values and beliefs. It will guide you in taking a proactive position in addressing diversity and equality. Aistear (NCCA 2009), Síolta (CECDE 2006) and the *Diversity and Equality Guidelines for Childcare Providers* (OMC 2006) provide good guidance and ideas for beginning the process of addressing diversity and equality. However, approaches to diversity are not a prescription of how to '*do*' diversity and equality. Your approach to work is tightly tied to your own understanding and acceptance of diversity. Having a knowledge of different approaches to diversity will give you the tools to recognise and evaluate what is happening in a setting and possibly change your thinking on ECEC practice.

Educational approaches outlined below are assimilationist, multicultural and intercultural approaches. We will also explore a fourth and more proactive approach, the anti-bias approach, in more detail.

ASSIMILATIONIST APPROACH

An assimilationist approach is based on the belief that it is better for minorities to be absorbed into the main or dominant culture and its shared value system. Minority cultures are perceived as deficient and there is an expectation of them to change. Assimilation does not acknowledge the child's individual and group identity, which can hamper a child's opportunity to flourish.

MULTICULTURAL APPROACH

The multicultural approach holds the belief that exposing children to other cultures, languages and customs at an early age will have a positive impact on their 'tolerance of others'. It usually focuses on the minority 'exotic' or 'touristic' aspects of a culture, such as food, festivals, dress, etc. This approach is somewhat naive as it usually fails to consider more complex social issues and hence does not address the negative impacts of prejudice, discrimination and unequal power.

INTERCULTURAL APPROACH

The intercultural approach contends that culture (beyond the exotic) and equality are not just minority issues but also *majority issues*. It is proactive and acknowledges the importance of assisting all people to become aware of their own cultural identity. Unlike the multicultural approach, it actively addresses racism and power relations and challenges stereotyping.

ANTI-BIAS APPROACH

The anti-bias approach to ECEC, developed by Louise Derman-Sparks and the ABC Task Force (1998) addresses 'all the areas of diversity' including gender, culture, disability, LGBT, class, etc. It is an activist approach and recognises the societal context and its influence on generating equality or inequalities. At the heart of the anti-bias work is a vision of a world in which each child is able to blossom, and each child's particular abilities and gifts are able to flourish (Derman-Sparks/ABC 1998).

This approach is value-based: differences are good, oppressive ideas and behaviours are not. It asks practitioners and children to confront troublesome issues rather than covering them up. The approach is integral to all aspects of daily life in the setting; it is not just activity-based (Murray and O'Doherty 2001).

It asserts that 'celebrating' diversity alone is not sufficient to address issues which go hand in hand with diversity and inequality such as discrimination. The approach proactively focuses on minority and majority children.

When faced with diversity issues, learners often ask: 'Where do we begin?' The anti-bias approach offers a four-goal structure, outlined below, for adults and children. The goals build on one another in a stepping-stone approach: hence before you can effectively address Goal 4 it is useful to work through Goals 1, 2 and 3. Using this structure you can begin your inquiry and progress to implementation in practice.

The aim of the adult goals is to build your own awareness, knowledge and understanding of diversity and equality, in order to engage effectively with children and adults.

The aim of the goals for children is to ensure that each child is actively recognised and respected in the ECEC setting and can comfortably engage with diversity issues, including being able to stand up for themselves and others in difficult situations.

Table 26.1 Anti-bias goals for adults and for children

Goals for adults	Goals for children
1 To be conscious of one's own culture, attitudes and values and how they influence practice	1 To support children's identity (individual and group) and their sense of belonging
2 To be comfortable with difference, have empathy and engage effectively with families	2 To foster children's empathy and support them to be comfortable with difference
3 To think critically about diversity, bias and discrimination	3 To encourage each child to think critically about diversity and bias
4 To engage confidently in dialogue around issues of diversity, bias and discrimination; and work to challenge individual and institutional forms of prejudice and discrimination	4 To empower children to stand up for themselves and others in difficult situations

Each goal should initially be interrogated separately by asking many 'why' and 'how' questions. This can happen at both individual and team level. See the *Diversity and Equality Guidelines for Childcare Providers* (OMC 2006) for further information and critical reflective questions such as:

- *Goal 1 for adults:* 'Can I stand back, examine and discuss objectively my own ethnicity and culture?'
- *Goal 1 for children:* 'Do I have the skills to create a setting which reflects and includes all children in the setting?'

Through consultation and 'equality proofing' by the éist Project (www.pavee.ie/edenn), the essence of the anti-bias goals is also embedded in Aistear and Síolta (particularly under the 'Standard and Theme of Identity and Belonging'). Equality proofing involves incorporating an equality perspective in all aspects of policy development (NESF 1996) (i.e. Aistear, Síolta). The ultimate objective and potential of equality proofing is to promote the development of a more equal society. Equality proofing is about recognising diversity and acting to ensure fair treatment and non-discrimination. It is about providing appropriate services to workers and end users. It is about meeting real needs (CWU 2008).

GETTING STARTED

The first part of this chapter focused on raising awareness and on building your knowledge base. The remainder of the chapter will focus on your beginning engagement with some of the anti-bias goals for adults and some for children.

This section offers you the opportunity to begin an exploration of your own personal beliefs and attitudes and to further build your knowledge base; all of which will inform how you acknowledge, recognise and engage effectively with diversity issues. Following this, we offer some scenarios for reflection on working with children. We provide some reflective questions which may at first seem 'awkward'. However, thinking about questions that put you 'on the spot' begins the process of working towards achieving the goals of the anti-bias approach.

To that end there are also four areas, already touched on, to keep in mind when engaging with the anti-bias goals: being personally reflective; building your knowledge base; developing skills; and working with others to critically reflect on diversity issues and implementation.

FOUR AREAS FOR ENGAGEMENT

1 *Personal reflection and understanding:* being aware of your own values and attitudes and how they affect your practice.
2 *Building your knowledge base:* exploring the historical context, research and approaches to diversity, and understanding diversity terminology: how stereotyping, prejudice, discrimination, oppression, racism, sexism and homophobia operate and the resultant consequences for a child's self-identity (both individual and group), self-esteem and well-being.
3 *Building your skills for practice:* recognising that to embrace children in all their diversity means creating an appropriate physical environment, addressing difficult situations in practice with adults and children and figuring out what actions to take.
4 *Critical reflection:* building learning communities in your teams or externally to actively explore concepts, attitudes and practice.

We shall now use these four areas to interrogate some of the anti-bias goals. It is not possible to address each goal in detail here: however, the vignettes offer ways to progress with an anti-bias approach. This work is ongoing and requires active engagement and commitment in order to support transformation practice and social justice for all children.

PERSONAL REFLECTION AND UNDERSTANDING

Ultimately the most important thing we bring to our practice is 'who we are' (Derman-Sparks/ABC 1998), which is often an overlooked resource (Urban 2010). As adults we are affected by our own social conditions and our identity. For instance, our own class, 'race', gender, sexuality, ability, etc. will impact on how we reflect critically on the way in which our biases influence our choice of curriculum goals. How we see and understand the world may restrict our ability to develop practices which are inclusive and transforming for particular groups of children. This engagement with self is not an easy task, but it is necessary if we are to uncover and change our conceptions and truly accept others in their diversity. When we see things differently we can choose different actions.

Personal Reflection using Goal 1 for Adults

To be conscious of one's own culture, attitudes and values and how they influence practice. Consider the following comment:

> I never considered myself to be racist or biased towards other people but I find myself challenged now on a daily basis. Am I judging other people by their behaviour or looks: do I really think Travellers are . . ., Roma are . . ., the English are . . . But now I am learning to look beyond the prejudice and see the person. I am learning the hard way about biased behaviour. I have to re-think my own views on people, not what society thinks but what am I going to do to change my way of thinking. (Practitioner attending anti-bias training)

Take some time to explore the personal reflection questions below, to engage with Goal 1 for adults. This can be done with a friend, colleague or a member of your learning community.

Personal Reflection Questions

- What were the first messages I learned about difference?
  - Where did the messages come from?
  - Were they positive, negative, mixed?
- Do I believe some of the messages about particular groups in society (Travellers, same-sex mothers, girls, boys, etc.) that declare them to be inferior in some way?

If so:

1 What are the messages?
2 Where did I learn them?
3 How might my belief of the messages affect my work with children and families?
4 How do I now go about dealing with them?

- Recall ways in which someone (teacher, adult) helped you learn about how to deal respectfully with difference.

Links

- *Síolta:* Component 14: 14.2.2; 14.2.4; 14.3.2; 14.3.4.
- *Aistear:* Theme: Identity and Belonging Introduction.

BUILDING YOUR KNOWLEDGE BASE

To engage confidently in dialogue around issues of discrimination, etc. with adults and children it is necessary to have an understanding of diversity terms, both descriptive (e.g. black, refugee) and conceptual (stereotype, prejudice, etc.).

Building your Knowledge Base using Goals 2 and 3 for Adults

- Goal 2 for adults: *To be comfortable with difference, have empathy and engage effectively with families.*
- Goal 3 for adults: *To critically think about diversity, bias and discrimination.*

Consider this experience:

> *Week one:* In our service I haven't seen the need to address the bigger issues of racism or inequality because for the two years I have been working these issues have never been raised by the children.
> *Two weeks later:* Well, well – work was very interesting today: I have noticed children talking about difference. In my previous entry I said I hadn't seen children this young noticing their differences and I didn't believe it but I have been proven wrong. Now I am listening more to the children as they are chatting and I am becoming more aware of the need to say something.
> (Learner journal comments during anti-bias training)

Through her training programme this learner began to build her knowledge base and awareness about diversity. This in turn supported her to recognise and address diversity issues in the setting.

Exploration Exercises using Goals 2 and 3 for Adults

Work with a colleague or learning community using the Glossary in the diversity and equality guidelines (OMC 2006) and begin to explore your understanding of diversity concepts. Take the terms 'stereotyping', 'prejudice', 'discrimination', 'racism', 'sexism' and 'oppression', read each definition and through discussion link your understanding of these terms with real situations. Sharing this exploration with others deepens understanding of concepts and of how they influence the way you look at situations and how they affect people's lives.

Links
- Síolta: Component 14: 14.2.4; 14.2.5; 14.3.1; 14.3.2; 14.3.4.
- Aistear: Theme: Identity and Belonging; Introduction, Equality and Diversity Principles p. 8; The Adult's Role p. 9; Thinking about my Practice pp. 15, 27, 51, 55, 59.

BUILDING YOUR SKILLS FOR PRACTICE AND CRITICAL THINKING

How we interpret the diversity and equality principles in ECEC policy documentation and how we work with diversity is what counts. Remember that it is not the human differences that cause problems; rather it is how we react to and how we treat those differences. Providing an appropriate equitable physical environment (OMC 2006), working through observation of the children and families and planning the implementation of curricular goals is essential in addressing diversity and equality in practice.

Building your Skills and Critical Reflection using Goals 1 and 2 for Children

- Goal 1 for children: *To support children's identity (individual and group) and their sense of belonging.*
- Goal 2 for children: *To foster children's empathy and support them to be comfortable with difference.*

Consider the following two scenarios.

Traveller-blind scenario:
A practitioner tells a Traveller boy starting in the setting not to say he is a Traveller as the other children won't like him. The Traveller boy tells his grandmother and asks her can he not be a Traveller any more. (Mother: Ireland, 2009)

What happened here?

The **aim** of this practitioner was: to protect the child.

The **result for the child** was: confusion – the Traveller child learns for the first time that there is a negative connotation to being a Traveller. This may have an effect on his self-esteem, his level of comfort and sense of belonging in the setting.

The **result for the other children**: the children don't learn about Traveller life and background. There is a lost opportunity to engage in positively recognising and respecting difference and in supporting children's development of empathy.

Traveller inclusion scenario:

The practitioner wants to support identity and belonging in the setting, so he works with the families and children to build a Family Wall (Murray and Urban 2012). All the children and families are represented on the wall. A Traveller boy brings pictures of himself with his horse. The children are fascinated and ask him about his background and ask, 'Do you own the horse?' 'Yes, and I have lots of horses.' The child shows his knowledge of horses and there is recognition of his life in the setting. The practitioner in this scenario uses the anti-bias goals to support his response by:

- representing all children in the environment (Goal 1)
- supporting each child's individual and group identity (Goal 1)
- supporting empathy and comfort with difference by providing accurate information (Goal 2)
- engaging in discussion and critical thinking (Goal 3).

The **result for the child** was: The Traveller boy is recognised and respected and his identity is affirmed. His home knowledge and experiences are utilised to the benefit of himself and the other children.

The **result for the other children** was: The other children find out about diversity in home life and in culture. Diversity is recognised.

Links
Goal 1 for children:
- Síolta: Component 14: 14.1.1; 14.2.1; 14.2.2.
- Aistear: Theme: Identity and Belonging: Aim 1 Goals 1–6.

Goal 2 for children:
- Síolta: Component 14: 14.2.2; 14.2.2; 14.3.5.
- Aistear: Theme: Identity and Belonging: Aim 2, 1–6; Aim 3, 4–5.

CRITICAL REFLECTION

Working together to explore diversity issues is both challenging and rewarding. There is no 'one cap fits all' approach to diversity work. It is 'messy' (Urban 2010) and complicated, so working together strengthens confidence in addressing new and complex issues.

Critical Reflection using Goal 4 for Adults and Children

- Goal 4 for adults: *To confidently engage in dialogue around issues of diversity and discrimination. Work to challenge individual and institutional forms of prejudice and discrimination.*
- Goal 4 for children: *To empower children to stand up for themselves and others in difficult situations.*

Critically reflect on the following two scenarios.

> Please, mam, don't speak your language to me when you collect me from school. My friends will hear you. (Four-year-old child to her eastern European mother, Ireland, 2006)

> Two children come out of pre-school; they are friends and chatting to one another: one child is white, one child is black. The white mother comes to collect her child and says come away from him, we don't mix with that kind. (Ireland, 2011)

To begin, outline:

- *what you think* is happening in the scenario
- *what you might do* in these situations (for children, families and staff).

Linking with the anti-bias goals outlined above, identify what knowledge/skill you might need to acquire to address these issues appropriately.

Links

Goal 4 for Adults:
- Síolta Component 14: 14.1.1; 14.2.4; 14.3.3; 14.3.4.
- Aistear: Equality and Diversity Principles p. 8; Identity and Belonging Introduction p. 25

Goal 4 for Children:
- Síolta Component 14: 14.2.4; 14.2.5; 14.3.4.
- Aistear: Theme: Identity and Belonging, Aim 3, Goals 5–6.

CONCLUSION

Working with diversity is 'messy', challenging and involves a commitment and a desire to be a critically reflective professional (Urban 2010). But how do we do that? A starting point is to build a solid diversity and equality knowledge base, learn how to become familiar with critically reflecting on your own attitudes and background, and explore how comfortable you are with difference: make the familiar strange and the strange familiar. Be able to recognise whether children are silenced or invisible in your service, know how to ensure that each child's identity and sense of belonging is affirmed and be able to engage effectively in addressing bias or discrimination with children and adults (Murray and Urban 2012).

Key Learning Points
- Diversity and equality is relevant to everyone, both minority and majority.
- An equality perspective includes the political, economic, cultural and affective systems.
- Children are affected by the prevailing biases in society.
- Working from an equality and diversity approach (anti-bias) should address personal beliefs, identity, empathy, critical thinking, and promotes social justice and active engagement against prejudice and discrimination.
- Diversity and equality is not about a 'how to do' approach. It is tightly bound up with your own attitudes and values and means equitably responding to all children and families attending your service.

References

Baker, J., Lynch, K., Cantillon, S. and Walsh, J. (2004) *Equality from Theory to Action*. Hampshire: Palgrave Macmillan.

CECDE (Centre for Early Childhood Development and Education) (2006) *Síolta: The National Quality Framework for Early Childhood Education*. Dublin: CECDE.

Connolly, P., Smith, A. and Kelly, B. (2002) *Too Young to Notice*. Belfast: Community Relations Council.

Crowley, N. (2006) *An Ambition for Equality*. Dublin: Irish Academic Press.

CWU (Community Workers' Union) (2008) *Equality Proofing*. London: CWU.

DECET (Diversity in Early Childhood Education and Training) Network (2011) *Diversity and Social Inclusion*. Brussels: DECET.

Deegan, J., Devine, D. and Lodge, A. (2004) *Primary Voices: Equality, Diversity and Childhood in Irish Primary Schools*. Dublin: IPA.

Derman-Sparks, L. and the ABC Task Force (1998) *Anti-Bias Education for Young Children and Ourselves*. USA: NAEYC.

Lodge, A. and Lynch, K. (eds) (2004) *Diversity at School*. Dublin: Equality Authority.

Mac Naughton, G. (2003) *Shaping Early Childhood: Learners, Curriculum and Contexts*. Berkshire: Open University Press.

Murray, C. and O'Doherty. A. (2001) '*éist*': *Respecting Diversity in Early Childhood Care, Education and Training*. Dublin: Pavee Point.

Murray, C. and Urban, M. (2012) *Diversity and Equality in Early Childhood: An Irish Perspective*. Dublin: Gill & Macmillan.

NCCA (National Council for Curriculum and Assessment) (2009) *Aistear: The Early Childhood Curriculum Framework*. Dublin: NCCA.

NESF (National Economic and Social Forum) (1996) *Equality Proofing Issues*. Dublin: NESF.

— (2005) *Early Childhood Care and Education*, Report 31. Dublin: NESF.

OECD (Organisation of Economic Co-operation and Development) (2006) *Starting Strong II*. Paris: OECD.

OMC (Office of the Minister for Children) (2006) *Diversity and Equality Guidelines for Childcare Providers*. Dublin: OMC.

Robinson, K. and Jones Diaz, C. (2007) *Diversity and Difference in Early Childhood Education: Issues for Theory and Practice*. London: Open University Press.

UN (United Nations) (1989) *Convention on the Rights of the Child*. Geneva: UN.

Urban, M. (2010) 'Dealing with Uncertainty' in M. Urban and C. Dalli, *Professionalism in Early Childhood Education and Care: International Perspectives*. London: Routledge.

Van Ausdale, D. and Feagin, J.R. (2001) *The First R*. USA: Rowman & Littlefield.

Woodhead, M. and Brooker, L. (eds) (2008) *Developing Positive Identities*. UK: Thanet Press.

Further Reading

Murphy Kilbride, K. (1997) *Include Me Too!* Canada: Harcourt Brace.

Murray, C. and Urban, M. (2012) *Diversity and Equality in Early Childhood: An Irish Perspective*. Dublin: Gill & Macmillan.

Useful Websites

Children's Database – www.childrensdatabase.ie

Diversity in Early Childhood Education and Training – www.decet.org

Equality and Diversity Early Childhood National Network (EDeNn) – www.pavee.ie/edenn

27

The Early Childhood Education and Care Sector in Ireland

Máire Corbett

Learning Objectives
After studying this chapter the reader should:
- Have gained an understanding of state funding programmes and schemes for the early childhood education and care (ECEC) sector.
- Have become aware of the variety of ECEC provision in Ireland.
- Have developed an awareness of the key structures and stakeholders in the ECCE sector.
- Be able to describe the contemporary developments and new players in the area of ECEC.

INTRODUCTION

The ECEC sector in Ireland is comparatively new and is evolving rapidly. Until relatively recently those working with very young children were considered to be simply caring for them, and their education was thought to begin when they started at a pre-school service at the age of 3 or 4 years. Today there is a much greater understanding and appreciation of how children learn, and the fact that they learn from birth, if not before birth. In this chapter we will describe the range of ECEC services in Ireland, along with how they are funded, the key players and how they relate to each other, and provide an overview of contemporary developments in the sector.

RANGE OF PRE-SCHOOL PROVISION IN IRELAND

When pre-schools were first established in Ireland the term 'pre-school' or 'play school' was used to refer to a service in which a group of young children played together in the care of an adult for a period of three to three and a half hours. When the Pre-school Services Regulations were introduced in 1996 the term came to refer to all services providing out-of-home care for children under 6 years of age. These

...ons require any person who is providing a pre-school service, apart from childminders caring for fewer than three children, to notify the Health Service Executive (HSE) of the service and be open to inspection. The types of service currently used in Ireland are as follows.

Crèche/Nursery/Day Care

These terms, which are used interchangeably, refer to a service that provides care and education to children from 3 months of age to school-going age. They may open for a full day or part time: full day services are generally open from 7–8 a.m. to 6–7 p.m., while a part-time service opens for a maximum of five hours. Children are generally divided by age, so there may be a baby room (under 12 months), wobbler room (1–2 years), toddler room (2–3 years) and pre-school/play school (3 years +). Many services also provide a before- and after-school service for children of school-going age. These age groupings are typical: however, depending on the number of children attending the service, there may be more rooms or perhaps as few as two rooms, e.g. a room for under 3s and one for over 3s.

Because maternity leave provision has improved in Ireland, babies are generally aged 7–8 months when they start at a crèche, though this can vary.

The Pre-school Regulations (DoHC 2006) require the adult:child ratio in full- and part-time day-care to be as follows.

- Children under 12 months: one adult to three children.
- Children aged 12–24 months: one adult to five children.
- Children aged 24–36 months: one adult to six children.
- Children aged 36 months–6 years: one adult to eight children.

The regulations (DoHC 2006) do not require staff to be qualified, but many staff do have training to FETAC Level 5 and increasingly some may be trained to a higher level.

Sessional Service

A sessional service is a setting that is open for a maximum of three and a half hours per day. In some cases this service can be provided in a larger full-day crèche facility, but a sessional service typically operates as a stand-alone service, meaning that it might open only from 9 a.m. to 12 p.m., for example. In some services two sessions a day may be provided, with a different cohort attending in the afternoon. The Free Pre-school Year scheme requires that children of qualifying age have access to five sessions per week. Children of all ages may be catered for, but the most common age range is from 2 years 9 months to school-going age.

The statutory ratios laid down by the Pre-school Regulations (DoHC 2006) for sessional services are:

- Children aged under 12 months: one adult to three children.
- Children aged 12 months–2½ years: one adult to five children.
- Children aged 2½–6 years: one adult to ten children.

The maximum group size in a sessional service, subject to the statutory space requirements being adhered to, is twenty children.

The regulations (DoHC 2006:45) also provide for a situation where a full day care service caters for children who do not attend on a full day basis: 'the adult:child ratio and group sizes for sessional services should apply'.

Staff in sessional services, while not required to by the regulations, tend to have qualifications equivalent to a minimum of FETAC Level 5. Most services offer a particular methodology such as Montessori, play-based, HighScope or Steiner, and practitioners are trained in the specific approach. Increasingly the curriculum provided is influenced by Aistear, the Early Childhood Curriculum Framework (NCCA 2009). Services that participate in the Free Pre-school Year Scheme (described later in this chapter) are required to have room leaders trained to FETAC Level 5 or Level 6 and a higher capitation is paid in respect of staff working in sessional services who have HETAC Level 7 or higher in a relevant discipline.

CHILDMINDING SERVICE

A childminding service is one where a person cares for children in his/her own home. Under the regulations (DoHC 2006) the maximum number of children a childminder may care for is five. Childminders who care for three children or fewer are not required to notify the HSE of the fact that they are caring for children in their own home: however, some childminders choose to do so, under the Voluntary Notification system supported by some County Childcare Committees (CCCs). Again, childminders are not required to have any qualifications, but some have completed a FETAC Level 5 or may have another relevant qualification.

DROP-IN SERVICE

A drop-in service may take two forms. The first is a service where a service is availed of for a short period, perhaps on a regular basis, for example in a shopping centre, hotel or gym. The other scenario is where a childcare service is set up for a one-off event, for example a conference or training course. Both of these types of service are required to be notified to the HSE and may also be open to inspection. Staff in such settings are often employed in a sessional service or crèche and may or may not be trained, as outlined previously.

SCHOOL-AGE CHILDCARE SERVICE

This type of service provides care for children of school-going age, in some cases before school and in some cases after school only. Some services will organise camps for school holiday periods. School drop-off and collection may also be arranged and provided. School-age childcare is not yet regulated in this country. There are some stand-alone school-age childcare settings where the only service provided is to schoolgoing children, but most of these services are provided by a full day care service which provides care for children from three months upwards.

MANAGEMENT STRUCTURES OF ECEC SERVICES

Each of the service types outlined above, apart from childminding, may be provided by a number of management contexts: community, private or workplace.

Community settings are of two main types: those in a family support centre, which will typically provide a variety of family support and community services; and services run by a committee drawn from the community, generally of parents, to operate a childcare service for the children in their own community. Many of these services were established in the past decade, availing of substantial capital grants, initially under the Equal Opportunities Childcare Programme (EOCP) and latterly under the National Childcare Investment Programme (NCIP). These grants were discontinued to new applicants in 2009 as a result of the economic downturn. Many community-based services are staffed partly by Community Employment Scheme participants, who are funded by a state training agency.

Private settings are also of two kinds. The most common are services set up by one or two people who run one setting as a crèche or sessional service. The other type of private setting is where one person or a group of people or a company operates several services or a 'chain' of services. Private services also benefited from the capital grants referred to above, but under the NCIP grants were capped at €100,000.

Workplace services are provided at or near a workplace as a benefit to its employees. Examples are hospitals, local authorities, government departments, semi-state bodies, etc. Some third-level colleges also provide for the childcare needs of students and staff. The premises may be provided by the organisation and in some cases the fees may be subsidised for parents. The management of such services may be provided by a private operator, either an individual or a consortium or a local community group.

HOW ECEC SERVICES ARE FUNDED

Three main funding programmes pertain to the ECEC sector in Ireland at present: the Free Pre-school Year Scheme; the Community Childcare Subvention (CCS) programme; and the Childcare Education and Training Support (CETS) programme.

The Free Pre-school Year Scheme (ECCE)

This scheme was introduced in January 2010 and provides for all children of qualifying age to avail of one year of free pre-school for either three hours per day, five days per week for thirty-eight weeks or for two and a quarter hours, five days per week for fifty weeks. The government pays a sum in respect of each child depending on the scheme the child is availing of, i.e. thirty-eight weeks or fifty weeks. This sum is referred to as capitation. The child must be aged between 3 years 3 months and 4 years 6 months on 1 September of the relevant year. The service must offer a programme for early learning that is influenced by the principles of Síolta, the National Quality Framework. Room leaders working in services offering the free pre-school year must hold qualifications to a minimum of FETAC Level 5. The scheme is a universal programme, so every child of qualifying age in the state benefits. As all ECEC providers can apply to deliver the scheme, private providers also benefit from the funding; and this was the first funding for private providers for ongoing running costs. Introduced as it was in a time of recession, the free pre-school year represented a positive step forward, recognising the benefits of early education for young children and ensuring that children have access to good-quality services. However, for some services the amount of capitation paid does not cover their costs and there is also anecdotal evidence to suggest that some displacement is taking place, as new services open to avail of the funding. The fact that the funding is only paid in many cases for thirty-eight weeks per year means that some staff are now seasonal workers and have to be laid off for the summer months.

Community Childcare Subvention Programme

This funding is only paid to community-based services and is aimed to enable parents experiencing disadvantage and those on low incomes to access affordable childcare. Parents qualify for the subvention payment based on their entitlement to social welfare/Family Income Supplement or a GP only medical card. The level of payment is tiered to reflect the means of the parent(s). The programme was introduced in its current form in September 2010, but was initially introduced in 2008.

Childcare Education and Training Support Programme

This scheme was first introduced in September 2010 and it aims to support parents who are availing of education and training through FÁS/SOLAS or the Vocational Education Committees. The programme is open to community and private services and places are available to parents for the duration of their training course.

Other Funding

In addition to the funding schemes and programmes above, some community services enter into local service agreements with agencies such as the HSE. While these agreements vary, they generally consist of a contract to provide some places for children who come to the attention of social workers or other local services in return for various levels of funding.

The Early Start programme, launched in 1994, provides pre-school services in primary schools in disadvantaged areas. It is funded by the Department of Education and Skills and services are staffed by a primary school teacher, with an assistant. The forty Early Start services have been evaluated, but are still operating in pilot phase mode. The Department of Education and Skills has also provided funding to pre-schools for Traveller children. Previously these pre-schools were segregated and just for Traveller children. However, over the past decade the thinking on segregation has changed and moves have been made to integrate Traveller children with other children to support all children's confident self and group identity (Síolta and Aistear).

STAKEHOLDERS IN THE ECEC SECTOR AND LINKS BETWEEN THEM

The ECEC sector is built on a solid foundation of voluntary support to community and private providers in the development of high-quality provision for young children. Over time a number of voluntary support organisations developed, especially in the context of the lack of state regulation in the area of education and care for young children. Some of these organisations could be depicted as having a child welfare focus, others support providers and others promote and support a particular methodology, such as Montessori, play-based, etc. Some of these organisations receive part of their funding from the state. These organisations are:

- National Children's Nurseries Association (NCNA)
- Irish Pre-school Play Association (IPPA)
- Childminding Ireland
- Barnardos
- Irish Steiner Waldorf Association (ISWA)
- Forbairt Naíonraí Teoranta (FNT)
- Montessori Ireland
- Border Counties Childcare Network (BCCN).

At the time of writing NCNA and IPPA are in the process of merging to form a new organisation which will be called Early Childhood Ireland.

These organisations are collectively known as the Voluntary Childcare Organisations (VCOs). While each of these organisations does receive some funding from the state, each also derives income from elsewhere. Some are member-based organisations (NCNA, IPPA, Childminding Ireland, ISWA, Montessori Ireland and FNT) so receive funding through membership fees, and they may be in receipt of some grants from sources such as the HSE. Each of the organisations is run by a voluntary board with paid staff who carry out the strategic plans of their organisation. Each of these organisations supports high-quality provision for children, in a variety of settings, ranging from crèches, sessional pre-schools, childminders in the home and hospitals, and with a variety of educational philosophies, such as Irish language pre-schools, Montessori services and Steiner services. This work of supporting high-quality provision is done through delivering training, on-site visits to services, quality improvement initiatives, compiling resources and publications, phone and email advisory services and the publication of bulletins and magazines. In 2009 some staff from NCNA, IPPA, Barnardos, Childminding Ireland, the BCCN and the ISWA were inducted as Síolta co-ordinators by the Early Years Education Policy Unit at the Department of Education and Skills and their role now includes awareness-raising in the ECEC sector about the principles and standards of Síolta. These co-ordinators also participate in the pilot phase of the formal roll-out of Síolta.

OTHER AGENCIES

HighScope is an organisation which supports services that use the HighScope approach to support children's early learning. The National Voluntary Childcare Collaborative is a co-ordination structure for the national voluntary childcare organisations. Using this structure, the national voluntary childcare organisations, as well as Children in Hospital Ireland, co-ordinate representation on the County Childcare Committees, and consider national childcare policy.

COUNTY AND CITY CHILDCARE COMMITTEES

In addition to the VCOs, the County and City Childcare Committees (CCCs) support and co-ordinate the development of ECEC services in their areas and administer the funding programmes and schemes outlined. The thirty-three CCCs were established following a recommendation made in the report of the Expert Working Group on Childcare 2000 (DJELR 1999). The CCCs bring together a range of local agencies such as the HSE, FÁS/SOLAS, local authorities, Enterprise Boards and Development Boards, in addition to ECEC providers and parents. Each county has a CCC: Cork, Limerick and Waterford have a City Childcare Committee and a County Childcare Committee; Tipperary has two CCCs (North and South); and Dublin has four CCCs: Dublin City, South Dublin, Fingal and Dún Laoghaire/Rathdown. They are fully funded by the state. However, plans to amalgamate some local authorities will have an impact on the CCCs, for example Limerick City and County, and North and South Tipperary. Each CCC operates independently of the others but many collaborate with each other on specific projects and meetings are held regularly in two groupings: the South and East region and the Border/Midlands/West region.

GOVERNMENT STRUCTURES IN RELATION TO ECEC

The Office of the Minister for Children was established in 2006 and its remit was subsequently broadened to include Youth Affairs in 2009. This office was located in the Department of Health and Children and the Minister for Children and Youth Affairs was a 'Super Junior Minister', meaning that the Minister had a seat at Cabinet, but not a vote. This welcome move brought together for the first time the various government departments that had a role in children's issues, for example Health, Education, Social Protectiton, and Justice, Equality and Law Reform. In March 2011 this was reinforced even further by the establishment of a full Department of Children and Youth Affairs, and Frances Fitzgerald TD was appointed Minister. At the time of writing the Department is being set up and roles and functions are being defined as they devolve from other departments. However, there can be no doubt that this move will strengthen the importance of matters affecting children and families since a full Minister now has a vote at cabinet meetings.

Following the abolition of the Centre for Early Childhood Development and Education, which developed Síolta, the Early Years Education Policy Unit (EYEPU) was established. It is located in the Department of Education and Skills, but is closely linked with the Department of Children and Youth Affairs.

Many of the funding schemes available to the ECEC sector are administered through Pobal (formerly Area Development Management (ADM)), a company which was established to administer government funding schemes across a range of sectors. Currently Pobal conducts compliance visits to all services in receipt of government funding.

Both the VCOs and the CCCs report to the Department of Children and Youth Affairs in line with the requirements of their funding programmes. Each also plays a role in influencing policy, in terms of various aspects of the funding schemes and also, in the case of membership organisations, in relation to the experiences and issues of ECEC providers and the families they represent. The organisations under the VCO and the CCCs also collaborate on a range of projects, such as training, network meetings and publications, though the extent of this collaboration varies.

The National Childcare Co-ordinating Committee is chaired by the Department of Children and Youth Affairs. It comprises representatives of the various government agencies with a remit in relation to ECEC, and also the VCOs. This means that national policy in the sector is influenced by all relevant stakeholders.

OTHER STAKEHOLDERS AND INFLUENCES ON PROVIDERS

HSE INSPECTORATE

As previously described, the Pre-school Regulations (DoH 1996; DoHC 2006) require most services providing out-of-home care for children to notify the HSE of their service. All such services are open to inspection by the HSE. Providers of services are notified of a date for their first inspection, but subsequent inspections are unannounced. The inspection team generally comprise a public health nurse and an environmental health officer. In theory, services are visited annually but in practice inspections frequently take place less often, due to local resourcing issues.

The pre-school inspectors have a big influence on providers and the relationship between providers and inspectors can range from very good to uneasy. This can depend on the interpretation of various aspects of the Regulations on the part of the inspector and the provider. In 2010 a set of national standards for the pre-school sector were published, with the aim of ensuring more consistency among inspectors.

CENTRAL GARDA VETTING UNIT

A vital part of ensuring high-quality provision of ECEC services for children is the requirement that all adults working with children are of the highest calibre. This, in part, involves ensuring that adults working with children do not have criminal convictions. The revised Pre-school Regulations (DoHC 2006) also require that staff are Garda vetted: however, for many years it was impossible to have prospective staff or volunteers Garda vetted. In 2007, following lobbying from several organisations, including the VCO, the Central Garda Vetting Unit was established in Thurles, County Tipperary. This means that all staff working in ECEC settings in Ireland can be vetted. However, under the child protection guidelines (OMCYA 2009) Garda vetting is only a small part of an overall child protection policy: recruitment, induction and ongoing support and supervision as well as an atmosphere of openness and trust are vital components to ensure the safety and well-being of children in ECEC settings.

START STRONG

The Start Strong organisation was born out of the Irish Childcare Policy Network (ICPN), which was set up in 2004. The ICPN was made up of a number of organisations with a common interest in promoting the necessity for high-quality childcare provision for children. Having successfully applied for funding from the Katharine Howard Foundation, the Irish Youth Foundation and Atlantic Philanthropies, ICPN became incorporated as Start Strong, employing a team of staff to further the aim of advancing high-quality care and education as a right for all young children in Ireland, reflecting research evidence of the benefits of this early intervention for all children, for the economy and for society.

PREVENTION AND EARLY INTERVENTION PROGRAMME

Jointly funded by Atlantic Philanthropies and the Department of Children and Youth Affairs, three projects – Young Ballymun, Preparing for Life (Darndale, Dublin) and the Childhood Development Institute, Tallaght West – were established in 2006 to promote better outcomes for children in these three areas of disadvantage. The initiative aims to provide a variety of programmes and strategies to be developed, with strong local input, and robustly evaluated. The interventions cover a variety of projects aimed at children of all ages and their families and communities. Substantial funding has been put in place to roll out this programme.

CENTRE FOR EFFECTIVE SERVICES

This agency was established in 2008 to promote an evidence-informed approach to policy making and service delivery of child, family and community services. It is based in Dublin and Belfast and is jointly funded by the Atlantic Philanthropies, the Department of Children and Youth Affairs and the Department of Community, Rural and Gaeltacht Affairs.

EQUALITY AND DIVERSITY EARLY CHILDHOOD NATIONAL NETWORK

This network was established in 2008 to support organisations, trainers and practitioners to work collectively towards the inclusion of an equality and diversity approach as a core element in ECEC training and practice. They have developed a Train the Trainer course to deliver a FETAC module in equality and diversity education for young children.

CHILDREN'S SERVICES COMMITTEES

As is evident, there have been several policy and strategy developments in Ireland relating to the lives of children. To ensure that these policies are carried out and that they make a difference there is a commitment to develop a Children's Services Committee under the aegis of each City or County Development Board in the country. To date seventeen of these committees have been set up. These committees will draw representation from all organisations and agencies in the local area who work on behalf of children and young people, with the intention of ensuring that local services are relevant and accessible.

NATIONAL EARLY YEARS ACCESS INITIATIVE

This is a collaborative partnership between Atlantic Philanthropies, the Mount Street Club Trustees, the Department of Children and Youth Affairs (OMCYA), the Early Years Education Policy Unit, the Department of Education and Skills, and Pobal. The initiative has approved funding for eleven projects over a period of three years. Each project was proposed by a consortium of local agencies and must focus (either directly or indirectly) on children from birth to 6 years and their families who are living in socio-economically disadvantaged communities.

WORKFORCE DEVELOPMENT PLAN

This plan was launched in 2010. The aim of the plan is to support the upskilling and professional development of staff in the ECEC sector. It is envisaged that the Workforce Development Plan will streamline all the strands currently providing education and training to the sector and ensure that all training delivered is consistent, of a high quality and accessible.

CONCLUSION

The ECEC sector in Ireland is diverse, evolving and exciting. Over the past ten years huge advances have been made, new projects and funding have been developed and the sector has progressed from being perceived as simply minding children to achieving recognition of the immense potential of young children and their learning, and of the importance of early intervention and the benefits this has for children, families and the community as a whole. There are numerous stakeholders, which have been outlined here. Some of these stakeholders, such as the national organisations that make up the NVCC and other organisations such as High/Scope Ireland, Montessori Ireland, the Border Counties Childcare Network and the CCCs, have a role in supporting service providers, developing and influencing policy and delivering training. Others, such as the HSE, the Department of Children and Youth Affairs, Pobal and Atlantic Philanthropies, are involved with funding. The HSE has a dual role in many ways as it provides some funding to some services and also controls the inspectorate function.

Key Learning Points
After reading this chapter the reader should:
- Know the variety of service provision in the ECEC sector and understand the difference between each type.
- Have an understanding of the key agencies and organisations active in the ECEC sector in Ireland.
- Have an awareness of their linkages and influences on each other.
- Know the key funders in the sector, both from government and from other sources.
- Have a knowledge of the various schemes and interventions currently being delivered in areas of disadvantage.

References
CECDE (Centre for Early Childhood Development and Education) (2006) *Síolta: The National Quality Framework for Early Childhood Education*. Dublin: CECDE. Available at: www.siolta.ie.

DoH (Department of Health) (1996) *Child Care Pre-School Services Regulations*. Dublin: DoH.

DoHC (Department of Health and Children) (2006) *Child Care (Pre-School Services) (No 2) Regulations 2006*. Dublin: DoHC. Available at: www.dohc.ie/legislation/statutory_instruments/pdf/si20060604.pdf?direct=1

DJELR (Department of Justice, Equality and Law Reform) (1999) *National Childcare Strategy, Report of the Partnership 2000 Expert Working Group on Childcare*. Dublin: Government Publications Office.

NCCA (National Council for Curriculum and Assessment) (2009) *Aistear: The Early Childhood Curriculum Framework*. Dublin: NCCA. Available at: www.ncca.ie/en/Curriculum_and_Assessment/Early_Childhood_and_Primary_Education/Early_Childhood_Education/Framework_for_Early_Learning/.

OMCYA (Office of the Minister for Children and Youth Affairs) (2009) *Children First: National Guidelines for the Protection and Welfare of Children*. Dublin: OMCYA.

Further Reading

Department of Education and Science (1999) *Ready to Learn: White Paper on Early Childhood Education*. Dublin: Government Publications Office.

Useful Websites

Barnardos – www.barnardos.ie
Border Counties Childcare Network – www.bccn.ie
Centre for Effective Services – www.effectiveservices.org
Childminding Ireland – www.childminding.ie
Children in Hospital Ireland – www.childreninhospital.ie
Citizens' Information – www.citizensinformation.ie/en/education/pre_school_education_and_childcare/
Department of Children and Youth Affairs (includes details of funding programmes and initiatives) – www.dcya.ie
Department of Health – www.dohc.ie
Forbairt Naíonraí Teoranta – www.naionrai.ie
Health Services Executive – www.hse.ie
High/Scope Ireland – www.highscope.ie
Irish Pre-school Play Association – www.ippa.ie
Irish Steiner Kindergarten Association – www.steinerireland.org
Montessori in Ireland – www.montessoriireland.ie; www.montessoriami.ie/
National Children's Nurseries Association – www.ncna.ie
Pobal – www.pobal.ie
Pavee Point/EDeNn Network – http://pavee.ie/edenn/welcome-to-edenn
Start Strong – www.startstrong.ie

28

The Application and Uses of Ethics in Early Childhood Education and Care

Noel Kavanagh

> ### Learning Objectives
> - To explain what is meant by 'ethics', 'theories of ethics', 'ethical guidelines' and 'codes of practice'.
> - To outline the central ethical theories and the assumptions underpinning them in order to properly contextualise their usefulness for the student.
> - To discuss how the application of these theories can assist and inform decision making in regard to ethical dilemmas as they arise in the student's future working life.
> - To explore the possible meta-ethical questions that may arise as a consequence of these ethical dilemmas.

INTRODUCTION

The aim of this chapter is to outline those philosophical theories of ethics that underpin and inform the elaboration of ethical guidelines in regard to working with young children.

WHAT IS ETHICS?

The term 'ethics' refers to that branch of philosophy that deals with questions about:

- how we ought to act in any given situation
- the nature of human values
- what constitutes the right thing to do.

These are questions that have preoccupied humans since the beginning of recorded history and that have led to many different theories of how or why we have the moralities that we have. So what are our morals based on?

DIFFERENT UNDERSTANDINGS OF MORALITY

There are many different ways in which philosophers have tried to figure out what the source of our capacity to be moral is.

- Is it the belief in a god that provides the bedrock of morality?
- Is it our capacity to feel sympathy for or empathy with others that provides us with the basis for our regard for others?
- Is it our inherent reason as human beings that allows us to make moral rules to live by?

All of these different approaches have had and continue to have a direct influence on the way in which morals and ethics in societies are formulated. It is vitally important for the student to understand the various influences that went into formulating society's morals. It is also essential in understanding the moral framework of individuals and the things that contribute to creating their world view as you encounter them in daily life. Knowing where they are coming from, as it were, will inform how you interact with them.

Since the beginning of Western thinking, many thinkers, from Augustine and Aquinas to Luther and Calvin, among others, have argued that religion is central to our moral making. They would argue that our moral rules and regulations come from the divine authority of a god; one can think of the Ten Commandments as a clear example of this type of interpretation.

Others, like David Hume, have argued that it is our ability to sympathise or empathise with others that allows us to be moral. This would mean that our ability to be moral is grounded in our emotional response to the suffering of others. Philosophers who support this view would consider that when we say we 'feel for someone' in their suffering, we are minded to try to ensure that we, or others, are not the cause of suffering and we create moral rules to ensure this.

Most philosophers would argue that it is the human capacity to reason that enables us to create moral rules. They would assert that all moral rules and regulations that govern our dealings with each other are a product of our ability to reason, and moral rules will therefore tend to be revealed as quite reasonable, given the particular situation.

The ban on smoking in public places is a prime example. Even though smokers were put out by the imposition of the smoking ban, generally speaking the success of the law was due to the fact that we all saw it as a rational and reasonable thing to do. It is the idea that beyond, or despite, our immediate self-interests, we can recognise that reason would dictate that we act differently. We ask ourselves in relation to our actions whether we would want everyone else to do such a thing.

Alternatively, it may suit me at a given moment in time to throw rubbish out of my car as I travel down the motorway, but I ask myself what would happen if everyone were to do this? Would that be desirable, or in my long-term interest? Therefore reason and self-interest come together.

Still other philosophers, Aristotle and John Stuart Mill, for example, would argue that the essential motivating factor in our ability to be moral is our desire for our own happiness, which leads to what they call an enlightened self-interest: I treat others well because if I do they will treat me well and everyone's happiness is secured. Therefore reason and self-interest come together. It is rational for me to act morally because everyone's happiness is achieved.

Still more philosophers of ethics, such as Immanuel Kant, maintained that we must act morally out of a sense of duty alone and that emotions such as sympathy, happiness and self-interest must not come into the equation. These thinkers would suggest that an ethics based on duty alone avoids the problems that they see as emerging from those theories. What if I do feel sympathy for animals but not for foreigners? Have I then no ethical obligations to foreigners? I may not see it as being in my self-interest to be caring toward my fellow human being. If doing good for someone else does not make me happy, should I pursue that act? Does my helping someone out always have to depend on how I feel about that person? Philosophers who argue for an ethics based on duty would tell us that it takes the emotion and therefore the subjectivity out of ethics.

Consider the following scenario: My frail and elderly mother-in-law has a next-door neighbour whose anti-social behaviour makes her life very difficult. When attempting to discuss the situation with the young man I am physically assaulted. Weeks later, while driving down a secluded section of road, I come across the young man. He has clearly now himself been the victim of a serious assault and is in desperate need of medical assistance. What do I do? I do not feel sympathy for the said individual. Perhaps I even feel that he has got what was coming to him. It would not be in my immediate self-interest to help him. However, have I a duty to help him? It can be argued that I ought to help him because it is simply the right thing to do: I have a duty of care to the person because he is a person, and my private and personal dealings with him should have no role in determining how I should act towards him. In the same way, a policeman or doctor is bound by duty to assist those in distress, whether they deserve to be helped or not: the person ought to be helped out whether they are a nice person or whether they are a distinctly unpleasant character. We can see this on our televisions night after night in those fly-on-the-wall shows about police and ambulance services out and about on weekend nights and the characters they meet. Often unhelpful, to say the least, they receive care from the police and ambulance services because there is a duty of care to the individuals concerned.

All of these competing and conflicting claims about the grounds of morality can prove frustrating for anyone trying to grapple with the complexities of trying to decide the 'right' thing to do in any given situation. This can be all the more difficult in the workplace when the welfare of others is concerned. It is for these reasons that professions such as early childhood education and care (ECEC) have elaborated codes of practice that provide a framework for understanding duties and obligations.

ECEC AND CODES OF PRACTICE

Most professions and services that seek to provide care for others have codes of practice under which they operate that provide clear ethical guidelines governing the exercise of the given profession. A code of practice is a specific set of written rules which sets out to explain how people working in a particular profession should behave. Those codes of practice tend to be written in terms of how a particular profession sees its role and the ethical theories that underlie and inform those codes. Given that the student's experience of ethics on placement and subsequently in the workplace will be wholly governed by elaborate codes of practice that are articulated in terms of duties to children, the focus of our attention must be on those ethical theories that reflect and inform the construction of those duties. Therefore we will argue that perhaps *deontological theory* is the best tool with which to understand the idea and role of duty as an ethic. We will also discuss its counterpoints in the ethical theories of *consequentialism*.

Why do I say the 'best tool'? Given that there are numerous theories of ethics that range from those attempting to explain why we are moral to those that try to establish what ought to be the basis for morality, any profession needs to pick the ethical theory or theories that most adequately articulate(s) what they feel suits the presuppositions of their task in hand. Given that most, if not all, codes of conduct, practice and ethical guidelines in the area of children are articulated in terms of rights, deontological theories of ethics could be said to suit best. If we take, for example, the code of ethics for Early Childhood Australia (see Useful Websites below) we can see that it holds as central (point 2) that the practitioner must respect and advocate for the rights of children as set down in the United Nations (UN) Convention on the Rights of the Child.

DEONTOLOGICAL THEORIES

Deontological theories of ethics assert the nature and role of duties in judging our actions. The word 'deontological' is derived from the Greek words for duty (*deon*) and *logos*, which means an understanding or rationale. There are various ways in which the duty-based approach to ethics is thought through. The most centrally useful in articulating a theory of ethics for our particular purposes are the rights-based theory of duty and the Kantian expression of duty.

A *rights-based theory of duty* tells us that because a person has a right therefore I have a duty to both respect this right and also a duty to uphold it; to make sure, as far as is possible, that others do not infringe on this right. (For example, Article 28 of the UN Convention on the Rights of the Child states that all children have the right to primary education, which should be free.) Therefore I am duty bound to respect, uphold and advocate for the rights of others. Under what circumstances? Under all circumstances, because the central features of the idea of rights are:

1 They are *natural* in that they are not created or invented by people: I have rights that are mine by virtue of me being human.
2 They are *universal* in that they do not depend on time or place.
3 They are *equal* in that they apply to all human beings.
4 They are what we call *inalienable*. They belong to me whether I like them or not. I cannot sell them to others or give them up.

For example, I cannot willingly give up my right to freedom by selling myself into slavery. I certainly can physically sell myself into slavery but I still, by virtue of the fact that I am a human being, have the right to freedom attached to me.

What we call the *Kantian expression of duty* comes from the work of the philosopher Immanuel Kant (1724–1804). He tells us that our entire moral decision making must be done in terms of an overall sense of duty. Yes, we certainly have duties to ourselves and others; the gifted footballer can be said to have a duty to themselves to develop and exercise this talent. We have a duty to others to keep our promises and to tell the truth. But, for Kant, all these particular duties must be based on something more foundational, a single principle that is based on reason, which he called the 'categorical imperative'. This differs from moral decisions that are made according to personal desire or self-interest. Take the following statement, for example: 'If I take care of my grandmother she might leave me her possessions in her will.' This is what Kant calls a 'hypothetical imperative': if I want this then I ought to do that. In contrast to this the categorical imperative simply tells us that we ought to do x because it is our duty.

What all duty-based approaches have in common is that they are non-consequentialist. What we mean by this is that they regard duties as being obligatory whether or not the consequences of those actions are beneficial.

CONSEQUENTIALISM

All consequentialist theories assert that the morality of an action must be assessed in terms of the consequences it produces. An action can be seen to be morally acceptable if its consequences can be deemed to be favourable. The consequentialist suggests that, in any given moral situation, the morality of our response should be weighed up in terms of the consequences it produces. If the consequences are more bad than good, we determine the action to be morally bad; if the weighing-up falls on the side of good consequences, we decide the action to be moral.

Let us explore the application of these approaches to an ECEC practice setting with an example.

Student Exercise

You are working in a Montessori school and you have come to the conclusion, based on your observations over time, that a child in your care is being neglected by its single parent. The child does not seem to be getting the proper nutrition it needs or the proper clothing; it does not seem to be getting the routine that it needs in terms of bedtimes and quite often the parent does not collect it from school in time. However, you are also keenly aware that parent and child seem to have a very close and loving bond. You do know that the parent has had serious addiction issues before and that the child was previously taken into care. The parent has said to you in conversation in the past that they felt that getting their child back was the only thing that was keeping them from relapsing into addiction. Would you report your concerns to the child protection social worker?

Under the consequentialist model you must now weigh up whether reporting your well-grounded suspicions of neglect is going to produce good consequences. The child will undoubtedly be parted from a loving parent; the parent may very well relapse into addiction. Nevertheless, the child's welfare is paramount: and, who knows, maybe this would do the parent good in that they would perhaps get the help they need in terms of educating them on how to ensure that the child has all it needs in terms of care?

It does seem that your dilemma of weighing up these consequences can be made easier by referring always to the clear code of practice that is articulated in terms of a duty; the duty of care to the child, which is considered to supersede all other considerations. It does seem, then, that the deontological position, which stresses the role of duty, is a vital aid to anchor the often complex and competing dilemma involved in ethical decision making.

REFLECTIVE PRACTICE AND ETHICS

If the early childcare student is to become a valuable practitioner in the field, their working experience will lead them to a possible re-evaluation of the governing ethics of their practice. This may involve a positive reinforcement of existing ethical practices or it may result in a concrete rejection of the presuppositions on which those practices were based.

For example, in your experience in the workplace your practice of adhering to and interpreting those codes of practice may lead you to reflect on whether they are achieving the stated aim. Are the rules and regulations actually, in effect, upholding the rights that are enshrined at the core of your work? Could a change in the rules mean that rights are more effectively upheld?

Perhaps reflection on those codes will reveal that they are indeed the best possible implement for achieving the desired result. This is to understand that moralities may shift and change according to the development of society at any given time: it is to understand that morals and values are, perhaps, not static. Our attitudes to what is culturally and morally acceptable obviously change over time. There was a period in time when slavery was considered in the Western world to be morally acceptable; that is no longer the case. It was once thought that women should not be afforded the basic rights which would naturally accrue to a man; this has now changed fundamentally.

However, in the childcare setting, ethical codes of practice are most commonly articulated in terms of duties based upon the established rights of the child which are, by and large, understood to be inviolable and therefore unaffected by social context. If there are certain fundamental rights that accrue to the child by virtue of their very existence, for example the right to not be economically exploited, those rights supersede any particular historical context of a specific culture at a specific time: it is simply the case that whether you are child X living in Western Europe in a multicultural liberal society in the twenty-first century or child Y living in southeast Asia in a mono-culture based on ancient traditions, neither makes any difference as to the rights that *ought* to accrue to you.

A quick glance at those codes of ethics that have been clearly articulated, for example the Early Childhood Australia Code of Ethics or, closer to home, the ECEC principles and standards of Síolta, shows that they both place the rights of children and advocating for the rights of children first and foremost. This is explicitly borne out by reference to the UN Convention in their principles and codes of practice.

Therefore any discussion of ethics in relation to early childhood must take account of the rights of children that are set down both in UN conventions and in Irish and European law. It is undoubtedly the case that the attractiveness of deontological theories of ethics in this particular field is due to their defence of the morality of duties and obligations and because they therefore provide a framework for understanding the adherence to those rules.

ETHICAL DILEMMAS AND ECEC

The intention of any module or text in ethics offered to students must seek to prepare them, as far as possible, for those experiences in the field that are commonly called 'ethical dilemmas'.

Those theories of ethics that talk in terms of the rightness or wrongness of actions in regard to the adherences to rules, obligations and duties will be of particular assistance to the student in understanding the value of those ethical guidelines that will govern their actions on placement and in their future working lives.

However, there will undoubtedly be times in your life in general and particularly in your work life where you will be faced with not knowing what course of action is the right one to take; that is the 'dilemma' part of an ethical dilemma. In those moments it seems to us that we are at an impasse. How do we know what is the right thing to do?

There may also be occasions when the 'dilemma' involves a questioning of the adherence to duty and a rule-governed response to a given situation. Codes of practice and ethical guidelines that are built on the notion of a rule-governed response are of necessity general in nature because they specifically do not take account of the particularities of a case. Yet ethical dilemmas quite often arise because of the particularities of a case, because the rule does not adequately take account of the lived situation.

When we have to make difficult ethical decisions they tend to be in regard to specific situations, not abstract generalities. The difficulty arises when we cannot tally up the rule with the particular case. Our ethical dilemma is that we do not know whether it will work out or not, whether we are doing the 'right thing'. Of course, what we desire is to know, in advance of making a decision, that it will turn out to be the right one. But we cannot be sure in advance. Yet we must decide. We have to make a decision without knowing, in advance, whether it is the right thing to do.

The Danish Philosopher Søren Kierkegaard (1813–1855) tells us that in order to live authentically we must make choices: we are faced constantly in life with the choice between one route or another, which he outlined in his famous book *Either/Or*. We cannot remain undecided, paralysed by what might seem to us the pros and cons of each course of action. There comes a time, Kierkegaard believed, when we have to make a 'leap of faith'. The philosopher Jacques Derrida (1930–2004), drawing on Kierkegaard's work, tells us that all ethical decisions require us to make a certain leap of faith because very rarely do we really know how things are going to work out. We fall back on the rule-governed response because it provides us with guidance: rules are, after all, guidelines for conduct; they are there to help us through these situations.

Yet Derrida would suggest that if we are truly being ethical we must not simply and blindly apply the rule to the situation; we must always put the rule to the test. If that puts us in an uncomfortable situation, so be it; that is the nature of ethics. We should not blindly adhere to a set of rules as if they were mathematical formulae. The question of the ethics of ethics in any given particular field must be seen not as the luxury of abstract academic musings but as central to the development of both the field of work and the personal development of the practitioner.

CONCLUSION

In this chapter we have outlined the basic theories of ethics as they inform codes of practice and ethical guidelines in this field. What we have hoped to do is to demonstrate that ethical theories can help us in the field to form a framework for what will inevitably be our own decision-making processes. They are therefore not to be seen as supplying easy solutions to problems and they point to the notion that the questioning student and practitioner is hopefully the better one.

Key Learning Points

- The philosophical theories of ethics that inform and support codes of ethics in practice.

- The role of ethical theories in assisting practitioners' decision making in the field.
- The role of ethics in assisting the articulation of any possible re-evaluation of the central tenets of accepted practice in order to facilitate the continuing development of the field.
- The role of ethics in forming the student as practitioner.

Further Reading

Charleton, M. (2007) *Ethics for Social Care in Ireland: Philosophy and Practice*. Dublin: Gill & Macmillan.

Hinmann, L.M. (2003) *Ethics: A Pluralistic Approach to Moral Theory*. Belmont: Wadsworth.

Norman, R. (1984) *The Moral Philosophers*. Oxford: Oxford University Press.

Useful Websites

Early Childhood Australia Code of Ethics – www.earlychildhoodaustralia.org.au/code_of_ethics/code_of_ethics.html

Internet Encyclopaedia of Philosophy – www.iep.utm.edu/

Síolta Standards – www.siolta.ie/standards.php

29

Practice Placement and Reflection

Deirdre Scott

Learning Objectives

After studying this chapter the reader should be able to:

- Recognise the contribution of placement to the education of the early childhood education and care (ECEC) student.
- Understand the importance of preparation prior to placement and the need to identify personal learning objectives.
- Examine the function of supervision in an ECEC placement.
- Explore the contribution of reflection to personal and professional development.

INTRODUCTION

This chapter addresses the role of practice placement for the ECEC student. Working alongside experienced practitioners in an environment catering for the needs of babies and children is a crucial part of the education process.

ECEC placement should provide students with the opportunity to:

- integrate theory with practice
- apply a range of practical skills
- begin to form a sense of professional identity
- experience supervision
- develop an ability to reflect on actions and learning.

Before examining each of these areas in more detail, the chapter provides an overview of the placement experience.

OVERVIEW OF ECEC PLACEMENT

The Model Framework for Education, Training and Professional Development in Early Childhood Care and Education Sector (DEJLR 2002:21) requires ECEC workers to have a minimum of 500 hours of supervised practice. To gain this experience, all ECEC undergraduate courses in Ireland require students to carry out practice placements. A practice placement is a period of time spent working, under supervision, in an early childhood service. Under the guidance of ECEC practitioners, the student can observe the day-to-day activities in a service catering for the needs of babies and children. Students are likely to experience at least two placement opportunities during their degree programme. The initial placement is an important step for students who have had limited contact with children or who have not had work experience of any type. ECEC students may undertake their first practice placement in one of the following areas.

- An early childhood setting in the private sector, where the service is run as a business for profit.
- A community childcare setting which has a management group consisting of parents, and which is not run for profit.
- A setting with a specific focus such as Montessori, Steiner or HighScope.

In their second placement a student may be placed in a setting with a different emphasis, perhaps working in the county childcare committee, with an advocacy and family support organisation such as Barnardos or Springboard or alongside a hospital play specialist. Occasionally students have gone abroad to work with voluntary organisations catering for children living in institutions, homeless children or children with specific health or social needs.

PLACEMENT PREPARATION

The preparation period prior to placement enables the student to address the following areas.

- Identification of personal learning objectives.
- Questions and concerns about placement.
- Pre-placement visit.
- Code of behaviour.
- Role of supervision.

While each college will have identified learning outcomes for placement, students need time to consider their personal learning objectives. These are simple statements of what a student wishes to accomplish on placement. Objectives can range from achieving practical tasks to overcoming personal challenges such as reading to children while other staff are in the room or writing up children's records. Whatever the objectives, it is most important that they are specific and measurable. One recommended method is to use the SMART guidelines (Drucker 1954). SMART is an acronym for Specific, Measurable, Attainable, Realistic and Time-specific.

Examples of objectives appropriate to an ECEC placement are:

- By the end of my placement I will be able to read, with confidence, and using props and actions, a story to a group of 3-year-old children.
- By the end of my placement I will have completed three art activities with 4-year-old children.
- By the end of my placement I will be competent in looking after the physical needs of babies under 12 months of age.
- By the end of my placement I will have an understanding of the role of the different people employed in the early childhood setting and knowledge of relevant policies and procedures.

Objectives may be revised while on placement if the student or supervisor feels that sufficient knowledge or expertise has been achieved. New learning objectives, perhaps addressing a situation identified as challenging by the student or a personal development issue identified by the supervisor or student, may be written.

In the preparatory stage students require the opportunity to discuss concerns they may have about working in the sector. While they may look forward to their introduction to the ECEC environment, many, naturally, have doubts about their ability or suitability for the work. Below is a list of questions about emotional and practical issues that have been posed by students in the past. These may help you identify your own concerns and may form part of a discussion with a lecturer prior to placement, or with the placement supervisor during supervision sessions, when you are required to reflect on your progress and learning.

1   What if I become attached to the children?
2   How do I prevent a child becoming too affectionate towards me?
3   What if I am unable to do the work required of me?
4   What if I become emotional if I learn things about children's circumstances?
5   What do I do if I see a staff member speaking crossly to a child?
6   What do I do if I feel I am not challenged or given responsibility?
7   What do I do if a child has bruises?
8   I have never handled a real baby: what do I do if I am asked to change a nappy?
9   How will I cope if the children or staff do not like me?
10 I heard a student was asked to clean the toilets: is this part of our work?

Pre-Placement Visit

Many colleges organise a pre-placement visit for students and this can be most useful. During the visit a student can present their CV along with their learning objectives. They can ask about their work timetable, expected dress code and code of behaviour for the agency, which may address the following issues.

- Communication with children, parents and colleagues.
- Dress code.

- Notification arrangements when a staff member is unwell or unable to attend work.
- Confidentiality.
- Keeping children safe and identification of the designated person for child protection.

The most important thing a student can do is to arrive on placement physically and emotionally prepared. Carrying out practical tasks as well as concentrating on relating theory to practice leaves many students exhausted, particularly in the first few weeks.

THE ECEC PLACEMENT EXPERIENCE

In this section of the chapter consideration is given to what the ECEC placement offers students. Returning to the five points made in the introduction, placement should enable the student to:

- integrate theory with practice
- apply a range of practical skills
- begin to form a sense of professional identity
- experience supervision
- develop an ability to reflect on actions and learning.

INTEGRATE THEORY WITH PRACTICE

Students are able to observe at first hand the implementation and relevance of material studied in college, whether subjects such as psychology, social policy, law, creative studies, learning and play, or modules related to professional practice. Examples include:

- How activities such as circle time, sand and water play and outdoor play are managed.
- How the Pre-School Regulations 2006 are adhered to.
- How Aistear and Síolta influence the curriculum and the pre-school environment.
- How the professional ECEC worker meets the needs of children.

APPLY A RANGE OF PRACTICAL SKILLS

Placement should provide scope for students to practise many of the skills introduced in college. These might include:

- Communicating with children and staff.
- Reading a story to a group of children, perhaps using puppets or other props.

- Planning, implementing and evaluating a range of activities for different age groups.
- Looking after the physical needs of children; feeding, changing and toileting according to the policies of the agency.
- Writing up a child's daily log.
- Carrying out child observations using a range of techniques.

PROFESSIONAL IDENTITY AND CAREER DEVELOPMENT

Working alongside ECEC practitioners, students are provided with an opportunity to observe the many roles taken by ECEC professionals, including:

- The professional ECEC worker who works directly with the children.
- The supervisor who has responsibility for day-to-day management of the ECEC setting.
- The manager who looks after policy issues, staffing, training, financial management and development work for the agency.

While on placement the student may also observe the importance of working closely with parents and other family members. In addition, ECEC practitioners engage very closely with a wide range of health, social care and educational professionals, including child psychologists, speech therapists, community development workers, pre-school inspectors, social workers and primary school teachers.

SUPERVISION

Supervision is described as: 'planned, regular periods of time that the student and supervisor spend together discussing the student's work in the placement and reviewing the learning process' (Fred and Jones 1987:63, cited in Parker 2004:65). Supervision provides the student with the opportunity to reflect on the events of the week with a view to:

- analysing their learning
- considering challenges encountered during the week, reflecting on how they dealt with them at the time, their feelings about the situation and how they would deal with the situation if it arose again
- acknowledging their achievements
- examining their attitudes, prejudices and practice
- discussing links between theory and practice
- identifying gaps in knowledge
- reviewing and perhaps amending learning objectives.

It is recommended that a student meet formally with their supervisor for one hour a week. The meeting should be structured in advance with an agreed agenda, as this enables the student to prepare. Preparation demonstrates a student's active engagement in their own personal and professional development.

During the meeting a supervisor may provide constructive feedback in the form of a compliment or questions. While students may react differently to these conversations, it is an important part of the supervision process, often leading to improved professional practice and greater self-awareness.

Discussions and decisions need to be recorded by both supervisor and student to ensure that any actions decided upon can be reviewed at the following supervision session.

MODELS OF REFLECTION

In this final section we look at reflection, which is an intrinsic part of placement. Reflection is a form of learning which encourages us to look more closely at an event. In reflection we ask: What happened? Why did it happen? What was happening before/after the event? How did I react to or feel about the situation? Without taking time to reflect, placement could become a merely task-focused experience.

We shall look at three key areas:

1 What is reflection?
2 Why do we reflect?
3 How do we reflect?

WHAT IS REFLECTION?

Reflection is something we do every day. We replay events or conversations and try to make sense of them, often thinking that if they were to be repeated we would act differently.

In a practice context reflection is more formal; we examine events at a deeper level.

> Reflection is an in-depth consideration of events or situations outside of oneself. The reflector attempts to work out what happened, what they thought or felt about it, why, who was involved and when, and what these others might have experienced and thought and felt about it. (Bolton 2010:13)

Many theorists have studied the contribution of reflection to our learning and self-awareness, for example Dewey in the early twentieth century, Kolb, who introduced the term 'experiential learning' in the 1980s, and Donald Schön in his book *The Reflective Practitioner* (1983).

To assist ECEC students to become reflective practitioners, models of reflection proposed by Melanie Jasper and Professor Graham Gibbs of Oxford University are discussed below.

These models of reflection are maps to guide us, to help us ask appropriate questions, to look at things from many different angles and to focus on particular aspects of our practice. In reflection it is important to acknowledge our achievements as well as areas where improvements are required in order to increase our self-awareness and ultimately our ability to work in a professional manner.

WHY REFLECT?

We reflect to learn: about ourselves, our practice and about the people we work with. The purpose is to gain insight, which can lead to action. Jasper (2007:43) describes it as:

experience + reflection + learning = change in behaviour or action

Reflection may, for example, provide increased knowledge about a child, which may then lead to the practitioner changing their communication method or the way they present an activity. Of course not all reflection leads to a change in behaviour or action: after taking time to reflect on a situation, a student or practitioner may feel affirmed in their practice.

Taking time to reflect on placement experiences in a purposeful way provides a student with an opportunity to address:

- How they met the needs of children in the ECEC service.
- How they applied the knowledge and skills developed in college along with identification of gaps in their learning.
- Their emotional response to the children and their own role in the service.

Examining what went well, what did not go so well and what would be done if the situation arose in the future is the very essence of reflection.

Of course reaching this level of analysis takes time and support and this is why supervision is such a key component of placement. Through sensitive questioning by a supervisor a student can be helped to gain insight into their personal and professional practice.

HOW TO REFLECT

Developing the ability to become a reflective practitioner, like learning any new skill, takes practice and commitment. People may be resistant to reflection as it may make them feel uncomfortable with an element of their practice or highlight action which they must take (Kilvington and Wood 2010:14).

Students require support and guidance to become reflective, otherwise they may become frustrated with the concept. Two possible models of reflection are Melanie Jasper's 5WH (What, Why, When, Where, Who and How) (see Table 29.1) and Graham Gibbs's 'reflective cycle'.

Table 29.1 Jasper's 5WH cues to guide reflection

WHAT	WHY
Happened? Did I do? Was I feeling? Was the result? Went well? Went badly? Went unexpectedly? Am I worried about? Did I learn? Do I need to know? Skills do I need to develop?	Did it happen? Did I act/think/feel this way? Is it significant?
WHEN	**WHERE**
Did it happen? Am I going to take action? Will I revisit my reflections?	Did it happen?
WHO	**HOW**
Was involved? Might be affected? Needs to know? Needs to take action?	Did it happen? Can I learn from it? Can I prevent it happening again?

Source: Jasper 2007:69.

Figure 29.1 Gibb's reflective cycle

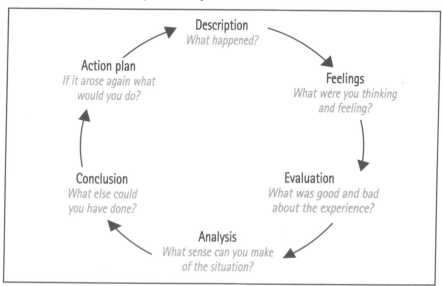

Source: Gibbs 2008.

Gibbs's reflective cycle (Jasper 2003:77) is a model that, more than others, requires a student to explore their emotional response to events. In the context of ECEC placements a student may encounter many situations where they feel emotionally challenged and it is important to examine not only their emotional response but why they reacted as they did. This is the personal and professional development process of practice placement. Indeed, the experienced practitioner also needs to reflect on practice in order to meet the needs of those in their care.

Case Study: Using Gibbs's Reflective Model
Situation: Montessori room in a community childcare service.
Jane, a second-year student, is in week eight of her first placement, working with 4-year-old children.

Description
Today I planned to do an art activity with the children split into two groups as there was insufficient space for the whole group. One of the childcare workers was to assist me while the other worker was to provide an alternative activity for the other children.

I had all my materials ready and my plan typed out to remind me of all the steps.

Feelings
I felt very nervous and apprehensive about my art activity.

I was nervous about how the children would respond to it. I was concerned about being able to manage their behaviour. I felt a bit intimidated about the workers observing and perhaps judging me. I was also a bit excited as this method – gloop – had not been used in the setting before.

Evaluation
Good points:
- The children loved the feel of the gloop. They played with it for longer than I thought they would.
- The childcare worker assisting with the activity thought it was a great idea and even called a worker from a different room to view it.
- I was then asked if I would do this with another group next week.

Bad points:
- The clean-up took longer than I anticipated so this made the second group a bit cranky as they were waiting their turn.
- The worker also felt a bit impatient as she had her activity completed and had to come up with another idea.
- I almost ran out of material and this caused me some anxiety.
- I did not think of an alternative in the event of a child not liking the texture of the gloop.

Analysis

I put a lot of energy into feelings of anxiety about how I would be viewed by staff. I asked myself whether I should have just repeated a project done by the student the previous year. Thinking about it now, I appeared to think more about the staff than the children and this is something I need to address. The children responded well to the activity even though there were one or two who did not like the texture of the gloop.

Conclusion

I believe I performed well although I was nervous.

Skills used:
• organisation and planning
• communication with children and staff
• patience
• observation of children.

Theory to practice:
• child observation
• developmental psychology – social interaction, language and fine motor skills.

Education and play – creative studies.
Increased confidence as I was asked to repeat activity.

Action plan

I need to consider the concentration span of younger children.
I need to focus on the needs of children and less on how I am perceived by staff – as they have always been very supportive to me.

In this example you can see where the student has gained insight, by moving through the reflective model. She recognises her anxieties and how they may impact on the children. She is also able to identify areas where she related college theory to practice and the skills she developed.

REFLECTIVE WRITING

It is recommended that reflections are written down, in a journal or in electronic format, in order to retain the information and learn from it. Jennifer Moon, who has written extensively on journal writing, cites the following reasons for keeping a journal.

• It helps learners focus their attention.
• It captures ideas for later consideration.
• It helps learners organise and clarify their thoughts. (Moon 2006)

Journals may be used for assessment purposes; and in some cases extracts from a journal can be incorporated into a reflective essay. Students should be clear about the use that is going to be made of the journal because its purpose may influence how the entries are written.

Journal entries can include drawings, diagrams or poems, for example, to capture an event or an emotion, or to question an action or event.

CONCLUSION

Reflective models provide a framework to help students engage in reflection. While a criticism levelled against using models is that they may be too restrictive, as students, or indeed practitioners, engage in regular reflection and writing they will develop their own style and become less reliant on specific models.

However, for the novice who is considering reflection and staring at a blank page, models offer a method of capturing their reflections, perhaps revealing insights into their practice and assisting with personal and professional development.

Key Learning Points

- Placement is a major learning experience for students. It enables them to integrate theory with practice, to become self aware, and to understand the ECEC sector.
- Planning for placement is a vital part of the process. Students require opportunities to identify their challenges and concerns and to write learning objectives that can be assessed at the end of a specified period.
- Supervision plays an important role for the placement student. In order to gain from it, however, students cannot be passive: they need to be able to discuss their emotions, their progress, identify their learning and examine challenges that may have arisen since the previous session.
- Reflection is a means of learning. There are many different theories of reflection and reflective models, which are maps to guide us towards becoming reflective practitioners.

References

Bolton, G. (2010) *Reflective Practice*. London: Sage.

DEJLR (Department of Equality, Justice and Law Reform) (2002) *Quality Childcare and Lifelong Learning: Model Framework for Education, Training and Professional Development in the Early Childhood Care and Education Sector*. Dublin: DEJLR.

Drucker, P. (1954) *The Practice of Management*. New York: Harper Brothers.

Gibbs, G. (1988) *Learning by Doing. A Guide to Teaching and Learning Methods*. London: Further Education Unit.

Healy, J. and Spencer, M. (2008) *Surviving your Placement in Health and Social Care*. UK: Open University Press.

Jasper, M. (2003) *Beginning Reflective Practice. Foundations in Nursing and Health Care*. Cheltenham: Nelson Thornes.

— (2007) *Professional Development, Reflection and Decision Making*. Oxford: Blackwell.

Kilvington, J. and Wood, A. (2010) *Reflective Playwork*. London: Continuum.

Moon, J. (2006) *Learning Journals: A Handbook for Reflective Practice and Professional Development* (2nd edn). London: Taylor & Francis.

Parker, J. (2004) *Effective Practice Learning in Social Work*. Exeter: Learning Matters.

Schön, D. (1983) *The Reflective Practitioner: How Professionals Think in Action*. Surrey: Ashgate.

30

The Future: Where are We Going?

Mark Taylor and Máire Mhic Mhathúna

Learning Objectives

After studying this chapter the reader should:

- Be aware that the capacity to develop high-quality early childhood education and care (ECEC) services now exists in Ireland.
- Understand that the Irish state needs to intervene to improve the pay and status of practitioners who hold ECEC degrees in order to create high-quality ECEC services.
- Recognise that private sector ECEC providers are unable by themselves to develop high-quality ECEC services.
- Appreciate the longer-term economic benefits arising from a high-quality ECEC service.
- Recognise the role of Irish culture in early years education and care in Ireland.
- Value the home language and culture of immigrant children and their families.
- Understand how culture and language may be developed in both the Aistear and Síolta frameworks.

INTRODUCTION

This book sought to introduce first- and second-year ECEC undergraduate degree students to a variety of ideas, theories and experiences, covering a broad range of academic and practice-related issues, to support their learning at college and on placement. Chapter contributors were asked to focus on the knowledge, skills and values which an undergraduate student needs to acquire in order to become a competent ECEC practitioner. The aim of this concluding chapter is not to review the material from previous chapters. Instead, we want to consider the future direction of ECEC in Ireland by examining two very different, but pertinent, issues.

First, there are likely to be many future initiatives in Ireland aimed at improving the quality of ECEC. While some of these initiatives will focus on areas such as the professionalisation and registration of practitioners, we suggest that younger children should always have the right to be educated and looked after by the best-qualified

ECEC practitioners. Specifically, we argue that the state needs to provide additional funding to make a career in ECEC a more attractive option for better-qualified practitioners. When this happens, improvements in ECEC are likely to occur; not only will children benefit, society will benefit too.

Second, we need to give careful consideration to the role of cultural beliefs, attitudes and behaviours that we think should define ECEC in Ireland. Specifically, we need to consider the place of Irish culture in its totality in our approach to ECEC. How is ECEC in Ireland qualitatively Irish; what do Irish practitioners and systems bring to ECEC that is distinctly 'our own'? In our view, Irish culture should be the foundation from which we embrace the contributions of other philosophies, systems and, of course, diversity within the Irish system.

IMPROVING THE PAY AND WORKING CONDITIONS OF ECEC DEGREE HOLDERS

The development of children is affected by their experiences during the pre-school years, so consideration needs to be given to how early years services can be safe, fun and stimulating environments. Opportunities to learn and develop through free and guided play and games are particularly rewarding for younger children. And notably, a significant part of providing an effective pre-school service is about having the right staff in place to make these opportunities available.

While pre-school workers need to have qualities such as warmth and empathy, their approach to work also needs to be informed by relevant professional and pedagogical theories and practices. This combination enables pre-school educators to help children to become more socially adept and better prepared to learn, now and in the future. There is evidence from other countries such as the USA and the UK to suggest that children's intellectual, social and behavioural development is enhanced if they attend quality pre-school services and that benefits from attendance can endure over time (e.g. Gormley 2008; Sylva et al. 2004, 2010).

Undoubtedly there are many people working today in Irish pre-school settings who provide a good service to young children. Nevertheless, we also know that the quality of pre-school settings is associated with staff having higher qualifications, particularly if there are trained staff present. For example, Whitebook and Ryan (2011:3) suggest that 'studies of publicly funded preschools [USA] that require that teachers hold a bachelor's degree and have specialised training in early childhood education, report positive child outcomes'. Children, therefore, benefit from engaging in developmentally appropriate activities where staff have received in-depth pedagogical training.

The creation of a highly qualified ECEC workforce is linked to two factors. First, a country needs to establish the capacity to generate graduates with ECEC degrees. And in this regard, Ireland has been spectacularly successful. Primarily by directing funding to the institutes of technology and a number of universities, the state has witnessed a rapid increase since 2002 in the number of third-level ECEC degree providers, ECEC undergraduate students and ECEC degree holders (see Department of Education and Science (2009:22–5), which outlines these changes).

Second, the creation of a highly qualified ECEC workforce is also linked to the demand from the workplace for highly qualified practitioners. Regrettably, at the time when Ireland was increasing the number of practitioners with ECEC degrees, not enough was being done by the state to make a career in ECEC a more attractive option for many graduates. Unfortunately, even the state's recently published workforce development plan for the ECEC sector (see Department of Education and Skills 2010) has little to say on practitioners who have earned an ECEC degree.

Students leaving ECEC programmes want to work with young children, but are cognisant of low status and poor pay in the pre-school sector – constraints which are acknowledged by the Department of Education and Science (2009:46) and the European Commission (2011:6). From an economics perspective, many highly qualified ECEC graduates face a high opportunity cost in choosing to establish a career in the pre-school sector. Since there is no sector-wide framework on pay or on career progression (including continuous professional development) for practitioners who hold ECEC degrees, those graduates who decide to work in ECEC often pay a high price in terms of sacrificing potential careers or training options in other fields. Therefore, the next obvious step is to make a career in ECEC a more rewarding choice for degree holders.

Poor pay and inadequate working conditions are factors influencing the quality of ECEC services. As the OECD (2006:216) noted: 'a strong link exists between the training and support of staff – including appropriate pay and conditions – and the quality of Early Childhood Education and Care services'. While Irish 'state funding of education and training provision in ECCE [early childhood care and education] has risen sharply in the past decade' (Department of Education and Science 2009:33), the state also needs to do more to make a career in ECEC an attractive career option for ECEC degree holders. Why the state needs to do more – especially by providing more funding to employ ECEC degree holders – becomes clearer if both the benefits of ECEC and the limitations of the private market are considered.

DOES THE STATE HAVE A ROLE IN FUNDING THE EMPLOYMENT OF HIGHLY QUALIFIED ECEC PRACTITIONERS?

The introduction of the Early Childhood Care and Education (ECCE) Scheme (i.e. the Free Pre-school Year) in 2010 demonstrates that the state recognises the benefits of ECEC for younger children and wider society. The objectives of the pre-school year were outlined in a press statement released by Barry Andrews, Minister for Children and Youth Affairs, in April 2009.

> The Government has, by announcing this decision, demonstrated our commitment to our children's social and educational development. It is a key building block in the realisation of our plan for a smart economy. The provision

of a year's free pre-school to all children will promote equality of opportunity at the most important developmental stage of children's lives. Regardless of income or ability to pay, all children will be entitled to avail of this pre-school service. (OMCYA 2009)

The introduction of the free pre-school year extends the state's expectations of ECEC. In addition to its traditional functions of enabling disadvantaged children to achieve equality of opportunity or assisting disadvantaged parents to get back into work or training, ECEC is increasingly seen by the state to be contributing to the development of a better-prepared workforce and a more socially adroit society. The benefits accruing from a quality pre-school service are not only 'private' (i.e. not only to the children receiving ECEC). Among other benefits, pre-school prepares children for later schooling, which in turn leads to a better-equipped workforce, laying the foundations for economic growth. Other merits include the socialisation function of ECEC, leading to increased social cohesion. Put simply, the level of welfare enjoyed by each member of society will increase because of the benefits which materialise from ECEC.

From an economics perspective, not only does ECEC benefit an individual child (economists call this a private benefit), it also benefits wider society (economists call this an external benefit) by contributing to the social and emotional development and cohesion of a group of children who inevitably, later in life, become the adult citizens of a nation. However, without state funding (e.g. the ECCE Scheme), many parents would be unable or unwilling to meet the costs of an ECEC place in the private market. In addition, without state intervention (e.g. information campaigns), many parents would have inadequate information (economists call this imperfect information) on the advantages of ECEC. As a result, children and society would be unable to benefit from the rewards of the ECEC experience, to the extent that is possible.

Or in the language of economics, without state intervention, the net social benefits (i.e. the sum of the private and external benefits, less the sum of the private and external costs) would not be maximised, as children and wider society would have a lower level of welfare than would otherwise be possible; when this happens, economists say that an inefficient level of ECEC exists. Consequently, where private and external benefits diverge, the private market by itself 'cannot be relied upon to produce an efficient allocation of resources' (Le Grand, Propper and Smith 2008:56). When this situation arises, a case can, therefore, be made for state intervention to ensure that a level of ECEC is provided which maximises the net social benefits.

In determining the extent to which the state should intervene, an effort must be made to consider the return to society from state expenditure on ECEC. In the USA they have endeavoured to do this by calculating the returns to society from investing in quality ECEC services, where practitioners hold a bachelor's degree and a certification of education. Traditionally, these types of study have focused on the returns to society from an investment in programmes targeting children from disadvantaged communities. For example, researchers at High/Scope Perry – an

ECEC programme in Michigan aimed at low-income African-American children who were assessed to be at high risk of school failure – found that forty years after its introduction, the public gained $12.90 for every dollar spent on the programme.

> Much of the savings came from dollars not spent on incarceration; there were also savings to the public in lower special education costs; taxes paid to public coffers because of higher earnings, and savings in public assistance costs. As to the benefit to the participants: program participants earned 14 percent more per person than they would have otherwise – $156,490 more over their lifetimes. The cost of the two-year program itself was $15,166 per child. (Calman and Tarr-Whelan 2005:13)

These gains would not have been possible on the High/Scope Perry programme without the public funding of highly qualified ECEC practitioners. And while the introduction of the free pre-school year in Ireland is a move in the right direction in terms of providing resources to recruit practitioners who have achieved particular levels of qualifications, arguably even more funding is required to recruit and retain practitioners with ECEC degrees. Put simply, employing a better-qualified workforce is likely to lead to increased levels of welfare for younger children and the wider society.

Moreover, rather than targeting ECEC resources to particular groups of younger children (e.g. those from deprived backgrounds), there is also evidence to suggest that all children benefit from an investment in quality pre-school services that every child can attend (i.e. universal services). Such an investment is also likely to offer the greatest level of returns to society. As Barnett (2010:9) notes, 'even a program that enrolled 75 percent of the children in poverty or 75 percent of poor and near-poor children is unlikely to surpass a universal program in terms of net economic benefits'. Similarly, Barnett (2004, cited in Calman and Tarr-Whelan 2005) calculated, through economic modelling, that a quality ECEC programme which was universal and which served all 3- and 4-year-olds in the USA would cost $50 billion, but over a subsequent forty-year period it would generate $213 billion in returns, for a net gain of $163 billion.

Furthermore, there is evidence to suggest that investing in pre-school education provides the largest return on educational investment. As the European Commission (2011:5) acknowledges, 'returns on investment in early childhood education are the highest, and particularly for those from a disadvantaged background, while educational investment at later stages tends disproportionately to benefit children from higher socio-economic backgrounds'.

Ireland could learn from other countries on how to attract graduates to work at the pre-school level. For example, the Early Years Professional Status (EYPS) was introduced in England in 2007 as part of a plan to improve early education by increasing the number of well-qualified graduates working with younger children. The intention is to have an early years professional working in every children's centre by 2010 and in every full day care environment from 2015. New Zealand is going even further, with their government announcing that 80 per cent of practitioners in teacher-led, centre-based early childhood education (ECE) services must be registered teachers by 2012. The 80 per cent target was meant to be achieved by 2010, but this goal was deferred due to a projected shortage of 1,100 registered ECE teachers, who already have parity of pay with primary and secondary school teachers. The specification of targets was deemed to be an integral element of a ten-year national plan to improve early years education: the benefits of quality in ECEC have long been recognised in New Zealand.

In summary, a key feature of ECEC is that it creates 'external' benefits (i.e. beyond the individual child) or externalities (to use the language of economics). Services which employ the best-qualified ECEC practitioners are also likely to generate the greatest returns. However, the private market, unaided, is unable to generate these returns. A case must, therefore, be made for the establishment of a national and implementable strategy, identifying clear milestones and an agreed timeframe, to maximise the benefits to children and society from ECEC. Such a strategy needs to recognise that ECEC can be used as a means to promote social justice. At the same time, there also needs to be an acknowledgement that ECEC benefits all children and society. A strong case can, therefore, be made for using state resources to employ a highly trained, professionally developing and commensurately rewarded workforce – the key element of a high-quality ECEC service. Ireland is developing a high-quality ECEC workforce. Now we need to find the resources to employ them.

IRISH CULTURE

Culture in the sense intended here is broad, encompassing language certainly, but also ways of being, ways of interacting and valuing aspects of behaviour such as oral culture. Irish people are well known for our love of talk and conversation, of a good turn of phrase and of storytelling (Kiberd 1996). Music, both vocal and instrumental, folk and more formal, is also culturally marked. We have a rich tradition of folk wisdom and strong connections to place. Some of these links are changed by families moving away from their own home areas or to different parts of the country, but each local area has its own heritage and lore. Heritage and traditions have the power to stifle or to empower, depending on social contexts and personal views, but they have the potential to keep us grounded in the past while also moving forward. This raises the question of how locally connected early years services are to their own communities. How can early years settings draw on the local heritage and tradition of the area in which they are situated? How can they draw on the wider linguistic and cultural heritage of Ireland?

Languages include both official languages of Ireland, Irish and English. The Irish language and culture are part of the heritage of Ireland and as such should be made real and available in appropriate ways to the children in our care. Children in Irish early years settings have a right to the totality of their heritage. Naíonraí opt to deliver their service through Irish. Other services decide to offer part of their sessions through Irish, roll call in circle time, some songs and rhymes in Irish, words of praise, etc. In this way, children learn through first-hand experience that there are a number of ways of saying things: English is one way, Irish is another way, yet both have a place in their lives and are valued. For some practitioners, there is a real challenge in accessing the Irish language. However, simple routines such as greetings, phrases for praising children, children's books and recorded songs and rhymes (see www.naionrai.ie for resources) can open up this area for children and provide first steps in accessing the rich children's tradition in Irish.

HOME LANGUAGE MAINTENANCE

Many of the children of immigrant parents attending early years services are learning English as an additional language. This clearly implies that they are speakers of other languages. Research by Cummins and others (Cummins 2000; Baker 2011) shows the importance of valuing and, where possible, providing support for the home languages of newcomer children. The experience in countries such as the USA, with longer histories of immigration than Ireland, shows that unless steps are put in place, immigrant children lose their home languages to the dominant societal language at an early age (Bernhard and Pacini-Ketchabaw 2010). International research shows that parents often experience schools as unsupportive of or oblivious to mother tongue retention and that their children's cultural and linguistic identity takes on a new and unfamiliar shape in a short period of time (Bernhard and Pacini-Ketchabaw 2010). Parents' capacity to explain the nuances of their home culture to their children often diminishes and becomes weakened over time. Minority children's 'cultural capital' (their understanding and knowledge of their own culture) is rarely considered as a valuable resource and the knowledge and experiences of families are ignored as vital founts of knowledge.

Early years training should include an awareness of the value and role of languages other than English in order to avoid the trap of considering monolingualism as the default or normal position. Additional languages are much more than mere add-ons to the status quo. Small-scale studies in Ireland (Mhic Mhathúna and Hill 2007; Dillon 2011) and larger-scale studies abroad (Cummins 2000) show that early childhood practitioners value diversity but find it hard to put supportive practices in place. The focus is often on surface-level inclusion through multicultural activities rather than on more deeply embedded practices that draw on and develop the knowledge of newcomer children. Due to the frequent presence of children from many language backgrounds in any one early years group, it must be recognised that specific language support is a challenge. However, strategies such as using/making dual-language books, CDs and videos of storytelling in diverse languages, involving parents in learning activities and employing bilingual staff on a temporary or more permanent basis offer useful ways of enabling all children to benefit from the diverse cultural and linguistic resources within the group.

AISTEAR AND SÍOLTA FRAMEWORKS

Aistear (NCCA 2009a) and Síolta (CECDE 2006), now being rolled out in practice, offer us opportunities to reflect on how we want to implement the new frameworks. The two frameworks follow a long tradition of naming new ventures in Irish. Edwards (2009) holds that naming is an important maker of identity and that names can be given by insiders or ascribed by outsiders. By choosing names in Irish for Aistear and Síolta, the symbolic nature of the Irish language is evoked. The two early childhood frameworks are marked as being Irish, but are open to influences from further afield.

Aistear and Síolta are broad frameworks, leaving wide scope for interpretation by the individual practitioner, the early years setting and in the wider society. The four main themes of Aistear and linked themes in Síolta, as outlined in the audit of similarities and differences between the two frameworks by the NCCA (2009b), will be examined in order to identify how culture and language may be developed through the framework statements.

- *Aistear:* 'The theme of Well-being is about children being confident, happy and healthy.' (NCCA 2009a)
- *Síolta Standard 1:* Rights of the Child. 'Ensuring that each child's rights are met requires that she/he is enabled to exercise choice and to use initiative as an active participant and partner in her/his own development and learning.' (CECDE 2006)

Both frameworks advocate for the well-being of children, physically, mentally, socially and emotionally. They propose that children should be given choice and opportunities to use their initiative. Research by Cummins (2000) and others (Baker 2011) indicates that it is necessary for children's well-being that their cultural and linguistic background is acknowledged and valued. There is a grave danger of lowering self-image and self-esteem if their home language and culture is not respected or if they are denied opportunities to use their home language. We concur with the principles of the Aistear curriculum statement and the Síolta standard and believe that all children in early years centres should also have the right to learn the Irish language as part of their heritage. This right should be included in official policy and guidance documents for ECEC settings.

- *Aistear:* 'The theme of Identity and Belonging is about children developing a positive sense of who they are and feeling that they are respected as part of a family and community.' (NCCA 2009a)
- *Síolta Standard 14:* Identity and Belonging. 'Promoting positive identities and a strong sense of belonging requires clearly defined policies, procedures and practices that empower every child and adult to develop a confident self and group identity, and to have a positive understanding and regard for the identity and rights of others.' (CECDE 2006)

Both statements emphasise the concepts of individual and group identity and the need to actively promote respect for all cultures. The statements can be interpreted in many ways, but they are open to the development of strong local and cultural connections and to the inclusion of the home languages and cultures of children from diverse cultures.

- *Aistear:* 'The theme of Communicating is about children sharing their experiences, thoughts, ideas and feelings with others with growing confidence and competence and in a variety of ways and for a variety of purposes.' (NCCA 2009a)
- *Síolta Standard 5:* Interactions. 'Fostering constructive interactions (child/child, child/adult and adult/child) requires explicit policies, procedures and practice that emphasise the value of process and are based on mutual respect, equal partnership and sensitivity.' (CECDE 2006)

The above statements are concerned with language and other means of expression such as art, music, song and dance. They indicate that children should be facilitated in expressing their thoughts in all their languages, including their mother tongue and any additional languages they may be learning. The emphasis is on process rather than outcome and the role of the adult is in supporting children to extend their learning.

- *Aistear:* 'The theme Exploring and Thinking is about children making sense of the things, places and people in their world by interacting with others, playing, investigating, questioning, and forming, testing and refining ideas.' (NCCA 2009a)
- *Síolta Standard 7:* Curriculum. 'Encouraging each child's holistic development and learning requires the implementation of a verifiable, broad-based, documented and flexible curriculum or programme.' (CECDE 2006)

Both statements advocate the active exploration of the environment through play, language and investigation in the context of a well-defined, broad-based curriculum. Children should be encouraged to understand that their experiences can be expressed in several ways and in many languages. Some of the learning opportunities to be provided by adults could include language-learning activities.

Taken together, the themes of Aistear and Síolta standards support a strong focus on language and culture, valuing both the local or Irish culture and the contribution of knowledge to be made by children and adults from diverse cultures.

CONCLUSION

Irish early years education and care is undergoing unprecedented change and development. On the one hand, there is increased regulation regarding health, safety, child development and management: on the other, flexible frameworks offer opportunities to consider issues, reflect on practice and make informed decisions. With increasing numbers of degree-educated students and the wealth of experience of practitioners, Irish early years education is in a good position to make positive contributions to the lives of children in its care. High-quality care demands that we continue the process of reflection, that we debate issues and that, above all, we place the rights and needs of children first.

Training at degree level in ECEC is a significant factor in providing high-quality education and care for young children. High-quality practice requires that practitioners continue to develop their skills through critical reflection on their practice and by keeping abreast of developments in theory, policy and practice. ECEC is a relatively young profession and its professional identity is becoming established. Degree-educated practitioners will be able to articulate the importance of providing the highest-quality ECEC for the youngest members of society and to explain the interplay between education and care in the provision of ECEC services.

At the same time, ECEC in Ireland has reached its 'tipping point': a critical mass of graduate-level practitioners are leaving college with knowledge, energy and enthusiasm, wanting to transform a sector that historically has been under-funded and under-qualified. And a critical mass of highly qualified practitioners makes a difference: the numbers are there for conversations to take place about professional identity, continuous professional development and the need for practice to be informed by evidence-based research.

And because we know that these conversations are occurring, eventually leading to a clearer specification of the practitioner's role, we are therefore confident that future graduates will find ECEC an interesting and exciting sector to work in. Also it seems that current research in science, psychology and economics is on the ECEC graduate's side: witness the evidence that a quality ECEC experience provides longer-term mental health, social and economic returns for individuals, the community and our country.

Some graduates may proceed to postgraduate study, thereby gaining a deeper appreciation of theories and research in regard to the education and care of young children. They may contribute to the field through their own research and recognise that future policy and practice developments should be grounded on a sound theoretical basis and on evidence-based research.

So we are also confident that the future for graduate-led ECEC practice in Ireland looks bright.

Key Learning Points
- By funding the expansion of ECEC undergraduate degree programmes in the 2000s, the Irish state has developed the capacity to create a high-quality ECEC service.
- However, to establish a high-quality ECEC service, the Irish state needs to do more to attract ECEC degree holders to work in the ECEC sector, by offering them higher pay levels and opportunities for continuous professional development.

- Ireland could learn from other countries, such as New Zealand, in terms of the steps which need to be taken to move to a high-quality ECEC service.
- Children will develop their understanding of Irish language and culture through first-hand experiences.
- The home languages of immigrant child should be valued and made visible in early years practice.
- Aistear and Síolta offer opportunities for reflecting on how language and culture may be developed.

References

Baker, C. (2011) *Foundations of Bilingual Education and Bilingualism* (5th edn). Bristol: Multilingual Matters.

Barnett, W.S. (2004) 'Returns to Preschool for All'. Paper presented at Economic Impacts of Child Care and Early Education: Financing Solutions for the Future, Legal Momentum/MIT Conference, Massachusetts Institute of Technology.

— (2010) 'Universal and targeted approaches to preschool education in the United States', *International Journal of Child Care and Education Policy* 4:1, 1–12.

Bernhard, J. and Pacini-Ketchabaw, V. (2010) 'The Politics of Language and Educational Practices: Promoting Truly Diverse Childcare Settings' in O. Saracho and B. Spodek, *Contemporary Perspectives on Language and Cultural Diversity in Early Childhood Education*. Charlotte, NC: Information Age Publishing, pp. 21–42.

Calman, L.J. and Tarr-Whelan, L. (2005) *Early Childhood Education for All: A Wise Investment*. New York: Legal Momentum.

CECDE (Centre for Early Childhood Development and Education) (2006) *Síolta: The National Quality Framework for Early Childhood Education*. Dublin: CECDE.

Cummins, J. (2000) *Language, Power and Pedagogy*. Buffalo, NY: Multilingual Matters.

Department of Education and Science (2009) *Developing the Workforce in the Early Childhood Care and Education Sector*, Background Discussion Paper. Dublin: Department of Education and Science.

Department of Education and Skills (2010) *A Workforce Development Plan for the Early Childhood Care and Education Sector in Ireland*. Dublin: Department of Education and Skills.

Department of Justice, Equality and Law Reform (1999) *National Childcare Strategy: Report of the Partnership 2000 Expert Working Group on Childcare*. Dublin: Stationery Office.

Dillon, A. (2011) *Teachers and Language Learning in Primary Schools: The Acquisition of Additional Languages in the Early Years*. Unpublished PhD dissertation, Dublin Institute of Technology.

Edwards, J. (2009) *Language and Identity*. Cambridge: Cambridge University Press.

European Commission (2011) *Early Childhood Education and Care: Providing All Our Children with the Best Start for the World of Tomorrow*. Communication from the Commission (COM(2011) 66 final). Brussels: European Commission.

Gormley, W.T. (2008) 'The effects of Oklahoma's pre-K program on Hispanic children', *Social Science Quarterly* 89:4, 916–36.

Kiberd, D. (1996) *Inventing Ireland: The Literature of the Modern Nation*. London: Vintage.

Le Grand, J., Propper, C. and Smith, S. (2008) *The Economics of Social Problems* (4th edn). Basingstoke: Palgrave Macmillan.

Mhic Mhathúna, M. and Hill, Ú. (2007) 'Intercultural Books in Practice', in *Vision into Practice* (2008), Proceedings of Centre for Early Childhood Development and Education Conference, Dublin Castle, February 2007. Dublin: CECDE, pp. 180–7.

NCCA (National Council for Curriculum and Assessment) (2009a) *Aistear: The Early Childhood Curriculum Framework*. Dublin: NCCA.

— (2009b) *Aistear: The Early Childhood Curriculum Framework and Síolta, The National Quality Framework for Early Childhood Education: Audit: Similarities and Differences*. Dublin: NCCA <www.ncca.ie/en/Curriculum_and_Assessment/Early_Childhood_and_Primary_Education/Early_Childhood_Education/Aistear_Toolkit/Aistear_Siolta_Similarities_Differences.pdf> accessed 12 July 2011.

OECD (Organisation for Economic Co-operation and Development) (2006) *Starting Strong 2: Early Childhood Education and Care*. Paris: OECD.

OMCYA (Office of the Minister for Children and Youth Affairs) (2009) 'Minister for Children and Youth Affairs Barry Andrews Welcomes Free Pre-school Year in Early Childhood Care and Education (ECCE)', press release, 7 April.

Sylva, K., Melhuish, E., Sammons, P., Siraj-Blatchford, I. and Taggart, B. (2004) *The Effective Provision of Pre-School Education (EPPE) Project: Final Report*, Longitudinal Study funded by the DfES 1997–2004. London: Institute of Education.

— (2010) *Early Childhood Matters: Evidence from the Effective Pre-School and Primary Education Project*. London: Routledge.

Whitebook, M. and Ryan, S. (2011) *Policy Brief – Degrees in Context: Asking the Right Questions about Preparing Skilled and Effective Teachers of Young Children*, NIEER Policy Brief 22 <http://nieer.org/resources/policybriefs/23.pdf> accessed 30 June 2011.

Further Reading
National Institute for Early Education Research (NIEER) online newsletter.

Useful Websites
Comhar Naíonraí na Gaeltachta: the agency for Irish-medium pre-schools in Irish-speaking areas – www.cnng.ie

Early Education (UK) – www.early-education.org.uk/

Mála Mór: story sacks in Irish – www.malamor.ie/web2

Forbairt Naíonraí Teo: the agency for Irish-medium pre-schools in Ireland, outside Irish-speaking areas – www.naionrai.ie

National Institute for Early Education Research (USA) – http://nieer.org/

Spraoi Online: resources in Irish – www.spraoi-online.com/books.asp

Start Strong (Ireland) – www.startstrong.ie/

Contributors to this Book

Jonathan Angus has been a Steiner Waldorf educator for over twenty years. He started his teaching career in early years, with experience both as an independent contractor (a.k.a. 'nanny') and in a Waldorf crèche. His most recent work with children is in the capacity of learning support. He was the founding facilitator of the Novalis Institute for Anthroposophical Studies in St Paul, Minnesota. For the last nine years he has been a director of the Early Childhood Education Programme, a Steiner kindergarten training programme in Ireland.

Carmel Brennan is Head of Practice with Early Childhood Ireland and a BA degree course lecturer in early childhood teaching and learning. She has worked as a second-level teacher and as a playgroup practitioner. Her particular interests in terms of teaching and research are children's socio-dramatic play, relationship building and assessment. Her PhD thesis (2008), 'Partners in Play: How Children Organise their Participation in Sociodramatic Play', is an ethnographic study of how children interpret and reconstruct their worlds through play. She has also edited the IPPA publication *Power of Play* (2004), presented papers at conferences organised by the Centre for Early Childhood Development and Education (CECDE), the World Organisation for Early Childhood Education (OMEP) and the European Early Childhood Education Research Association (EECERA), and published in their journals.

Máire Corbett, while initially trained as an AMI Montessori teacher, has worked in a variety of roles in the education and early years sectors. She has taught in mainstream primary schools and with children with additional needs, she ran a successful Montessori school and crèche, has been a childminder and managed a community-based early years centre. She has worked with the National Children's Nurseries Association (now Early Childhood Ireland) since 2001, as regional support worker, advisory team leader and early childhood specialist. She has also been a guest lecturer in Mary Immaculate College. She completed her MA in Integrated Provision for Children and Families with the University of Leicester in 2009. Her research interests include supporting young children's emotional development and the importance of outdoor play for children.

Mary Daly is an education officer with the National Council for Curriculum and Assessment (NCCA) and was a member of the team that developed *Aistear: the Early Childhood Curriculum Framework*. She continues to work in the NCCA, supporting the implementation of Aistear and redeveloping the infant level of the Primary

School Curriculum, starting with the language area. Mary has completed a degree in Early Childhood Studies and a PhD at University College Cork. Her main publication is *Developing the Whole Child: The Importance of the Emotional, Social, Moral, and Spiritual in Early Years Education and Care* (2005). She has worked in the area of early years education and care in Ireland for the last ten years.

Dr Áine de Róiste is a senior lecturer in social care, Cork Institute of Technology, and a registered psychologist of the Psychological Society of Ireland. Áine undertook her doctoral research on early interventions with infants at risk at the University of Glasgow and worked in the UK in this sector. She is a co-author of the textbooks *Young People in Contemporary Ireland* and *Social Care in Ireland: An Integrated Perspective* and collaborated with CIT colleague Joan Dineen on the research report on *Young People's Views about Opportunities, Barriers and Supports to Recreation and Leisure in Ireland* commissioned by the Office for the Minister for Children and Youth Affairs (formerly the National Children's Office).

Maresa Duignan is Early Years Education Specialist in the Early Years Education Policy Unit of the Department of Education and Skills. Formerly Assistant Director of the Centre for Early Childhood Development and Education (CECDE), she has been centrally involved in the development and publication of national policy in the field of early childhood care and education, including *Quality Childcare and Lifelong Learning: A Model Framework for the Education, Training and Professional Development of the Early Childhood Care and Education Sector in Ireland* (2002) and *Síolta, the National Quality Framework for Early Childhood Education* (2006). Her particular research interest is the professional preparation and practice of adults working with young children in ECEC settings, and she has recently completed a doctorate in education.

Elizabeth Dunphy (E&D) is a senior lecturer in early childhood education at St Patrick's College, Drumcondra. She was an infant/primary teacher for almost two decades and was intensively involved at management level with CECDE from its inception until its closure in 2008. She acted in an advisory capacity with the development of Aistear and was the author of the background paper on the assessment of early learning which informed the guidelines for good practice that accompany Aistear. Her most recent publication is a chapter jointly written with Therese Farrell in D. Harcourt, B. Perry and T. Waller (eds), *Young Children's Perspectives: Ethics, Theory and Research* (2011, Sage).

Anne Fitzpatrick (BSocialScience CQSW MSocialScience, Diploma in Montessori Education) is a tutor and lecturer on the BA Early Childhood Education and MA Child, Family and Community programmes in Dublin Institute of Technology (DIT). She has extensive experience of working with children and families in a range of early years and additional needs settings. Her current teaching areas include professional practice in the early years, child protection and working with families in early years services. Her research interests are parent–educator relationships in early years services and the professional development of early educators.

Arlene Forster is a Curriculum and Assessment Director with the NCCA. She has taught in the early years sector in Northern Ireland and in the Republic of Ireland. Since joining the NCCA, Arlene has led the development of *Aistear: The Early Childhood Curriculum Framework*. She also led the development of *Assessment in the Primary School Curriculum: Guidelines for Schools* and worked in the area of reporting information on children's progress to parents. Arlene has a particular interest in learning through play, young children's literacy development, and assessment. She has co-authored a number of published articles on Aistear and on pedagogy in early childhood education in Ireland.

Dr Geraldine French lectures on early childhood education at DIT. She has conducted evaluations in early childhood settings (Barnardos, and the Katharine Howard Foundation with the HSE), and literature reviews and publications (Barnardos, CECDE and NCCA). Her research interests include quality in early childhood settings, with a particular focus on interactions for early learning.

Margaret Gilmore is a senior lecturer in social care at the Institute of Technology, Sligo. She trained as a medical doctor with particular interest in paediatrics before joining IT Sligo, where she has been involved in the development of the Social Care and Early Childhood BA programmes. She is involved with local community groups, particularly the management committee of Sligo Family Support (incorporating Lifestart) since it began over twenty years ago, supporting parents and early childhood initiatives.

Dr Ann Marie Halpenny is a lecturer in psychology in the School of Social Sciences and Law in DIT and tutor to students on the BA (hons) degree course in Early Childhood Education. She has extensive research experience in the field of children, families and communities. Her doctoral research involved a study of post-separation child–parent relationships, with a particular focus on children's perceptions of closeness and security with resident and non-resident parents. Most recently she has collaborated on a major study of Irish parenting and discipline practices and beliefs, which involved accessing the views of both parents and children and was commissioned by the Office of the Minister for Children and Youth Affairs.

Professor Nóirín Hayes (PhD) is a senior lecturer at DIT. She is a developmental psychologist lecturing in the areas of children and childhoods, children's rights, early education and research methods. She is a founder member of the Centre for Social and Educational Research (CSER) at DIT, where she leads a number of research projects in the field of early childhood and is research supervisor to a group of PhD students. She is a founder member of the Children's Rights Alliance and the author of a number of books, reports and articles on practice and policy in early childhood education, children's rights and childhood.

Moira Jenkins (BCL MA LLM) teaches law on the Early Years Education and Social Care degrees at Cork Institute of Technology. Previously (1999–2005) she lectured in legal skills and constitutional law at University College Cork. She practised as a solicitor and then as a barrister in Melbourne, Australia, mainly in crime, juvenile justice and child protection, before returning to Ireland. She is admitted as a barrister and solicitor of the High Court of Australia and as a solicitor in the Supreme Court of England and Wales. She has postgraduate degrees in law and modern theatre studies and current research interests include social care advocacy and vulnerable adult protection and child law. She has extensive community/voluntary sector work experience both as an employee and board director.

Dr Noel Kavanagh is a lecturer in philosophy at the Department of Humanities, Carlow College. A native of Kildare, he entered third-level education as a mature student in 1992, taking his degree, master's and PhD at the National University of Ireland, Maynooth. He is a member of the Royal Irish Academy's Committee for Philosophy and Ethics. His primary area of interest is the concept of love in philosophy and culture. Current areas of research include phenomenological psychology and the interconnections between philosophy and psychoanalytic thought.

Joan Kiely is a senior lecturer in education at Coláiste Mhuire, Marino Institute of Education, Dublin, where she works in the area of early childhood education. She is a former primary school teacher and spent many of those years in infant classes and also as a learning support teacher. Research interests are learning in the early years, oral language and play. Joan has written a number of online courses for teachers, focusing on teaching in the early years and on the work of a learning support teacher.

John McGarrigle (MA MSc) is Course Director of Early Childhood Education and Care at the Wexford Campus of Carlow IT. He studied psychology at Liverpool University and trained as a primary school teacher in the UK in the 1980s before working with children and young people in a variety of educational and community settings. Research interests include teaching and learning, pedagogy, narrative and community psychology.

Máire Mhic Mhathúna is a lecturer in early childhood education at DIT. She has also worked as a primary school teacher and as a Naíonra practitioner. Her research interests include child language, second language acquisition, literacy and the Irish language. Her PhD thesis was on storytelling as a vehicle for second language acquisition. She has published on these topics in Irish and international journals. She was the principal investigator on two projects on Irish language maintenance in Gaeltacht areas. She has served on the board of CECDE and is currently a director of Forbairt Naíonraí Teo.

Joe Moynihan lectures on the Early Years Education and Social Care courses at Cork Institute of Technology. His research interests include technological literacy, multicultural education, disability, higher education, educational psychology and childhood cultures. He is a strong advocate for new forms of early education research and its relevance for early education practitioners. He can be contacted at joe.moynihan@cit.ie.

Colette Murray (MSc) is currently the co-ordinator of the National Pre-school Education Initiative for Children from Minority Groups. For much of her professional life she has advocated in the éist Project (Pavee Point) for the rights and needs of Traveller children in early childhood and education. She has also led the debate on the inclusion of a diversity and equality approach in early childhood education in Ireland. She has worked as a practitioner, trainer, lecturer, advocate and researcher. She established the Equality and Diversity in Early Childhood National Network (EDeNn) and is a founding member of the European Diversity in Early Childhood Education and Training (DECET) Network. Colette is author of a number of publications on diversity and equality in ECEC.

Claire Nolan (BA ECS MA) graduated from University College Cork (UCC) in 2002 with a BA (hons) degree in Early Childhood Studies. In 2004, she was awarded a master's research scholarship by Waterford Institute of Technology and graduated in October 2007. Claire currently lectures on the BA (hons) Early Childhood Studies and BA Social Care degree courses at Waterford Institute of Technology. Claire is currently studying for a PhD in education at UCC. Her research interests include: children's rights; locating the voice of the child in research; children's experiences of family change; pedagogy in early childhood; impact of domestic violence on children.

Gerard O'Carroll is a lecturer in early childhood education in the Institute of Technology, Tralee. He has a background in language teaching, has studied and worked abroad in higher education and currently teaches language acquisition and language development. Research interests revolve around inclusive education and the interface between therapies and pedagogy for children with learning difficulties. Gerard worked for many years in the International Office in IT Tralee and has a keen interest in international developments in education. He plays an active role in parent, teacher and therapist support in conjunction with Down Syndrome Ireland.

Doireann O'Connor is a lecturer in early childhood care and education at Sligo Institute of Technology. Before entering academia, she worked in the ECEC field, holding a variety of practitioner, management and policy positions. She has produced an anthology of traditional Irish children's games, songs and rhymes; a number of publications with organisations and government agencies on early years care and education, out-of-school education and community development; and a large volume of launched reports, evaluations, strategic plans and other documents relevant to the fields of early childhood education and community development in Ireland today.

Maura O'Connor (PhD) is a lecturer in education at St Patrick's College, Drumcondra, Dublin, where she specialises in early childhood education. She has worked as a primary school teacher and school principal. She has written numerous articles on ECEC in Ireland and has presented at several national and international conferences. Her latest publication is entitled *The Development of Infant Education in Ireland, 1838–1948: Epochs and Eras* (London and Berne: Peter Lang). Her research interests include early years teaching and learning, the history of education and childhood studies.

Jan Pettersen is a lecturer at DIT, where he teaches early childhood education (pedagogy), ICT in the early years, business and management, research methods and outdoor play. He has worked as a practitioner in the early years sector at different levels for more than a decade. Jan is currently working on his PhD thesis, entitled 'ICT in the Early Years: An Exploratory Study of Young Children and Technology'.

Deirdre Scott lectures on the BA Early Childhood Care and Education and the BA Applied Social Studies programmes at Institute of Technology Sligo. For the last twenty years she has provided bespoke training for the early childcare sector including FETAC Levels 5 and 6. She was a member of the inaugural Sligo County Childcare Committee, where she served as vice-chairperson and chairperson of the training committee. She is a Keeping Safe Child Protection trainer for the HSE. Her other interests are in the area of reflective practice and the creation of the reflective practitioner.

Karen Smith teaches social policy and social theory in the School of Social Science and Law, DIT and runs a module on Childhood Inequality in a Global Context in the School of Social Justice, University College Dublin. Her main teaching and research interests lie in the area of childhood studies. She was awarded a PhD in 2009 for a study examining discourses of childhood in Irish social policy.

Patsy Stafford has been a lecturer in early childhood education and mathematics education at Froebel College of Education since 1998. Before that she taught for thirteen years at pre-school and junior primary school level in New York City and California. Patsy's research interests include early numeracy, block play and integrating numeracy and literacy.

Dr Jennifer (Sturley) Pope (PhD) is a lecturer in ECEC at the Department of Reflective Pedagogy and Early Childhood Studies, Mary Immaculate College, Limerick. Her professional interests are in the areas of child health and well-being, the care and education of the under-three age group and research methods. She has a PhD in paediatric epidemiology from UCC.

Dr Mark Taylor is a lecturer in the School of Business and Humanities, Institute of Technology Sligo. Before moving to academia, he worked as a social worker and as a social and health care planner. He teaches social policy to ECEC students. His research interests include examining the role of the state in ECEC. He is a management committee member for an ECEC community project in Sligo.

Máire Uí Chonghaile has taught in Gaelscoileanna for over twenty years and completed a thesis on the topic of immersion education. She has tutored on early childhood courses organised by the Irish National Teachers' Organisation (INTO), Na Naíonraí Gaelacha, Forbairt Naíonraí Teoranta and FÁS. She has lectured on the BA degree course in Early Childhood Studies, University College Cork and is currently a senior inspector with the Department of Education and Skills.

Dr Dorit Wieczorek-Deering has been a full-time lecturer in child development, psychological adjustment during the early years and research methods at undergraduate and postgraduate courses in the School of Social Sciences and Law,

DIT since 1995. She was brought up in Munich and completed her third-level education at Trinity College Dublin. She obtained her MSc in child and adolescent psychoanalytic therapy, whilst her PhD was based on a prospective study of determinants of infant–mother attachment. Her research pursuits include attachment, temperament, parenting, the transition to day care and longitudinal research of child development.

Index